Hang Separately

Hang Separately

Cooperative Security between the United States and Russia, 1985–1994

by Leon V. Sigal

A CENTURY FOUNDATION BOOK

2000 ◆ The Century Foundation Press ◆ New York

The Century Foundation, formerly the Twentieth Century Fund, sponsors and supervises timely analyses of economic policy, foreign affairs, and domestic political issues. Not-for-profit and nonpartisan, it was founded in 1919 and endowed by Edward A. Filene.

LIBRARY OF CONGRESS CATALOGING-IN-PUBLICATION DATA

Sigal, Leon V.
    Hang separately : cooperative security between the United States and Russia, 1985-1994 / Leon V. Sigal.
        p. cm.
    Includes bibliographical references and index.
    ISBN 0-87078-450-1 (alk. paper) –ISBN 0-87078-456-0 (pbk. : alk. paper)
        1. United States–Relations–Russia (Federation) 2. Russia (Federation)–Relations–United States. 3. United States–Foreign relations–1981-1989. 4. United States–Foreign relations–1989-1993. 5. Russia (Federation)–Foreign relations–20th century. 6. Soviet Union–Foreign relations–1985-1991. 7. National security–International cooperation–History–20th century. 8. Nuclear arms control–International cooperation–History–20th century. I. Title.
    E183.8.R9 S56 2000
    327.73047'09'048–dc21

00-009977

Manufactured in the United States of America.

FOREWORD

Perhaps because it happened so suddenly, the breakup of the Soviet Union was as much a source of confusion as of celebration among Western observers. Initially, there was an understandable skepticism about whether the changes would be permanent. But, while recognizing that some political forces in Russia still emphasize the desirability of a return to the good old days, the prevailing view among scholars now is that the USSR has been consigned to the dustbin of history. Why this happened, however, remains a contentious matter among Russia scholars.

In general, foreign policy experts search for historical examples that can illuminate the present and give some clues to the future. When they do so, they usually find plenty of evidence that great changes in international affairs usually take centuries or at least generations. Within this tradition, states and peoples likewise evolve, but they do not always move neatly from one category into another. Change, at least in the eyes of scholars, also follows a certain logic of development and makes sense in terms of what has gone before. Moreover, so-called national character or even the basic agenda of governments does not totally alter without enormous upheaval, usually war or revolution. Unfortunately, this process of looking back in order to understand the likely effects of change has provided scant help in dealing with recent and current events in Russia: It has failed to provide a clear picture of what has happened and why. As a result, caution has become the watchword for both scholars and policymakers. In this sense, it may not be surprising that, in the West over the past decade, prudent policy toward Russia often involved more watching and waiting than action.

The cascading events that resulted in the breakup of the Soviet empire and the dissolution of the USSR itself put this response to change to its greatest twentieth century test. Beginning in the late 1980s, the world's attention was riveted on decisions being made first in Moscow and subsequently in Prague, Budapest, Warsaw, and elsewhere. The stakes for the globe in general, and for the West in particular, were very high. This book focuses on the actions of policy-makers in the nation that, arguably, had the most at stake of all: the United States.

Frozen in a nearly half-century-long cold war with the Soviet Union, America was confronted with an opportunity of unprece-dented importance. Would it watch and wait? Or would U.S. leaders seize the moment and form a great new partnership intended to increase the chances of success for the forces of democracy and com-mon security in the new Russia?

Leon V. Sigal, director of the Northeast Asia Cooperative Security Project at the Social Science Research Council and a for-mer member of the *New York Times* editorial board, addresses these questions directly in *Hang Separately*. His conclusion is unambigu-ous: Constrained by outdated notions about foreign policy and by domestic political divisions, much of the American establishment was paralyzed and unable to agree on bold action to match the sweep-ing changes taking place in Eastern Europe. Bringing a journalist's skills to the tale of U.S.- Russian relations during the period 1985–94, he tells a story of missed opportunities and lack of imagination. Sigal argues that the guiding philosophy behind foreign policymaking—a traditional "realist" view of international relations—made fresh think-ing rare in the first place and even more rarely appreciated when it did occur. He concludes that the United States and its allies would have reaped great benefits from policies premised on a stronger com-mitment to cooperative security. This is an important argument and one that is part of the continuing discussion about the premises of American foreign policy. Its implications for the recent history of U.S. policy toward Russia are likely to be the subject of debate for decades to come.

But this book is not just another early installment in that debate. Perhaps Sigal's greatest accomplishment in the pages that follow is that his reporting makes sense of the events of this critical period of recent history. More than a case study, the book not only sets a high standard for recapitulating key decisions but also offers a context that helps to explain the thinking that propelled decisionmakers.

The Century Foundation has supported many books about the great transition under way after the end of the cold war, including Elizabeth Pond's *Beyond the Wall*, Richard Ullman's *Securing Europe*, James Chace's *The Consequences of Peace*, Jacques Gansler's *Defense*

Conversion, Jonathan Dean's *Ending Europe's Wars,* Steven Burg's *War or Peace?,* John Ruggie's *Winning the Peace,* Michael Mandlebaum's *The Dawn of Peace in Europe,* and Tony Smith's *America's Mission.* We also published a series of reports—Russia in Transition—on developments at the heart of the former Soviet Union. Over the next several years, we plan to add new installments to our work in this area, including books by Henry Nau, Robert Art, Michael Mandlebaum, William Durch, and Walter Russell Mead.

Sigal's work, which is an especially important contribution to the first generation of such research and writing on this subject, is certain to find a permanent place in future discussions on this important topic. On behalf of the Trustees of The Century Foundation, I commend him for this accomplishment.

RICHARD C. LEONE, *President*
The Century Foundation
July 2000

CONTENTS

PREFACE

Today politicians and pundits are posing the question, Who lost Russia? It is the wrong question. Russia is not lost, and Russia was never America's to lose. Many who raise this question are convinced that Russia's democrats and reformers have been vanquished forever and that the country is on a downward sprial to hell. They regard corruption and Chechnya as symptoms of Russia's irredeemable decline and fall. Others see signs of hope in Russia's pluralist politics, budding entrepreneurship, and a new generation of Russians who reject the past even as they face an uncertain and daunting future. Trends in Russia point in many directions, and extrapolating any single trend is likely to lead to the wrong conclusion.

The questions for Americans to ask are, What interests does the United States have in Russia? What has the United States done to advance its interests in Russia in the recent past? How can it better realize them in the future?

The answer to the first question is that Russia still matters more to American security than any other country in the world. The only threat to the survival of the United States is the spread of nuclear arms, and the principal danger comes from Russia, not Iran or North Korea, because its vast nuclear stocks are not securely under state control. Moreover, a peaceful, democratic Russia remains the key to the future security of all of Europe.

The United States has abiding interests in reducing the nuclear dangers in Russia and nurturing its fragile democracy. The best way to satisfy these interests is to try to cooperate with Russia and see whether it reciprocates. Yet Washington's willingness to cooperate with Moscow was fitful in the decade from 1985 to 1994, as this book documents.

In this respect, Benjamin Franklin's admonition to the thirteen American colonies on the day that the Declaration of Independence was signed applies with equal force to American relations with Russia today: "We must all hang together, or assuredly we shall all hang separately."

From 1989 until 1995, I had an unusual vantage point for observing Soviet-American cooperation—the editorial board of the *New York Times*, where I wrote about American policy toward the Soviet Union. I have had the benefit, dating back to my work on arms control in the Department of State from 1979 to 1981, of conversations with friends in Washington, and a few in Moscow, as well as with senior officials in both capitals. But I have chosen to rely, whenever possible, on publicly available documents and memoirs in order to allow readers to check my interpretations and draw their own conclusions.

This work would not have been possible without the support of the W. Alton Jones Foundation and The Century Foundation. I am grateful to them, and especially to George Perkovich and to Morton Halperin and Richard Leone for securing that support. I am indebted to the Social Science Research Council for its help and hospitality, and especially to Kenneth Prewitt and Craig Calhoun. I owe thanks as well to Thomas Graham for his judicious comments and to Steven Greenfield for his perspicacious editing. This book is dedicated to my son, Jake, who is learning better than many adults in Washington to use his words, and to my wife, Meg, who keeps teaching me the deeper meaning of cooperation.

New York City
June 15, 2000

UNCOOPERATIVE AMERICA

I think the cold war is not over.

—National Security Adviser Brent
Scowcroft, January 22, 1989[1]

The superpowers are not in touch with each other's reality.

—German chancellor Helmut Schmidt to
Secretary of State George Shultz, May 1982[2]

Since the end of the cold war, the United States has proved surprisingly unwilling to think and act cooperatively about its security. In dealing with strangers, it has tried threats to get its way when promises seemed more likely to succeed. Whether trying to get Japan to open its markets or to keep Iran from acquiring nuclear weapons, it has resorted to coercion, including threats of military force. The United States also has had difficulty making promises and keeping them, whether the pledge entailed paying its share of dues to the United Nations or easing its economic embargo on North Korea to comply with the October 1994 Agreed Framework that halted nuclear arming by Pyongyang.

Of course, cooperative strategies are not always appropriate for achieving American aims abroad. Sometimes conciliation alone may not suffice. It has to be combined with coercion, or at least the threat of coercion. Yet a compelling case can be made for trying cooperation in pursuit of American national interests.

Nowhere has the American propensity to coerce rather than cooperate been more pronounced—or more profoundly misguided—than in dealing with the Soviet Union and its successor state, Russia. From 1985, when Mikhail Gorbachev came to power in Moscow, until now, American willingness to cooperate has been fitful at best.

Russia's future matters to the United States. If policymakers or citizens were asked to name the gravest danger to American security, they would probably answer, "the spread of nuclear arms." Leakage of nuclear arms and material from Russia is the principal source of that danger. If they were asked what would best advance America's national interest in a secure and stable Europe, their reply upon reflection might be, "a peaceful and prosperous Russia."

"Cooperative threat reduction," in the apt phrase of Senators Sam Nunn and Richard Lugar, is needed to reduce the nuclear risk in Russia. For Russia to transform itself into a peaceful and prosperous part of Europe, thoroughgoing political and economic cooperation between the United States and Russia also is essential.

Russia has to be brought into, not left out of, the world's political, economic, and security arrangements. While aid on a scale equivalent to another Marshall Plan may have been more than Americans were willing to provide, more modest and timely aid than the United States offered in the past decade was politically and economically feasible. Such aid might have helped stabilize Russia's currency sooner and taken the edge off the worst of its people's economic insecurity. Deeper U.S. economic engagement still could be of help now.

Political engagement is much more imperative. A democratic Russia would be far less likely to threaten its neighbors than an authoritarian one. Yet the United States acted as if a market economy, not democracy, mattered more to Russia's future. Worse yet, the United States did not do much to build democratic institutions in Russia or to support the more democratically inclined leaders there. In fact, it sometimes took steps that undermined them.

So long as its political and economic fortunes remain in doubt, Russia will pose more of a proliferation menace than will so-called rogue states like Iran. Iran has no weapons-grade nuclear material and will not be able to produce a bomb on its own for at least five years. By comparison, Russia has as many as 22,000 warheads and enough nuclear material—plutonium and highly enriched uranium— to make tens of thousands more. With corruption rife, a serious risk remains that nuclear controls could loosen, especially at Russia's civilian nuclear installations, allowing weapons-grade material to seep out and end up in Iran or another country.

The Moscow coup of August 1991 momentarily galvanized American concern about "loose nukes" in the former Soviet Union. Since the coup, American security has depended more on nuclear reductions than on nuclear deterrence. The fewer nuclear warheads in Russia, the safer the United States would be. To stop the spread of

nuclear arms after the Soviet Union broke apart, the challenge was to
negotiate deeper cuts in arms, to coax the other ex-Soviet states into
ceding custody of their warheads to Russia, and to mount a sustained
effort to convince Russia to dismantle as many nuclear warheads as
possible, dispose of the uranium and plutonium they contained, and
tighten controls over the warheads and material that remained. Deep
cuts in Russia's nuclear arsenal required cooperative security arrangements to reduce the sense of isolation and threat felt by many
Russians. Controlling and disposing of Russia's nuclear stockpile also
took thoroughgoing political and economic engagement. That collaboration was vital to help Mikhail Gorbachev, Boris Yeltsin, and
their allies overcome entrenched resistance in Moscow. It will remain
vital in the future.

Yet since 1985 cooperation has been slow to take hold and difficult to sustain. The United States never kept its end of the "grand
bargain"—timely economic and technical aid to speed the transformation from communism to political pluralism and open markets. It
did little to help Gorbachev arrange the end of empire in Eastern
Europe, gain politburo acquiescence to a unified Germany in NATO,
or withdraw from Afghanistan. Only in the Persian Gulf did the
United States cooperate, enabling it to assemble a winning coalition
against Iraq that included the Soviet Union.

The United States also has resisted deeper cuts in nuclear arms,
cuts that the Soviet Union was—and still is—ready to accept. The
Bush administration slowed strategic arms reductions to a crawl,
holding up the signing of the START I Treaty that mandated deep
reductions until July 31, 1991. To his credit, President Bush unilaterally withdrew all but a few tactical nuclear arms based overseas
after the August coup, a move that Moscow reciprocated, but even
that prudent step was not motivated by the need to control Soviet
"loose nukes." In his last days in office President Bush finally signed
a START II Treaty mandating deeper cuts, only to have the Senate
put off ratification for three full years. Negotiations to make even
deeper cuts are just now being contemplated. President Bush also
ordered American bombers off alert, as well as the missiles slated for
elimination under START I, but many more missiles armed with
thousands of nuclear warheads remain on hair-trigger, ready to
launch at a moment's notice.

Under President Clinton, Washington's hesitation about security cooperation, and its rush to expand NATO eastward in violation

of understandings with Moscow, only fueled a reaction in Russia, where START II remained unratified until May 2000 and broader security cooperation has become politically more precarious. The United States has been grudging in providing aid for Russian disarming. Some members of Congress, outraged at Russia's involvement in building nuclear reactors in Iran, even tried to cut off aid for dismantling Russian warheads and controlling the extracted nuclear material. American reluctance to keep its commitments could harm future relations with Russia.

When the United States tried it, cooperative security with Russia worked. It also proved far less costly than containment. Yet the United States did not try cooperative security in any sustained way.

COOPERATION AND THE END OF THE COLD WAR

Cooperative security is slighted in contemporary American accounts of U.S.-Soviet relations after Gorbachev came to power. In the American foreign policy establishment, the prevailing view of how the cold war ended is that containment brought about the collapse of the Soviet Union and the nonviolent transformation of Eastern Europe. By this interpretation, a commonplace among realists, a weakened Soviet Union had little choice but to accept the collapse of empire and the unification of Germany. This conclusion is simple, satisfying, and wrong. It overlooks the fact that the Soviet Union, while stagnating economically and overrated militarily, was still strong enough to carry on without radical change. The steepest decline in growth occurred in the 1970s, when Brezhnev was building up Soviet conventional forces. Indeed, in the 1970s some realists fretted that the United States, not the Soviet Union, was in decline. Soviet economic performance improved slightly in the early Gorbachev years, which just as easily might have strengthened the argument for muddling through rather than radical reform. Realists also fail to explain why in the late 1990s a much weaker Russia became less cooperative than the Soviet Union had been under Gorbachev.

A rival interpretation, put forth by liberal critics of realism, is that détente succeeded where containment had failed, sapping the Soviet system from within. Yet Brezhnev's response to détente casts doubt on that proposition. To him, détente was the fruit of the Soviet military buildup. Washington, acknowledging the fact of nuclear stalemate, had to come to terms with Moscow. Far from feeding an impulse to reform the system, détente in the Brezhnev era produced self-satisfied stasis and the stifling of dissent both at home and throughout Eastern Europe.

Both the realist and liberal interpretations overstate the importance of external influences on Soviet foreign policy and understate the predominantly domestic impetus for change. Responding to what he called a "crisis" of stagnation, Mikhail Gorbachev adopted an increasingly radical program of internal reconstruction.[3] To accomplish that, he and his reform-minded allies revolutionized Soviet foreign policy by embracing new values—the values of European social democracy. Gorbachev redefined Soviet national interests, abandoning Marxist-Leninist dogma for "new thinking." The essence of new thinking was his rejection of class struggle for what he called "common security," a concept Soviet reformers had imported from Western Europe.[4]

Common security had immediate resonance in its birthplace, West Germany, but it was foreign to all but a few Americans. In a larger sense, the American foreign policy establishment was slow to absorb the implications of Soviet new thinking. Liberals who had favored relaxing the confrontation with the Soviet Union welcomed Gorbachev's new line as confirmation of their long-held hopes. Most realists initially dismissed the change as cosmetic, intended to buy time, a "breathing space" for the Soviet Union to revitalize its economy and renew its global rivalry with the United States. Ideologues on the right wing of the Republican Party warned it was a tactic designed to lull the United States into letting down its guard.

Skepticism about Gorbachev's aims and his chances of achieving them reigned among the conservative realists who occupied high government office in the latter years of the Reagan administration and throughout the Bush administration. It also prevailed among realists who tried to influence them from the outside.

Ronald Reagan was a notable exception. Neither realist nor conservative, he was a true believer and a radical who thought of the world in ideological terms, as a contest between freedom and communism. Acutely attentive to the big picture, he recognized the significance of the changes sought and wrought by Gorbachev and the reformers. To him, the cold war ended with their break from Marxist-Leninist orthodoxy. By 1987, over the opposition of most administration officials,

he was prepared to declare victory over the "evil empire" and cooperate with the Soviet leadership in disarming.

Reagan's successor had enough political leeway to follow in his
footsteps. But George Bush, a realist and a conservative, was skeptical
about Gorbachev's intentions and his staying power. Gorbachev
sensed that and tried to subdue Bush's skepticism by sheer force of
personality. On December 7, 1988, minutes after delivering his historic address laying out new thinking to the United Nations General
Assembly and announcing a unilateral cut of 500,000 Soviet troops,
he had lunch with President Reagan and President-elect Bush. He
told Bush, "I know what people are telling you now that you've won
the election: you've got to go slow, you've got to be careful, you've got
to review, that you can't trust us, that we're doing all this for show."
Gorbachev attempted to talk the president-elect into rejecting that
view: "You'll see soon enough that I'm not doing this for show and
I'm not doing this to undermine you or to surprise you or to take
advantage of you. I'm playing real politics. I'm doing this because I
need to. I'm doing this because there's a revolution taking place in
my country. I started it." Bush, whom Secretary of State George
Shultz described as "a reluctant presence," remained unpersuaded.[5]

Gorbachev had good reason for making his earnest appeal.
American cooperation—political, military, and economic—was essential for the second Russian Revolution to succeed. It would take
decades, not a brief breathing space, to transform the Soviet polity
and economy, a monumental task that reformers could accomplish
only in a relaxed international environment. Politically, Gorbachev
and the reformers wanted to break the conservatives' grip on power.
To do that, they needed to dispel the specter of encirclement by gaining membership in Western institutions, acknowledgment of the
Soviet Union's legitimate interests, and deference to its great-power
status. Militarily, they needed the United States to agree to arms reductions and not to take advantage of deep cuts in Soviet defense spending and the resulting disintegration of the Red Army. Economically,
they wanted to integrate the Soviet Union into the global economy,
putting an end to the autarky that had long sheltered its firms from
competition at the price of prolonging its backwardness. They needed
American aid to negotiate the perilous transition from a command to
a market economy, especially to introduce monetary reforms and
head off hyperinflation. They also needed trade with the West to satisfy pent-up popular demand for consumer goods while keeping

Soviet-style monopolies from gouging customers. Above all, they needed the West to lift the cold war embargo in order to obtain the technology and investment that would permit factories to retool.

Moscow, acting on the basis of common security, did most of the accommodating. Washington was a reluctant partner.

IMPEDIMENTS TO COOPERATION

What accounts for American reluctance to cooperate? Congress and the executive agencies have been politically unwilling to pay the price of cooperation. Yet this unwillingness was abetted by a narrow conception of the way the world works, one subscribed to by most American foreign policy practitioners and members of the press and the academy who try to influence them. That conception is *realism*. That shared image lies at the core of the approach to the world embraced by the foreign policy establishment.[6]

The question of theory is not merely academic. The scholarly discourse informs the public discourse, both because American foreign policymakers are schooled in realism and because some of the leading scholarly advocates of realism took part in the public debate that affected official and popular attitudes toward cooperation with the Soviet Union and later Russia. As a theory, realism has much to recommend it. Well reasoned and parsimonious, it has considerable explanatory power. By drawing practitioners' attention to the security dilemma, that policies aimed at increasing one state's security tend to decrease another's, realism is a prescription for self-limitation. Like any theory of state behavior, it does not always work. That is why it is critical for analysts of international politics to be conscious of their theoretical assumptions and to use more than one approach to any question. Yet, for most foreign policy practitioners and even many scholars, realism was not just one theory of international politics among many, all of them subject to disputation or disproof. It was dogma, the one true faith. The foreign policy establishment's belief in realism has impeded decisionmakers from adopting policies better suited to advancing American interests after the cold war, especially policies toward Russia.

Realists start from the premise that the new world order, like the old, is anarchic. That leads either to hegemony, the domination of other states by a sole superpower, or to a balance of power. War and peace are explained by the operation of the balance of power. Even when they have no hostile intent, states may go to war. To deter war, they threaten war. They arm and ally to dissuade potential foes from waging war against them. Lack of preparedness invites aggression, but even the prudent precautions that a nation takes to defend itself may be mistaken by its neighbors as a sign of hostile intent. Realists call that "the security dilemma." Consequently, the threat of force remains immanent in relations among all states, especially the most powerful ones. So does the risk of war. Sometimes, while mobilizing their armed forces in order to deter, states may stumble into war inadvertently. Sometimes, too, they may act in the belief that war is inevitable and go to war sooner rather than later, when they expect the military balance to be less advantageous. Deterrence of premeditated war, in short, may lead to preemptive or preventive war.

The core contention of realism can be stated succinctly: without a functioning system of international governance, states seek autonomy and control rather than interdependence and cooperation. Under conditions of anarchy, insecurity is the rule. Each state has to look to itself to provide for its own survival, preparing for war in order to prevent war.

Realists hold that all states seek survival, that they value national security above all else, and that, on balance, military preponderance makes them secure. They view conflict as endemic in international affairs.

Realists consider cooperation improbable and precarious. In the view of a leading realist scholar, Kenneth Waltz, cooperation will occur "only in ways strongly conditioned" by the anarchy of the international system.[7] Dispute settlement will fail without a credible threat of force.[8] In theory, realism does not rule out cooperation among rival nations. In practice, noncooperation is a premise, not a hypothesis, for many realists.

On the realists' assumption that war remains likely, states have to concern themselves with relative, not absolute, gain. While cooperation may make states better off, as Waltz puts it, "States that feel insecure must ask themselves how the gain will be divided. They are compelled to ask not 'Will both of us gain?' but 'Who will gain more?'"[9] The unceasing struggle for advantage, realists contend, severely constrains cooperation.

So does striving for autonomy. States try to reduce their dependence on others for fear of being denied or of leaving themselves vulnerable to coercion. To avoid such vulnerability, especially with respect to weapons or to food, oil, and other critical resources, states seek self-sufficiency and avoid interdependence. The imperial drive to widen their span of control impedes cooperation and generates conflict.

The precariousness of cooperation, in the realists' view, is evident in international law, which is more circumscribed than domestic law because law is rooted in morality and norms that are not widely shared across cultures and societies. For realists, the norm of international relations is normlessness. "Law is regarded as binding because it represents the sense of right of the community," writes E. H. Carr. "International law is a function of the political community of nations. Its defects are due, not to any technical shortcomings, but to the embryonic character of the community in which it functions."[10] Law enforcement is unlikely, realists add, because states will not pay the price, whether it entails alienating an ally or fighting a lawbreaker.

In contrast to realism, which views a state's behavior as highly competitive, taking advantage of other countries to maximize its own relative gain, *cooperative security*, as the name suggests, emphasizes cooperative behavior by states. A state acting in accordance with this approach takes the interests of other states into account and satisfies those interests, even at some sacrifice to its own, whether by diplomatic give-and-take leading to negotiated agreement, by mutual adjustment, by unilateral action that is then reciprocated, or by unilateral action that consciously serves both sides' interests.[11] Cooperative security is another name for common security.

Cooperative security proponents contest the core contention of realism, that war is an ever-present possibility in international relations. They argue that what distinguishes the period since 1985 is the *absence of threats of military force in the relations among the major powers.*

Several conclusions flow from this argument. With a wider margin of security, the great powers no longer need be as preoccupied with relative as opposed to absolute gains from cooperation. They feel less need to assert control for the sake of autonomy and are more willing to cooperate, to tolerate the risk of vulnerability from interdependence.

Domestic political tides ebb and flow, and the intentions of the great powers change with them. Even in the absence of such change, nations still arm against uncertainty, raising neighbors' mistrust. Under these conditions, one purpose of cooperative security is to prevent threats to the peace from arising in the first place. Another is to facilitate mutual reassurance among states that have no intention of going to war. Achieving these purposes requires extensive engagement, both economic and political. It also requires collaboration and reciprocity on military matters.

Proponents of cooperative security start from the same assumption as realists: that the anarchy underlying relations among nations can lead to conflict. They part company from the realists over the potential for cooperation.[12]

Cooperative security's advocates also differ from classical liberals, who hold that economic interdependence and democratization will necessarily give rise to peace. Free trade does give people a stake in avoiding war. In a democracy, the will of the people can restrain the state from waging war. Yet free trade does not always yield benefits that are conducive to cooperation. It is also a source of vulnerability and conflict. The period of the greatest economic interdependence in Europe, for instance, came in the years just before World War I. Moreover, democracies do wage war, though seldom with one another. India, a democracy, started more wars than any other country after World War II. The United States, a democracy, went to war on numerous occasions over the past half century. Economic interdependence and democratization may be necessary conditions for peace. They are not sufficient conditions.

Thoroughgoing political and economic engagement also is needed. Such engagement increases the domestic political stakes of military cooperation. Of course, economic ties can generate conflict as well, but the more intricate the interdependence, the less likely it is that economic rivals will resort to war to settle disputes. Indeed, over time, economic engagement can foster formation of a security community in which the very idea of war or the threat of war no longer plays any part in the relations among member nations.[13]

In Europe and elsewhere, the major powers, including the United States, have attained their aims by reciprocity, not unilateral assertion, by reassurance instead of deterrence, and by promises instead of threats. Yet the United States remains reluctant to try cooperative security when it should. The reason for that failure is the predominance of realists among the makers of American foreign policy.

2

GORBACHEV'S NEW THINKING UNREQUITED IN EASTERN EUROPE

By breaking the rules of the game, he has disrupted the game as such. He has exposed it as a mere game. He has shattered the world of appearances, the fundamental pillar of the system. . . . He has said that the emperor is naked. And because the emperor is in fact naked, something extremely dangerous has happened.

—Vaclav Havel, leading Czech
dissident, October 1978[1]

In 1985, when I said there was going to be a revolution, everybody cheered. They said, yes, we need a revolution. But by 1987, our revolution was on, and the cheering began to die down. Now in 1988, the revolution still goes on, but the cheering has stopped.

—Mikhail Gorbachev to Ronald Reagan
and George Bush, December 7, 1988[2]

To the radical reformers who rose to power in Moscow under Mikhail Gorbachev, common security was a foreign policy imperative, driven in part by their desire to transform the Soviet Union politically and economically. To the conservative realists who held power in Washington under George Bush, common security was either a sign of Soviet weakness or propaganda aimed at dividing the West and giving the Soviet Union breathing space to gird itself for a renewed struggle with the United States. Misreading Gorbachev's willingness to cooperate, they were slow to reciprocate.

That was evident in the grudging American response to the revolutions in Eastern Europe. Aided and abetted by Gorbachev, reform Communists ousted hard-liners from power. Gorbachev's dramatic withdrawal of 50,000 crack Soviet troops opened the way to the over-throw of these Communist regimes. Soon protesters took to the streets across Eastern Europe. When the regimes sought Soviet support for a crackdown, Gorbachev stayed their hand.

From conversations with Soviet new thinkers, it was possible to anticipate these developments more than a year in advance.[3] The American intelligence community did not. When change came, the Bush administration's reaction was mostly skeptical, even dismissive. So was the dominant reaction among Soviet experts in the United States. President Bush stopped short of reciprocating Soviet conventional force cuts. He welcomed the revolutions in Eastern Europe without crowing about them. But he kept setting higher hurdles for Gorbachev to clear before he would consider cooperating.

PERESTROIKA

Mikhail Gorbachev revealed his determination to transform the Soviet Union even before he became general secretary of the Communist Party. In a December 10, 1984, speech to an ideological conclave in Moscow, he introduced *perestroika* into the Soviet political lexicon. The term was "an inspired choice," writes Archie Brown, "precisely because it did not carry ideological baggage."[4] Orthodox Communists could regard perestroika, or restructuring, with equanimity because it avoided the negative connotations of the term "reform."

Perestroika consisted of six radical reforms, all of which were intended to reduce the role of the state in the life of the individual and the economy and diminish the Communist Party's role in the workings of the state: *glasnost* or exposure of what is hidden, democratization, the rule of law, decentralization, privatization, and the introduction of markets.

Glasnost was an expansive concept that initially meant greater transparency in the state and party in order to stimulate feedback from the public and the press and promote bureaucratic responsiveness to high-level initiatives. After the Chernobyl disaster, it came to mean freedom of expression and freedom of information, opening up the state, the party, and the Red Army to criticism from below.

Democratization was at first aimed at improving productivity by empowering workers to elect their own managers and team leaders.

It later meant subjecting hidebound apparatchiks in appointive offices to multicandidate elections by secret ballot and eventually opening the way to pluralist democracy by ending the Communist Party's monopoly of power.[5] It also was invoked to depoliticize the armed forces, which were legally obliged under the 1977 constitution to safeguard the country's "socialist gains"—in short, to preserve the party's monopoly of power.[6]

The rule of law had special meaning for Gorbachev, who was trained as a lawyer and whose family had personally experienced the years of Stalin's, and the party's, arbitrary rule. Both of his grandfathers were arrested during the purges of the 1930s.[7]

Two other reforms revolutionized the economy as well as the polity: decentralization, freeing many state enterprises from the dictates of planners in Moscow's ministries, and privatization, allowing cooperatives and privately owned firms to enjoy some of the legal rights previously reserved for state enterprises.

A final reform followed from these two: the introduction of markets, which would compel state enterprises to compete with one another and with private firms at home and abroad.[8]

Gorbachev first used the terms glasnost, democratization, and decentralization in his December 1984 speech, calling for a "deep transformation" of economic and social relations. The speech staked his claim to the party's general secretaryship on a platform of reform. Yet his break with orthodoxy was enough of a concern to the standpatters who dominated higher party circles that they delayed the publication of his speech in *Pravda* and ran it only after excising its most radical points.[9] Three months later, with the backing of a coalition of moderates and reformers fed up with stagnation, Gorbachev was chosen general secretary.[10]

A FOREIGN POLICY DRIVEN BY DOMESTIC RECONSTRUCTION

From the start, Gorbachev realized perestroika could not succeed unless he revolutionized Soviet foreign policy as well. "Soviet diplomacy must help the country's domestic development," he told foreign ministry officials on May 23, 1986. Recent foreign policy thrusts had been a failure, in his view, that gained little ground in the third world and needlessly antagonized the West, reinvigorating anti-Soviet sentiment and triggering a substantial buildup of conventional forces that further disadvantaged Moscow militarily. Even worse, Soviet foreign policy was increasingly out of touch with global trends.

Gorbachev was well aware of latent bureaucratic opposition, especially to reducing arms. "It is necessary," he went on, "to keep a careful watch to assure that our fundamental proposals aimed at disarmament and the limitation of the arms race are reinforced within the shortest possible periods of time by concrete recommendations at the appropriate negotiations." Gorbachev then pointedly warned the diplomats, many of whom owed their rise to longtime foreign minister Andrei Gromyko and were resistant to major departures from Gromyko's policies: "We must not allow persistence in defending a particular position to develop into senseless stubbornness, so that the Soviet representatives will be called 'Mr. Nyet.'"[11]

Within a year, seven of nine deputy foreign ministers, eight of sixteen regional bureau chiefs, seven of ten ambassadors-at-large, and 68 of 115 ambassadors were replaced.[12] Personnel changes were not confined to the foreign ministry. When a German teenager, Mathias Rust, piloted a Cessna under the vaunted Soviet air defenses and landed just outside the Kremlin on May 28, 1987, he punctured the prestige of the military. Gorbachev seized the opportunity to sack Defense Minister Sergei Sokolov, who was resisting defense budget cuts, and replace him with a relatively junior officer, Dmitri Yazov. His shakeup of the top brass extended to the chief of the Soviet general staff, all the first deputy chiefs, all the military district commanders, the commander and chief of staff of Warsaw Pact forces, all the commanders of groups of forces and fleets, the first deputy minister, and fourteen of sixteen deputy ministers—a drastic turnover that rivaled Stalin's 1937–38 purge.[13]

For Gorbachev foreign policy was inextricably tied to domestic reform. He wanted to slash the defense budget to free up resources for domestic reconstruction. "So far, we are applying intellectual resources to defense; now we are going to devote them to technological renewal and industrial development," he told Prime Minister Felipe González of Spain on May 20, 1986.[14] "We cannot resolve the tasks of perestroika if we allow the army to remain as it is," he exhorted the politburo in November 1988. "All our best scientific-technical resources go there."[15] The reallocation of resources posed a direct challenge to managers in the military-industrial complex, whose attitude toward the economy was summed up by Dmitri Ustinov, the politburo member in charge of the defense industry under Leonid Brezhnev: "The only thing the country needs for its survival is bread and defense."[16] For years, apparatchiks like Ustinov had exaggerated the threat of Western encirclement to create a siege mentality and had exploited it to consolidate their control and commandeer resources in the Soviet system. Gorbachev saw the need to break this pernicious linkage between domestic politics and foreign policy. He was increasingly outspoken in condemning foreign policy-making as the narrow preserve of the bureaucracy and in encouraging public involvement. "The bureaucratic manner of conducting world politics," he said in Belgrade on March 16, 1988, "was a source of many calamities for which the popular masses had to pay."[17] His remark was aimed at domestic, not just foreign, audiences.

Only a benign international climate would allow reformers to mount their radical challenge at home. To foster such a climate, Gorbachev was determined to end the cold war. That required a revolution in Soviet foreign policy. Gorbachev and his advisers recognized the need to end decades of autarky and integrate the Soviet Union into the world economy. Trade and investment from the West were essential to Soviet economic reform. Neither would be forthcoming without an end to cold war enmity.

Finally, Gorbachev acted in the misguided hope that the conversion of defense plants to domestic production could serve as the engine of economic reform. Conversion presupposed a relaxation of international tension. Gorbachev, writes Clifford Gaddy, held the "stubborn belief that a key to reform was to take what he perceived to be the defense-industrial complex's secret of success and apply it to the rest of the economy. He did not know that in trying to extend the methods of the military economy to the civilian sector, he was doing exactly what would not work."[18] The output of the military-industrial complex included not only tanks and aircraft but also consumer goods like refrigerators. The fact that some of these goods were of higher quality than those manufactured in other Soviet factories convinced Gorbachev that the military-industrial complex had somehow solved the problem of quality control. It had, but in grossly inefficient ways. Goods that failed to meet the exacting standards of defense ministry inspectors were simply discarded, or else dumped into the consumer sector. The military-industrialists were known in Moscow as "the metal-eaters" for good reason: their method of quality control was to produce more and reject all but the best. That was possible because they could afford to be wasteful. Not only could the ministry of defense commandeer more inputs, but it also had first claim to the very best of everything from raw materials and semifinished goods to skilled labor and scientific talent. In contrast, managers in the civilian sector had to line up for resources, often doing deals under the table to jump the queue or scrounging to get what they needed. That familiarized them with a market of sorts—the black market. They also grew accustomed to the critical condition underlying any market economy, scarcity, which implied that every input or investment exacted a price. Although the best and the brightest managed the military-industrial complex, they were less able than managers in the civilian sector to meet the test of the market. Gorbachev's notion of revitalizing the economy by converting defense industries to civilian production made little economic sense.[19]

However wasteful it may have been in purely economic terms, conversion had an unintended political benefit. It reduced the military-industrial managers' resistance to reform by giving them a stake in it. Crudely put, conversion helped buy them off by keeping their enterprises afloat.

Gorbachev also made some military converts by changing the terms of the defense budget debate.[20] Military strength depended on the nation's economic vitality, he argued, and national security required the Soviet Union to reinvigorate and modernize production. The thrust of his critique, however, was a frontal assault on the military-industrial complex: economic power mattered more to the nation's well-being than military strength. As he told a Central Committee meeting in May 1986, "We are encircled not by invincible armies but by superior economies."[21]

Domestic reform, however he justified it, was certain to encounter determined resistance from entrenched interests in the military-industrial complex, the armed forces, the party, and the economic ministries whose power and perks depended on preserving the command economy, who thrived in a climate of economic protectionism and foreign encirclement, and who could block the implementation of reform at every turn.

Foreign policy, by contrast, was easier to change. Gorbachev and his high-level appointees could control contact with other governments. They could also articulate new lines of policy somewhat freer from the constraints of collective leadership.

NEW THINKING

For innovations in foreign policy, Gorbachev reached out to circles of *institutchiki* in the civilian think tanks, to members of the scientific community, and to the intelligentsia.[22] Many of his advisers had long been in contact with American and European nongovernmental organizations and with Europeans in the socialist international.[23] The concept of interdependence in the nuclear era came from Andrei Sakharov, Fedor Burlatsky, and Georgy Shakhnazarov. Far-reaching ideas about common security came from the Institute of Economics of the World Socialist System under director Oleg Bogomolov, especially from Vyacheslav Dashichev; from the Institute for World Economy and International Relations (IMEMO) under director Aleksandr Yakovlev; and from the Institute of Europe, formed in March 1988 under director Vitaly Zhurkin. Innovations in military strategy and arms control came from Zhurkin's deputy, Sergei Karaganov; from Alexei Arbatov, Vladimir Baranovsky, Andrei Kokoshin, Andrei Kortunov, Georgy Kunadze, and retired General Mikhail Milshtein of IMEMO's arms control department; from Evgeny Velikov, vice president of the Soviet Academy of Sciences; from Roald Sagdeev, director of the Institute of Space Research; and from the Institute of the United States and Canada under director Georgy Arbatov, who had served on the Palme Commission.[24]

The most influential of the innovators were Eduard Shevardnadze, Gorbachev's surprise choice to replace Gromyko as foreign minister on July 2, 1985; Aleksandr Yakovlev, whom he put in charge of ideology and promoted from director of IMEMO to full politburo membership within three years with responsibility for Eastern Europe; Georgy Shakhnazarov, Gorbachev's special assistant from 1988 to 1991; and Anatoly Chernyaev, who served as his top aide and close confidant starting in 1986. Shevardnadze and Yakovlev both were named to the Defense Council, the top military policymaking organ, putting them in position to offer competing policy alternatives to those of the military.

Gorbachev gave a bland name to the revolution in Soviet foreign policy. He called it "new thinking." He first used the term outside the Kremlin's inner councils in a January 15, 1986, letter to President Reagan that called for the phased elimination of all nuclear weapons by the year 2000 and rejected the notion of strategic parity. In phase one, he proposed that all Soviet and U.S. intermediate-range missiles be withdrawn from Europe. By dropping earlier Soviet insistence on compensation for British and French nuclear forces, he accepted the "zero option" banning such missiles, first proposed by President Reagan in 1983.[25] He even loosened the linkage to U.S. abandonment of Reagan's pet program, the Strategic Defense Initiative, or "Star Wars," although he still conditioned the cuts on an end to "development, testing, and deployment" of antimissile defenses. All but ignored by the letter's recipients in Washington was his passing reference to "new political thinking."[26]

Gorbachev had unveiled the core of his new thinking in Paris in autumn 1985. At a dinner hosted by President François Mitterrand on October 2, he first spoke of "reasonable sufficiency." If disarmament was not yet possible, "then at least there should be a negotiation about a reasonable sufficiency of armaments, primarily nuclear ones, and about maintaining strategic stability at the lowest possible level of this sufficiency." The next day, in a break with Marxist-Leninist orthodoxy, he questioned the applicability of the idea of class struggle to international politics. "We hold that it is not by force of arms but only and exclusively by force of example that one must prove the correctness of one's ideology," he told a group of French parliamentarians. "I believe that in the present situation it is especially important not to emulate medieval fanatics and not to spread ideological differences to inter-state relations." He also expressed doubt about deterrence. "Europe's security cannot be ensured by military means, by military force," he said. "So far, fear of unacceptable retribution is one of the obstacles to war, to the use of military force. Everyone understands, however, that it is impossible to build a lasting peace on fear alone. But the entire question is where to search for the alternative to fear or, to use military language, deterrence."[27]

Nuclear abolition was one of five critical concepts in his new thinking. To realists in Washington it sounded suspiciously like Soviet calls in the 1950s for "general and complete disarmament." The difference was that Gorbachev meant what he said. Four other concepts made a complete break with the past: common security, global interdependence, reasonable sufficiency, and freedom of choice. Embedded in each was a critique of longtime Soviet policy, and indeed of traditional Marxist-Leninist dogma.[28]

For Gorbachev these ideas were more than means to an end in the nuclear era; they were ends in themselves. "Some people say that the ambitious goals set forth by the policy of perestroika in our country have prompted the peace proposals we have lately made in the international arena. This is an oversimplification," he wrote in 1987. "True, we need normal international conditions for our internal progress. But we want a world free of war, without arms races, nuclear weapons, and violence not only because this is an optimal condition for our internal development. It is an objective global requirement that stems from the realities of the present day."[29]

Gorbachev promulgated these concepts in his report to the twenty-seventh party congress in 1986. The report provoked a "stormy reaction," according to Foreign Minister Shevardnadze.[30] Opening the congress on February 25, Gorbachev spoke of the dangers of nuclear war, environmental pollution, and depletion of natural resources, problems "on a global scale, affecting the very foundations of the existence of civilization." Instead of conflict between the capitalist and socialist worlds, the usual refrain at party congresses, his theme was interdependence: "We are realists and are perfectly aware that the two worlds are divided by many things, and deeply divided, too. But we also see clearly that the need to resolve most vital problems affecting all humanity must prompt them to concerted action."[31]

Gorbachev then introduced the idea of common security. Common security was the antithesis of the Marxist-Leninist doctrine of class struggle, which held that international politics was inherently antagonistic, pitting two irreconcilable social systems, capitalism and socialism, against one another. This doctrine identified the national interest of the Soviet Union with support for Marxist-Leninist parties and national liberation movements abroad. The form of class struggle had been revised in Nikita Khrushchev's time, when the idea of the inevitability of war was abandoned in favor of "peaceful coexistence." While acknowledging the need to avoid war with the United States and its closest allies, peaceful coexistence was compatible with Soviet support for wars of national liberation. Gorbachev's concept of common security went much further, calling into question the ends, the means, and the ultimate outcome of the struggle—namely, the irreconcilable differences in class interests, the use of force, and the inevitable triumph of socialism. "The situation created by nuclear confrontation calls for new approaches, methods, and forms of relations between the different social systems, states, and regions," he declared. "The task of insuring security is more and more taking the form of a political task and can be resolved only by political means." That spelled an end to the threat and use of force, including wars of national liberation. In contrast to reports to the 1971, 1976, and 1981 party congresses, which featured lengthy discussions of Soviet support for liberation movements, Gorbachev's report contained just three sentences on the subject and not one word of support.[32] Gorbachev dropped a specific reference from earlier drafts to the need to withdraw from Afghanistan, but he called the war a "bleeding wound."[33] It would take him three years to stanch that wound: the politburo decided to withdraw in November, and the last Soviet units pulled out on February 15, 1989.

Gorbachev's February 1986 report was more explicit about the implications of common security for Soviet-American relations. "Security," he asserted, "can only be mutual." The endless quest for advantage led to instability. That deviated sharply from the decade-old party line that détente had been made possible by Moscow's military spending. He also took issue with the Brezhnev formula of "equal security," which was intended to justify a buildup of Soviet conventional and nuclear forces to match, and in some instances outnumber, NATO's: "In our time, genuine equal security is guaranteed not by the highest possible, but by the lowest possible level of strategic balance, from which it is essential to exclude entirely nuclear and other types of weapons of mass destruction." In his report, Gorbachev also made reasonable sufficiency the measure of Soviet military might. No longer did he tie the concept to negotiated ceilings as he had in Paris. As a standard for how much is enough, reasonable sufficiency challenged the need for numerical equality in arms.

Gorbachev would later supplement reasonable sufficiency by introducing "defensive sufficiency," which required the Soviet armed forces to "rule out the possibility of surprise attack."[34] Surprise attack and preemptive strikes endangered stability by raising the likelihood of inadvertent war in a crisis. Especially destabilizing were "counterforce" doctrines, aimed at destroying the other side's missiles and command and control, and the high-yield nuclear warheads and accurate means to deliver them on target. Such weapons were pushing both sides down a slippery slope from retaliating against a nuclear first strike to launching on warning or even preempting—striking first in the last resort. Also destabilizing were conventional weapons like highly mobile tank divisions and "deep strike" aircraft and doctrines of the offensive, which put a premium on seizing the initiative in any near war crisis. In demanding "defensive sufficiency," Gorbachev renounced the offensive and counterforce doctrines that had been so prevalent in Soviet military thinking in the 1960s and 1970s.

"Freedom of choice" was implicit in Gorbachev's report when he called for East bloc unity but added, "unity has nothing in common with conformity."[35] As early as March 13, 1985, he had urged Eastern European leaders, in Moscow for the funeral of Konstantin Chernenko, to assume "full responsibility for the situation in their own countries" and not to count on Soviet intervention.[36] He made it explicit in a confidential speech to foreign ministry officials on May 23, 1986, which called for a fundamental change in relations with Eastern Europe, "respecting those countries' experience" and "understanding their national peculiarities." That left room for many roads to socialism: "It is impermissible to think that we can teach everyone. No one gave us that right."[37] Gorbachev promptly followed up politburo endorsement of freedom of choice and renunciation of the use of force in Eastern Europe with a hastily convened secret meeting of the Council of Mutual Economic Assistance (COMECON) on November 10–11, 1986, at which he urged Eastern European leaders to adopt perestroika in order to shore up their own legitimacy and, breaking with the Brezhnev doctrine, made a firm commitment to nonintervention.[38] To Communists who had been kept in power by the Red Army the message was unmistakable.

He soon made it clear to everyone else, first during an April 1987 visit to Prague, when he publicly referred to the "unconditional principles" of the "independence of each party, its responsibility to its people, the sovereign right to decide questions of the development of the country," then on March 19, 1988, in a joint declaration with former Communist reprobate Yugoslavia that affirmed "the impermissibility of interference in internal affairs irrespective of pretext," and finally in his report to the nineteenth Communist Party conference on June 28, 1988, when he called for "managing normal civilized relations among *all* peoples and states on the basis of democratic principles of equal rights, non-interference in the affairs of one another, and recognition of the sovereign right of peoples to determine their own destiny."[39]

New thinking was motivated in part by a determination to dispel the enemy image of the Soviet Union held abroad. Yet it was not meant just for foreign consumption. It reoriented Soviet policy in favor of cooperative security. A policy paper approved by the politburo on August 29, 1989, confirmed this: "The radical change in the foreign policy course of the Soviet Union associated with new thinking and recognition of the reality of an integral interdependent world of our times permitted [us] to evaluate in a new way the significance and prospects for the activity of the UN and other instruments of international cooperation of states [and] to begin a decisive restructuring of our line relating to them." The paper set out "a long-term strategy" for bilateral relations: "the strengthening and broadening of constructive cooperation with the United States, its translation into multilateral measures, without which it would be unrealistic to count on a practical raising of the effectiveness of international organizations and a realization of their decisions."[40] The Soviet Union would follow this line in the Persian Gulf in 1990 when it backed the American-led coalition against its own ally Iraq.

That was just one of the profound programmatic implications of Gorbachev's report to the 1986 party congress, as Foreign Minister Shevardnadze later summarized in his memoirs:

> Our guidelines were precise: to stop the preparations for nuclear war; to move Soviet-American relations onto a track of normal, civilized dialogue; to reject the dead, brutally rigid positions in favor of intelligent, mutually acceptable compromises; to move our affairs toward a balance of interests; to strive for the confinement of military capabilities to the level of reasonable sufficiency; . . . to seek ways to end nuclear tests and dismantle the American and Soviet intermediate-range missiles in Europe; to bring Soviet troops out of Afghanistan; to create a security system in Europe on the basis of the Helsinki process, radically cutting nuclear and conventional arms; to defuse regional conflicts; to normalize relations with China; to build relations with our neighbors on a basis of respect of their interests and the principles of noninterference in their internal affairs.[41]

New thinking was not mere rhetoric; it was Soviet foreign policy.

Edging beyond Gorbachev's formulations, Shevardnadze and Yakovlev elaborated new thinking. "We are fully justified in refusing to see in peaceful coexistence a special form of the class struggle," Shevardnadze told a July 27, 1988, collegium of senior Soviet diplomats. "The struggle of two opposing systems is no longer the decisive tendency of the contemporary age." When Yegor Ligachev, a one-time supporter of reform who aligned with the conservatives as Gorbachev turned more radical, contested this line in an August 7 speech in Gorky, he was rebutted by Yakovlev within a week: "Marxism as such is the interpretation of the common interests of mankind from the point of view of history and the perspective of the development of all mankind, not only that of individual countries or classes, peoples or social groups."[42] The conservatives' assault on Yakovlev at a Central Committee plenum in September prompted Gorbachev to shift his responsibilities in the Central Committee secretariat from ideology to foreign policy. At the same time he demoted Ligachev from his post as head of the Central Committee secretariat to the thankless task of supervising agriculture.[43]

The culmination of new thinking came on December 7, 1988, when Gorbachev addressed the UN General Assembly. Instead of a world divided into socialist and capitalist camps, his theme was integration. He spoke of a global network of communications and its implications: "Today, the preservation of any kind of 'closed' society is hardly possible." He also spoke of a global market, arguing that "no state, whatever its social system or economic status, can normally develop outside it." In place of class interests, he foresaw "an era when progress will be shaped by universal human interests," which necessitated "the freeing of international relations from ideology." Class conflict no longer justified a call to arms. In this "new world order," he said, "the use or threat of force no longer can or must be an instrument of foreign policy." That self-restraint applied to conventional as well as nuclear arms. The doctrinal shift was capped by his ringing declaration, "Freedom of choice is a universal principle; it should not be subject to any exceptions." Gorbachev believed that the Eastern Europeans would choose some form of democratic socialism, but he would not compel them to.

New thinking in foreign policy was a prerequisite for domestic reform. "The time has come, so to speak, to 'economize' our foreign policy," Shevardnadze told a meeting of foreign affairs personnel on July 4, 1987, echoing Gorbachev's May 1986 speech, "since, until it is wholly linked with the economy, it will be unable to help in restructuring our domestic economy and society overall."[44] At the same time the survival of new thinking in foreign policy depended on domestic reform. "Perestroika," Shevardnadze told the Supreme Soviet on October 23, 1989, "predetermines the need for a fundamentally different foreign policy. But the reception given to this policy and the external response to it depend directly on the consistency and irreversibility of perestroika."[45]

Gorbachev could not go it alone. He needed cooperation, especially from the United States. Asked in late 1988 what he would tell president-elect George Bush if he met with him, Georgy Arbatov, a prominent adviser to Gorbachev and a leading new thinker, replied, "I'd tell him that President Gorbachev needs a partner and President Bush should be that partner."[46] The courtship was unrequited.

WASHINGTON'S SKEPTICISM ABOUT NEW THINKING

Gorbachev's pathbreaking speech of December 10, 1984, on perestroika got little notice in Washington. His visit to London a week later did spark interest. His main theme was integration of Eastern and Western Europe. "Europe is our common home," he told members of Parliament. "Home and not a 'theater of military operations.'"[47] He impressed Prime Minister Margaret Thatcher enough for her to endorse his bid for the general secretaryship: "I like Mr. Gorbachev. We can do business together."[48] He also impressed West German foreign minister Hans-Dietrich Genscher, who told the World Economic Forum in Davos on February 2, 1987, "If we refuse to cooperate, we act against our own interests. The West has no reason to fear cooperation. We can have only one guiding principle: Take Gorbachev seriously. Take him at his word!"[49]

Such rapport was lacking in Washington, where few recognized early on how radical Mikhail Gorbachev would prove to be at home and abroad and still fewer understood how ripe for revolution Russia was.[50] Gorbachev's invitation to cooperate initially received a cool reception in the American foreign policy establishment. Some realists dismissed new thinking as mere rhetoric or window dressing. "It's old poison in new bottles," said Helmut Sonnenfeld, who had been a senior aide to Henry Kissinger.[51] To others the change was designed to buy the Soviet Union time, a brief "breathing space" to revive itself for a new assault or to lull the West into lowering its guard.[52] That realist interpretation reflected Henry Rowen's influential case against cooperation: "We have been told before about the 'good guys' in the Kremlin who need Western support only to find that they were largely figments in the minds of hopeful Westerners." Rowen ruled out helping Gorbachev. "The collective interest of the West lies in letting the Soviet system decay," he argued, "because even small increments of outside support might enable that system to continue in ways that are dangerous to our health."[53]

By 1989, when the magnitude of the shift became undeniable, realists contended it would soon run its course and be reversed, its architects ousted from power by orthodox Communists. Rather than reciprocate Gorbachev's concessions and do whatever else they could to help Moscow's reformers, realists preferred to step up American demands and "lock in" the gains. When the second Russian Revolution eventually proved irreversible and the Soviet Union disintegrated, realists saw the outcome as a necessary result of Russian weakness. Even today, they ignore what Gorbachev's new thinking was fundamentally about—cooperative security. These gross misreadings are signs of the unreality of realism.

A handful of Soviet experts were notable exceptions. Early on, they came to appreciate the profound transformation under way in Moscow. Archie Brown at Oxford and Jerry Hough at the Brookings Institution anticipated Gorbachev's rise to power and his radicalism. Moshe Levin described the deeper trends in Soviet society that spawned radical reform.[54] Michael MccGwire, Raymond Garthoff, and John Steinbruner at Brookings grasped the significance of Soviet changes in military doctrine and arms control policy and the need for American reciprocity. Robert Legvold and his colleagues at Columbia University, Marshall Shulman and Jack Snyder, soon joined the others in recognizing the significance of Gorbachev's new thinking.[55] These experts kept in contact with Gorbachev's reformist allies, giving them an advantage over those who reported on the Soviet Union at a distance. That intimacy sensitized them to the daunting political obstacles that Gorbachev faced at home and helped them distinguish his strategic goals from his tactical retreats and advances.

American officials were slower to discern the distinction and recognize the direction and magnitude of the transformation. Jack Matlock, for one, recalls his reaction in October 1985 to Gorbachev's rejection of the relevance of ideological differences to Soviet foreign policy and to his new standard of reasonable sufficiency in military might: "These statements were intriguing but too cryptic for us to discern precisely what they might mean in practice."[56] Matlock dates the "authoritative renunciation of class struggle as a basis of foreign policy" to a speech Foreign Minister Shevardnadze gave to Soviet diplomats in July 1988, more than two years after Gorbachev's initial pronouncement.[57] His view is a useful benchmark because he was a well-placed Soviet watcher, as a staff member of the National Security Council (N.S.C.) in 1983–85 and ambassador to Moscow subsequently, and because he was more open-minded than most American officials.

Other officials, including many analysts at the Central Intelligence Agency, were too cautious or dogmatic to heed what Gorbachev was saying and doing. "The C.I.A. had been unable to perceive that change was coming in the Soviet Union," Secretary of State Shultz complained to National Security Adviser Frank Carlucci on January 4, 1987. "When Gorbachev first appeared at the helm, the C.I.A. said he was 'just talk,' just another Soviet attempt to deceive us. As that line became increasingly untenable, the C.I.A. changed its tune: Gorbachev was serious about change, but the Soviet Union had a powerfully entrenched and largely successful system that was incapable of being changed; so Gorbachev would fail in his attempt to change it. When it became evident that the Soviet Union was, in fact, changing, the C.I.A. line was that the changes wouldn't really make a difference."[58] Colin Powell's meetings with Gorbachev as Ronald Reagan's national security adviser had convinced him that "this man meant what he said." By April 1988 Powell was no longer relying on the C.I.A.'s Soviet assessments. "I had seen what was happening up close and began to pay less and less attention to the experts," he relates. "Our professionals were reluctant to predict a future bearing no resemblance to the past."[59] Pessimism persisted in intelligence assessments of the Gorbachev revolution. "Disruptions, such as widespread reform-related work stoppages or a drastic drop in performance indicators, might strengthen conservative opposition," read a December 1988 national intelligence estimate. "Such trends, coupled with continuing nationality turmoil, could force the leadership into a major retreat."[60] An April 1989 national intelligence estimate said, "If Gorbachev were to be ousted from office in the next few years, he most likely would be replaced by a more orthodox figure favoring a distinctly more cautious course on domestic and foreign policy."[61] That same month, the C.I.A.'s Office of Soviet Analysis warned of the possibility of a hard-line coup or reversion to repression by Gorbachev in order to stave off his overthrow.[62] "They thought Gorbachev would fail, and he did," recalls Powell. "They did not think he would fail from the left for not being revolutionary enough, but instead from the right for abandoning the Soviet dream, now turned nightmare."[63]

President Bush came into office doubtful about Gorbachev's motives and staying power. He was determined to hold the line on foreign and defense policy and to go slow on cooperation. So were most top officials and much of the bureaucracy. Notwithstanding Powell's private assessment, for instance, the Pentagon contended in its 1990 defense guidance that "fundamental Soviet objectives in the Third World do not appear to have changed" and that global war remained a possibility.[64] "The changes with which American policy had to deal were revolutionary, but they fit a familiar cold war frame of reference," says Robert Hutchings, N.S.C. director for European affairs in the Bush years. "Eastern Europe, where the cold war began, was also where it had to end. This judgment, which contradicted the then-conventional wisdom that the United States needed to 'meet Gorbachev halfway' and reach an 'understanding' on the future of Eastern Europe, formed the basis of an American grand strategy. . . ."[65] The best defense, in short, was a good offense.

Secretary of State James Baker had the same cold war frame of mind: "All along, containment had been premised on the notion that the more leverage we could exert on the Soviets, the more we could pressure them to make the hard choice in favor of internal change."[66] In Baker's view, "Gorbachev's strategy was to weaken Western cohesion through high-profile, publicly attractive proposals and thus to gain economic benefits from the West." The administration's response, said Baker, was to go beyond freeing Eastern Europe and to try to transform the Soviet Union itself: "We wanted to attack his strategy by having proposals of our own—initiatives designed to open the Soviet system to Western influence, to institutionalize stability and predictability and prevent a reversal of reform, and finally to foster what we euphemistically called 'legitimate political arrangements' in the U.S.S.R. By that, we meant 'democratization.'"[67]

As late as the Malta summit in December 1989, the White House was characterizing its policy toward Gorbachev as "tough love," as if the Soviet leader were a reform school parolee remanded for recidivism. In their authoritative inside account of the diplomatic negotiations leading to German unification, N.S.C. staff members Philip Zelikow and Condoleezza Rice quoted National Security Adviser Brent Scowcroft, "Once you say the cold war is over, you can never take it back." In their interpretation, "Once the words were spoken, it would be hard to hold back massive reductions in defense spending."[68] It would also make it more difficult to maintain a substantial American troop presence in Europe, another administration aim.

American officials were understandably more sensitive to their own domestic political constraints than to Gorbachev's. More surprisingly, the same was the case with most of the American foreign policy establishment, including the community of Soviet experts, who were either involved in government decisionmaking or tried to influence it from the outside. These constraints were apparent in contrasting realist and liberal assessments made in early 1990. In an op-ed in the *Washington Post,* Paul Nitze, doyen of the realists, argued that Soviet goals remained unchanged, but Gorbachev was merely "awaiting the eventual emergence of conditions" that "will give communist parties a decisive edge in dealing with a potentially fragmented world."[69] Strobe Talbott, Washington editor of *Time,* articulated the liberal point of view. "A new consensus is emerging, that the Soviet threat is not what it used to be. The real point, however, is that it never was."[70] Both assessments understated the fundamental shift in Soviet foreign policy to common security.

The slowness of the American foreign policy establishment to acknowledge that shift put political limits on cooperation. It was only when transnational alliances formed between American and Soviet officials that cooperative security could begin in earnest. For such alliances to succeed, officials had to satisfy not only their own but also their allies' domestic political needs. American officials and those who tried to influence them were slow to try and often undermined the very Soviets who were most inclined to cooperate with the United States. In a larger sense, cooperative security required outside help with the internal political transformation of the Soviet Union. American help seldom extended beyond lip service. Much more American aid flowed to Eastern Europe than to the Soviet Union. Had the United States done as much for those forces in the Soviet Union that American officials could regard as their allies, that would have been better for its long-term security—and Eastern Europe's.

Even today, looking back on the Gorbachev years, much of the American foreign policy establishment believes that the United States compelled the Soviet Union to change, or else that it inspired Moscow to change by taking a principled position and standing firm. Both views see the American impact as decisive and underestimate the importance of Soviet new thinking.

In the first interpretation, the much-vaunted Reagan defense buildup is credited with forcing Gorbachev to retrench and reform by straining the Soviet economy to the limits. That claim is contradicted by the facts. The Soviet Union did not increase military spending in response to the Reagan buildup. When the chief of the Soviet general staff, Nikolai Ogarkov, led the charge for a hike in military outlays to meet the technological challenge from the United States, the civilian leadership, concerned about starving the consumer sector of resources in the wake of the Polish crisis, sacked him in September 1984.[71] Moreover, Gorbachev had already embraced perestroika before becoming general secretary in 1985, and reformers had begun working out the program he adopted even before the Reagan presidency. Far from prompting Gorbachev to look for a way out of the military competition, the Reagan buildup reinforced opponents of reform in the military-industrial complex.

Others take a different tack. The United States, they contend, inspired the Soviet Union to change by resolutely sticking to principle. Jack Matlock denies that "Gorbachev changed the direction of Soviet foreign policy mainly on his own initiative. In fact, the wide-ranging proposals for ending the cold war that Reagan made in January 1984, more than a year before Gorbachev came to power, prefigured what actually happened." Matlock had a hand in formulating Reagan's proposals from 1983 to 1986, so his emphasis is somewhat understandable, but he overreaches in asserting that "Gorbachev recognized, gradually, that the U.S. proposals were consistent with reform in the Soviet Union, and he then adjusted Soviet policy to fit them."[72] No doubt, American officials assiduously pressed for one-sided arms cuts, an end to the military competition in the third world, human rights, and a freer flow of information, but it was the Soviet radicals who had embraced these ideas before 1985 and persuaded a reform-minded Gorbachev to adopt and implement them over strong internal opposition.

Neither account of the American influence on Soviet policy is warranted. Instead, the United States, by remaining reluctant to reciprocate and by rejecting cooperative security, made it more difficult for the reformers to transform Russia.

NEW THINKING IN PRACTICE: THE REVOLUTIONS OF 1989

By the summer of 1986 Gorbachev was frustrated by the American reaction to his foreign policy initiatives. "We would have a good idea," his close aide Anatoly Chernyaev recalls, "but nobody in the world would believe us, because Brezhnev also used to use these pretty words. Gorbachev still remembers the response he got to the idea of a moratorium [on nuclear testing]: he put forward a globally important idea, and people said it was some kind of utopianism, that he wanted to trick the West."[73] Gorbachev kept looking for ways to puncture the enemy image of the Soviet Union prevalent in the American foreign policy establishment. He embraced a strategy laid out in a 1985 IMEMO paper by Aleksandr Yakovlev: make substantive arms control proposals that would compel the cold warriors in Washington to reciprocate.[74] In an interview with *Time* in August 1985, Gorbachev described the strategy in his own words: "If all that we are doing is indeed viewed as mere propaganda, why not respond to it according to the principle of 'an eye for an eye, a tooth for a tooth'? We have stopped nuclear explosions. Then you Americans could take revenge by doing likewise. You could deal us yet another propaganda blow, say, by suspending the development of one of your new strategic missiles. And we would respond with the same kind of 'propaganda.' And so on and so forth. Would anyone be harmed by competition in such 'propaganda'?"[75]

As Gorbachev soon made clear, new thinking went beyond thoughts to deeds. In a passage that overshadowed the rest of his speech to the UN General Assembly on December 7, 1988, he stunned onlookers by announcing a unilateral reduction of 500,000 troops over the next two years. Six tank divisions stationed in central Europe numbering 5,000 tanks and 50,000 troops would be withdrawn and disbanded, and Soviet forces in Europe would be cut by 10,000 tanks, 8,000 artillery pieces, and 800 combat aircraft.

The troop cuts opened the way to the revolutions in Eastern Europe. That was not Gorbachev's intention, but he was aware of the potential and willing to live with the consequences. Indeed, within days of his speech, a K.G.B. assessment of the Warsaw Pact predicted that "chances for survival of the allied regimes were small," according to Lieutenant General Leonid Shebarshin, chief of foreign intelligence.[76] Gorbachev and his fellow reformers believed that perestroika could not succeed in the Soviet Union without reform in Eastern Europe. He also believed that reform Communists—"mini-Gorbachevs," Fedor Burlatsky called them—would come to power in Hungary, Poland, and Czechoslovakia and that reformation along social democratic lines in Eastern Europe would serve as a model for the Soviet Union.[77] It was their own choice, however. Although

Gorbachev tried to influence that choice, he repeatedly renounced the use of force to overturn the outcome. He was prepared to let Poland be Poland.

For years, Eastern European radicals like Vaclav Havel, Adam Michnik, and Jacek Kuron had been trying to open some space for social and political activity outside the Communist Party—"civil society" they called it. Pressure for change beneath the surface burst forth in East Berlin on June 9, 1987, when youths listening to a rock concert being held on the western side of the Wall were dispersed by East German police and took to the streets chanting, "Gorbachev! Gorbachev!" and "The wall must go!"[78] Unaware of Gorbachev's pledges of nonintervention, Eastern Europeans by the thousands braved threat, truncheon, and worse to demonstrate against party rule. The revolutions could not have happened without them.

Yet Gorbachev's role was decisive. It was not until 1989—after Gorbachev began withdrawing Soviet troops from Hungary on April 25, the Soviet Communist Party was routed in first-round elections for the Congress of Peoples' Deputies, and perestroika turned radical—that the uprisings in Eastern Europe picked up steam, outpacing the capacity of policymakers to react to, let alone absorb, their impact. This brief chronology tries to capture the rush of events:

April 5: Roundtable talks between the Communist government and the opposition in Poland end with agreement on political reform; parliamentary elections are scheduled for June.

April 17: Solidarity is legalized in Poland.

May 2: Hungary rips a hole in the barbed wire along its border to Austria, breaching the Iron Curtain. East Germans by the thousands begin traveling to Hungary on tourist visas. Refused exit to Austria, some start a sit-in at the West German embassy in Budapest.

June 4: In free elections, Solidarity wins 99 of 100 seats in the Polish Senate. In the Sejm, or lower house, thirty-three of thirty-five party and government leaders, running uncontested, are denied seats when their names are crossed off a majority of ballots. That same day, in stark contrast, China sends in troops to clear demonstrators from Tienanmen Square.

July 19: General Wojciech Jaruzelski is elected president of Poland by parliament by a one-vote margin.

August 9: Hungary stops repatriating East Germans, and more flee to Hungary. A month later, on September 10, Hungary formally annuls its 1969 protocol with East Germany requiring their repatriation and announces it will allow the 60,000 East Germans in Hungary to enter Austria.

August 24: Poland's Communists agree to join a Solidarity-led government under Prime Minister Tadeusz Mazowiecki.

October 6–7: Gorbachev visits East Germany. Crowds chant "Gorby! Gorby!" Two days later, the first mass march in Leipzig proceeds peacefully.

October 17: East German party boss Erich Honecker, in power since 1971, is ousted by Egon Krenz.

October 23: Reform Communists call all-party elections in Hungary after renouncing Marxism-Leninism, renaming the party the Hungarian Socialist Party and calling the country a republic, no longer a Soviet-style "people's republic."

November 9: East Germany announces liberalized travel rules, and East Germans rush west, breaching the Berlin Wall. The same day, Bulgarian party chief Todor Zhivkov, in power since 1954, is toppled.

November 24: Czechoslovak party head Milos Jakes is deposed.

December 9–10: Czechoslovak president Gustav Husak, in power since 1968, resigns after several weeks of demonstrations. A coalition government, dominated by non-Communists, takes power.

December 22–25: After troops fire on demonstrators, Romanian dictator Nicolae Ceausescu, in power since 1965, is overthrown, court-martialed, and executed.

December 28–29: Former dissident Vaclav Havel is inaugurated president of Czechoslovakia, and Alexander Dubcek, deposed after the "Prague Spring" of 1968, is named to chair parliament.

Political intermediation by Gorbachev and Shevardnadze helped stay the hand of repression, liberating the forces of change. As Polish Communists moved to form a coalition government with Solidarity, hard-line party chief Mieczyslaw Rakowski conferred by telephone with Gorbachev, who supported a course of national reconciliation.[79] The Soviet leader thereby acquiesced in the ouster of Communists from power in Poland and formation of a Solidarity-led government. On May 18, on a tour of the Great Wall of China, Gorbachev responded to a reporter's question about the future of the Berlin Wall: "We must work to improve the international atmosphere and I hope that would create conditions when all unneeded walls would disappear."[80] In a speech to the Council of Europe on July 6, he made it clear that Poland would be the rule, not the exception: "Social and political orders in one country or another have changed in the past and may change in the future. But this is the exclusive affair of the people of that country and is their choice. . . . Any interference in domestic affairs and any attempt to restrict the sovereignty of states—friends, allies, or anyone else—are inadmissible."[81] A week before Czechoslovak party boss Jakes was deposed, Gorbachev knocked out the props under the Prague regime by notifying it that he would repudiate the 1968 Soviet invasion. He convened a meeting of Warsaw Pact leaders in Moscow on December 4 and did just that in a declaration signed by all but Ceausescu. It was a ringing endorsement of new thinking: "The illegal disruption of the process of democratic renewal in Czechoslovakia had long-term negative consequences. History showed how important it is, even in the most complex international situations, to use political means for the solution of any problems, and to observe strictly the principles of sovereignty, independence and non-interference in internal affairs, which is in accordance with the tenets of the Warsaw Pact."[82]

These principles did not extend to relations among the constituent republics of the Soviet Union. Yet, as the spirit of liberation from Moscow spread from Eastern Europe into the Soviet Union itself, Gorbachev seemed undecided whether to apply them there as well. On April 9, 1989, army and interior ministry troops brutally suppressed demonstrations in Tbilisi, Georgia, killing at least nineteen civilians. The politburo had reviewed the decision at a hastily convened airport meeting upon Gorbachev's and Shevardnadze's arrival home from London.[83] When Lithuania on May 18 asserted sovereignty, its right to override Soviet laws, followed on July 28 by Latvia, Gorbachev at first resisted pleas to use force. After elections brought the Sajudis national front to power and Lithuania declared independence on March 11, 1990, he approved military maneuvers to pressure Baltic leaders into negotiating. That eventually led to "Bloody Sunday" of January 13, 1991, when an elite K.G.B. unit spearheaded military and paramilitary troops in storming a broadcasting tower in Vilnius, Lithuania, killing 14 and wounding 580.[84] On January 19, 1990, the army launched an attack in Baku, Azerbaijan, to put down demonstrations and remove the Azerbaijan National Front from power, killing dozens of people.[85]

Throughout 1990 Gorbachev came under mounting opposition from conservatives, stirred by the loss of Eastern Europe and determined to resist secessionism in the Soviet Union. Gorbachev appeared reluctant to face down domestic critics of new thinking, leaving it to Shevardnadze to rebut them. At a February 1990 Central Committee plenum, for instance, the Soviet ambassador to Poland, Vladimir Brovikov, denounced Gorbachev's foreign policy: "Our country, the mother of us all, has been reduced to a sorry state. It has been turned from a power that was admired in the world into a state with a mistake-filled past, a joyless present, and an uncertain future. All this is so much fun for the West which, while extolling us, lets out emotional whoops about the collapse of 'the colossus with clay feet' and the downfall of communism and world socialism. Yet we are trying to present this as a dizzying success for perestroika and the new thinking in international affairs." Shevardnadze returned fire in *Izvestia* a few days later: "We know what they admired. We sent troops into Czechoslovakia and destroyed the progressive trends there. Do they think the world admired that? We 'restored order' in Hungary in 1956. We went into Afghanistan. What was it called at the time, 'internationalist duty'? The correct word is invasion. Did the world admire that too? At the U.N., 128 countries voted against us, passing resolutions that condemned our Afghan policy. Such was their 'admiration.'"[86]

By backing perestroika for Eastern Europe, Gorbachev was undermining the rationale for a divided Germany. That did not escape the attention of the East German leadership. In contrast to Bonn's concept of a single German nation partitioned into two states, the East German regime had staked its claim to existence on the basis of two separate states and two different nations, each with its own values, one capitalist and one socialist. A highly placed social scientist in the East German Communist Party posed a telling question early in 1989, "What right to exist would a capitalist G.D.R. have alongside a capitalist Federal Republic? In other words, what justification would there be for two German states once ideology no longer separated them?"[87] Honecker's successor, Egon Krenz, made the same point to Gorbachev in Moscow on November 1: "De-ideologizing state relations would in this case mean a renunciation of the defense of socialism."[88]

The liberation of Eastern Europe did not lead Washington to cooperate with Moscow. Instead, secessionist movements in the Soviet Union and Gorbachev's responses to them were seized upon by the uncompromising realists in the Bush administration as the pretext to resist reciprocity and justify distancing Bush from Gorbachev on the grounds that the Soviet leader had turned conservative or was about to be toppled from power. That was the bureaucratic and domestic political context in which the administration addressed the question of how to gain Soviet acquiescence to German unification.

3

UNCOOPERATIVE SECURITY: GERMAN UNIFICATION

The oracle of our times has proclaimed unity,
Which can be forged only with iron and blood,
But we try to forge it with love,
Then we shall see which is more lasting.

—Fedor Tyutchev, nineteenth-
century Russian poet

Mikhail Gorbachev and his reform-minded allies may have been ready to live with a liberated Eastern Europe, but they had much more reason to worry about a unified Germany. Like many others in Europe, Russians had bitter memories of German invaders in World War II and deep unease about Germany's revival.[1] Gorbachev was moved by more immediate feelings. One was apprehension that opponents of perestroika could successfully exploit the issue of German unification to weaken him at home, much as Republican critics assailed Harry S Truman with the question of "who lost China?"[2] The other was fear that events in Germany could get out of control, that Germans might vent their anger on the 380,000 Red Army troops garrisoned there and provoke a violent reaction. That would jeopardize establishment of a cooperative security order in Europe.[3]

Yet Gorbachev believed that good relations with West Germany were essential for the security of a reforming Soviet Union. Alone among the countries of Europe, West Germany gets more than mere mention in his 1987 book, *Perestroika*. He also appreciated the "truly historic significance" of a rapprochement between the longtime rivals: "Europe's development is impossible without active cooperation by our two states."[4] To deny Germany what it wanted would antagonize it and impede such active cooperation. Although

35

Gorbachev preferred a reformed East Germany, once he recognized that no East German regime could survive without being propped up by Moscow, he was prepared to live without one.

Despite the political pitfalls at home, Gorbachev remained open to unification and firm in his refusal to consider the use of force to prevent it. The first hint that he did not regard the division of Germany as permanent came in a July 1987 conversation with West German president Richard von Weizsacker. "History would decide what would happen in a hundred years," he told the West German president. "Or perhaps fifty?" retorted von Weizsacker, and Gorbachev nodded.[5] This was intended to be a "signal" that Gorbachev was open to the possibility, says his close aide, Anatoly Chernyaev, and was understood to be one by Foreign Minister Hans-Dietrich Genscher, who accompanied von Weiszacker.

"I can affirm," says Chernyaev, "that inwardly he was already then, and some time earlier even, convinced that without a resolution of the German question and without a restoration of historically conditioned normal relations between the two great nations of Europe, no healthy international situation would result."[6] Eduard Shevardnadze shared that view "as far back as 1986" by his own account.[7] "The division of Germany was not a natural state," he writes. "Did the Soviet people win the last war to continue living under the permanent danger of having to withstand yet another military threat coming from German soil? One must look the truth in the face: This was a major threat as long as a split Germany existed, as long as a mass-scale military confrontation persisted in Central Europe."[8] Gorbachev and Shevardnadze had internalized the logic of cooperative security and were applying it to the German question.

As Gorbachev and Shevardnadze reconciled themselves to a united Germany, they asked for various quid pro quos that would help them sell the policy at home. West Germany did most of the reciprocating. The United States was unwilling to give much in return. The Soviet Union, in short, embraced cooperative security. So did West Germany. The United States did not.

The unification of Germany without any use or threat of armed force is sometimes seen as the high point in the post–cold war history of cooperative security.[9] That claim stands in need of qualification when it is applied to American behavior.

AMERICAN FORESIGHT AND MYOPIA

The Bush administration was at once farsighted and myopic about German unification. Much sooner than most outside experts, top officials foresaw how the pace of change in Eastern Europe would put unification on the international agenda and with it the future of NATO. The United States backed unification even before the West German government did, but on one condition: that a united Germany remain in NATO. That was arguably prudent; its neighbors were anxious to moor Germany to one security structure or another, lest it float off on its own, unsecured and insecure.

Yet the Bush administration did too little too late to make unification politically more manageable for the Russians. That would have meant assuring Moscow of its rightful place in Europe, making provision for its security in a changing international system, and giving political and financial backing to perestroika. With the Warsaw Pact on the verge of disintegration, the future of NATO was a critical issue in Moscow. To most Russians NATO was an antagonist. To have a united Germany join it was anathema. In contrast, the Conference on Security and Cooperation in Europe (CSCE) included all the members of NATO and the Warsaw Pact, plus most European neutral nations. American support for turning CSCE into a United Nations for greater Europe could make NATO's eastward expansion more bearable by guaranteeing the Soviet Union a prominent place in Europe. A combination of conventional arms cuts by NATO, limits on a united Germany's armed forces, and Germany's reaffirmation of its commitments not to arm itself with weapons of mass destruction and not to reopen the question of its borders could provide security assurances to Moscow. Support for perestroika could take the form of substantial American aid on condition of Soviet reform and, at a minimum, relaxation of cold war controls on trade to allow export of Western technology. Such measures would have constituted a comprehensive program of cooperative security with respect to Germany.

President Bush stopped well short of that. Moscow was entitled to a seat at the negotiating table as one of Germany's four occupying powers, but Bush actually considered circumventing the four powers altogether, then did his best to circumscribe their role. He temporized before responding to Gorbachev's requests, then left most of the reciprocating to Germany. In the end, he did provide a few security assurances, but he resisted efforts by Western Europeans to construct a new concert of power or even to strengthen CSCE much, and he offered little or no aid for Soviet reform.

A September 1989 Central Intelligence Agency estimate warned against "Western actions that could be presented by his [Gorbachev's] opponents as attempts to 'take advantage' of Soviet internal instability and hurt Gorbachev."[10] Yet the president's resistance to cooperative security had that very consequence: it undermined Washington's principal allies in Moscow, Mikhail Gorbachev and Eduard Shevardnadze, and fed an ultranationalist reaction by Russians.

KOHL'S POLITICAL FORTUNES TAKE PRIORITY

Almost from its inception in 1989, the Bush administration was aware that ending the division of Europe would have profound implications for the domestic politics and internal political transformation of, and hence American relations with, a major power in Europe. The country it was preoccupied with was not the Soviet Union but West Germany. Polls showed Chancellor Helmut Kohl's Christian Democrats might lose the next election to the opposition Social Democrats. That prompted Bush administration worries about future German support for NATO and for a continued presence of American troops and nuclear arms in Germany.

Germany was a divided nation on a divided continent. But geography is not destiny. West Germany had had choices, and it had chosen first to ally itself with the United States and then to try to reach an accommodation with the Soviet Union. The policy of accommodation, *Ostpolitik,* had won unquestioned acceptance in all three major parties by the 1980s.

Gorbachev's embrace of common security had special resonance in West Germany, where the idea had originated. First introduced into the platform of the Social Democratic Party by Egon Bahr and then picked up by the Free Democratic Party and the Christian Democratic Party, common security was now a widely accepted plank in West German foreign policy.[11] "On the basis of our liberty protected in the alliance," as Richard von Weizsacker, a Christian Democrat, expressed the consensus, "we must concentrate our efforts on a good relationship with the Eastern leading power."[12] To overcome Germany's division, Washington wondered, would Bonn try to better its relationship with that leading power at NATO's expense?

More immediately, the Bush administration was encountering criticism in West Germany for slowing START, strategic arms reduction talks aimed at deep cuts in nuclear weapons, and for wanting to deploy a follow-on to Lance, a short-range nuclear missile capable of reaching East Germany and Czechoslovakia. "The shorter the range," jibed Christian Democrat Volker Rühe, "the deader the Germans." Another criticism was more telling: Lance made no sense given the political developments in Eastern Europe.

The incoming Bush administration commissioned a review of Western European policy chaired by Rozanne Ridgway, assistant secretary of state for European and Soviet affairs. Like most reviews ground out by an interagency committee, National Security Review 5 (NSR-5) reproduced existing policy. It also reflected the European Affairs bureau's interest in maintaining good relations with allied governments. German unification would trouble U.S. relations everywhere but in Bonn, and even raising it there was premature. In an undiplomatically blunt passage, NSR-5 warned, "The Germans themselves do not wish to increase the salience of this issue at this time. Nor do the other Europeans. There is no more inflammatory and divisive issue, and it serves no U.S. interest for us to take the initiative to raise it."[13]

The National Security Council (N.S.C.) staff disagreed. On March 20, 1989, National Security Adviser Brent Scowcroft sent the president a memorandum written in response to NSR-5 by two N.S.C. staff members, Philip Zelikow and Robert Blackwill. "Today, the top priority for American foreign policy in Europe should be the fate of the Federal Republic of Germany," it began. Kohl "is now lagging in the polls behind an opposition that, as currently constituted, has too little regard either for nuclear deterrence or for conventional defense." It urged Bush to "help keep Kohl in power."[14]

The authors had two proposals in mind. One was to offer an ideological alternative to Gorbachev's "common European home," what they called a "commonwealth of free nations" based on common democratic values. The other was to have the United States take the lead in raising unification. The memo made a prescient point: "Even if we make strides in overcoming the division of Europe through greater openness and pluralism, we cannot have a vision for Europe's future that does not include an approach to the 'German question.'" Scowcroft proposed going beyond lip service: "The formal allied position has long been that we want the German people to regain their unity through self-determination. I think we can, working with Bonn, improve on this formula, make it more pointed, and send a clear signal to the Germans that we are ready to do more if the political climate allows it."

Left unstated was the trouble that would cause the Social Democrats. By putting downward pressure on wage rates, upward pressure on housing prices, and tremendous strains on social services, unification would adversely affect the opposition party's working-class constituency. Unification also would antagonize the Soviet Union, with adverse consequences for the Social Democrats' long-standing commitment to *Ostpolitik.*

On March 26 President Bush returned the paper with sentences on the priority to accord to Germany highlighted in his own hand and the notation, "Read this with interest!"[15]

German domestic politics, not Soviet domestic politics, continued to preoccupy officials close to the president. For some, Lance became a litmus test for German loyalty to NATO. In May, as the Lance controversy heated up in Bonn, Scowcroft forwarded another memorandum by Robert Blackwill to Bush arguing that if the allies identified themselves more closely with Germany's national aspirations, it would be easier to persuade the German people to envision their future with NATO. At the same time, Secretary of State James Baker was being urged by his top aide on Germany, Robert Zoellick, "to get ahead of the curve" on unification.[16] According to Zoellick, administration officials decided it was far more important to reelect Kohl than to protect Gorbachev and Shevardnadze.[17]

BUSH MOVES THE GOALPOSTS

President Bush soon faced criticism at home and abroad for temporizing instead of responding to Gorbachev's initiatives. Even Ronald Reagan joined in, complaining to "friends" about the president's "foreign policy indecisiveness."[18] The *New Yorker* caught the mood: "Gorbachev has thrown away the cold war script, and the Bush people don't seem to know it." It contrasted Ronald Reagan's "disregard for facts and capacity for magical thinking which were almost winningly child-like" to Bush's "overdetached jaded professionalism." It came to a stinging conclusion: "With the passing of time, what at first appeared to be professional detachment is looking more and more like a tenuous grasp of reality."[19]

Bush's response to the criticism was largely rhetorical. In a commencement address at Texas A&M University on May 17, 1989, he spoke of going "beyond containment." Speechwriters had drawn the phrase from an April draft of National Security Directive 23 on Soviet policy, which recommended that the United States move "beyond containment to the integration of the Soviet Union into the international system." That recommendation was never adopted. Had it been, NSD-23 would have marked a major change from the administration's policy of integrating Eastern Europe into the Western bloc and leaving the Soviet Union out. "By accident, not by design, the speech resonated with a central tenet of the 'new thinking': that an end to the Soviet Union's isolation from the international system was now possible," wrote insiders Philip Zelikow and Condoleezza Rice. "Actually, 'beyond containment' relied on the Soviet Union to continue to make concessions at a time it was really the United States that was on the defensive."[20]

U.S. policy, as set forth in NSD-23, was not seeking to help Gorbachev but to test him, and to cooperate only if he passed the tests: "The United States will challenge the Soviet Union step by step, issue by issue and institution by institution to behave in accordance with the higher standards that the Soviet leadership itself has enunciated. Moscow will find the United States a willing partner."[21] Among the tests Moscow would have to pass before Washington would cooperate were "deployment of a force posture that is smaller and less threatening," democratization of the Soviet Union, and adherence to "self-determination for the countries of East-Central Europe."

The administration's aim, said Robert Hutchings, director for European affairs on the N.S.C. staff, was to raise the bar, "to shift the international agenda away from Gorbachev's 'common European home' toward a new and radical agenda for ending the cold war."[22] President Bush made that evident in a May 31 speech in Mainz, when he told German listeners that the cold war was not yet over: "The cold war began with the division of Europe. It can only end when Europe is whole." Gorbachev's vision of a "common European home" made room for socialism and a Warsaw Pact. Bush's did not: "Let Europe be whole and free." That was "the new mission for NATO." He also set a tough test for Gorbachev in Germany. "Nowhere is the division between East and West seen more clearly than in Berlin.

There the brutal wall cuts neighbor from neighbor, brother from brother. It must come down."[23] Hutchings, an author of the policy, summed it up: "Rather than seeking a strategic partnership with a reform-minded Soviet leadership, the United States, in effect, held its bilateral relationship with the Soviet Union, and East-West relations generally, hostage to the end of Soviet domination of the countries of Eastern Europe."[24]

That may have been the highest bar the administration raised to U.S.-Soviet cooperation, but it was not the only one. In a speech at the Center for Strategic and International Studies in Washington on May 4, 1989, Secretary of State Baker stressed the need to "test the application of Soviet 'new thinking'" to see if it would be "translated into enduring action."[25] He repeated the theme to reporters en route to see Gorbachev in Moscow on May 11. "We want to test the new thinking across the whole range of relationships," he said. "*If* we find that the Soviet Union is serious about new global behavior, *then* we will seek diplomatic engagement in an effort to reach mutually beneficial results." An end to Soviet commitments in the third world ranked high on the list. Baker carried a letter from the president that specified, "A constructive contribution by your government in support of a diplomatic solution in Central America will be a key near-term test."[26] Bush was determined not to meet Gorbachev halfway.

American strategy did not go down well in Moscow. Shortly before Baker's arrival, Shevardnadze complained to aides, "Are the Americans willing to do *nothing* to help us? Are *we* the ones who have to make all the moves? We take these huge steps and all we hear from Washington is, '*More! More! You must do more!*'"[27]

Bonn had a better idea: try reciprocity. "We ought not ask too much of Gorbachev," Horst Teltschik, Kohl's closest foreign policy adviser, wrote in June 1989. "Our visions ought not to push us to make maximum demands before their time has come," he advised. "It is wiser to offer dialogue and cooperation in order that the reforms be carried out successfully."[28] Bonn practiced what it preached. In October 1988 Chancellor Kohl had taken seventy business and banking leaders with him on a visit to Moscow. A consortium led by Deutsche Bank had extended a $1.7 billion line of credit for exports. In preparation for Gorbachev's return visit on June 12–15, 1989, Alfred Herrhausen, chairman of Deutsche Bank and a close personal adviser of Kohl's, went to Moscow to discuss ways of deepening economic cooperation.[29]

The turnout in Bonn for Gorbachev was tumultuous. He and Kohl had a heart-to-heart talk in the chancellor's bungalow overlooking the Rhine. After reminiscing about their experiences as youths in wartime, they spoke movingly about their aspirations for the future. The river of history, Kohl told Gorbachev, was flowing toward German unity, as the Rhine flowed down to the sea. One could not reverse its course any more than one could dam the Rhine. Gorbachev, in turn, spoke of Soviet economic troubles. If he were to ask for urgent help, would the chancellor give it? Yes, said Kohl. It was not a specific quid pro quo but a meeting of the minds, which Kohl later called "the decisive moment" for unification.[30] "Even in East Germany," Anatoly Chernyaev reflected, "it was understood at all levels that West Germany would now have priority in Soviet German policy. It would become the most important partner in the construction of a new Europe. The bottom line for the East Germans was clear: the Soviet Union would no longer prevent unification. . . ."[31] The Bonn Declaration of the two leaders spoke of "respect for the right of self-determination of peoples" as a "building brick" of "a Europe of peace and cooperation—in which the United States and Canada also have a place." It also called for "unlimited respect for the integrity and security of each state. Each has the right freely to choose its own political and social system."[32] Gorbachev and Shevardnadze understood its implications. In drawing up the declaration, Shevardnadze told Foreign Minister Genscher on June 12, "I am convinced that all the communist nations will arrive at democracy."[33] That was eight days after the Tienanmen massacre.

On July 29 Baker and Shevardnadze met in Paris. Referring to President Bush's backing for reform during his trip to Poland and Hungary two weeks earlier, Baker told his Soviet counterpart that "in supporting that reform process we were not trying to create problems for the Soviet Union" but added that if Moscow were to use force in Eastern Europe, that would create serious problems for U.S.-Soviet relations. Shevardnadze responded reassuringly that reform in Poland and Hungary, far from being a threat, was beneficial for perestroika. Decisions on "the pace, the movement, the process" there would be "left up to them." The use of force "would be the end of perestroika."[34] That had implications for Germany as well.

By fall 1989 East Germany was literally bankrupt. The regime of Erich Honecker kept begging Moscow to maintain its supply of subsidized oil, cut back since 1982, but it had become more of a burden than reformers in Moscow cared to shoulder. They hoped the refugee crisis might prompt Honecker to reform, but reform would require economic belt-tightening that was almost certain to build up explosive political pressures or inspire further flight to the West. With 85 percent of the populace living within reach of Western television, East Germans had acquired a taste for Western goods. Increasingly, workers were demanding their pay in deutsche marks in order to buy those goods in special state stores. After years of heavy borrowing from West Germany to finance imports of blue jeans, Volkswagen Golfs, and other goods to buy off popular dissatisfaction, East Germany had run up an astounding $26.5 billion foreign debt. By 1989 its current account deficit was $12.1 billion. The interest it owed on that foreign debt came to $4.5 billion—representing more than 60 percent of its hard currency earnings for the year.[35] The bill for "jeans and Golf communism," East Germany's brand of "goulash communism," had come due.

In August Hungarian foreign minister Gyula Horn telephoned Shevardnadze to ask about opening the border with Austria and allowing the refugees to cross. In the hope that their departure would ease strains on East Germany's economy, Shevardnadze raised no objection.[36] Hungary opened the border on September 10. Two weeks later, Shevardnadze conferred with East Germany's foreign minister and encouraged him to liberalize travel policies.[37] The first mass demonstration was held in Leipzig on September 25.[38] The next day, Shevardnadze asked Hungary's foreign minister how many refugees might flee East Germany. One or two million, he was told. That did not faze Shevardnadze, who said they should be allowed to go because they could not be stopped by force.[39]

At the same time that he was opening an escape valve for East Germany, Shevardnadze, acting on instructions from the politburo, warned Bonn against unilaterally changing the status quo. Soviet conservatives were incensed when Chancellor Kohl told a Christian Democratic Union party conference on September 11 that the "idea of one Germany" was closer than ever and delegates spoke out for restoring Germany's 1937 borders. Shevardnadze's speech to the UN General Assembly on September 26 used language inserted from Moscow: "Now that the forces of revanchism are again becoming active and are seeking to revise and destroy the postwar realities in Europe, it is our duty to warn those who, willingly or unwillingly, encourage those forces."[40]

On October 6–7 demonstrative crowds greeted Gorbachev in East Berlin. In a speech marking the fortieth anniversary of the founding of the German Democratic Republic (G.D.R.), he pointedly spoke of "new thinking" and quoted an 1870 poem by Fedor Tyutchev contrasting Bismarck's efforts to forge German unity "with blood and iron" to unifying "with love."[41] In private with Honecker he discussed how difficult it was to reform the Soviet Union. "Those who are late will be punished by life itself."[42] It was a thinly veiled warning.

His visit did little to discourage East Germans from taking to the streets of Leipzig on October 9. Nor did fear of a police crackdown.[43] On the eve of the demonstration, a senior member of the East German politburo, Egon Krenz, telephoned the Soviet ambassador, Vyacheslav Kochemasov, to say that Honecker had told him to fly to Leipzig with top officials of the security ministry and the army and to carry out "necessary measures." Kochemasov, thinking that Krenz intended to disregard Honecker's instructions and wanting assurance of Soviet backing, told him, "As I understand it the most important thing is to avoid bloodshed."[44] The Soviet military commander was ordered not to intervene.[45] The next day 70,000 protesters marched peacefully. "Gorby! Gorby!" they chanted. "Wir sind das Volk!" (We are the people!) "We're staying here!" And, in a sardonic reference to the East German national anthem, "Germany, united fatherland!"[46] The slogans were life-threatening imprecations to a demoralized Communist Party that claimed to speak for the people and had been exiling dissidents.

Within a week, Krenz sent a high-level party emissary to Moscow to inform Gorbachev of plans to topple Honecker. Gorbachev wished the plotters well and stood aside.[47] On October 17 Krenz ousted Honecker. On October 25, in Helsinki, Gorbachev said of Eastern Europe, "We have no right, moral or political, to interfere in events happening there. We assume others will not interfere, either."[48] Yet he still did not regard unification with any sense of urgency. "His inaction," says Vyacheslav Dashichev, "stemmed from his illusion that the G.D.R. leadership under Egon Krenz . . . would be able to carry out the political and economic reforms needed to save the socialist G.D.R."[49]

Popular protests did not abate. More than 500,000 demonstrated in East Berlin on November 4. Three days later, the Volkskammer (People's Chamber) voted down a partial easing of travel restrictions as inadequate, and the government of Prime Minister Willi Stoph resigned. Shortly thereafter, Krenz telephoned Gorbachev, who advised him to open the border between the two Germanys to ease unrest.[50] Anatoly Kovalyov, Shevardnadze's deputy, instructed

Ambassador Kochemasov to treat the travel law as "an internal responsibility of the G.D.R."[51] In a comedy of errors, new travel regulations were promulgated before border guards were issued new orders. When crowds rushed for the exits on November 9, unsure border guards gave way. The wall was breached.[52]

A *Pravda* dispatch called the G.D.R.'s action "a bold and wise political step" that "graphically confirms its will for renewal" along the lines of "new thinking." The reason for the relaxed reaction in Moscow, said Aleksandr Tsipko, an Eastern European specialist on the Central Committee staff, was the assumption that the end of Honecker's rule "would lead to the setup of a truly democratic socialist state."[53] Gorbachev had a candidate to replace Honecker who was well-regarded by reformers in Moscow, Hans Modrow.[54] By early 1990 Moscow knew better: the East German Communist Party was crumbling, leaving a vacuum of power that would soon be filled by West German politicians.

President Bush's reaction was not to "beat my chest and dance on the Wall" but to repeat the mantra that he had no intention of taking advantage of the Soviet Union. "We are handling it in a way where we are not trying to give anyone a hard time," Bush told reporters in the Oval Office on November 9. Yet in private he was encouraging Kohl to do just that. His deliberately low-key public response outraged the Republican right wing. That domestic political price was little enough to pay for the liberation of Eastern Europe. It was still a far cry from cooperative security.

KOHL'S RUSH TO UNIFY

Kohl also was worried about trouble at home. His drive to unify Germany had aroused unease throughout Europe, notably in Britain and France. Russia's retrenchment and Germany's growing power called into question Britain's aloofness from the European Community and its "special relationship" with the United States. They also weakened the pillars of France's foreign policy: a quasi-independent nuclear deterrent, a quasi-allied stance in NATO, and Franco-German cooperation in the European Community. Their effect, Dominique Moïsi told a seminar at Harvard, was to devalue France's nuclear deterrent, or *force de frappe,* while revaluing the

German mark.[55] President François Mitterrand's own reaction was muted, but French sentiment was epitomized by a bon mot from former cabinet member Simone Weil: "I like Germany so much that I prefer two of them." Former prime minister Edward Heath articulated the establishment view in Britain with customary reserve: "Naturally we expressed our support of German reunification because we knew it would never happen." But resentment of Germany in right-wing circles was more visceral. A cabinet ally of Margaret Thatcher denounced plans for European monetary union as "a German racket designed to take over the whole of Europe," and the prime minister's own unflattering characterization of Teutonic traits, "angst, aggressiveness, assertiveness," leaked to the press from her meeting on unification with academic advisers.[56]

The reaction in Europe posed a problem for Kohl at home. "International disapproval could be a big vote-getter for Kohl's political opponents," said Zelikow and Rice, reflecting the Bush administration's view. Under the circumstances Bush could serve as a shield for Kohl. On October 23 Kohl telephoned Bush to seek his support. A day later, Bush told New York Times reporter R. W. Apple, Jr., "I don't share the concern that some European countries have about a reunified Germany." He did not think "we ought to be out pushing the concept of reunification, or setting timetables," he noted. "But the subject is much more front and center because of the rapid changes that are taking place in East Germany."[57]

Kohl now decided to accelerate those changes. Addressing the federal parliament, the Bundestag, on November 8, one day before the opening of the Berlin Wall, he went out of his way to put unification on the agenda in East Germany: "Our fellow Germans do not need lectures—from anybody. They themselves know best what they want. And I am sure, if they get an opportunity, they will decide in favor of unity." He then turned something that East Germany had relied on for its survival into a weapon for its undoing: its desperate need for West German loans to meet its short-term financial obligations. Kohl promised economic aid, but only on condition of "thoroughgoing reform." The reform he had in mind was an end to the Communists' monopoly of power through "binding free elections."[58]

On November 11 Gorbachev spoke to Kohl by telephone and urged caution. A "historic transition towards other relations and

another world" was under way, he said. "We must not, through our
own clumsiness, allow this shift to be endangered—let alone prod
developments towards an unanticipated path, towards chaos, by rush-
ing them."[59]

On November 17 Moscow's hope for reform in East Germany,
Hans Modrow, became prime minister. He promptly proposed an
alternative to unification, that the two Germanys negotiate a "treaty
community" like the European Community. East German polls still
showed strong support for preserving the G.D.R., but on November
19 demonstrators in Leipzig took up a new rallying cry, "Wir sind
ein Volk!" (We are *one* people!)

As one people, Germans were now free to move from east to
west, and they were doing just that at the rate of two thousand a day.
More than 130,000 East Germans, 1 percent of the populace, would
go west that November, putting a strain on jobs, housing, and social
welfare in West Germany. That alienated the Social Democrats' trade
union constituency. It also threatened to draw voters to the far-right
Republikaner at the Christian Democrats' expense.

On November 28 Kohl tried to stanch the hemorrhaging by forcing the pace of unification—having the East Germans stay home by
bringing East and West Germany together. He presented a ten-point
plan to the Bundestag, trumping Modrow's proposal for a treaty community with an open appeal for unification. "I am sure that unity
will come if the people in Germany want it." Kohl made some concessions to Soviet as well as allied sensibilities: a pledge to embed
unification "in the all-European process and in East-West relations"
and to expedite the strengthening of CSCE.

In his eagerness to outflank Foreign Minister Hans-Dietrich
Genscher, his coalition partner and leader of the Free Democratic
Party, Kohl did not reveal the contents of the speech to him in
advance. That left West Germany's allies in the dark as well, much to
their irritation.[60] Elsewhere Kohl's speech was read as an assertion of
German independence, said N.S.C. staffer Robert Hutchings. "It was
meant to send a signal to Paris, London, and Moscow, but also to
Washington—virtually on the eve of the president's meeting with
Gorbachev off Malta—that Bonn intended to assert primacy on the
German question and not defer leadership on this issue to the Four
Powers individually or collectively."[61]

Kohl's ten points omitted two other points that Washington considered imperative: NATO membership and acceptance of the postwar

German-Polish border. A day later, Secretary of State Baker provided an American counterpoint by setting out four principles on unification. "Self-determination should be pursued without prejudice to its outcome." If Germans chose unification, it had to come "within the context of Germany's continuing alignment with NATO and an increasingly integrated European Community," as the result of a "peaceful, gradual," and "step-by-step process," and with respect for the inviolability of existing borders in accordance with the Helsinki Final Act.[62] As if to underscore its four principles, Washington also agreed to a request from Moscow for a meeting of the four-power ambassadors.

The ten points posed risks for Kohl at home, according to Rice and Zelikow: "He could be very exposed politically in the F.R.G. [Federal Republic of Germany], especially if the German public believed that he had triggered an international crisis." The day after his speech, Kohl appealed by telephone to Bush for support. "Germans—East and West—are listening very carefully. Every word of sympathy for self-determination and unity is very important now." Again, Bush was ready with a word or two. "I feel comfortable," he told reporters on November 29. "I think we're on track."[63]

Gorbachev, like Kohl, was preoccupied with the domestic political repercussions of unification. On November 6, he told Ambassador Kochemasov in East Germany, "Our people will never forgive us if we lose the G.D.R."[64] The day Germany unites, he said to Mitterrand during a meeting in Kiev on December 6, "there would be a two-line announcement that a marshal had taken over my position."[65] It was a comment that Mitterrand and Thatcher would propagate to try to slow the drive for German unity.[66] Yet what counted for Gorbachev were the terms and conditions under which unification took place. His stance was misconstrued by the French and British leaders, according to his close aide, Anatoly Chernyaev. "Their assumption was that the U.S.S.R. had a great interest—both practical and ideological—in such a delay," he wrote. "He realized that resistance to the inevitable, particularly violent resistance, was bound to cause that very chaos which he wished to prevent."[67] Although the issue of Soviet intervention never came up in the politburo, Shevardnadze would later recall that "our opponents" were demanding that the Soviet Union "start the tank engines."[68] The question facing Washington was, what, if anything, should Bush do to ease Gorbachev's predicament?

GORBACHEV'S NEEDS AT MALTA

President Bush had not been eager for a U.S.-Soviet summit, but on July 18, 1989, under mounting criticism at home for his standoffishness, he invited Gorbachev to an "interim" meeting, a prelude to a full-fledged summit.[69] The December 2–3 shipboard get-together off Malta gave Bush a chance to meet Gorbachev's political needs, in keeping with cooperative security, but Bush confined himself mostly to rhetorical reassurances. He professed support for perestroika and recalled his restrained reaction to the liberation of Eastern Europe. "We have not responded with flamboyance or arrogance," Bush noted. "I have conducted myself in ways not to complicate your life. That's why I have not jumped up and down on the Berlin Wall." He pledged similar restraint on Germany: "We will not undertake any premature actions, or attempts to hasten a solution of the unification question."[70]

Gorbachev sought something more concrete: a lifting of cold war economic impediments to Soviet-American trade. With right-wing Republicans in Congress up in arms about rising tensions in Lithuania, Bush was unwilling to go that far. Instead, he promised to increase "technical cooperation," to set a date for granting most-favored-nation trade status, and to seek observer status for Moscow in the General Agreement on Tariffs and Trade (GATT). The Soviet leader tried to make the most of it. "You tell me you support perestroika," he said. "I was going to ask you today to go beyond words. But you have done so."[71]

Gorbachev surprised and pleased the Americans with his unsolicited comment that U.S. troops were a force for stability and should remain in Europe. "We accept your role in Europe. It is very important that you be there."[72] At the same time, he sought American support for CSCE to replace NATO and the Warsaw Pact as the main pillar of European security. He wanted negotiations on unification to take place in CSCE, where opposition from Germany's neighbors might slow unification: "We should do everything within the Helsinki context rather than ruining what has been done." All Europeans agreed, he said, even Kohl. Bush did not. He would not even consent to a summit meeting of CSCE members. Although Baker tried to sound more responsive in a December 12 speech in Bonn calling for a somewhat expanded role for CSCE, the Bush administration wanted NATO as the cornerstone of European security in the belief that it would ensure the United States the preeminent place in Europe after the cold war.

Urging that they should "work together" to integrate Europe, Gorbachev showed his pique at Bush's attempt to counter his vision of a "common European home" by speaking of a Europe "whole and free," which left no room for socialism. In a revealing exchange, Gorbachev took umbrage at the U.S. assertion that "the division of Europe should be overcome on the basis of Western values." He warned that if "policy is made on that assumption the situation could become quite messy." Gorbachev restated his support for self-determination, the idea that each country should be free to choose its own political, cultural, or economic system.[73] Kohl's ten-point plan had "gone too far ahead," he said. "There is an emotional side to this. The process should not be forced."[74] Afterward, sitting at Bush's side at a joint press conference, Gorbachev conceded that unification was coming but warned against any "artificial acceleration" of the "processes that are going on."

According to Zelikow and Rice, "Gorbachev's relaxed demeanor convinced the Americans that the Soviet leader was malleable on the German question."[75]

Not everyone was as pleased with the results of Malta. Sergei Akhromeyev, former chief of the Soviet general staff and military adviser to Gorbachev, accused him of failing to give a "concrete answer" to the German question and blamed the foreign ministry, which "was not ready for a serious discussion."[76] That was mild compared to the reaction of others in Moscow who accused Gorbachev and Shevardnadze of a sellout.[77]

The U.S. invasion of Panama later that month further inflamed Gorbachev's critics and put his reformist allies on the defensive. "Against the background of the Soviet Union's concessions and 'good behavior,' it looked like an affront, a slap in the face, and more and more people said so," recalled Pavel Palazchenko. Shevardnadze thought the outcry could be contained, but he worried about the reaction of the hard-liners if unrest spread in the Soviet republics: "They would say immediately, why don't we use force to restore order—see what the Americans did in Panama? And that's a foreign country!"[78]

In December, as the East German Communist Party and state showed signs of falling apart, raising fears of anarchy, Gorbachev, Secretary of State Baker, and French president Mitterrand each met with Modrow to try to shore up his standing. Gorbachev's support was not unalloyed: he told Modrow on January 10, 1990, that "in principle" the Soviet Union was not opposed to unification.[79]

Kohl, meanwhile, was doing his best to undermine the new East German leader. In Berlin, Baker saw Christian Democratic campaign posters plastered everywhere with the message, "One people; one nation!" Kohl went to Dresden to begin talks with Modrow on forging new social, cultural, and economic ties between the two Germanys and seized the moment to address cheering crowds about German nationhood. Even Baker thought Kohl's rush to unification seemed rash. In a note to Bush on December 20, 1989, he warned that some might question "whether the chancellor's domestic political interest is leading him too far, too fast on the issue of unification; he's tapping emotions that will be difficult to manage."[80]

Yet President Bush's impulse was to push for unification as rapidly as possible and to limit the Soviet role in the process. As one of the four occupying powers, the Soviet Union retained substantial rights in Germany, which entitled it to a say in any settlement. On January 12, 1990, Foreign Minister Shevardnadze proposed four-power talks on the German question.[81] Britain was receptive to asserting four-power authority over unification, but West Germany was adamantly opposed. The United States persuaded Britain to deflect the Soviet initiative.[82] The State Department policy planning staff and Robert Zoellick, Baker's principal adviser on the issue, endorsed the idea of "two-plus-four talks" first put forward by France's foreign minister, Michel Jobert. The aim was to subordinate the four powers to the two Germanys. Even that went too far for Raymond Seitz, assistant secretary of state for European affairs, who objected that it would slow down unification, would invite "the Soviets into an essentially German affair," and would alienate Germans by casting the United States as an opponent of German self-determination. Seitz was not alone. "I was dubious about the proposal," said Brent Scowcroft. "It would let the Soviets work their opposition from inside the process."[83] Yet two-plus-four talks reduced the risk that Kohl would deal directly with Gorbachev without the Americans and concede neutrality in exchange for unification. On January 18 Kohl hinted at just such a possibility in an interview in the *Washington Post*.[84] "If the Germans work out unification with the Soviets," Zoellick warned, "NATO will be dumped and will become the obstacle."[85]

GORBACHEV ACQUIESCES

Unification posed a far graver risk to Gorbachev. Self-determination for Germany could have nasty repercussions at home, where separatism was threatening Soviet disunion and stirring demonstrations and violent repression in the Baltics and in Azerbaijan. Still, reconciliation with Germany could pay off in security and economic terms. A January 1990 memorandum from the Institute of Economics of the World Socialist System made that case: "In principle, the reunification of Germany does not contradict the interests of the Soviet Union. A military threat from that side is not very likely if one considers the radical fracture in the consciousness of the German nation that occurred with the national catastrophe of the last war. In the economic sphere, the Soviet Union can obtain tremendous gains from cooperation and interaction with Germany."[86]

At this point, Gorbachev decided not to block unification but to try to make the best of it. On January 26 he convened his senior advisers on Germany. He laid down the terms of discussion at the start of the four-hour meeting: everything could be considered except the use of armed force. Chernyaev recommended that, instead of propping up Modrow by inviting him to Moscow, they seek a "mutual understanding" with Kohl, who, he said, was a reliable partner. Chernyaev favored German ties to NATO and thought that Kohl would link unification to development of the "all-European process." He proposed talks by a "group of six," the four powers and the two Germanys, similar to the French four-plus-two idea. Foreign Minister Shevardnadze backed Chernyaev, but Valentin Falin, a German specialist in the party's international department, argued against abandoning East Germany or its Communist Party. To accept inclusion of East Germany in the NATO sphere, he said, was to succumb to fatalism. Yet the East German state was falling apart, reported K.G.B. head Vladimir Kryuchkov, and the Communist Party was defunct. Aleksandr Yakovlev, who headed the Central Committee secretariat, backed his deputy, Falin. Falin tried to highlight the difference between a confederation of two sovereign states and direct absorption of East Germany by West Germany, but his distinction was lost on the others. Prime Minister Nikolai Ryzhkov favored a middle course, not to block change but to work more closely with Britain and France so that "not everything should be given away to Kohl." Gorbachev summed up. All had accepted the "group of six." The Soviet Union would orient itself toward Kohl, who had just made good on a pledge to deliver $100 million in food two weeks after an urgent Soviet request. A united Germany's membership in NATO was unacceptable, he said. Unification should not bring NATO closer to the Soviet border. He directed Marshal Akhromeyev to examine plans for removing Soviet troops as part of a withdrawal of all foreign forces from Germany. But he was not ready to abandon East Germany just yet. Instead, he decided to invite Modrow to Moscow.[87]

When they met on January 30, Modrow was blunt. "The majority of the people in the German Democratic Republic no longer support the idea of two German states and it seems that it has become impossible to preserve the republic."[88] Modrow got Gorbachev's backing for unification through confederation. That became the fulcrum of the Soviet Union's opening stance in negotiations on unification, which also included a peace treaty, the evolution of NATO from a military alliance into a purely political institution that eventually could be absorbed into CSCE, and, in some formulations, a neutral, demilitarized Germany with no foreign troops on its soil.

A neutral or demilitarized Germany was not desirable. By joining NATO and subordinating its armed forces to NATO's integrated command, Bonn had limited its military freedom of action. A united Germany outside NATO would have its own independent command structure, might build up its armed forces to levels far in excess of what it would need if it remained in NATO, might even seek nuclear arms of its own. A scaled-down, residual American troop presence, if acceptable to the German and American people, was compatible with cooperative security in Europe. It was simplistic, however, to regard CSCE as a threat to displace NATO. As the Bush administration belatedly recognized in 1992, CSCE could be strengthened and, if it proved workable, could have NATO units serve as its military arm, much as the armed forces of member nations do for the United Nations. That would help meet Gorbachev's needs, something President Bush was unwilling to do.

Not satisfied with a token troop presence, Bush was determined to keep a sizable contingent of American forces in Germany. To that end, in his State of the Union address on January 31, 1990, he announced a new proposal for negotiations between NATO and the Warsaw Pact on conventional forces in Europe that would reduce U.S. and Soviet troop levels to 195,000 apiece in Central Europe yet allow the United States to retain another 30,000 troops elsewhere in Europe. That would entail a Soviet cut of 370,000, while the United

States would have to withdraw just 60,000. In a letter to Gorbachev delivered that day, Bush wrote of his intention "to retain a substantial military presence in Europe for the foreseeable future, regardless of the decisions you take about your own forces."[89] Even if the Red Army withdrew, 225,000 American troops would remain. Gorbachev would have political difficulty explaining that away in Moscow.

Later that day, Secretary of State Baker met with Bush on Germany. His notes for the meeting read, "Soviet statements [were] now recognizing unification will happen, but making clear the *terms* will be at issue."[90] The two men were not about to yield on one key term, keeping a united Germany in NATO. They had yet to secure Bonn's commitment to NATO membership, however. If the price for Gorbachev's acceptance of unification was Germany's neutrality, would Kohl yield? The signs were not reassuring. Asked in an interview in mid-January whether a unified Germany would remain a member of NATO, he had replied that it was too early to say.[91] When Kohl was consulted about accepting an American troop presence in Germany, he had consented, but he was noticeably noncommittal on NATO.[92] Bush and Baker decided to insist on a quid pro quo, as Zelikow and Rice related: "The United States would help make unification happen, *if* the West Germans stood with the Americans on the issue of NATO."[93]

On January 31 West Germany's foreign minister, Hans-Dietrich Genscher, said in public what other Germans were brooding about in private: trying to incorporate East Germany into "NATO's military structures would block intra-German rapprochement." Sensitive to politics in the Soviet Union and East Germany, Genscher supported NATO membership for a united Germany, but within limits. "What NATO must do is state unequivocally that whatever happens in the Warsaw Pact there will be no expansion of NATO territory eastward."[94] Genscher, a Free Democrat, was not speaking for his coalition partner, Chancellor Kohl. Both were vying for support from not only the West German electorate but also East German voters, who Genscher thought would favor neutralism for a united Germany and who were scheduled to go to the polls for their first free election ever on March 18.

To Robert Hutchings, N.S.C. director for Europe, Genscher's speech "underscored the danger that, left to themselves, the Germans might pay—and make others pay—an unacceptable and unnecessary price to win Soviet acceptance of unification." He was appalled: "Preemptive capitulation as regards the G.D.R. was one thing, arguably within the purview of the foreign minister–presumptive of a united Germany; preemptively sacrificing the future security of the new democracies of Central Europe on the altar of German unification, quite another."[95]

Secretary of State Baker was more inclined to reciprocate for Soviet acquiescence to unification. On February 2, when Genscher in person repeated his proposal of no NATO expansion, Baker accepted the formulation. Scowcroft was miffed. "This was an unfortunate 'concession' to Genscher," he said, "one which could have created serious difficulties."[96]

Baker then flew to Moscow, where Gorbachev's stance on Germany was under attack by politburo member Yegor Ligachev, who warned of the "approaching danger" of unification and urged Gorbachev to "prevent a prewar Munich." Shevardnadze's frank appraisal of Gorbachev's political predicament impressed Baker, who later told his staff, "The odds have got to be against his survival, although we aren't about to say that in public." Baker's assessment made him determined to consolidate American advances. "We can gain a great deal if we lock in agreements that are in the U.S. interests."[97]

One agreement he hoped to lock in was a unified Germany in NATO. While Baker, consonant with cooperative security, was prepared to make concessions to gain Soviet acquiescence, President Bush was not. With Shevardnadze, Baker distinguished between the internal aspects of unification, which were matters for the Germans alone to resolve, and the external aspects, which affected the security of other nations. The Germans, he said, "would never accept" having the four powers deal with the external aspects on their own. He proposed a two-plus-four process instead, to convene once the two Germanys settled internal matters after the March 18 election. He made the case for a Germany firmly secured in NATO, citing the risk that a neutral Germany could become "militaristic" and acquire nuclear arms.

Baker then made a key concession to Soviet sensitivities. Drawing on Genscher's idea, he "promised that if a united Germany were included in NATO, there would be ironclad guarantees 'that NATO's jurisdiction or forces would not move eastward.'"

Next, Baker tried to convince Gorbachev himself. The Soviet leader took little persuading. France and Britain might worry about a powerful Germany in Europe, but "for us and for you, regardless of the differences, there is nothing terrifying in the prospect of a unified

Germany," he told Baker. "We are big countries and have our own weight." He also accepted the two-plus-four idea. Turning to NATO membership for Germany, Baker framed the alternatives for Gorbachev: "Would you prefer to see a united Germany outside of NATO and with no U.S. forces, or would you prefer a unified Germany to be tied to NATO, with assurances that NATO's jurisdiction would not shift one inch eastward from its present position?" He was still weighing these possibilities, Gorbachev replied, but "certainly, any extension of the zone of NATO is unacceptable." Baker said, "I agree." Gorbachev saw advantages in a U.S. troop presence in Germany. "We don't really want to see a replay of Versailles, where the Germans were able to arm themselves. . . . The best way to constrain that process is to ensure that Germany is contained within European structures."[98]

In Washington, however, the White House began backing away from the Genscher formula. On the basis of the January 31 decision by Bush and Baker, the N.S.C. staff composed a letter for Bush to send Kohl linking Bush's support for German self-determination to Kohl's commitment to NATO membership and an American troop presence in a unified Germany. Subsuming all of Germany under NATO protection and rejecting demilitarization of the eastern part, it proposed instead that "a component of a united Germany's membership in the Atlantic Alliance could be a special military status for what is now the territory of the G.D.R."[99] According to Scowcroft, "The proposal differed from Genscher's in that *all* of a united Germany would be inside NATO territory and jurisdiction and thus covered by NATO's security guarantee."[100]

The draft was cabled to Baker in Moscow, who publicly tried to edge away from the commitment he had just made to Gorbachev. With a united Germany in NATO, he told reporters, "you will have the G.D.R. as part of that membership," but "some sort of security guarantees with respect to NATO's forces moving eastward or the jurisdiction of NATO moving eastward" would be needed. He added a further qualification: "Some special arrangements within NATO respecting the extension of NATO forces eastward. That's all I meant there."[101]

Kohl was due in Moscow on February 10, 1990. Bush sent the letter to Kohl on February 9, accompanied by a message from Baker rehearsing what the chancellor might expect to hear in Moscow. Baker recounted the choice he had posed to Gorbachev between a united Germany outside NATO with no U.S. troop presence and a united Germany in NATO "with assurances that NATO's jurisdiction would not shift one inch eastward from its present position."[102]

With Gorbachev, Kohl dwelled on the economic advantages of amicable relations between a united Germany and the Soviet Union. East Germany, a major Soviet supplier, was not making good on its contracts, he argued, but rapid unification would assure more reliable delivery of higher-quality manufactures at lower prices as well as entrée to the European Community for Soviet exports. Gorbachev reaffirmed his commitment to self-determination. It was up to the Germans themselves to decide whether they wanted to unite, at what pace and under what conditions, and to choose their own form of government. Kohl then said that Germany had to remain in NATO but could accept restrictions on NATO forces. The East German army could be converted into an equivalent of West Germany's border police. A unified Germany would forgo nuclear, chemical, or biological weapons and renounce all border claims. Gorbachev confined himself to citing various options without proposing that Germany be neutralized or demilitarized. He endorsed the two-plus-four process, or "the six" as he preferred to call it. He asked only whether East German subsidies for Soviet forces could be paid in deutsche marks.[103] Gorbachev repeated in public what he had told Kohl, that "the question of unity of the German nation should be decided by the Germans themselves," with the proviso that East-West relations not be adversely affected or "the European balance" upset.[104]

Kohl publicly proclaimed the meeting a "green light" for unification. His aim in doing so was to rally support for the Christian Democrats in the upcoming East German election. Yet his public pronouncement left Gorbachev open to attack by opponents of cooperative security in the politburo, the Red Army, and the foreign ministry. In their "official" version of events, Soviet diplomats tried to downplay the breakthrough, insisting that, while the Germans were free to choose unity, their decision had to be linked to "the overall European development" and claiming, incorrectly, that a unified Germany in NATO had been "categorically rejected." In a slap at Kohl two days later, Shevardnadze complained about politicians "who want to play a game of political speed chess."[105]

One fact was undeniable, however: Gorbachev had acquiesced to unification. All that remained was to give him the requisite political cover. The realists who ran the Bush administration were unwilling to engage in cooperative security, however. They figured they could get what they wanted from Gorbachev without paying the price of accommodating his political needs.

THE NINE ASSURANCES

Accommodating Gorbachev was decidedly in America's interest. Embittering Russia was no way to guarantee a secure Europe for long. Nor was encouraging Gorbachev's downfall. Even weakening Gorbachev would jeopardize perestroika. "The German question is a visceral one among the Soviet population, and criticism of Gorbachev's policy is beginning to emerge from people like politburo member Ligachev and from some military officials," Robert Blackwell, the national intelligence officer for the Soviet Union, warned on March 1, 1990. "Such criticism is no major threat to Gorbachev now. But if it were to appear that Soviet troops were being forced to retreat from the G.D.R., he had 'lost' Germany, and the security environment for the U.S.S.R. was now more threatening, the domestic fallout—when combined with other complaints—could pose a threat to his position."[106]

Gorbachev did not lack political leverage. He could confront the German people with a choice between unity and NATO, putting Washington's principal objective in jeopardy. A February 15 poll found 58 percent of West Germans preferred a united Germany that was nonaligned, a stance endorsed by the Social Democrats.[107] Gorbachev also could delay the Red Army's withdrawal, risking anarchy, even a clash between German and Russian troops. Alternatively, by refusing to cede Soviet rights as an occupying power, he could trigger an international crisis that would divide the NATO allies and endanger the Kohl government. That was the preferred strategy of senior Soviet officials who were unsympathetic to Gorbachev's conciliatory course. One of them, Valentin Falin, the German expert in the party secretariat, warned readers of *Der Spiegel* "not to pretend that we are unable to defend [our] interests legally—and not only legally." Alluding to Soviet four-power rights, he went on, "The Germans are intelligent enough to understand that it cannot be in their interest to bring about a confrontation."[108]

NATO and Warsaw Pact foreign ministers met in Ottawa on February 12–13. The European Community had sided with the Soviet

Union in favor of a CSCE summit to address the German question, but when NATO ministers caucused in Ottawa, Baker, backed by Genscher, fought off the idea. Also in Ottawa, Sevardnadze accepted unequal troop ceilings in Europe in bilateral meetings with Baker. He, the British, and the French all gave their formal assent to a limited mandate for two-plus-four talks: "to discuss the external aspects of the establishment of German unity, including the issues of security of the neighboring states." After getting Genscher's approval, Baker met last-minute resistance from Scowcroft, who had been led to believe that Kohl was not firmly behind two-plus-four. Baker had to arrange for Bush to call Kohl for his okay.[109] Other NATO allies expressed outrage at being left out.[110]

So did Poland, which had yet to get a firm German guarantee of its present border. President Wojciech Jaruzelski suggested that Soviet troops might have to remain in Poland and maintain lines of supply to their forces in East Germany until the border issue was settled. Poland's prime minister, Tadeusz Mazowiecki, sent a note to the four powers asking them to change two-plus-four into two-plus-five. Germany's border mattered to Moscow as well: Poland had been shifted westward after World War II, and parts of East Prussia contiguous to the Baltic republics had been ceded to the Soviet Union. Königsberg, birthplace of Goethe, was now Kaliningrad. Although most Germans were satisfied with the current boundary, called the Oder-Neisse line after two rivers marking it, Kohl was in no hurry to concede the point. He feared retaliation by a small but well-organized minority of Germans expelled from East Prussia, Silesia, and Pomerania during the war, mostly Christian Democrats, who had irredentist claims and could defect to the right-wing Republikaner.

Kohl was now drawing up unification plans that conditioned economic and currency union on East Germany's adopting a market economy. That would permit the deutsche mark to become the de facto currency in East Germany, which in turn might convince East Germans to stay home. As Kohl told a caucus of Christian Democrats on February 6, "If the DM doesn't come to Leipzig, then the Leipzigers will come to the DM."[111]

Political union then could be accomplished by invoking Article 146 of West Germany's Basic Law, which would require all-German elections to select delegates to a national assembly that would draft a new constitution for Germany. In early February Kohl's advisers opted to invoke Article 23 instead, which permitted "other parts of

Germany" to join the Federal Republic as individual *Lander* (states), as the Saarland had done in 1957. Meeting with Kohl on February 13–14, however, Modrow balked at economic union, accusing Bonn of annexation, another anschluss.

Getting Moscow on board also suffered a setback when West Germany's defense minister, Gerhard Stoltenberg, publicly repudiated Foreign Minister Genscher's commitment not to extend NATO jurisdiction to eastern Germany. Stoltenberg rejected neutralization or demilitarization and proposed that Bundeswehr (federal army) deployments there remain outside the NATO command structure. Genscher thought the Soviets would never accept German membership in NATO under those conditions; to insist on them could lead to Gorbachev's downfall. Kohl intervened and forced Stoltenberg to back down. He had the two ministers jointly affirm on February 19 that "no formations or institutions of the Western Alliance should be moved forward to the present territory of the G.D.R." That applied to both "NATO-assigned and non-assigned military forces of the Bundeswehr." As the U.S. embassy in Bonn reported, that would leave eastern Germany not only "de-NATOed" but also "demilitarized."[112] This concession showed Bonn's willingness, consistent with cooperative security, to extend itself far more than Washington to satisfy Moscow.

Kohl was due to meet President Bush at Camp David on February 24. The White House was still preoccupied with German accession to NATO. The time has come, Scowcroft and Blackwill advised the president, "for an honest and unadorned talk with Kohl about his bottom-line on security issues, despite the difficulty of pinning the chancellor down." They urged Bush "to cement a historic bargain: Kohl's pledge not to alter the form and substance of Germany's security commitments to NATO in exchange for a U.S. promise that the two-plus-four process will not interfere with German unity." A package of inducements might make this bitter pill go down easier in Moscow, but swallow it Moscow would: "In the final analysis, Soviet leverage to influence the fate of Germany is marginal, however much Moscow complains."[113] Margaret Thatcher, for one, disagreed with this realist assessment. When Bush telephoned her just before he saw Kohl, she opposed stationing NATO troops in eastern Germany because that would be unacceptable to Gorbachev: "NATO would be moving [east]. He's got to have some reassurance. That is the price for staying in NATO." Even she wanted CSCE strengthened.[114]

At Camp David, Kohl accepted NATO membership and an American troop presence. Under pressure from Bush, Kohl also backtracked further from Genscher's proposal—and Baker's commitment—to Gorbachev and Shevardnadze not to extend NATO jurisdiction to the east. You must stay, he told the Americans, even if the Soviets leave, but NATO units, including German forces dedicated to NATO, could not be stationed on East German soil. He mentioned two other possibilities that disturbed Bush. "If West Germany is a member of NATO, should it be done in the way we are handling France?" That raised the prospect of a German military command structure outside NATO, and Bush was quick to reject it. Kohl also questioned the need for U.S. nuclear forces in Germany, noting that those were an issue in Germany and in Eastern Europe, but Bush opposed any change. To firm up the German stance, Baker sent Genscher a note on February 28 reiterating that NATO forces, as distinct from NATO jurisdiction, would not extend eastward.[115] Ruling out the Soviet idea of negotiating a peace treaty in CSCE, which would slow down unification, Kohl endorsed the two-plus-four process, to begin after the East German elections. Bush expressed worry about the Soviet reaction, then dismissed the concern: "To hell with that. We prevailed and they didn't. We can't let the Soviets clutch victory from the jaws of defeat." When Kohl mused whether Soviet assent might just be a matter of money, Bush said, "You've got deep pockets."[116] Bush remained an uncompromising realist. Cooperative security with Moscow was now up to Bonn, without much help from Washington.

The Bush administration did make an exception for the Polish border. "We worried," recalled Hutchings, that Kohl "did not want to go down in history as the chancellor who gave up Germany's 'eastern territories' once and for all."[117] Poland's cause had been taken up not just by France and other American allies uneasy about unification but by the Polish-American community. American presidents had long ago absorbed the lesson of ethnic politics that Mayor Edward J. Kelly of Chicago taught Secretary of State James Byrnes in 1946. When Byrnes expressed concern about Moscow's reaction to an anti-Soviet demonstration by Chicago's Poles, the mayor replied, "The hell with the Russians. I haven't got any *Russians* here. I have *Poles* in Chicago."[118]

Kohl was opposed to adding Poland to the two-plus-four: "If we coordinate between the U.S. and the F.R.G., we *might* solve the issue vis-à-vis Poland not through participation, but through consultation." President Bush took that as an invitation to intercede. In secret mediation on March 23 he personally wangled a commitment from Kohl to draft a treaty with Mazowiecki defusing the border question.[119] Bush had no problem with cooperative security, so long as it had a constituency of Polish-Americans.

As Bonn opted for rapid unification and Washington backed away from its commitment not to expand NATO eastward, Gorbachev and Shevardnadze dug in their heels. In a letter to the foreign ministers of the two-plus-four on March 2, Shevardnadze said pointedly, "It is extremely important, in my view, that no one party among our 'six' act unilaterally." Asked by a reporter four days later, "What is the U.S.S.R.'s attitude to any form of participation by a united Germany in NATO?" Gorbachev replied, "We cannot agree to that. It is absolutely ruled out."[120]

The March 18 election in East Germany produced a stunning upset. The Alliance for Germany, backed by Kohl, won with 48 percent of the votes. The Social Democratic Party, which had led in the polls, got 22 percent, and the former Communists, just 16 percent. The massive turnout, 93 percent of the electorate, gave a firm mandate to the first freely elected government after a half century of authoritarian rule. Yet, in a less than ringing endorsement of democracy, Bonn and Washington would keep that government at arm's length while instead taking the vote as a mandate for uniting Germany.

Two days later, Shevardnadze spoke to Baker about German unification at a celebration of Namibian independence. "We don't want to see a neutral Germany. We want to see your troops remain. But we have a problem with NATO. It's an imagery problem. It would look as if you had won and we had lost." He went on, "The short-term problem is, how can we explain this domestically? The long-term problem is, how do you know that what we'll see ten years from now is going to be what we want? I have no problem with any current German leaders, but my nagging doubt is about who will replace them."[121]

The German question was an "inside-the-beltway" problem in Moscow. Polls commissioned by the foreign ministry showed only a minority of Soviet citizens, even in the military, opposed to a united Germany in NATO, but experts in the foreign ministry and on the Central Committee staff did not share Shevardnadze's penchant for common security.[122] The German specialists in Moscow resembled most American Sovietologists in their unremitting hostility to the object of their attention. Earlier, they had held out hopes for a government in East Germany that could withstand pressure for rapid unification, but the election dashed those hopes. Now, although they could no longer resist unification, they still balked at the external aspects.

At the same time, conservative opposition in the politburo to cooperative security crystallized around Yegor Ligachev, who warned of "NATO approaching the borders." Gorbachev also came under fire for his conciliatory course in the Baltic republics after the nationalist movement Sajudis won a majority of seats in Lithuania's legislature in a Union-wide election on February 24 and Lithuania declared independence on March 11. That election also swept a loose bloc of reform candidates into the Soviet Congress of People's Deputies. A Communist Party plenum had endorsed a stronger presidency in February, but the politburo was still the Soviet leader's power base. Gorbachev was forced to tack, siding temporarily with Ligachev and the conservatives on unification. Chernyaev has discussed Gorbachev's use of compromise as a tactic "because he finds it necessary to pacify his opponent and believes that afterwards things will take care of themselves and agreement will be reached." In contrast to the peremptory style of his predecessors, his "tendency to seek compromise" and "his calculated readiness to accept what he does not approve of," Chernyaev wrote, "make Gorbachev as a person and a politician at once strong and weak."[123]

When Shevardnadze tabled a position paper suggesting that a unified Germany in NATO was conceivable if certain conditions were met, among them creation of a pan-European security system, it was assailed by Ligachev. On April 2 the politburo instructed the foreign minister to oppose West German absorption of the East and to insist on a peace treaty in his April 4–6 meetings with Baker and Bush. Even Shevardnadze's opponents were willing to reaffirm the right of self-determination and the need for cooperative security. "Emphasizing the impermissibility of any kind of interference, direct or indirect, from outside in the internal affairs of the countries of Eastern Europe, and the unconditional right of their peoples to freedom of choice," his instructions read, "at the same time call for collaborative efforts with the United States to ensure favorable conditions for the democratic development of the deep transformation in these countries." Shevardnadze was further instructed, however, to preserve "existing security mechanisms and structures in Europe in the period of establishment of new all-European structures of collective security" and to invite direct ties between NATO and the Warsaw Pact "in the interests of strengthening mutual confidence on the continent."[124]

The politburo relented somewhat on May 16. Instead of a peace treaty, it instructed Shevardnadze to insist on a series of conditions for relinquishing Soviet four-power rights in his talks with Baker in Moscow. He was told to "emphasize that for us the inclusion of a united Germany in NATO is unacceptable—politically and psychologically. We cannot agree to what would in that case inevitably be a destruction of the balance of power and stability in Europe."[125]

Washington seemed oblivious to politics in Moscow. Bush had more political leeway to be accommodating on German unification than did Gorbachev. Many of the administration's early moves were made out of full view, so that public discussion was belated and muffled. Until this point debate had been confined to the foreign policy establishment, where the main issue was the desirability of restoring a powerful Germany. President Bush had long since decided that issue. Debate was just beginning to break out in the press, where a handful of critics bitterly decried the administration's stance. Perhaps the shrillest critic was *New York Times* columnist Abe Rosenthal, who equated unification with revival of Nazi Germany. He attacked the *Times*'s own editorials for supporting unification. The *Times* was initially hesitant out of concern that unification would weaken Gorbachev and "disrupt the process of change in the East and improvement in East-West relations," but it soon backed a united Germany in NATO.[126] Seeking to "ease Moscow's military withdrawal pains," it spoke out strongly in favor of cooperative security: "Some Americans want to use the [two-plus-four] talks to drive the Soviet Union out of Europe. Their vision is dangerously short-sighted. The talks will secure a peaceful Europe only if they are truly inclusive, satisfying Moscow's security interests and drawing the Soviet Union into Europe economically and politically, even as it withdraws militarily."[127] Editorial opinion elsewhere had less to say about taking into account Soviet security and political concerns, but the few newspapers that did take a stand on German unification were mostly supportive of meeting Moscow's needs.

Right-wing Republicans in Congress were quick to criticize any conciliatory gesture by the administration. Some critics were inspired by anticommunism, long a staple of right-wing politics in the United States, but visceral anti-Soviet sentiment was on the wane with the collapse of Soviet rule in Eastern Europe and the rise of the reformers in Moscow. More compelling on the Republican right than anticommunism was unilateralism, the belief that the United States should go it alone in the world, unfettered by allies and unobliged to cooperate with onetime foes.

While the right wing of the G.O.P. opposed cooperative security, moderate Republicans and most Democrats were urging Bush to help Gorbachev. "Does anyone really suppose that detente, so skillfully nourished at Malta, would survive the incorporation of all of Germany in NATO and the arrival of American forces at the Polish border?" wondered McGeorge Bundy, national security adviser to Presidents Kennedy and Johnson.[128] Other realists in the foreign policy establishment, doubtful that common security would impel Gorbachev to accept a united Germany in NATO or that NATO could survive the demise of its raison d'être, the Soviet threat, looked for alternatives. George Kennan, dean of America's Soviet experts, urged postponement of any decision to unify Germany.[129] Henry Kissinger argued that Germany might take the form of a confederation, with the eastern portion integrated into NATO but disarmed.[130] Samuel Huntington proposed a united Germany in NATO but substantially disarmed.[131] Zbigniew Brzezinski, who had taken a hard line on the Soviet Union as President Carter's national security adviser, contemplated stationing NATO troops alongside Warsaw Pact forces in Germany for a period of perhaps two decades.[132] Before Malta, over lunch in the White House, he urged Bush to be generous with aid to Moscow.[133] Unlike Poland, the Soviet Union had no constituency in the United States, but support for accommodation in parts of the foreign policy establishment gave President Bush considerable room for maneuver.

Despite his political leeway, Bush, ever the conservative realist, remained uncompromising. He drove a hard bargain, one that could put Gorbachev out of business. In the words of Zelikow and Rice, "the Americans had decided that the U.S. objectives for Germany were more important than protecting Gorbachev."[134] N.S.C. staffers now argued that if a settlement could not be negotiated by autumn, the Soviets "must know that, after a given date, the West will declare the game over, devolve their own four-power rights, and deploy legal arguments to the effect that all four-power rights—including the Soviets'—have now lapsed."[135] That would put Moscow in the awkward position of having to tell the German people that it alone was insisting on retaining its occupation rights in a united Germany.

On May 5 the two-plus-four ministers convened for the first time. After conferring with Shevardnadze on the eve of the talks, Baker cabled Bush about German membership in NATO: "I suspect that Gorbachev doesn't want to take on this kind of an emotionally charged political issue now, and almost certainly not before the party congress."[136] At the talks Foreign Minister Shevardnadze endorsed the Germans' right to self-determination but reiterated opposition to NATO membership for a united Germany. He proposed a new CSCE center on the "prevention of nuclear danger" to be located in Germany. One of its functions would be to monitor the "military-strategic situation in Germany." He wanted unification "synchronized" with creation of a new all-European security architecture built around CSCE. While such arrangements were negotiated, he proposed that four-power rights remain in place, in effect decoupling the internal and external aspects of unification. "If we are put in straitened circumstances in matters affecting our security," he warned, "our political flexibility will be greatly restricted since emotions will boil over in our country, the ghosts of the past will come forward, and nationalistic tendencies will be reborn." He ended with a plea for cooperation: "Attempting to gain one-sided advantages, put our partner in a position of isolation, ignore his interests, be clever, or get the better of each other have always ended badly. They are all the more out of place in issues connected with Germany and with European stability and security." Having made the case of his opponents in Moscow, he then agreed to a press statement that unification would proceed "in an orderly way and without delay."[137]

Kohl would brook no delay. In advance of local elections in East Germany on May 6, he announced that East German marks would be converted into deutsche marks on generous terms. Dismissing Bundesbank concerns that such a conversion rate would ignite inflation and throw the economy into recession, he pledged not to raise taxes. An increase in government debt as a result of subsidizing East Germans would lead interest rates to rise, further slowing growth. Already, ordinary West Germans were recoiling at the high cost of monetary union. The Social Democrats capitalized on the public reaction in elections in Lower Saxony on May 13 to gain ground at the expense of Kohl's Christian Democrats. The next day, Kohl, worried that disillusionment would grow as time passed, spoke of advancing the date of unification and holding all-German elections in 1990, when the next West German election was scheduled.

Bush was due to host Gorbachev from May 31 to June 3. In preparation for the summit meeting, Washington began putting together an "incentives package." One incentive was American forbearance in the Baltics. After Lithuania's declaration of independence in March, Moscow had begun military maneuvers, deployed special units of K.G.B. troops, and imposed a cutoff of oil and natural gas to put psychological pressure on the republic to back down. Demands to impose sanctions began reverberating in Congress, but on April 24 President Bush rejected this course.[138] When President Vytautas Landsbergis of Lithuania spoke darkly of "another Munich," Bush, furious but unfazed, secretly encouraged Kohl and Mitterrand to write Landsbergis to indicate that he favored suspension of Lithuania's declaration of independence and a negotiated resolution of the dispute. After Prime Minister Kazimiera Prunskiene, a nationalist whose ardor was tempered by prudence, endorsed the initiative, Bush met with her on May 3. She agreed to suspend independence if Moscow opened talks.[139]

Bush had taken domestic political risks on Lithuania in order to cooperate with Moscow, but he was unwilling to do much on aid or trade, an urgent priority for Gorbachev. On May 4 in Bonn, Shevardnadze, on Gorbachev's instructions, had asked for a line of credit, hard currency that Moscow could use to purchase foreign goods and buy off rising discontent at home. On May 8 Moscow got more specific. It wanted 20 billion deutsche marks (about $12 billion) in credits, with a guarantee by Western governments to repay the loans. The guarantee was essential for Moscow to obtain more credits from financial institutions because of growing doubts about its creditworthiness. It was short of foreign exchange and had not been making prompt payments on its outstanding debts. Without informing the cabinet, Kohl dispatched his foreign policy aide, Horst Teltschik, to Moscow, accompanied by representatives of two leading German banks. On May 14 they saw Prime Minister Nikolai Ryzhkov and Foreign Minister Shevardnadze, who asked for an unconditional credit of $2.5 to $3.3 billion to meet current payments and another $16.6 to $25 billion over the longer term. The loan would be paid off over ten to fifteen years, with no payments due for five years.

Kohl disclosed the request to Bush in Washington on May 17 and said his government would be willing to guarantee a loan of 5 billion deutsche marks (about $3 billion). Bush refused to provide any credits. Kohl begged him to reconsider, but Bush was adamant, citing Lithuania as the reason. He was also reluctant to make loans without a firm Soviet commitment to economic reform. Kohl pleaded with him to help Gorbachev, not wait for him to be overthrown, but Bush would not budge.[140]

Moscow also wanted to limit the Bundeswehr, Germany's armed forces. Negotiations on conventional forces in Europe (CFE) were nearing agreement on troop cuts for NATO and Warsaw Pact members, including a higher ceiling for U.S. than for Soviet forces. NATO members had already committed themselves to further CFE talks to lower the ceilings on forces in Central Europe, but Shevardnadze in meetings with Baker on May 16–17 asked for numerical and geographic limits on German forces to be set now in two-plus-four talks rather than be put off until CFE II. Aware of long-standing West German objections to being singled out for limits on its forces, Baker rejected the idea.[141] The United States also kept backing away from its earlier commitment to limit NATO expansion. In working-level talks with the Soviets on May 18, Robert Zoellick offered not to station NATO forces in eastern Germany during a transition period while Soviet forces withdrew. A temporary limit on NATO deployments in the east, a transition period for Soviet withdrawal, and a follow-on to CFE were three of the nine assurances in an "incentives package" that Washington had worked out with Bonn.[142]

Zoellick also promised the start of new arms control talks on short-range nuclear forces. Deployment of a follow-on to the Lance missile was dead, but talks would provide for a decent burial. President Bush had called for a review of NATO strategy, Zoellick noted, which would lead to changes in its force posture.

Bonn had already agreed to a sixth assurance, reaffirmation of its commitment not to possess or produce nuclear, biological, and chemical weapons. West Germany was the source of two more assurances, that it would resolve the border question and that it would arrange economic ties with the Soviet Union, satisfying East Germany's contractual commitments and debt obligations in the bargain.

A final assurance concerned the future of European security. The United States committed itself to modest enhancement of CSCE, including a meeting of CSCE ministers in September followed by a CSCE summit, conditioned on the conclusion of a CFE accord. Almost all of America's allies were willing to do more to build up CSCE, securing the Soviet Union a place in the new Europe.

There was less to the nine assurances than the Bush administration tried to make of them. "We had already planned to take all these steps individually," says Baker, "but by wrapping them in a package and calling them the 'nine assurances,' we greatly enhanced their political effect. . . ."[143]

Later the same day, as Zoellick's working group met, Baker, in a one-on-one meeting with Gorbachev, repeated the nine assurances. Gorbachev was frank about a quid pro quo for a united Germany in NATO. "Why should we do this? What's in it for us?"[144] He said the Soviet Union needed $15 to $20 billion in loans and credits over the next few years and asked for an American contribution. Baker was unreceptive. He noted how difficult it was to justify spending U.S. taxpayer money when the Soviets were subsidizing Cuba and squeezing Lithuania.

Baker cabled Bush his impression that Gorbachev was feeling pressured at home and that "Germany definitely overloads his circuits right now." He recommended against forcing the issue just yet: "We ought to let the process go forward, continue to try to meet Soviet concerns, but not press them to accept our objective. It's best to let it happen." One concern, he felt, had to be met: "We probably will have to get more specific on how and when Bundeswehr limits are going to be achieved if we want a CFE agreement."[145]

Upon his arrival at the White House on May 31, Gorbachev wasted no time getting to the point: he wanted American help for perestroika. A U.S.-Soviet trade agreement was essential. Conceding that Lithuania was a problem for Americans, he promised to pursue peaceful dialogue. When talk turned to Germany, Bush repeated the nine assurances, then made the case for a united Germany in NATO. Gorbachev first suggested that Germany be a member of both alliances. During a transition period of several years' duration, each alliance would be transformed into more of a political institution. Bush then noted that, under the Helsinki Final Act, all nations had the right to choose their allies. Shouldn't Germany? Gorbachev assented, "The United States and the Soviet Union are in favor of Germany deciding herself in which alliance she would like to participate" after the two-plus-four reached a settlement. Bush reformulated the point: "The United States is unequivocally advocating Germany's membership in NATO. However, should Germany prefer to make a different choice, we will respect it." As his aides recoiled, Gorbachev agreed.[146] Once again, he had shown his support for self-determination and cooperative security.

After the session, Bush, having taken the temperature in Congress, decided to go ahead with a trade agreement. Deferring to Gorbachev's wishes, he decided not to link the agreement to Moscow's actions in Lithuania. He insisted on another condition, however. He would not submit the agreement to Congress until a new Soviet law was enacted liberalizing emigration.

At Camp David, Gorbachev renewed his plea for aid. Bush again refused. He wanted more economic reform, movement on Lithuania, and a reduction in Soviet subsidies to Cuba before bilateral aid was possible. Still, he promised, the G-7 would consider multilateral aid for Moscow at its July summit meeting.

POLITICAL WINDOW DRESSING BY NATO

With something to show for his efforts, but not much, Gorbachev returned home to a hostile reception in Moscow. Now the contrast sharpened between the position he and Shevardnadze were taking in private and the formal Soviet negotiating position.

On June 5, in Copenhagen, Baker again took up the issue of unification with Shevardnadze. The Soviets had suggested the idea of an agreement between NATO and the Warsaw Pact. What did he have in mind? Shevardnadze mentioned a commitment to "no first use" of nuclear weapons. Baker demurred. He was more receptive to Shevardnadze's suggestion that the United States say in public what Baker had been telling him in private, that it no longer considered the Soviet Union an enemy. Shevardnadze promised a more specific reply in ten days. He also repeated his desire to have Germany accept a limit of 200,000 to 250,000 on its armed forces now, but he was willing to defer codifying it until all the other members of NATO and the Warsaw Pact accepted limits on their armed forces in CFE.[147]

Kohl thought NATO had to show that it was ready to adapt to the post–cold war world. Over dinner in the White House on June 8, he broached the idea of a nonaggression treaty with the Warsaw Pact. Bush rejected it, fearing it would prop up the Eastern alliance. Kohl again brought up the possibility of aid, but Bush remained non-committal.

Shevardnadze had more of a package to propose when he met with Genscher in Münster on June 18. To build up CSCE, he wanted to add a secretariat, a crisis prevention center, and a military monitoring center. He dropped insistence on retaining four-power rights during a transition period, but he still wanted a treaty signed by NATO and the Warsaw Pact to regulate their relations, a pledge that membership in one alliance not preclude membership in the other, renunciation of first use of nuclear weapons by both alliances, elimination of all short-range nuclear arms, a ceiling on German troop levels, and reductions in NATO troops in Germany as Soviet troops withdrew.[148]

Moscow's German specialists had adopted a much tougher negotiating position for the two-plus-four. During an interim settlement that would remain in force for five years, "the competence of the Warsaw Treaty and NATO respectively shall not extend to territories that did not fall within their scope"; eastern Germany would be demilitarized until NATO and the Warsaw Pact were both dissolved or Germany withdrew from both alliances; and German forces would be limited qualitatively as well as quantitatively—"structurally modified to render them incapable of offensive action." Restrictions would be imposed on domestic political activity in Germany to prevent a revival of Nazism.[149] Tabling the proposal in the two-plus-four, Shevardnadze told Baker in Berlin on June 22 that "we were guided by our domestic situation." Baker's response was blunt: "In the final analysis Germany will unify, and we are prepared, with others, to grant Germany the sovereignty it deserves and it is due. We are going to make every effort to accommodate your security concerns as we move forward, and I hope you will not be isolated in opposition to German sovereignty." Shevardnadze was just as blunt in reminding Baker what was at stake. The situation in Moscow was very difficult, and some decisions had to be made collectively, he said, alluding to his April 2 instructions from the politburo. Backing off, Baker said Soviet concerns would be addressed, as had been done in the nine assurances. These assurances were not public, replied Shevardnadze, so a lot would depend on the message that NATO sent at its July summit.[150]

President Bush had raised public expectations about the London summit in a speech on May 4. In preparation for it, Robert Blackwill and Philip Zelikow of the N.S.C. staff drew up a list of initiatives and a draft communiqué to satisfy Shevardnadze.[151] As political gestures designed to downplay NATO's anti-Soviet character, NATO would invite Warsaw Pact members to establish diplomatic liaison offices, Gorbachev would be asked to address NATO, and the NATO commanding general would hold talks with his Soviet counterpart. In a change of strategy, NATO would move away from forward defense.

Members would seek to cut conventional forces by half in CFE II, which postponed the urgent question of limits on German forces. NATO would replace its nuclear doctrine of flexible response with one of "minimum deterrence," abandoning reliance on early first use of nuclear weapons. The United States would eliminate its nuclear artillery in Europe, withdraw three-fourths of its nuclear arms, and leave no more than a thousand air-delivered warheads. It also would propose phased global elimination of all short-range nuclear forces except for air-delivered ones in upcoming talks. It would seek regular summit meetings of CSCE and creation of a small secretariat, a center for crisis management, and a CSCE parliament, the Assembly of Europe. That fell far short of a proposal by West Germany and Italy to make CSCE the central structure in "an all-embracing European security architecture."

In interagency deliberations in early June, State Department representatives added a joint declaration by NATO and the Warsaw Pact to the list of initiatives to be proposed. More significantly, Arnold Kanter of the N.S.C. staff suggested the possibility of changing NATO doctrine to renounce first use of nuclear weapons. After all, NATO's conventional strength had long been adequate to deter and withstand a Warsaw Pact attack.[152] With the Warsaw Pact now moribund and the Red Army in retreat and falling apart, the alliance could do without the threat to use nuclear weapons and could reduce its nuclear forces accordingly.

Interagency committees watered down the initiatives, one by one. The change in nuclear doctrine was strongly opposed by Paul Wolfowitz, under secretary of defense, and Ronald Lehman, director of the Arms Control and Disarmament Agency (A.C.D.A.). Instead, Blackwill, Kanter's N.S.C. colleague, drafted a sentence for the communiqué: "Alliance nuclear weapons will truly become weapons of last resort." The effect was to change the rhetoric to save the doctrine. A draft of a NATO–Warsaw Pact joint declaration by the Soviet foreign ministry was trashed by the N.S.C. staff: "There are at least a dozen major ideas in the Soviet proposal which we consider so unacceptable as to be nonnegotiable." On June 18 the interagency European Strategy Steering Group, chaired by Deputy National Security Adviser Robert Gates, agreed to propose permanent diplomatic liaison at NATO for members of the Warsaw Pact and accepted the initiatives on CSCE. Even though the Pentagon raised no objections, the State Department blocked proposals to eliminate nuclear artillery unilaterally, withdraw three-fourths of the American warheads in Europe, and propose a global ban on short-range nuclear arms. Anticipating opposition from Britain, A.C.D.A. director Lehman objected to calls for replacing the doctrines of flexible response and forward defense. The draft communiqué was reworded to say that NATO would be "moving away from 'forward defense' toward a reduced forward presence and modifying 'flexible response' to reflect a reduced reliance on nuclear weapons." A cabinet-level meeting the next day accepted these changes. It also approved a NATO pledge of nonaggression and invited the Warsaw Pact to reciprocate as a substitute for a NATO–Warsaw Pact declaration. It agreed to seek "further far-reaching reductions of offensive capabilities," but it dropped a pledged cut "by as much as one-half in some instances." Most substantive changes were excised. What was left was mostly political window dressing.

Instead of the usual turgid bureaucratic prose, the draft communiqué read more like a press agent's blurb to dramatize the birth of a new NATO. To avoid transmitting it to Brussels, where it would be translated back into bureaucratese, Bush sent it directly to Kohl, Thatcher, Mitterrand, Italian prime minister Giulio Andreotti, and NATO secretary-general Manfred Woerner. The "lively draft" left Thatcher unhappy. "We should not adopt a declaration which contains some eye-catching propositions before we have really worked out the underlying strategy," she wrote Bush. She also opposed the liaison missions: "Won't people ask, what is the point of defense and security if we are letting those who were so recently our bitter foes—and at worst could become so again—so close to the innermost councils of our defense and preparedness?" In reply, Bush expressed "worry that if we say nothing about the future of flexible response and our strategy for deterrence at this summit, we will just allow the advocates of no first use and denuclearization to set the terms for the debate, including in Germany."[153] The way to preserve nuclear strategy, he maintained, was to revise public rhetoric. Thatcher was unpersuaded. She wanted a new draft. Bush deflected that. "We will be able to work on the specific language of the document in London," he wrote her. He gave Mitterrand a similar response when the French president objected to the wording on nuclear strategy, to the limited role for CSCE, and to the political role for NATO implied by inviting the Warsaw Pact to send representatives there.[154]

At the July 5–6 summit, Thatcher argued against the language on NATO nuclear doctrine in her characteristically undiplomatic way. "To me the expression 'weapons of last resort' is very clear. Last resort: last means last and nothing else and yet I am told that it is not so, that the expression is ambiguous. But I have often read confusing words in communiqués and found them very confusing; but to be told that clear words are confusing is, to me, a new dimension of diplomacy. Of course, as colleagues round this table will know, I never had much use for diplomacy anyway, and I've got on very well without it."[155] The British did succeed in further weakening NATO's pledge to seek more far-reaching conventional force reductions, but the "last resort" language remained.

The president flew on to Houston for the G-7 summit on July 9–11. A month earlier he had told Gorbachev that the G-7 would consider aid for the Soviet Union, and it did, but Bush was still opposed. With Britain, Japan, and Canada also unwilling to provide aid, the G-7 instead asked the International Monetary Fund to undertake a study of Soviet economic needs for completion by year's end.

On the flight to Houston, Bush had sent a note to Gorbachev. "As you read the NATO declaration, I want you to know that it was written with you importantly in mind, and I made that point strongly to my colleagues in London," he wrote. "I hope today's NATO declaration will persuade you that NATO can and will serve the security interests of Europe as a whole."[156] That was Bush's bottom line on cooperative security. He had gone as far as he would go for Gorbachev. Anything more would be up to Kohl.

COOPERATIVE SECURITY AT STAVROPOL

A summit between Chancellor Kohl and President Gorbachev was scheduled for July 15 in Moscow. Even before that climactic encounter West Germany had moved to accommodate the Soviet leader. At a two-plus-four meeting on June 9, Bonn had accepted a road map for resolving the Polish border question, in which Moscow had a stake. It agreed that a united Germany would consist of "the territory of the Federal Republic of Germany, the German Democratic Republic, and the whole of Berlin." It promised to renew this pledge in a binding treaty with Poland, renounce territorial claims against any country, and amend any part of the West German Basic Law that might conflict with this commitment. The four powers would take note of these pledges and "state that the provisional character of Germany's borders has ended."[157]

Kohl next tried to line up substantial aid for the Soviet Union at a June 25–26 summit meeting of the European Community. President Mitterrand of France joined in the appeal, but Prime Minister Thatcher blocked agreement. The following day, Kohl went ahead on his own, extending a line of credit of $3 billion. The West Germans pledged to cover the upkeep for Soviet forces in eastern Germany as well, at an expected cost of $850 million.[158]

Kohl also was prepared to satisfy the demand for a ceiling on Bundeswehr troops if Gorbachev accepted German membership in NATO. The Germans had told Scowcroft at Houston the ceiling would be 350,000 to 370,000, but en route to Moscow, Kohl and Genscher revisited the issue. Kohl proposed 400,000, the defense ministry figure, and Genscher 350,000. In the end, they split the difference and settled on a ceiling of 370,000 troops.[159]

Gorbachev, meanwhile, was embroiled in domestic political wrangling of his own. The twenty-eighth congress of the Communist Party, which Gorbachev and the reformers had once intended to be a showdown with party conservatives, convened on July 2 with the conservatives on the rampage. Gorbachev was flayed for having "lost" Eastern Europe. Again he left it to Shevardnadze to answer the charges. The foreign minister rose to the challenge: "Soviet diplomacy did not and could not aim to prevent the elimination in other countries of administrative-command systems and totalitarian regimes which were forced upon them and alien to them. That would have contradicted the logic of our own actions and the principles of new thinking," he told delegates.[160] "My personal fate was on the line," Shevardnadze recalled. "In my circumstances, it was especially important to see some encouraging response from 'the other side.'"[161] NATO's London declaration came in handy. Putting the best spin on it he could, Shevardnadze cited it as evidence of Western reciprocity.

Having withstood the conservatives' onslaught at the party congress, they decided to take advantage of disarray in the party to clinch the deal on unification on their own, once the party congress adjourned, without consulting the politburo. "The moves in July were never discussed there," said Shevardnadze's close aide, Sergei Tarasenko. "The opposition would have been too great."[162]

Kohl and Gorbachev met on July 15, accompanied only by Horst Teltschik, Anatoly Chernyaev, and translators. Kohl set the tone at the outset. They had been too young to fight in World War II, he began, but they were both old enough to have memories of those years. It was time to address that history. He remembered the war well, responded Gorbachev, but it no longer mattered who had won and who had lost. Germany and Russia were now living together in one world. Kohl then raised the three issues he wanted to resolve: withdrawal of Soviet troops from East Germany, united Germany's membership in NATO, and future limits on Germany's armed forces. In response Gorbachev spoke of common security. He recalled trying to disabuse President Bush of the idea that he favored "dislodging the U.S. from Europe." At Malta, "I stated firmly that the presence of U.S. forces in Europe is stabilizing." He also took note of the London summit. "Now the political context is better than two or three months ago," he said, citing "the present transformative movement of NATO" and its "accent on the political sphere of activities." He gave Kohl a paper outlining a proposed treaty of cooperation and friendship between the U.S.S.R. and Germany. Then he proposed the basis of a deal. First, a united Germany should consist of the territory of East and West Germany and Berlin within current borders. Second, Germany would have to reiterate its pledge to renounce nuclear, chemical, and biological weapons. Third, NATO military structures should not extend to East German territory. Fourth, four-power rights would end. Kohl asked whether Germany would be fully sovereign at the time it unified. That was obvious, replied Gorbachev, but an agreement would have to be worked out to permit Soviet troops to remain in Germany for a "three to four year period." Kohl agreed. "A unified Germany will be a member of NATO," Gorbachev declared. "De facto the former territory of the G.D.R. will not be a sphere of NATO activity as long as Soviet forces are located there." Assuming agreement on a transitional arrangement, Gorbachev said, four-power rights would end once a settlement was reached in two-plus-four talks. "The sovereignty of a unified Germany in any case will not be in doubt."[163] Teltschik was ecstatic. "What a sensation!" he wrote in his diary. "We hadn't expected such a clear promise from Gorbachev."[164]

In an especially astute use of inducements for cooperative security, Kohl offered aid to repatriate Red Army troops. Housing and employment were in short supply back home, so the aid would expedite the troops' departure. West Germany also assumed East

Germany's financial obligations to the Soviet Union. In a separate meeting, Finance Minister Theo Waigel drew the line on additional aid; that would have to be provided multilaterally.

The two leaders then flew to Gorbachev's home in Stavropol. En route the Soviet leader asked the German chancellor about cutting the Bundeswehr. Kohl, as agreed with Genscher, offered to set the ceiling at 370,000. Gorbachev said he had expected a lower number, but Kohl responded that deeper cuts would mean ending conscription and relying on a professional army.

On July 16 the leaders met again, this time with ministers present, and reviewed the results of the previous day's talks. Gorbachev reaffirmed that Germany would be fully sovereign and, as such, could choose to be a member of NATO, but he did not want this point emphasized in public. NATO "structures" would not extend to former G.D.R. territory while Soviet troops remained there, which would make Germany's membership in NATO more tolerable in Moscow. This restriction, Kohl and Genscher underscored, would last only as long as Soviet troops were stationed in Germany. Bundeswehr units in the east would not be integrated into NATO, but in the meantime the commitment to mutual defense under Articles 5 and 6 of the North Atlantic Treaty would apply to the entire territory of a united Germany. According to Genscher, Gorbachev approved with the proviso that "no foreign troops could ever be deployed in these territories. The chancellor accepted this restriction."[165] Separate agreements would be concluded to allow the temporary stationing of Soviet troops and to settle financial arrangements for their departure. Shevardnadze asked for a ceiling of 350,000 troops. In response, Genscher restated the agreed position of his government: in conventional force negotiations Germany would declare that it would accept a troop ceiling of 370,000 for CFE II once other participating states accepted similar limits. Gorbachev agreed.[166]

Announcement of the accord caught Washington off guard. Reporters traveling with Secretary of State Baker to a two-plus-four meeting in Paris witnessed his surprise and annoyance and concluded that the administration had been left in the lurch. Pavel Palazchenko, an adviser to Shevardnadze, recalls being asked by reporters whether the deal at Stavropol was a snub to the rest of the two-plus-four: "I told them frankly, though not for attribution, that the two-plus-four and our other attempts to work out a formula on the NATO membership issue with the United States and other Western allies had not been particularly productive, and that therefore striking a deal directly with Kohl was all that remained for us to do."[167]

The two-plus-four meeting was anticlimactic. Its task, said Shevardnadze, was to turn the agreement on principles into an accord for the meeting of foreign ministers on September 12 in Moscow. At a NATO foreign ministers' meeting on August 10, ten days after Iraq invaded Kuwait, Genscher reported that the date for unification was being advanced to October because monetary union was causing East Germany's economy to implode. With East Germans able to spend deutsche marks on Western goods and the Soviet Union unable to afford hard currency for East German goods, manufacturing in the east was grinding to a halt.

On August 27 Shevardnadze wrote Genscher that unless the Germans provided more help, it would take at least five to seven years to withdraw the Soviet troops, not the three to four years agreed to in July. Kohl decided to stand firm on the costs of the troops stationed in the east but to be generous on housing for the returning troops. He could afford to be: at the prevailing rate of exchange, construction costs in Russia were a pittance. On September 5 Soviet officials submitted a bill for 36 billion deutsche marks (more than $20 billion) in all: DM 3.5 billion to cover the costs of stationing troops in the east, DM 3 million for transporting them home, DM 500 million for retraining them, DM 11.5 billion for constructing houses and schools back home, and DM 17.5 billion in compensation for Soviet-owned real estate in the G.D.R. After much haggling, on September 10 Gorbachev spoke to Kohl by telephone. He was frank about his political need to have something to show for agreeing to German unification. Gorbachev's asking price came down to DM 15 billion, and Kohl agreed to DM 12 billion plus an interest-free credit of DM 3 billion.

That was not quite all. In August Moscow submitted another request for subsidized food, and Bonn agreed to provide about 1 billion deutsche marks' worth (about $600 million). The sum would be used to purchase East German produce not easily sold in Western Europe, in effect subsidizing East German farmers.[168]

The text of a final settlement was worked out in the two-plus-four in early September. The main sticking point was the extent of NATO activities to be permitted in East Germany. The West Germans first proposed that American, British, or French forces "shall not cross a line" into the former East Germany, except for access to

Berlin.[169] Other allies interpreted the Stavropol statement to mean limiting the stationing of foreign forces in the east but not the movement of forces in and out or military exercises and overflights. The allies did pledge not to redeploy their nuclear weapons into eastern Germany, a largely symbolic gesture since only German forces would be stationed there and U.S. nuclear warheads to be turned over to the Bundeswehr in the event of war remained in American possession. The Soviets wanted to exclude all dual-capable weapons from the east, but the United States and Great Britain refused, contending that would prevent any NATO aircraft and artillery from being deployed there since all are capable of being nuclear armed. The Soviets proposed that foreign forces would be "neither stationed nor deployed" in eastern Germany until Soviet forces departed. West Germany was amenable, on the understanding that "deployed" did not preclude transit or training, just large-scale exercises, but the United States and Great Britain were opposed. The bitter squabble among the allies delayed completion of the declaration until the eve of the signing ceremony, when the two-plus-four ministers adopted an "agreed minute" to the treaty recognizing the obvious, that "any questions with respect to the application of the word 'deployed' . . . will be decided by the government of the united Germany."[170]

The ministers signed the Treaty on the Final Settlement with Respect to Germany in Moscow the next day, September 12. On October 3, 1990, the Federal Republic of Germany absorbed the German Democratic Republic. Four-power rights in Germany came to an end. Germany was unified.

A DOMESTIC BASE FOR COOPERATIVE SECURITY

Throughout the unification controversy, the United States bridled at cooperative security. The Bush administration was prepared to bargain with the Soviet Union, but it approached diplomatic give-and-take in a realist frame of mind, acting in accord with Thucydides' dictum, "The strong do what they will, the weak do what they must."[171] Soviet and West German leaders acted under a different assumption, that the best way to provide for their security was to cooperate, trying to take each other's interests into account instead of taking advantage of one another.

Nothing makes this clearer than their stands on NATO expansion into eastern Germany. The Bush administration treated NATO as if it were an end in itself, not a means to another end, enhancing American security by reducing the risk of war in Europe. Arguably, a better means to that end was to help with Russian reconstruction. Most officials in Bonn thought so. In an effort to reassure Russia, West Germany was willing to go so far as to accept temporary limits on its sovereign right to defend the eastern part of a united Germany. In February 1990, after talks with West Germany's foreign minister, Secretary of State Baker had assured Gorbachev and Shevardnadze that "NATO's jurisdiction would not shift one inch eastward from its present position." The Bush administration began backing away from that pledge almost immediately. The Clinton administration reneged on that commitment altogether when it decided to expand NATO into Eastern Europe.

Some U.S. officials even claimed that Baker's commitment was not binding because Gorbachev had failed to get it in writing. Such attempts to justify expansion of NATO eastward are worse than cynically deceitful. They are dangerously self-deceptive. The security of the United States—and of Eastern Europe—was best assured by cooperating with Russia. Breaking one's word is no way to cooperate.

NATO expansion gratuitously antagonized America's allies in Moscow and aroused Russia's nationalists, making cooperative security politically precarious. "The issue is not just whether Czechs, Hungarians, and Poles join NATO. The problem is more serious: the rejection of the strategy for a new, common European system agreed to by myself and all the Western leaders when we ended the cold war," Mikhail Gorbachev wrote in March 1999. "I feel betrayed by the West. The opportunity we seized on behalf of peace has been lost. The whole idea of a new world order has been completely abandoned."[172]

Bonn was willing to go much further than Washington in helping perestroika. The West Germans insisted that Gorbachev be invited to the July 1991 G-7 summit in London. They spearheaded efforts to secure Soviet membership in the European Bank for Reconstruction and Development, the International Monetary Fund, and the World Bank. Most of all, they gave some $40 billion in aid of their own, nearly 3 percent of West Germany's GDP. This was comparable to the sum that the United States gave Western Europe under the Marshall Plan.[173] As the American ambassador to Moscow at the time, Jack Matlock, concluded, "In the final analysis it was the German concessions that gave Gorbachev what he needed for an agreement."[174]

Cooperative security, in order to succeed, has to rest on a firm domestic political base. In the Soviet Union, where Gorbachev and Shevardnadze were challenging a long-held belief in the inevitable antagonism of capitalism and communism, that base was bound to be shaky. They could shore up their base with evidence of Western reciprocity. Concrete acts were forthcoming from West Germany, where cooperative security was rooted in the political consensus on *Ostpolitik*, but not from the United States, where the administration was in the thrall of realism.

Although it had political leeway to cooperate, the Bush administration felt constrained by unilateralists on the right wing of the Republican Party to limit support for the Soviet Union. Cooperation also received lukewarm backing from the foreign policy establishment. Above all, most administration officials were themselves disinclined to help Gorbachev because of their own shared images of the Soviet Union and of international politics. These shared images were shaped by realist convictions that nations pursue their interests regardless of who is in power—indeed, regardless of the nature of their domestic political and economic systems—and that as great powers the United States and the Soviet Union were doomed to rivalry. Yet, in making NATO the point of its policy, the Bush administration was prepared to intervene in domestic politics abroad, keeping Helmut Kohl in power even if that meant sacrificing Mikhail Gorbachev. American security would have been better served if it had tried to meet Gorbachev's domestic needs as well as Kohl's.

4

FROM RIVALRY TO ALLIANCE
IN THE THIRD WORLD

*We were both struck with the thought that we were perhaps
at a watershed of history. The Soviet Union was standing
alongside us, not only in the United Nations, but also in
condemning and taking action against Iraqi aggression.
That cooperation represented fundamental change. . . .
Compared to the period we had just come through, the era
ahead seemed like a new world order.*

—Brent Scowcroft[1]

The third world was the battleground of the waning years of the cold
war. An end to Moscow's meddling in regional conflicts was high on
Washington's agenda, along with human rights and arms control. "A
litmus test of Soviet seriousness in response to our concerns would be
whether they are moving seriously toward a real pullback from one of
the positions gained in the 1970s" was the way Secretary of State
George Shultz expressed it in a March 1983 memo to President
Reagan. "Here I was thinking of Afghanistan, Angola, or Cambodia,"
Shultz recalled.[2] It would take a year for Shultz's agenda to become
administration policy.[3] Jack Matlock, who helped write the president's
speech articulating that policy, says, "He had in mind the political reality that the U.S. Senate was unlikely to ratify a major arms reduction
treaty if the Soviet Union invaded another country, just as Congress
would refuse to eliminate barriers to trade if the Soviet regime seriously
violated its citizens' human rights. If Soviet society remained closed,
arms treaties would be much more difficult to verify."[4]

For realists in the Reagan and Bush administrations, intervention in regional conflicts served as the "acid test" of new thinking.[5]
For militant ideologues, that, along with Moscow's support for clients
in Cuba and Nicaragua, became a convenient cudgel for clubbing

anyone who wanted to improve U.S.-Soviet relations, especially by concluding arms control agreements.

An end to Soviet intervention in regional conflicts was central to Gorbachev's new thinking as well. Under its doctrine of peaceful coexistence, the Soviet Union had sought to limit direct conflict with the United States and its close allies in order to avoid nuclear war, but it had continued to wage class struggle by supporting wars of national liberation. Gorbachev's new thinking rejected the very idea of class struggle and replaced it with common security. Not a recent convert to nonintervention, he was against the Afghanistan invasion from the outset. In the 1970s, while he was still working in Stavropol, he befriended Eduard Shevardnadze, a fellow rising star in nearby Georgia. "We spoke of the many absurdities of our life and came to the conclusion that we just couldn't go on like this," Shevardnadze recalls. As candidate members of the politburo in December 1979, "we learned from the newspapers that Soviet troops had invaded Afghanistan and hastened to meet to discuss it. We agreed it was a fatal error that would cost the country dearly."[6]

If Moscow's readiness to withdraw from Afghanistan and cut off support for its clients elsewhere was a valid test of cooperative security, so was Washington's willingness to facilitate an end to rivalry in the third world. Gorbachev passed the test in Afghanistan. Reagan and Bush did not. By contrast, the United States was willing to defer to the Soviet Union's interests for the sake of their common good in allying against Iraq. As a result, the war in the Persian Gulf became the high point of cooperative security.

No Fig Leaf to Cover Withdrawal from Afghanistan

To roll back what they supposed were Soviet gains in the third world in the 1970s, the Reagan administration backed insurgencies around the globe. To devotees of what became known as the Reagan Doctrine, this was a way to sap Soviet strength. Their assumption was that it would be costlier for Moscow to wage counterinsurgencies to protect pro-Soviet regimes than to wage insurgencies against them.[7] Yet U.S. support for the mujahideen imposed only marginal costs on Moscow without exerting any demonstrable influence on Gorbachev to withdraw from

Afghanistan. His decision was informed by his belief in common security, which led him to reject the ends and means of wars of national liberation and to ease antagonism with the United States.

National Security Decision Directive 75, issued on January 17, 1983, laid the foundation for the Reagan Doctrine. The administration's Soviet policy consisted of three elements: "external resistance to Soviet imperialism; internal pressure on the U.S.S.R. to weaken the sources of Soviet imperialism; and negotiations to eliminate, on the basis of strict reciprocity, outstanding disagreements." NSDD-75 defined U.S. objectives in Afghanistan: "to keep maximum pressure on Moscow for withdrawal and to ensure that the Soviets' political, military, and other costs remain high while the occupation continues"; in short, to bleed the Soviet Union.[8] NSDD-166, signed in March 1985, set a more radical aim of driving the Soviets out of Afghanistan "by all means available."[9] An annex listed covert action to be taken in pursuit of this aim.

Covert assistance, including arms, for the purpose of "harassing" Soviet forces in Afghanistan was first authorized by the Carter administration on July 3, 1979, six months *before* Moscow committed itself to large-scale military intervention.[10] The Reagan administration stepped up arms aid to $80 million for fiscal year 1982 and raised additional funds from Saudi Arabia.[11] In April 1985 President Reagan signed an intelligence finding to expand covert action, approving funds to train Afghans in urban terrorism and sabotage and in propaganda operations and to supply small arms, plastic explosives, and a transmitter for Radio Free Afghanistan.

Even before the latest American aid could reach Afghanistan, Gorbachev was taking his first steps to leave. In the course of canvassing a wide array of experts on domestic policy before becoming general secretary, Gorbachev also had solicited advice on Afghanistan.[12] Barely a month after taking office, he ordered a secret reappraisal of Afghanistan policy. Just after the Central Committee plenum of April 1985, Gorbachev subsequently disclosed, the politburo had done a "hard, impartial analysis of the situation and already at that time began to seek a way out."[13] Having given the military six months to try to turn the tide of battle on the ground, in late May he authorized a new negotiating proposal that would open the way to a settlement of the war.[14] In early June 1985 he also had the Central Committee secretariat secretly order the first drawdown of Soviet forces in Afghanistan.[15] The C.I.A. was unaware of this development. It had penetrated the Soviet defense ministry and was privy to military plans for escalating the war, but it did not have the same access to the officials close to Gorbachev who were planning his exit strategy.[16]

That month Gorbachev responded to a letter from President Reagan criticizing Soviet actions in the third world. "Without saying so," Reagan recalled, "Gorbachev implied that the Soviets would like to extricate themselves from the war in Afghanistan and urged us to convince the Pakistanis not to support the Afghan rebels."[17] Reagan was unresponsive, leading Gorbachev to complain to him on December 24, "With regard to Afghanistan, one gets the impression that the United States's side intentionally fails to notice the open door leading to a political settlement."[18]

On the eve of the October 1985 party plenum, Gorbachev stunned Afghan leader Babrak Karmal in Moscow by telling him that Afghanistan lacked a revolutionary base and urging him to work out a power-sharing arrangement with the opposition. The Soviet Union would continue to supply arms, he said, but Karmal would have to defend himself. Soviet troops would be withdrawing.[19] Karmal's recalcitrance would lead to his demotion seven months later.[20] On October 17, 1985, Gorbachev won approval in principle from the politburo to withdraw once a friendly government was in place in Kabul. His top aide, Anatoly Chernyaev, later expressed regret that the decision was not made public at that time.[21]

One consequence of not going public was that resistance to withdrawal persisted in the politburo commission, chaired by Shevardnadze, that was deputized to implement Afghanistan policy. Aleksandr Yakovlev, a member of the commission, recalled in 1991 that Sergei Akhromeyev and Valentin Varennikov, the military representatives, and Viktor Chebrikov and Vladimir Kryuchkov, from the K.G.B., would offer "seemingly objective and reasonable arguments," but "when you put them all together, day after day, . . . it became apparent that they were deliberately holding things up, spinning things out in order to put off the moment when it would be possible to say: That is it, we are getting out."[22]

Gorbachev and Shevardnadze kept up the pressure. In his political report to the twenty-seventh party congress on February 25, 1986, Gorbachev spoke of common security. In a phrase that was dropped from his report only to be restored at Shevardnadze's insistence, Gorbachev called the war "a bleeding wound" and expressed a desire to withdraw Soviet forces "in the nearest future."[23] He noted, "The

time scale for their step-by-step withdrawal has been worked out with
the Afghan side" and could be put into effect "as soon as a political settlement has been achieved which will provide for a real end to and
reliably guarantee a non-renewal of the outside armed interference
in the internal affairs of the Democratic Republic of Afghanistan."[24]

On March 14, 1986, just two weeks after Gorbachev's speech to the
twenty-seventh party congress, Reagan sent a message of his own to
Congress. Denouncing "continuing Soviet adventurism in the developing world" as "inimical to global security and an obstacle to fundamental improvement of Soviet-American relations," he called for stepped-up
efforts "to convince the Soviet Union that the policies on which it
embarked in the '70's *cannot work*."[25] The rousing rhetoric failed to drum
up congressional support for the largest peacetime defense budget ever
proposed in American history—$320 billion. For the first time in years,
Congress made significant cuts in funding for defense.

Three days earlier, at the urging of members of Congress from
both parties, the president had secretly boosted aid to the Afghan
insurgents, including extensive targeting data from satellite recon-
naissance, communications intercepts, and more than $300 million
in additional covert military assistance.[26] Part of that sum, it was disclosed on March 30, 1986, was to be spent on arming the insurgents
with Stinger antiaircraft missiles. That was done despite objections
from those in the intelligence community who preferred to keep
American involvement more plausibly deniable and from those in
the army who did not want to deplete its stocks of shoulder-fired
Stingers and who feared the technology would be compromised if
some were sold on the black market or captured on the battlefield
and then reverse-engineered.[27] The Stingers would not score their
first success until September 26, 1986, when three Soviet Hind helicopters landing at Jalalabad airport were shot down, and would not
be deployed in significant numbers until mid-1987.[28]

Although the Reagan administration would later try to take
credit for driving the Soviets out of Afghanistan, the decision to leave
already had been made in Moscow and was beginning to be implemented. The main effect of the rhetoric and the Stingers was to make
life more difficult for Gorbachev, putting "sticks in the spokes," as
he told Shultz, and leaving him vulnerable to attack at home for
yielding to American pressure.[29]

In contrast to reluctant backing for the contras in Nicaragua,
Congress was enthusiastic about covert action in Afghanistan. A

bipartisan majority appropriated some $2 billion for the mujahideen in the 1980s. At times, as with the Stingers, congressional support preceded and exceeded administration requests.[30] A rare exception was a covert action authorized in October 1984 by William Casey, director of central intelligence, on his own authority, to encourage cross-border raids into the Soviet Union. When Casey's program of harassment, sabotage, and subversion in Uzbckistan and Tajikistan was uncovered in 1986, Congress curtailed it, although the Afghan rebels still mounted occasional forays on their own.[31]

The mind-set in Washington had another, more subtle effect. With few exceptions, American officials dismissed the idea that the Soviets would ever agree to withdraw from Afghanistan. Many top officials preferred to see them stay and be bled dry. "The focus was entirely on waging the war in Afghanistan to wear down the Soviets," said Raymond Garthoff. "This high-level inattention to the negotiations later led to some difficulty in the final negotiation in 1988."[32]

A cooperative security approach would have led the United States to seek a graceful exit for the Soviet Union. Instead the Reagan and Bush administrations kept up the pressure throughout 1987, 1988, and 1989 without providing Gorbachev the political cover he sought for his retreat from Afghanistan. One form of cover was an international agreement on Afghanistan. A second was backing for an internal political settlement there. A third was cessation of the American supply of arms to the Afghan resistance.

Proximity talks between Pakistan and Afghanistan had begun in June 1982 with Diego Cordóvez, UN under secretary-general, as go-between. Neither the United States nor the Soviet Union were party to the talks, although a Soviet high-level "observer" participated in the talks. In a major breakthrough on May 28, 1985, the observer, Andrei Kozyrev, told Cordóvez that the Soviet Union would sign an agreement, as coguarantor with the United States, committing it to withdraw.[33] On December 11, 1985, after a bitter intramural struggle, the Reagan administration agreed to sign as coguarantor on condition that the accord contained an acceptable timetable for Soviet withdrawal. American willingness to act as coguarantor rested on a widespread belief in the administration that Moscow would never agree to a timetable.[34] The end of external aid for the mujahideen and the composition of the postwar Kabul government also were issues that remained unresolved.

Although President Reagan had called for negotiations in October 1985 to achieve "an end to violence, the withdrawal of foreign troops, and national reconciliation," over the next two years Moscow tried without success to engage Washington in talks.[35] Ambassador Arthur Hartman informed Secretary of State Shultz that the Soviets "wanted to talk about Afghanistan. They were ready to discuss a timetable for withdrawal and a government of national unity that would include the Afghan freedom fighters and even leaders of armed Afghan groups outside of Afghanistan." Shultz declined to talk: "We would be premature to engage on the agenda as they stated it, I thought. We would not accept a government broadened out of the present regime. Nevertheless, it was a important blink, and I was encouraged."[36] Shultz's tough stance shielded him from attack by the Republican right for his readiness to engage in arms control talks with Moscow.

Gorbachev continued to pursue his version of Vietnamization in Afghanistan over the opposition of his Afghan ally. On May 4, 1986, Moscow helped engineer Babrak Karmal's ouster as party general secretary, though not as president, and his replacement by intelligence chief Mohammed Najibullah. On July 31 Gorbachev announced the withdrawal of six regiments. "We have been at war in Afghanistan six years already. If we don't change our approach we will be there another 20–30 years," Gorbachev told the politburo on November 13, 1986. "We need to wrap up this process in the near future."[37] The politburo decided to set a time frame for withdrawing all Soviet troops, one and a half to two years hence. In hopes of forming a coalition government in Kabul that would broaden the regime's base and prolong Najibullah's rule, it also decided to have Karmal removed from the presidency but not to have Najibullah replace him. Shevardnadze proposed summoning Najibullah to Moscow to inform him of the decisions. During the Afghan president's December 11–14 visit, Gorbachev told him that Soviet troops would be "out of Afghan territory in one and a half to two years."[38] Najibullah balked at yielding the presidency to a potential rival, but upon his return home he told a party plenum that the regime was prepared to join the mujahideen in a process of "national reconciliation" and held out the possibility of a coalition government for all groups willing to "accept a compromise" with the regime. On January 5–7, 1987, Shevardnadze went to Kabul and endorsed the new line. He emphasized that the connection between national reconciliation in Kabul and an accord in Geneva was "a very immediate one, very

direct and close."[39] Yet opposition to a rapid Soviet withdrawal continued in Kabul. So did resistance to forming a coalition government. Although Marshal Akhromeyev and others in Moscow fought
to broaden the base of the Kabul government first, by May 1988
Shevardnadze convinced Gorbachev that it would slow the Soviet
withdrawal.[40]

During talks in Moscow on April 13–15, 1987, Shultz resisted a
plea from Gorbachev to endorse "a modified version" of the government in Kabul now headed by Najibullah. "Solutions are not for
one or the other to make alone, but only in common," Gorbachev
said. Shultz recalls his reaction, "At the right time, I thought, but
not quite yet. The Soviets must leave."[41] The C.I.A.'s assessment that
"the Najibullah regime will not long survive the completion of Soviet
withdrawal even with continued Soviet assistance" became the prevailing wisdom in Washington.[42] Although Shultz did not share that
assessment, he was not about to leave himself open to charges of
propping up a Soviet-installed regime in Kabul, even if it led ultimately to a Muslim fundamentalist one.[43]

Gorbachev now exploited glasnost to undermine bureaucratic
resistance to withdrawal. Starting in summer 1987, a series of articles by Artyom Borovik in *Ogonyok* provided graphic reportage of the
Soviet involvement in Afghanistan for the first time. Publication had
high-level authorization. "The difficulties, the maneuvering in the
commission and the politburo increased," Aleksandr Yakovlev
recalled in December 1991. When Yakovlev, among others, proposed
"showing what was really happening," Gorbachev "came down firmly
on our side. Why not show it? he said. Why keep it all secret? Let's
show it. On the whole, this process of glasnost—applied to the war—
helped us a very great deal in bringing closer the withdrawal."[44]

Yet the Afghan government continued to resist the troop withdrawal with the connivance of sympathizers in Moscow. "The implementation was sabotaged," according to Yakovlev. "The evacuation
was hampered."[45] Suspecting that others in Moscow were sending
Najibullah mixed signals, Gorbachev arranged for another face-to-
face meeting. On July 20, 1987, he shocked Najibullah by saying in no
uncertain terms, "No matter what else you may have heard, I hope
you are ready in twelve months because we will be leaving whether
you are or not."[46]

That fall the Soviets told the United States as well. At a meeting
in the State Department on September 16, 1987, Foreign Minister

Shevardnadze drew Secretary of State Shultz aside. "We will leave Afghanistan," he said in the privacy of Shultz's back office. "It may be in five months or a year, but it is not a question of it happening in the remote future. I say with all responsibility that a political decision to leave has been made."

Shultz appreciated the "immense importance" of this private assurance. Yet he remained unwilling to ease the Soviets' exit. Shevardnadze again asked for help in arranging an internal settlement in Kabul: "A neutral, nonaligned Afghanistan is one thing," he told Shultz. "A reactionary fundamentalist Islamic regime is something else." Shultz sensed that Shevardnadze "was clearly worried about the Islamic republics in the Soviet Union." Still trying to shield himself from attack by the G.O.P. right wing, Shultz refused. His reply stressed "the importance of a short timetable for withdrawal of Soviet troops and disproportionate numbers to be withdrawn at the beginning, known as 'front-end loading.'" Beyond saying that "our interest was in a neutral, nonaligned Afghanistan being governed by Afghans," however, Shultz was noncommittal.[47]

In an address to the UN General Assembly five days later, President Reagan berated the Soviets for "prolonging a brutal war" and "propping up a regime whose days are clearly numbered." It was as if the Shevardnadze-Shultz exchange had never taken place. After recalling his demand that Moscow set a date for withdrawal, he made a "pledge" to be "helpful" if the Soviet Union wanted a "genuine political settlement."[48]

The president did not honor that pledge, even though, in Shultz's own words, "in mid-November the Soviets were practically begging us to help them get out of Afghanistan."[49] The secretary of state accepted Shevardnadze's assurances at face value, but others in the administration did not and remained determined to give the Soviets no easier way out. "Most of us at C.I.A. did not question that the Soviets badly wanted out of Afghanistan," recalled Deputy Director Gates, "but we did not think they could or would take out all of their forces or do so under conditions that imperiled their client, Najibullah's government."[50]

Gates was wrong. Gorbachev decided to set a timetable for withdrawal without arranging an internal political settlement in Kabul first. Shevardnadze went to Kabul in January 1988 and publicly declared that the U.S.S.R. "would like the new year of 1988 to be the last year of the stay of Soviet troops in your country."[51] On February 8,

1988, a statement broadcast on Moscow evening news in Gorbachev's name set a date of May 15, 1988, for the start of the Soviet pullout and a deadline of March 15, 1989, for complete withdrawal. Forming a coalition government in Kabul, it said, was a purely internal Afghan issue.[52] The public pledge to a war-weary populace greatly reduced Soviet leverage to secure the conditions that Gorbachev attached to a pullout, the signing of the Geneva accords on Afghanistan and an end to outside interference.

Far from reciprocating, the United States abruptly took an even less accommodating stance. When Shultz came to Moscow for talks shortly thereafter, the main issue was whether to terminate American military assistance to the Afghan resistance as part of the Geneva accords to settle the war. By then mujahideen stocks of arms were ample. In a fractious meeting with Shevardnadze on February 20, 1988, that ran well past midnight, Shultz insisted that the United States would not end aid unless the Soviet Union withheld assistance from the Kabul government. That violated an understanding reached in Geneva, Shevardnadze was quick to note. It was one thing to send arms to a legitimate government recognized by the United Nations, and quite another to aid those trying to overthrow it.[53] Shultz was unmoved.

In a meeting with Gorbachev the next day, Shultz reversed course on another critical issue, an internal political settlement in Afghanistan. Faced with Washington's repeated refusal to give backing for an interim government in Kabul before Moscow withdrew its troops, Gorbachev had abandoned the quest and set a deadline for withdrawal. Now it was Pakistani president Mohammad Zia ul-Haq's turn to move the goalposts. He insisted that Moscow undermine Najibullah by forming a coalition government that included outright opponents of the regime. Shultz, at Zia's behest, proposed that an internal political settlement precede international settlement of the conflict. Gorbachev refused. "That government is not going to be formed in Moscow or Washington, much less in Pakistan."[54]

Shultz obliquely confirmed that the United States did renege. "In December 1985," he wrote, "our negotiators in Geneva had taken the position that upon Soviet withdrawal from Afghanistan, our support for the mujahideen, having served its purpose, would cease." The Kabul government would still be entitled to military assistance. The withdrawal, which was viewed as hypothetical in 1985, no longer seemed so by 1988, and administration officials, feeling heat from right-wing Republicans, had a change of heart. "As the possibility of a Soviet withdrawal became increasingly real, and as the Soviets made clear their intention to continue supplying arms and other support to their allies in Kabul," said Shultz, "this position seemed to me incomplete and unwise, to say the least."[55]

When Shevardnadze revealed in public on January 6 that the United States had previously agreed to cut off arms to the mujahideen, Shultz offered a rebuttal the next day. Washington would desist from sending arms only if Moscow did so. That would leave the Afghan regime at a disadvantage. "The negative symmetry," Pavel Palazchenko points out, "could not just be U.S.-Soviet. The resistance received most of its weapons from Pakistan, Saudi Arabia, and other countries. The Americans refused to discuss how that flow could be halted."[56]

On March 12, 1988, Anatoly Dobrynin, director of the Central Committee's international department, sent word to Ambassador Jack Matlock that "Gorbachev feels betrayed by the U.S. demand for simultaneous cessation of arms to Afghanistan and by Zia's insistence on a change of government in Kabul before signing in Geneva." Moscow was aware of Washington's belief that Najibullah would not outlast the Soviet departure. "Our assessment is that you may be right, and we are willing to let nature take its course: *Que sera, sera*," Dobrynin said, "but nature must take its course after we leave and not be pushed by us beforehand."[57]

On March 20, 1988, with Gorbachev under hard-line assault at home, Shevardnadze returned to Washington to prepare for the Moscow summit. Shevardnadze's aide, Anatoly Adamishin, in talks with Under Secretary of State Michael Armacost, proposed a private understanding that left both sides free to arm their surrogates in Afghanistan.[58] Pakistan objected because the arms supply line would run through its territory in contravention of the draft peace accords. It wanted assurances that Moscow would not accuse it of violating the accords. In a three-hour meeting two days later, Shevardnadze pleaded with Shultz to end the supply of arms to the mujahideen. Shevardnadze argued his case "in strong and emotional terms," said Shultz. "The Soviets had done everything we asked: announced their intent to withdraw, set a date, and established a short, front-end-loaded withdrawal schedule. All we needed to put an international imprimatur on an historic agreement, he argued, was 'this one last piece.'" Shultz turned Shevardnadze down.[59] In Moscow a day later, Shevardnadze got a call from Ambassador Matlock urgently requesting a meeting.

Matlock brought a letter from Shultz accepting the Adamishin-Armacost formula that left both sides free to arm their allies in Afghanistan.[60]

Pakistan was still holding out for a coalition government in Kabul. On March 30 it relented. It had no problem committing itself "to prevent within its territory the training, equipping, financing, and recruiting of mercenaries from whatever origin," as stipulated in the Geneva accords. Pakistani president Zia called President Reagan. Asked how he could reconcile signing the Geneva accords while still supplying arms, Zia replied, "We'll just lie about it. That's what we've been doing for eight years."[61]

Some right-wing critics objected to signing accords that did not provide for Najibullah's overthrow, but the administration went ahead, convinced that Soviet withdrawal would lead to his fall. Four accords were signed in Geneva on April 14, 1988. Three involved Afghanistan and Pakistan: one on the Interrelationships for the Settlement of the Situation Relating to Afghanistan, another on Non-Interference and Non-Intervention, and a third on Voluntary Return of Refugees. Washington and Moscow signed the second as "observers" and a fourth agreement of their own, a U.S.-Soviet Declaration on International Guarantees. In signing, Shultz qualified the American commitment to act as a guarantor of noninterference: "It is our hope that the Soviet Union will contribute to this process by ending the flow of arms to its client regime in Kabul. But we have made clear to Soviet leaders that, consistent with our obligations as guarantor, it is our right to provide military aid to the resistance. We are ready to exercise that right, but we are prepared to meet restraint with restraint."[62]

The Bush administration was initially no more ready than the Reagan administration to ease Gorbachev's exit from Afghanistan. In February 1989, as factional fighting raged unabated in the country, Gorbachev made a private appeal to President Bush to convene an international conference to end it. Bush refused. On May 10, with the new secretary of state, James Baker, in Moscow, Shevardnadze renewed his appeal for a cutoff of American arms to the mujahideen, to no avail.[63] Baker told Shevardnadze that "there will be no peace in Afghanistan as long as Najibullah stays. The mujahideen will never accept him. So if peace comes, it won't come with Najibullah in power."[64]

The next day, in their first encounter, Baker and Gorbachev made little headway on Afghanistan. A remark by Gorbachev caught

Baker's attention, however. Commenting on the complexity of the factional fighting, the Soviet leader said, "So maybe we should let them stew in their own juices." Baker did not react, said Gorbachev's translator, Pavel Palazchenko, "but he often quoted those words later. They became a kind of code for a policy of diminished interest."[65]

Diminished interest became the basis of cooperation of sorts. In February 1990 Shevardnadze proposed a peace plan consisting of a cease-fire, internationally supervised elections, and an end to U.S. and Soviet arms shipments. In May Baker accepted that approach as the basis of negotiation.[66] He and Shevardnadze further narrowed their differences in Irkutsk in August and in Houston in December. The administration did not ask Congress for funding for the mujahideen in 1991, and Soviet support for Kabul declined. On September 10, 1991, just after a failed coup in Moscow, Russian president Boris Yeltsin told Baker that he and Gorbachev would accept a January 1, 1992, cutoff date for arms shipments to Kabul.[67] The Najibullah government fell in April 1992, prompting an upsurge in the bloodletting, with little American and Soviet involvement.[68] Leaving the Afghans to "stew in their own juices," said Pavel Palazchenko, "seemed to be the most realistic option, but it also indicated how difficult it was to develop cooperative U.S.-Soviet policies now that the cold war was on the way out and the old assumptions were no longer valid."[69]

While the Soviet Union tried to engage in cooperative security in Afghanistan, the United States did not reciprocate—at some sacrifice to its own interests. Enthusiasm in Congress and the administration for supplying Stinger missiles and other arms persisted long after the costs exceeded the benefits. By the early 1990s, Stingers were credited with shooting down two NATO aircraft in Bosnia, and the C.I.A. had to buy back Stingers from the Afghans at inflated prices to keep more from being sold abroad.[70] Maintaining the flow of aid to the mujahideen also proved costly to American efforts to prevent proliferation. Washington's reliance on Pakistan to wage the proxy war made it reluctant to confront Islamabad over its manufacture of nuclear arms. With Washington's help, Muslim fanatics gained ascendancy in the mujahideen. All these adverse consequences were well understood in the American government at the time. Yet the administration decided it was better to take the risks than to give Gorbachev and Shevardnadze a fig leaf to cover their retreat from Afghanistan.

Gorbachev and Shevardnadze got little credit in Washington for ending Soviet intervention. Nor did Washington interpret their willingness to withdraw as an example of their putting common security into practice. National Security Adviser Brent Scowcroft's reaction typifies that of realists in the American foreign policy establishment: "The few positive regional changes which had occurred seemed to me to stem more from Soviet failures than from a general change of attitude about regional superpower competition. The withdrawal of troops from Afghanistan, for example, was a clear case of overextension. When it was obvious they could not prevail they decided to cut their losses."[71]

ALLIES IN THE PERSIAN GULF

In contrast to Afghanistan, where Soviet cooperation went unreciprocated, there was concerted action in the Persian Gulf. In allying against Iraq, the United States and the Soviet Union made important concessions to each other's interests. That was the glue that held the uneasy Gulf coalition together. Yet each side still harbors grievances about the extent to which it gave more than it got in return.

Cooperation began fortuitously. Secretary of State Baker and Foreign Minister Shevardnadze were meeting in Irkutsk on August 2, 1990, just as Iraqi troops stormed into Kuwait. Slipped a note that the invasion had been detected by U.S. intelligence, Baker told Shevardnadze, "The State Department has just received information that Iraq has crossed the border into Kuwait." In disbelief, Shevardnadze instructed his senior aide, Sergei Tarasenko, to check with Moscow. "I could not imagine that Saddam Hussein would dare to invade Kuwait," he recalled. "There had been no signals or indications of this at all. In the past, Iraqi troops had often crossed their neighbor's borders, had stayed briefly, and then had returned to their own territory."[72]

Iraqi infidelity prompted realignment. After the meeting, Baker's top aides, Dennis Ross and Robert Zoellick, headed to Moscow for previously scheduled talks with Tarasenko. They were joined there by Peter Hauslohner, a member of the policy planning staff, who proposed that Baker and Shevardnadze issue a joint statement condemning Iraqi aggression. Ross framed it as a defining moment of the post–cold war order. "We've talked about an evolution from competitors to cooperation. Now we've got to talk about partnership," he told his Soviet counterpart, Tarasenko. "If we've really entered a new era, nothing is going to demonstrate it more than our being together, and nothing is going to demonstrate more clearly that we *haven't* entered a new era if we can't be together."[73] Tarasenko concurred. He phoned Shevardnadze, who agreed and said he would speak to Gorbachev.

Ross and Tarasenko drafted a joint statement denouncing the invasion of Kuwait as "brutal and illegal" and demanding Iraq's immediate withdrawal. It invited all nations to join in embargoing all arms shipments to Iraq, declared that the United States and the Soviet Union "are prepared to consider further actions," and concluded, "Governments that engage in blatant aggression must know that the international community cannot and will not acquiesce in nor facilitate that aggression."[74] A 4 a.m. call from Ross awoke Baker, who decided to cut short a trip to Mongolia and return to Moscow. "I knew that flying to Moscow was a risky proposition," said Baker. "Shevardnadze had just warned me that a meaningful joint statement would be a tougher sell than he had realized." Baker opted to try: "If I *didn't* go to Moscow, there was no chance of getting a statement."[75]

By mid-morning Tarasenko returned with a very different text. "I had a tough time with the ministry," he reported with some understatement.[76] Gone was any reference to joint steps, an arms embargo, and "further actions." After much back-and-forth with Ross, the language on the arms embargo remained bracketed for the foreign ministers to resolve.

That evening Baker and Shevardnadze conferred for ninety minutes at a Moscow airport. "I've come here because I thought it important to demonstrate that we can and will act as partners in facing new challenges to international security," Baker told him. "While it is easy to talk about partnership, taking the unusual step of issuing a joint call for an international cutoff of arms would send a signal to the world and to the Iraqis that U.S.-Soviet partnership is real."[77]

Shevardnadze was under pressure not to cooperate. Opposition to common security was building in the armed forces, the K.G.B., the Supreme Soviet, even within the foreign ministry. Resistance to taking sides against longtime client Iraq was spearheaded by Yevgeny Primakov, a member of the presidential council, who had maintained close ties to Saddam Hussein and was maneuvering to replace Shevardnadze as foreign minister.[78] "My colleagues reminded me of the Treaty of Friendship and Cooperation with Iraq and our special relations," Shevardnadze said. He took up another of his colleagues' preoccupations with Baker: "The thought of the eight thousand Soviet citizens stationed in Iraq filled me with alarm," he wrote, "and I was obligated to do everything so that not a single one would be harmed." Yet Arabists in the foreign ministry seemed parochial to Shevardnadze. "There are people who look at events from only one 'foxhole.'. . . My position dictated that I keep the whole front line in view." He was ready to break with Iraq for the sake of common security. "When perestroika began, we advanced a number of new ideas for reorganizing international relations, new methods of guaranteeing peace and security and safeguarding the rights of individuals and nations," he recalled. "If the world community could not stop the aggression against Kuwait, then it would have gained nothing from the end of the cold war, from the renunciation of confrontation."[79]

Without first obtaining Gorbachev's approval, the foreign minister decided on his own to endorse concerted action, including an arms embargo on Iraq.[80] Shevardnadze's commitment proved impossible for his opponents in Moscow to shake, or convince Gorbachev to undo, no matter how hard they tried.

Toward the end of the airport meeting, Shevardnadze raised another concern: "There are rumors the U.S. intends to make military strikes against Baghdad." Baker assured him that was not so, but Shevardnadze wanted a commitment that "the U.S. is not going to take immediate military action and we're not going to be faced with something that is unexpected."[81]

The unexpected did not take long to surface. On August 4, the very day of the airport meeting, President Bush decided to dispatch substantial U.S. air and logistical forces, some 100,000 troops in all, to Saudi Arabia to deter further aggression and to prepare for more massive troop deployments to expel the Iraqis from Kuwait.[82] Upon his return to Washington, Baker discussed with the president "the delicate task of breaking the news to the Soviets." Baker reached Shevardnadze on August 7 and told him "the troops would begin deploying the next day." According to Baker, "I went out of my way to make clear that this deployment was temporary and that our troops would leave Saudi Arabia once the crisis had been resolved. We had no intention of seeking a permanent U.S. presence." This was disingenuous. For more than a decade the Soviet Union had watched American infrastructure in Saudi Arabia being built for just such an eventuality. Shevardnadze was "furious," recalled Baker. "Are you *consulting* us or are you *informing* us?" he wondered. "Well, Eduard,"

Baker replied, "I'm *talking* with you because this is not something we want to do by ourselves."[83]

Having broken faith with Shevardnadze, Baker renewed his effort at accommodation: "I would like to explore with you whether Soviet forces would want to participate with us in the multinational force. That would demonstrate resolve and make the use of force less likely."[84] Baker's improvised attempt to restore cooperative security caused consternation in Washington. It was made "on the spur of the moment," said Scowcroft. "We had worked for decades to keep Soviet forces out of the Middle East and it was premature to invite them in. Cheney, Powell, and I opposed it, although a Soviet naval presence in the international flotilla was less objectionable."[85] President Bush had initial misgivings as well, but he was won over by Baker's insistence that "we needed the Soviets more than anyone else." Baker thought "it was naive, as well as dangerous to our interests to believe we could continue to shut them out of the Middle East." On August 8 he telephoned Shevardnadze to say that Bush had "absolutely no problem" with having Soviet troops in the coalition. The foreign minister called back a few days later to turn down the offer.[86] Public reaction to the debacle in Afghanistan ruled out a Soviet troop commitment. In the end, Moscow would send just a few ships to monitor the blockade.

The alliance nearly foundered again in mid-August when U.S. intelligence detected five tankers bound for Yemen laden with Iraqi oil. Defense Secretary Dick Cheney, Chairman of the Joint Chiefs of Staff Colin Powell, and Scowcroft all were determined to enforce the embargo, and the president's first impulse was to let the navy open fire on the lead ship, but Baker opposed unilateral action. The Security Council had approved sanctions without provision for armed enforcement. On August 18 Baker won Bush's approval to delay intercepting the tanker if the Soviets agreed to a Security Council resolution authorizing military means to enforce the embargo. On August 20 Shevardnadze asked for five days' delay to try to convince Saddam Hussein to withdraw. Baker persuaded a "clearly frustrated" President Bush to go along with the request. Bush feared it would demonstrate lack of resolve. "We're going to be much worse off losing the Soviets than losing that ship," Baker replied.[87] Bush agreed to hold off for three days. When he telephoned Margaret Thatcher at 3 a.m. to inform her about the delay, she was her usual, gracious self: "Well, all right, George, but this is no time to go wobbly."[88] On August

25 the Security Council voted 13-0, with Soviet support, to outlaw all trade with Iraq and authorize "all appropriate measures" to enforce the embargo.

Around the same time, President Bush asked Scowcroft about arranging a get-together with Gorbachev. Bush felt that a meeting "would reinforce our message to Saddam that the United States and the Soviet Union were standing together in rock-solid opposition to the invasion." The Soviet leader, he knew, "had been very sensitive about the potential use of force, which made it more pressing that I talk with Gorbachev sooner rather than later." Bush's other concern was the interest expressed by Gorbachev and Shevardnadze in "a Middle East peace conference which would include trying to solve the question of Israel's occupied territories—the very linkage of the Gulf crisis with the Arab-Israel confrontation we had been trying to avoid." That would enrage the hard-line Shamir government in Israel, which could jeopardize the Gulf coalition. Scowcroft worried that Gorbachev would try "to straddle: stand strong beside the United States, but work diligently behind the scenes to protect Saddam and the Soviet investment" in Iraq.[89] A one-day meeting was set up on neutral ground, in Helsinki, on September 9, 1990.

On September 6 Gorbachev had a long conversation with Tariq Aziz, Iraq's foreign minister. "I advise you to move as quickly as possible to a search for political ways out of the crisis," he told Aziz and noted the many calls for "tough measures" against Iraq. "Do you have any new proposals?" But Aziz was in no mood to offer any. Iraq "is not afraid of confrontation with the Americans," he replied. "We know that confrontation could lead to a wide-scale conflict, the consequences of which would affect not only the Arab region but the entire world. That prospect does not frighten us, though." Gorbachev was stern: "It is unrealistic after all that has happened, after the Security Council has passed five resolutions and a large U.S. military contingent has been sent into the Persian Gulf zone, to talk about negotiations without displaying a readiness to withdraw Iraqi troops from Kuwait." Adamant, Aziz expressed confidence that the confrontation would "bring Iraq success" and reproached Gorbachev for talking "the same language as the Americans."[90]

Three days later, Bush and Gorbachev conferred, with only Scowcroft and Chernyaev in attendance. "I do not want this to escalate and I do not want to use force," Bush reassured Gorbachev. "But if he [Saddam] does not withdraw, he must know the status quo is

unacceptable." If the coalition did have to resort to force, Bush
expressed hope it would have Gorbachev's backing. Disavowing any
intention to leave substantial U.S. forces in the Gulf after the crisis,
Bush added a qualification: "Any residual security presence to keep
Saddam Hussein under control should be multilateral."

Besides trying to impress Gorbachev with his self-restraint, Bush
moved beyond unilateralism in a much more far-reaching way. For
years it had been U.S. policy to try to keep the Soviets out of the
Middle East. Scowcroft "winced" when Bush said that if Gorbachev
were to decide to send troops of his own, "I have no problems with
that." In an even more open break with past U.S. policy, the president
went on to say, "The world order I see coming out of this is US and
Soviet cooperation to solve not only this but other problems in the
Middle East. . . . I want to work with you as equal partners in dealing
with this." The president then previewed his address to a joint session
of Congress: "I want to go to the American people tomorrow night to
close the book on the cold war and offer them the vision of this new
world order in which we will cooperate."[91]

Gorbachev shared Bush's conviction that the Gulf crisis was a
test of cooperative security between the United States and the Soviet
Union, but he was not prepared to settle for fine words about partnership in a new world order. He wanted something more specific. In
Eastern Europe and on the matter of German unification, he began,
the main burden had been on the Soviet Union to end old thinking. "In the Gulf, the United States is in a more difficult position. I
understand that, perhaps more than our people." The difficulty lay
on the home front: "Your people expect you to act decisively and
win." That put Gorbachev in a political bind. "We have condemned
Iraqi aggression and supported the UN. We are as one here," he said
pointedly. "But it was difficult for us at first because you decided to
send forces first and then told us."[92]

Now that Iraq's troop disposition showed it was not about to
attack Saudi Arabia, Gorbachev saw a need to seize the diplomatic
initiative. "Backing Saddam Hussein into a corner is wrong. He must
be allowed to save face." The Soviet leader had a proposal to make: if
Iraq released the hostages and withdrew from Kuwait, the United
States would promise not to attack and would reduce its forces, which
would be replaced by an Arab peacekeeping force. Then an international conference on the Middle East would be convened. Bush was
noncommittal. He raised no objection to reviving the Mideast peace

process, only to its auspices. A U.S.-Soviet plan, he cautioned, "would look like a condominium of just the two of us trying to find a solution. But the idea is interesting and we must do some thinking."[93]

In contrast, Shevardnadze was broaching the possibility of a peace conference with Baker at the same time, but Baker rejected it out of hand. "Eduard, that would be a disaster," he argued. "It would look like Saddam had delivered, that he would have gotten something nobody else could have. It would be a great victory for him and would send the message that his way of doing business works. It would put the moderate Arabs on the defensive and cause all kinds of problems with the Israelis. We simply can't do this."[94] Dennis Ross prepared a draft of a joint statement committing the United States and the Soviet Union to consider "additional steps" if the Iraqis refused to withdraw from Kuwait. When Baker showed him the draft, Shevardnadze proposed that Ross work on it with Tarasenko.

After lunch the U.S. delegation held a contentious caucus. Bush and Scowcroft had the impression that Gorbachev was "dug in" on the idea of linkage and would insist on convening a Middle East peace conference.[95] But Shevardnadze's acceptance of the thrust of the draft statement had convinced Baker and Ross that linkage should be resisted. "You can't do that. This will absolutely undercut what we're trying to do," Ross said with some passion. "Well," the president responded, "I just don't think he's gonna accept anything less than that." Baker seconded Ross, "We cannot be talking about an international conference. That would be a big victory for him [Saddam] and it would be a disaster for our friends in the Arab world." The president was unpersuaded: "Well, I am afraid we're going to find we have to do this. We need a joint statement, and Gorbachev is gonna want that in there." Baker rejoined, "We've already *got* a draft and it's not even mentioned. Don't worry about it." The president was adamant, "Well, I've *got* to worry about it. I put all those kids out there. Nobody else did it—*I* did it. And I've gotta take every step to be sure that I don't put their lives at risk needlessly. If I can get them out of there without fighting, I'll do it." There was silence. Agreeing to a peace conference for the sake of partnership with Gorbachev or keeping the Gulf coalition together was open to argument, but it was more difficult for aides to take issue with a president who was keenly aware of the unique responsibility he had as commander in chief. Then John Sununu, White House chief of staff, broke the silence. "Well, maybe we can put a reference to an international conference in there." Baker bristled, "Get off of it, John." Finally, the president decided, "Look, Jimmy, if you can get the statement without it, fine."[96]

The joint statement drafted by Ross and Tarasenko committed the two sides to collaborate "to resolve all remaining conflicts in the Middle East and the Persian Gulf" but without any explicit reference to a Mideast peace conference. Overriding Yevgeny Primakov's objections to a phrase about Iraq's isolation and attempts by others in the Soviet delegation to water down the language demanding unconditional withdrawal by Iraq and calling for additional steps if it did not, Gorbachev signed on.[97]

Gorbachev had even more pressing domestic concerns on his mind than opposition to a break with Iraq. When Baker saw him in Moscow three days later, just after the two-plus-four had reached agreement on German unification, he asked for aid for economic reform. "In six to nine months, things will get better for us. But we need help now. We have to meet the people's needs during this period of transition. I understand there's a limit to what you can do, but can you get some money from the Saudis for us?" Gorbachev mentioned a figure of $4 to $5 billion. Baker secured a $4 billion line of credit from Saudi Arabia two weeks later.[98]

Bush returned home to address a joint session of Congress on September 11. "Out of these troubled times," he declared, "a new world order can emerge." In a call to arms that resounded with liberal internationalism, Bush spoke of "a world where the rule of law supplants the rule of the jungle, a world in which nations recognize the shared responsibility for peace and justice, a world where the strong respect the rights of the weak."[99]

Meanwhile, Baker flew from Moscow to Damascus to get Syrian president Hafez el-Assad to join the coalition. Dennis Ross had vehemently opposed the visit on the grounds that Assad would join on his own out of hatred for Saddam Hussein. Assad had told Egyptian president Hosni Mubarak that he would commit at least one division and had extracted a pledge from Saudi Arabia to underwrite the costs. "When you go to Damascus," Ross argued, "you're doing something he wants very badly, and you won't get anything from him that he isn't already prepared to do." Baker considered canceling the trip but reconsidered after President Bush told him, "I don't want to miss the boat again." After expelling Iraq from Kuwait, he intended to get comprehensive peace talks started between Israel and its Arab neighbors. In going to Damascus on September 14, Baker wrote, he had "a more long-term purpose in mind. There was no way to move a comprehensive Mideast peace process forward without the active involvement of Syria, and I believed that there could well be an opportunity to begin laying the groundwork with Assad for a new effort to revive the peace process."[100]

Baker, accompanied by Ross and Ed Djerejian, the American ambassador to Syria, forged linkage of another sort—not to an Iraqi withdrawal but to Assad's commitment of troops to the Gulf coalition.[101] "In the event of military action," Baker said, "we will need to know what you would be willing to do with your troops that are going to Saudi Arabia, and with your troops on the Syrian-Iraqi border." Assad gave no direct answer at first, but after some prodding he indicated willingness to send up to 100,000 troops: "We will commit as many as is required." To ensure that Assad lived up to his pledge, Baker committed the United States to reviving the Mideast peace process. "Assad is a realist," wrote Baker. "He didn't have to be told that joining the coalition would reinforce his clout in the Arab world and help settle old grudges with Saddam. He also understood intuitively that it would make it easier for the United States to deal with Syria. But I wanted him to understand that the stakes were much higher than simply a warming in bilateral relations. In my view, a successful outcome in the Gulf would open up new avenues for reviving the prospects for peace in the region." Similarly, Baker did not need to tell Assad that the only hope for Syria to regain its sovereignty over the Golan Heights rested on peace with Israel. Baker told Assad, "We're optimistic that the circumstances that bring Syria, Egypt, and the Gulf states together in a major Arab coalition can augur well for the future of the Arab-Israeli peace process." Linkage gave Assad a stake in the outcome. "The most urgent objective had been achieved," concluded Baker. "Syria was firmly committed to the coalition."[102]

In October Moscow and Washington each acted unilaterally to secure the outcome it preferred. On October 4 Yevgeny Primakov flew to Baghdad bearing an offer from Gorbachev of a diplomatic settlement. The trip made Bush "uneasy," especially after Shevardnadze sent word to U.S. officials that he had objected to Primakov's going and had been overruled. Gorbachev sent Primakov to Washington on October 18–19 to brief President Bush, which did little to lessen his unease. Saddam Hussein offered to withdraw from Kuwait if he could retain complete control of the contested oil fields and two islands offshore. "I'd die before leaving" under threat of an ultimatum, he told Primakov. "I'm prepared to die, but this battle is not confined to one country alone." Primakov tried to extricate the five thousand Soviet citizens held hostage in Iraq. He also detailed what the coalition would be willing to do in return for Iraq's withdrawal. "Rather than insist on Saddam's unconditional withdrawal," Bush protested in a letter to Gorbachev, "this approach would offer him significant 'face-savers' that he would inevitably present as a 'reward.'"[103]

Washington, on its own, took an irreversible step to expel the Iraqis forcibly from Kuwait. On October 11 Bush convened his war council to marshal U.S. forces and consider plans for retaking Kuwait. By October 30, when the president next met with his military advisers, some 250,000 troops were en route to the Gulf or already there. "The existing pipeline was full," said Scowcroft. "If we were going to stop at 250,000, which was our present commitment, the military had to know so they could turn off the spigot." The president decided to dispatch substantially more troops. That made war unavoidable if the Iraqis did not withdraw within the next four months. As Colin Powell, chairman of the joint chiefs of staff, told him, "Mr. President, you need to understand that if we go through this buildup, we will not be able to have a rotation policy of bringing up troops and relieving them."[104] If they did not fight, the troops in the Gulf would have to be withdrawn by spring. Further, the Arabs in the coalition were adamantly opposed to initiating hostilities during the holy season of Ramadan, so the fight to liberate Kuwait would have to begin by February at the latest, leaving insufficient time for economic sanctions to work.

The announcement was delayed until November 8, two days after congressional elections. It caught Secretary of State Baker off guard. He was in Moscow to line up Gorbachev's support for a Security Council resolution threatening "other appropriate means" if Saddam did not yield. Baker laid out the case for armed force with Shevardnadze that morning. Threatening to use force might make Saddam a hero, Shevardnadze replied. "Maybe we should just tighten the sanctions." Baker's rebuttal was blunt: "This guy will let everybody in the country starve before he'll give this up." Holding the coalition together for very long also was a problem. Left unspoken was Baker's concern that sanctions without military force would lead to a negotiated settlement, not Iraq's unconditional withdrawal.

Shevardnadze worried about the use of force: "We learned from Afghanistan. Don't listen to military men who give you these simplistic views that you'll succeed. You need to *know* that you'll succeed. Are you really sure you've thought this through?" In what Baker later called "an extraordinary exchange of military information from one former foe to another," he had General Howard Graves brief Shevardnadze in considerable detail on the U.S. strategy for defeating Iraq.[105]

Shevardnadze left to lobby Gorbachev before his meeting with Baker. "From our talk in the car," recalled Pavel Palazchenko, who accompanied the foreign minister, "I gathered that Shevardnadze was cautious about Baker's idea. He wanted to cooperate with the Americans but he clearly had doubts, which he did not discuss with me."[106] Gorbachev was still holding out for a settlement, short of war. To Baker's surprise and dismay, he proposed two UN Security Council resolutions, one to authorize the use of force but only after a six-week hiatus and a second to order the start of hostilities. "We'd never get a second resolution," Baker replied, "and we'd embolden Saddam to make a token withdrawal which could result in a partial solution." Baker made a counterproposal, a single resolution that provided for a pause and a deadline for Saddam Hussein to withdraw, after which the use of force was authorized. The next morning Baker cabled the president about his "rather extraordinary discussions." In his assessment, Shevardnadze "came close to our position that a UN [Security Council] resolution authorizing force should be passed this month. Gorbachev is close but not there yet."[107]

That assessment was borne out when Gorbachev sent Bush a letter proposing two resolutions instead of one. Bush insisted on a single resolution that would not become operative until the first of the year. "I am firmly convinced," he replied, "that the only way to achieve our end is, ironically, to convince Saddam that military action is imminent."[108] Shevardnadze remained committed to cooperation. The day after Baker's departure from Moscow, Soviet foreign ministry officials began formulating a "pause of goodwill" along the lines that Baker had suggested.[109]

Gorbachev acceded when he saw Bush on November 19, on the eve of the meeting of the Conference on Security and Cooperation in Europe in Paris. "After much thinking," he told Bush, "I decided we need one resolution, but one which would combine your idea and mine. The first part would set a deadline for an ultimatum. The second part would say 'all necessary measures' can be used."[110] He agreed to a vote on the ultimatum within the month, while the

United States was still chairing the Security Council. Gorbachev stressed the need to pursue a Middle East peace but without linking the issue to the Gulf.[111] He made one request: he wanted announcement of their accord delayed. That led reporters to mischaracterize the meeting as "chilly" instead of cordial and to speculate about renewed conflict between Moscow and Washington.

Two short-lived disputes did follow the meeting. The U.S. draft of the Security Council resolution made no mention of a "pause" to give Iraq time to withdraw. Washington reworded it after Moscow protested.[112] On November 28, one day before the resolution came to a vote in the Security Council, Baker flew to New York to see Shevardnadze. Gorbachev wanted to push back the deadline for the use of force to January 31 from January 1. At France's suggestion, the United States and the Soviet Union agreed to split the difference. That would give coalition forces more time to get ready. The deadline was set for January 15.[113]

Moments before the air campaign was due to be launched on January 16, Gorbachev made one last attempt to avert war. Baker awoke Shevardnadze's successor, Aleksandr Bessmertnykh, that night in Moscow to alert him to the allied military plans. Bessmertnykh called back a half hour later with a request from Gorbachev for a twenty-four-hour postponement to allow a final plea to Saddam Hussein. Baker, who had not made the call until just before the bombing commenced "for that very reason," turned him down. "We're at H-hour," he said. "You can't call off an operation of this size."[114] Weeks before the deadline expired, U.S. covert operations already had swung into action against Iraq. Now the bombing began.

Two days later, Bush had a long conversation with Gorbachev. The Soviet crackdown in Lithuania had led to bloodshed in Vilnius five days before, and the Soviet leader was besieged by hard-line opponents in Moscow. "His tone was somber as he tried to talk me into halting the air campaign," recalls Bush. Gorbachev pleaded, "We have demonstrated US-Soviet cooperation. Stop in time. Think of the casualties."[115] Bush was not about to agree to a bombing pause then, or ever, until the Iraqis fled from Kuwait.

Differences over the war persisted, but U.S.-Soviet political cooperation reached a pinnacle in late January 1991, when Bessmertnykh came to Washington. The Soviet foreign minister pressed for a diplomatic solution to the war. "We've been rather passive when it comes to political steps at the point when military action is going on," he told

Baker. Moscow was weighing introduction of a resolution in the Security Council calling for a halt to the bombing, which was taking its toll both of noncombatants in Iraqi cities and of political support elsewhere. "There is a growing position in many countries that the bombing is becoming more destructive and there's no search at the same time for anything else." Baker opposed a pause in prosecuting the war. Bessmertnykh turned to the postwar political concerns. The secretary of state was more amenable to this discussion. "It's very important that we begin thinking about the post-crisis security structures," he said. He had in mind a joint statement. Baker suggested that Bessmertnykh prepare a draft.

On January 28 the Soviet foreign minister returned with drafts of two joint statements, one on the Gulf War and the other on Mideast peace. "The language of both was largely unacceptable, the handiwork of Saddam's friends in the foreign ministry," recalled Baker. Instead of rejecting it, however, he suggested they find mutually acceptable language. "I knew that Saddam's defeat would bring fresh opportunities for progress on Arab-Israeli matters."[116] Dennis Ross and Oleg Derkovsky led the drafting, and the foreign ministers gave their approval without vetting the statement with the rest of their governments.[117] The United States secured continued Soviet commitment to the goal of "Iraq's withdrawal from Kuwait." In return, the Americans accepted Soviet language on a cease-fire with just minor tinkering: "The ministers continue to believe that a cessation of hostilities would be possible if Iraq would make an unequivocal commitment to withdraw from Kuwait. They also believe that such a commitment must be backed by immediate, concrete steps leading to full compliance with the Security Council resolutions."

In a startling case of cooperative security, the United States, together with the Soviet Union, now went well beyond the cease-fire to put peace in the Middle East on the agenda. The joint statement read,

> The ministers agreed that establishing enduring stability and peace in the region after the conflict, on the basis of effective security arrangements, will be a high priority of our two governments. . . . In addition, dealing with the cause of instability and the sources of conflict, including the Arab-Israeli conflict, will be especially important. Indeed, both ministers agreed that without a meaningful peace process—one

which promotes a just peace, security, and real reconciliation for Israel, Arab states, and Palestinians—it will not be possible to deal with the sources of conflict and instability in the region. Both ministers, therefore, agreed that in the aftermath of the crisis in the Persian Gulf, mutual U.S.-Soviet efforts to promote Arab-Israeli peace and regional stability, in consultation with other parties in the region, will be greatly facilitated and enhanced.[118]

The statement made no linkage to Iraqi withdrawal. Nor did it commit the United States to an international conference. It did, however, allow a postwar role for the Soviet Union in the Middle East, ending an American policy of exclusion. The statement was sure to cause trouble with the government of Yitzhak Shamir in Israel, which was opposed to peace with the Palestinians, to a peace conference, and to a Soviet role in the region.

Bessmertnykh was eager to release the statement, but Baker wanted to delay for two days. With the president's State of the Union address scheduled for that evening, he said, "Believe me, Sasha, this won't get two lines in any American newspaper." The Soviet foreign minister was insistent: "If I get back to Moscow and this hasn't been issued yet, I'm going to face a lot of opposition." The Arabists back in Moscow would try to alter it, he warned. "They're going to see the old words are missing, and we'll have a problem. Let's finish it now and make it a fact."[119] Baker agreed.

Brent Scowcroft was holding a background briefing for reporters on the contents of the State of the Union address when he was blindsided by a reporter's question: "The Soviet Union and the United States just put out a joint statement on the Gulf saying that if Iraq pledges to withdraw from Kuwait, the war can stop. Does that mean you aren't insisting anymore that Iraq should go completely from Kuwait, that they only have to pledge that they will do so?" Scowcroft issued a firm denial: "No, they have to leave Kuwait."[120] Nuances were quickly lost in the noise. The notion that American bombing would continue until the last Iraqi left Kuwait was absurd. So was the notion that bombing could not resume if Iraq reneged on its pledge to withdraw. No reporter bothered to ask about the reference in the statement to a Middle East peace.

Scowcroft ended the briefing and stomped off to alert the president. "It was the first I had heard of the statement and I was furious," wrote Bush. "It implied that we would accept a cease-fire for Saddam's promise; that we were, in effect, prepared to take something less than the unconditional withdrawal we had been demanding since the invasion. To make matters worse, the statement also linked a cease-fire more closely to negotiations over the Palestinian question." He feared it would "panic" the coalition partners. It also surprised leaders on Capitol Hill.[121] Yet the president never backed away from the joint statement.

The president's commitment to peace in the Middle East also was the main motivation for ordering a halt to the war short of occupying Baghdad. Having the United States tied down in Iraq would have impeded a Middle East peace process made possible by the war. It was not a reason top officials were inclined to share with reporters, however. Instead, officials crowed about a "five-day war" and talked about the need to head off criticism of a "turkey shoot" of Iraqi forces retreating north along the "highway of death."[122] The president himself defended his decision by saying that he expected Saddam would be toppled. "I did have a strong feeling," Bush told reporters on June 13, 1994, "that the Iraqi military, having been led to such a crushing defeat by Saddam, would rise up and rid themselves of him. We were concerned that the uprisings [by Shiites and Kurds] would sidetrack the overthrow of Saddam, by causing the military to rally around him to prevent the breakup of the country." Another reason he cited was geopolitical, avoiding a power vacuum in Iraq that could benefit Iran. "It was never our goal to break up Iraq," said Bush.[123] Occupying Baghdad and trying to restore order in postwar Iraq would tie the United States down, delaying his efforts to seek a comprehensive peace in the region. That was the main reason he ordered a cease-fire as soon as he did, which helped make the war a high point of U.S.-Soviet cooperation.

On February 9, barely two weeks before the ground assault was due to commence, Gorbachev announced he was sending Primakov to Baghdad in a bid to forestall it.[124] On February 13 Primakov presented a proposal to Saddam Hussein: announce willingness to withdraw by a definite time in return for a cease-fire. On February 15 Bessmertnykh telephoned Baker to say that the particulars of the proposal were contained in a letter Gorbachev had just sent to Bush and that Saddam was sending Tariq Aziz to Moscow to explore it further.[125]

That sparked fears of a separate peace. The White House did not share those fears. "I believed these attempts by Gorbachev to mediate were aimed primarily at salvaging some influence and bolstering his ever-weakening political strength at home," commented Scowcroft. "He was fighting for his political survival and was looking for a major foreign policy coup to burnish his reputation."[126] Watching a television news report on the morning of the 15th, Bush said, "my heart sank" upon hearing that Iraq had announced it would withdraw. The president was not about to settle for that; his aim was to destroy Saddam's armed forces, especially the Republican Guard. Within hours Bush denounced the overture as a "cruel hoax" and "impulsively" upped the ante by calling for the overthrow of Saddam Hussein.[127] The last-minute maneuvering made the president more anxious than ever to get on with the ground war. "The meter is ticking," reads his February 18 diary entry. "Gosh darn it, I wish Powell and Cheney were ready to go right now. But they aren't, and I am not going to push them, even though these next few days are fraught with difficulty. Little turns of diplomatic mischief, but I will not order the military to go until they say they're ready."[128]

That day, a letter arrived from Gorbachev about his talks with Aziz. The administration cast about for a nonnegotiable demand to kill off the overture. "We debated the idea of giving the Iraqis ninety-six hours to withdraw from Kuwait, which we felt was a 'test' of immediacy," said Scowcroft. It was also a test the Iraqi army could not pass without abandoning its equipment in Kuwait. It was unenforceable, however. The next morning, the Bush administration found another way to raise the bar unilaterally. "We decided we would announce four criteria beyond the UN resolutions with which the Iraqis would have to comply to show their good faith," recalled Scowcroft: "no cease-fire until the withdrawal was complete, no more launching of Scuds, no use of chemical weapons, and an immediate swap of POWs."[129] On February 21 Gorbachev called Bush to say that Iraq was willing to withdraw, but only after an allied cease-fire. The administration decided to issue "an ultimatum," said Scowcroft, "to keep from being nickeled and dimed to death." For an administration that was unwilling to settle for less than the defeat and destruction of the Iraqi army, "there was always the danger that Saddam would say okay."[130] It was a risk the president was prepared to run in order to prevent a negotiated settlement. Gorbachev reacted with "obvious irritation" to the rejection of his last-ditch proposal. "What is the priority?" he asked Bush over the phone on February 22. "Are we trying for a political solution or to continue military operations to culminate in ground operations?"[131] Despite this strong disagreement, the alliance held firm.

Early in the Gulf crisis, on August 23, 1990, as he fished with President Bush in the waters off Kennebunkport, Maine, National Security Adviser Scowcroft had mused about U.S.-Soviet cooperation and the potential for creating a "new world order." Scowcroft's "ruminations" made their way into a presidential address and many a pundit's prose. The new world order, which once had had an ominous ring, would soon become a term of disparagement, passed off as mere hyperbole. That put its expositor on the defensive. "The phrase, as we thought of it," wrote Scowcroft, "applied only to a narrow aspect of conflict—aggression between states."[132] Yet Scowcroft's narrow construction obscures the main point: creation of a new world order required the United States and the Soviet Union to engage in cooperative security. For a time at least, during the Persian Gulf war, they did.

5

"DOOMED TO COOPERATE"

What are you going to do now that you've lost your best enemy?

—Mikhail Gorbachev to Colin Powell, Chairman
of the Joint Chiefs of Staff, April 22, 1988[1]

Nuclear weapons cast a dark shadow over Russian-American relations from the start of the cold war. They still do today.

The conflict between the United States and the Soviet Union was fundamentally ideological in character, which made the cold war inherently unlimited. To ideologues on both sides, the only way to assure security was to destroy the enemy or bring about a fundamental transformation of its political and economic system. Many ideologues believed war was inevitable.

Once the United States and the Soviet Union had the Bomb, however, the conflict became life threatening to both countries. To realists on both sides, the Bomb imposed limits on the ends as well as the means of the conflict.[2] Victory in all-out war was potentially self-destructive. So was a rollback of communism from Eastern Europe. Limited war or political and economic competition became the only prudent ways to wage the struggle, and deterrence became the sole stated purpose for nuclear arming.

Yet nuclear deterrence had a deadly logic all its own, which was also inherently unlimited. To deter nuclear attack, both sides deemed it necessary to threaten nuclear retaliation. Inasmuch as the cost of a nuclear war was prohibitive, neither side would risk it. Yet that calculus conveniently ignored the irrationality of retaliating for a nuclear first strike with a nuclear second strike. A second strike made no sense unless it could eliminate the other side's nuclear forces and preclude the launching of yet a third strike. That led ineluctably to the conclusion that, for nuclear deterrence to work, retaliation had to be automatic or mad. Even if the threat of retaliation ruled out nuclear war, however, that seemed to leave the world safe for war waged by lesser means. That was the source of gnawing anxiety for the United States, which was committed by treaty to deter any attack by the Soviet Union on the allies in Western Europe. It did not have the capability to do that by conventional military might alone, at least in the 1950s, so it chose to rely on a threat to initiate nuclear war. For the United States to carry out that threat would be suicidal. Yet deterrence might still work if Soviet leaders could not be sure the United States would shrink from first use of nuclear weapons in the event of war. Thomas Schelling called it "the threat that leaves something to chance," a cosmic bluff that led to a preoccupation with "credibility," the willingness to run seemingly irrational risks to shore up an incredible threat. Deterrence, in short, did not work very well in theory.

What happened in practice was in many ways worse. Because of the chance that the cosmic bluff could be called, each side drew up detailed war plans to destroy the other with nuclear weapons. Those war plans fully reflect the deadly logic of deterrence: in the event that war breaks out, nuclear weapons confer enormous, perhaps decisive, advantage on the side that strikes first. The most urgent targets are the other side's nuclear weapons and command and control. Concern about a disarming first strike led the United States to keep some of its bombers airborne at all times and to put others on alert, ready to take off at a moment's notice. This hair-trigger posture raised the risk of inadvertent or accidental war in a crisis, a risk familiar to any moviegoer who has seen *Dr. Strangelove*. Although in theory aircraft could be turned back once they were en route, in practice that was exceedingly unlikely. Once the other side detected the takeoff of a large flight of bombers, it would launch its own. Once that happened, neither side's bombers could be recalled.

The advent of ballistic missiles heightened fears of a disarming first strike and sped up the arms race. The superpowers amassed more and more warheads—in excess of fifty thousand at the peak in the 1970s—to attack each other's missile sites, only to find they had more and more sites to attack.[3] They then tried to make their missiles more survivable by burying them underground beneath tons of concrete, only to have the boosting of warhead yields and improvements in accuracy render the missiles vulnerable again. Although some would survive attack, the dispersal of missiles made command and control an Achilles' heel. They also deployed missiles aboard submarines at sea, which made command and control problematic and set off a silent competition in antisubmarine warfare. The precariousness of the nuclear balance led both sides to adopt plans and procedures to shoot first as a last resort if war seemed imminent, in the desperate hope of destroying enemy missiles before they could be launched. Although it is not widely understood, some of these potentially self-defeating plans and practices persist to this day.[4] The doomsday machine has yet to be dismantled.

That was not all. After the Soviet atomic bomb test in 1949, the United States and its allies had begun a massive buildup of conventional forces. By the late 1960s the buildup offset the earlier Soviet advantage.[5] That, too, was not widely understood. To redress its disadvantage, especially in the air, the Soviet Union deployed more of its best forces close to the dividing line in Germany, thereby reducing its reliance on long and vulnerable lines of supply through Eastern Europe. It also formulated a new military doctrine of rapid and decisive offensive operations, as well as plans for prompt initiation of war.[6] So did NATO.[7] The principal effect of these military postures and plans was to raise the risk of unintended war in a crisis.

Nuclear weapons only aggravated this instability. Starting in 1961, the United States deployed thousands of warheads in Western Europe. Organizationally, these nuclear forces were so inextricably tied to NATO ground and air forces that any war in Europe was likely to escalate uncontrollably. In theory, deterrence all but precluded premeditated nuclear war, but in practice, the danger remained that in an intense crisis in which war seemed imminent, the very steps taken to deter war could provoke it. Worse yet, as forces were deployed and put on alert, the interaction of the two sides' nuclear operations could lead inadvertently but inexorably to nuclear war.[8] The military balance, in short, was fraught with crisis instability.

The Cuban missile crisis brought that home to top leaders of both superpowers.[9] In October 1962 the United States had a nuclear advantage so overwhelming that it conceivably could have launched a successful disarming first strike. When Nikita Khrushchev tried to offset that disadvantage by deploying medium-range missiles in Cuba, the United States nearly went to war in order to remove them. Had the crisis lasted much longer, it would have been difficult to control the nuclear interactions of the two sides and keep the conflict from escalating.

The crisis over Cuba was also a reminder of the buffering effect of geography. The cold war was waged not between next-door neighbors but at a distance. Only in Europe were American and Soviet forces deployed in such proximity.

That danger ended with President Gorbachev's decision to withdraw substantial forces in December 1988. Over the next three years, as the Warsaw Pact and the Red Army fell apart, the possibility of premeditated Soviet attack on the West evaporated, relaxing requirements for nuclear deterrence as well.

At the same time, however, signs of Soviet disunion raised the risks of loss of nuclear control. Moscow tried to cope with the dangers by proposing radical reductions and by withdrawing many of its 20,000 tactical nuclear warheads from exposed positions in Eastern Europe and in unstable Soviet republics. Yet most in Washington remained largely oblivious to the new nuclear dangers until just months before the failed putsch against Gorbachev and Yeltsin in August 1991.

Today, nuclear control, not nuclear deterrence, has become the main source of insecurity. With the dissolution of the Soviet Union, the likelihood of premeditated war sank. With the disintegration of the Soviet infrastructure, however, the risk of losing nuclear control rose to alarming levels. The new nuclear dangers take four forms. Above all, the risk is unacceptably high that a few bombs' worth of nuclear material, neither fully accounted for nor adequately secured, could find its way into the hands of would-be proliferators. Second, with hundreds of nuclear technicians at the mercy of the market, the risk has grown that some would sell their nuclear know-how to the highest bidder. Third, the collapse of the Red Army could tempt Russian military planners to rely on nuclear weapons to counter threats along their borders. As Russia's nuclear infrastructure deteriorates, aggravating military fears for the survivability of its nuclear forces, and Russia's nuclear forces remain at high levels of alert, the risk of unauthorized nuclear use rises. Fourth, Russia lacks the capacity to maintain the thousands of warheads and launchers it has, raising the risk of accident.[10]

Remedying these problems requires far closer cooperation between the United States and Russia than American officials or most members of the foreign policy establishment were willing to support in the cold war or have been willing to envision since.

BEYOND ARMS CONTROL TO COOPERATIVE SECURITY

One form of cooperation that persisted through the latter years of the cold war was arms control. Arms control always involved a modicum of collaboration and mutual reassurance. Even that was too much for some Americans who believed that the United States should act on its own in the world, unfettered by friend or foe alike. To ideologues on the right wing of the Republican Party, some of whom held high office in the Reagan administration or seats in Congress, arms control was anathema. Many of them believed war with the Soviet Union was inevitable. That belief ruled out any cooperation, especially on arms control. If war was inevitable, any limits on arming were inherently untrustworthy. Even worse, they feared, such limits might lull Americans into a false sense of security and inhibit efforts to acquire the capabilities necessary for a disarming first strike—missiles accurate enough to target enemy missiles and defenses robust enough to shoot down the enemy missiles that survived. To these ideologues, a unilateral military buildup, free of arms control constraints, was America's best hope of surviving a war.

To most realists, by contrast, arms control was essential in the nuclear era. It assured ample deterrence while damping down excesses in the arms race that could put deterrence, or even survival, at risk. To many American citizens who were neither ideologues nor realists, arms control did not go far enough to reduce the risk of nuclear war. They favored nuclear disarmament.

Throughout the late 1980s, while the American foreign policy establishment continued to debate the wisdom of arms control, a handful of American and Soviet experts quietly began to explore the need to defuse the nuclear time bomb by moving beyond arms control to cooperative security.

Although it required cooperation between potential foes, arms control was premised on the possibility of conflict and the resulting need to arm in order to deter premeditated war. Arms control, Thomas Schelling and Morton Halperin wrote in their pathbreaking 1961 book, *Strategy and Arms Controls*, "rests essentially on the recognition that our military relation with potential enemies is not one of pure conflict and opposition, but involves strong elements of mutual interest in the avoidance of a war that neither side wants, in minimizing the costs and risks of the arms competition, and in curtailing the scope and violence of war in the event that it occurs." Distinguishing arms control from disarmament, they contended that arms control complements deterrence and that both must be intrinsic to military strategy in the nuclear age: "It is the responsibility of military force to deter aggression, while avoiding the kind of threat that may provoke desperate, preventive, or irrational military action on the part of other countries." That requires cooperation and reassurance. "In short, while a nation's military force opposes the military force of potentially hostile nations, it also must collaborate, implicitly if not explicitly, in avoiding the kinds of crises in which withdrawal is intolerable for both sides, in avoiding false alarms and mistaken intentions, and in providing—along with its deterrent threat of resistance or retaliation in the event of unacceptable challenges—reassurance that restraint on the part of potential enemies will be matched by restraint on our own."[11] Such cooperation is conditioned and constrained by the security dilemma: the predicament that prudent precautions taken by a nation to defend itself will be countered by its rival, leaving both sides more insecure, but that lack of preparedness may invite aggression.

In contrast to arms control, cooperative security starts from the premise that premeditated war is out of the question. Once countries recognize that they have no intention of waging war on one another, mutual deterrence is no longer salient. That relaxes the security dilemma. Yet the military postures, plans, and practices of deterrence remain. To unwind those postures requires countries to undertake far more thoroughgoing forms of military collaboration and reciprocity than arms controllers contemplated in order to reassure one another that they have no intention of going to war. It also demands extensive engagement, both political and military, to prevent threats to the peace from arising in the first place. That is what is meant by *cooperative security*.[12]

By the late 1980s premeditated war between the United States and the Soviet Union was inconceivable. Mikhail Gorbachev's recognition of the need to demonstrate that and to end the cold war led him to reduce Soviet conventional forces and restructure them into a more defensive posture.[13] The August 1991 Moscow coup underscored the critical need to secure control of nuclear arms and the material for making them. The fewer the warheads, the easier it was to control them.

Once nuclear control took priority over nuclear deterrence, nuclear safety lay in the radical reduction of nuclear forces, the dismantling of warheads, and the safe storage and disposal of the uranium and plutonium extracted from them. That applied especially to so-called tactical nuclear warheads, such as nuclear artillery shells, which were more susceptible to accident, theft, and misuse and less amenable to control. Safety also lay in lengthening the nuclear fuse by taking nuclear forces off hair-trigger alert—for instance, by separating warheads from launchers and ensuring that it would take hours or days, not minutes, before they could be ready to strike— or, better yet, standing down most of the nuclear force so that it would take weeks to ready for action. Cooperative security also required intrusive, on-site verification to monitor compliance and impede violations. Verification included an accounting of all warheads and fissionable material to establish a baseline for subsequent reductions and international inspection of all civil nuclear facilities and excess nuclear material.

Cooperative security required a number of other interlocking actions.[14] Conventional forces had to be reduced and restructured, with reductions concentrated in capabilities like tanks and motorized artillery essential for mounting a rapid offensive. The remaining forces had to be reorganized and repositioned to favor the defense over the offense. It was necessary to disengage forces from the central front in Europe and demobilize them to a point where preparing for war would give ample time for the other side to take defensive precautions, eliminating the possibility of surprise attack. Confidence-building measures would subject military exercises to observation and regulation, limiting the forces involved and reducing the likelihood that exercises could be a precursor to an attack. An open-skies agreement to allow monitoring by satellites and aircraft and on-site inspections would assure sufficient transparency not only to verify compliance but also to give timely warning of any change in the status of the forces. These arrangements, taken together, writes Michael Mandelbaum, can be understood "not as a formula for abolishing war but rather as a method of buying time," especially "to extend the warning time for an attack in Europe from the minutes of the cold war to the years" it would take to mount an offensive after these arrangements are put in place.[15]

Beyond that, cooperative security required extensive political and economic engagement, including economic aid and technical assistance to ease Russia's transition to market democracy, educational and other exchange programs, aid for scientific research and training, and the like. The aims of such engagement were to eliminate the causes of war inherent in a Soviet-style state and to develop the sort of relationship with Russia that now exists between the United States and Canada. Under those circumstances, the very idea of war would be truly unthinkable.

Top Soviet leaders embraced the idea of cooperative security in the late 1980s. American leaders resisted it until after the 1991 Moscow coup, then pursued it fitfully. Instead of embracing cooperative security, the United States continued to hold out the possibility of a resumption of the cold war by adopting what the Clinton administration later called the "hedge strategy." That strategy aroused suspicion in Moscow, which undermined nuclear cooperation. The consequence is that today Americans still live under the shadow of a potential loss of nuclear control in Russia, which poses the single greatest threat to their security.

RONALD REAGAN, NUCLEAR RADICAL

Throughout the 1980s, the debate in the American academy and the rest of the foreign policy establishment was largely about the theory of deterrence and the value of arms control. The detailed nuclear operations of the superpowers received fleeting attention.[16] Nevertheless, one stark fact was widely appreciated: nuclear war posed the only clear and present danger to the United States. Most experts concluded that nuclear deterrence was the way to forestall that danger. They disagreed about how many or what sort of nuclear arms would suffice to deter attack. Other people, mostly outside the foreign policy establishment, came to a radically different conclusion—that safety lay in nuclear abolition. Ronald Reagan was one of them.

Reagan was a man of strong beliefs, and one of them was that the world should get rid of all nuclear weapons, starting with the United States and the Soviet Union.[17] He intuitively grasped two essential points understood by all presidents since Truman, that the nuclear balance is inherently precarious and that nuclear deterrence is potentially suicidal. He put his insight into words: "A nuclear war can never be won and must never be fought."[18] That insight opened the way to a radical reduction in nuclear arms.

One reason that Reagan found abolition attractive was its simplicity. He liked goals that could be expressed in a single sentence.

Presidents, after all, make speeches for a living; they do not negotiate arms control agreements. Proposals that are simple to articulate, however one-sided and nonnegotiable they may be, are likelier to win public approval. Yet the attraction of nuclear abolition for Reagan went beyond its popular appeal. It was his profound moral conviction. That set him apart from almost all his advisers.

Reagan had another vision that, in his mind, was compatible with nuclear abolition and even more popular: that defenses would replace offenses.[19] He expressed this hope in his March 23, 1983, speech unveiling his Strategic Defense Initiative (SDI). "This could pave the way for arms control measures to eliminate the weapons themselves."[20]

Reagan did not appreciate that his dream of defenses against nuclear attack was much more likely to impede nuclear arms reductions and make nuclear abolition all but impossible. Were the United States to begin deploying large-scale defenses against ballistic missiles, it would raise Soviet fears of an American preemptive strike in a crisis. No foreseeable form of defense was technologically capable of making the United States impregnable against a Soviet first strike: the Soviets had more than enough ballistic missile warheads to overwhelm any defenses. If the United States were to shoot first, however, defenses could make a difference. A first strike would destroy large numbers of Soviet warheads before they could be launched, better enabling antimissile defenses to defeat, though not eliminate, the retaliatory force that managed to survive. The Soviet military planners' response to SDI would not be to reduce their nuclear weapons but to build more, and to devise other ways to deliver them. It is far cheaper to take countermeasures or to build more attacking warheads and overwhelm the defenses than to build more interceptors and defend against a massive attack.

SDI would preclude hopes for nuclear abolition. Getting rid of all nuclear arms necessitated extensive security cooperation and political and economic engagement between the United States and the Soviet Union. The strategic suspicions aroused by SDI would hardly be conducive to cooperative security.

Reagan's answer was to share the secrets of antimissile defense with Moscow. Yet that required a degree of cooperation and trust that would be difficult to realize once the United States went ahead and tried to develop, test, and deploy SDI.

SDI was also expensive. Nevertheless, building modest antimissile defenses might have made some sense once all ballistic missiles were eliminated—as insurance against cheating. No rival would have much incentive to rearm by building a small force of nuclear-tipped ballistic missiles in secret if it knew that such a force could not overwhelm the defenses. Yet that begged the question of how to eliminate all such missiles in the first place.

Even the elimination of all ballistic missiles would leave the United States unprotected against other, less technologically demanding means of delivering nuclear warheads, from aircraft to cargo ships. Reagan's solution to that problem was disarmingly simple: nuclear abolition.

Inveterate optimist that he was, he may not have appreciated how difficult it might be to abolish nuclear weapons altogether, but Reagan was right to recognize that reduction to very low levels, a few hundred warheads for each side, was both practical and desirable for American security.

What made their summit meetings all the more remarkable was that Mikhail Gorbachev embraced Ronald Reagan's abolitionist vision and was willing to cooperate in realizing it. He was unwilling, however, to acquiesce in rewriting the Anti-Ballistic Missile (ABM) Treaty in order to permit SDI. Unlike Reagan, Gorbachev recognized the contradiction between cutting down nuclear arms and putting up strategic defenses. That contradiction would block agreement at the Reykjavik summit between Reagan and Gorbachev.

The two leaders' convictions about abolition are critical to understanding why the United States and the Soviet Union made progress on arms control from 1985 until 1988 but failed to cooperate more fully. So is the determined opposition of their bureaucracies. While the bureaucrats continued to duel and feud, the leaders and their closest foreign policy advisers were secretly searching for common ground.

Few of Ronald Reagan's advisers shared his enthusiasm either for abolition or for ballistic missile defenses. Nor did most members of the arms control community and the foreign policy establishment.[21] Some administration officials like Director of Central Intelligence William Casey, Secretary of Defense Caspar Weinberger, and Assistant Secretary of Defense Richard Perle were unilateralists who did not believe in cooperating with the Soviet Union in arms control or anything else.[22] Nor did they think much of extending nuclear protection to America's allies. To them the proposed deep cuts and "Star Wars" were the means to block further agreements with the Soviet

Union and to undo the most important agreements still in place. They did not want to abide by the still unratified SALT II Treaty and were determined to stretch the interpretation of the ABM Treaty beyond the breaking point.

Other officials, like Paul Nitze and the joint chiefs of staff, were nuclear conservatives who opposed abolition and strategic defenses as threats both to nuclear deterrence and to arms control. Intent on keeping intact the ABM Treaty he had helped negotiate and doubtful about the effectiveness of space-based missile defense, Nitze tried to kill SDI with kindness. He devised criteria for deploying defenses that could never be met.[23] Deep cuts contradicted the joint chiefs' nuclear war plan, the Single Integrated Operational Plan (SIOP). In the Defense Guidance for fiscal years 1984–88 approved in March 1982 and in National Security Decision Directive 32 signed by the president, the chiefs were ordered to prevail in a protracted nuclear war. That required destroying as many Soviet missiles as possible before they could be launched and holding Soviet leaders and everything they valued at risk. It also meant shooting first. "We were being told by our commander-in-chief," said one of the chiefs, "to be ready, on a moment's notice, to destroy all the Soviet Union—everything, everywhere, of any conceivable consequence or time-urgent value. At the same time we were supposed to climb on board the reductions bandwagon."[24] The chiefs also saw efforts to erode the ABM Treaty as a source of needless strategic uncertainty and opposed diverting resources to SDI that otherwise could be spent to procure weapons with enough accuracy to destroy Soviet missiles in their silos.

To National Security Adviser Robert McFarlane, who played a critical role in its inception, SDI was leverage for deep cuts in Soviet nuclear arms, in particular, for disproportionate cuts in Soviet heavy missiles armed with ten warheads.[25] Yet SDI would provide leverage only on the assumption that Soviet leaders believed an impregnable defense could be built and would be willing to accept reductions that put them at a disadvantage rather than add to their military burden by building defenses of their own or by adding more missiles to overwhelm SDI. McFarlane tacitly acknowledged that when he called his stratagem "the greatest sting operation in history."[26]

Secretary of State George Shultz recognized the strength of Reagan's convictions about SDI and chose not to challenge them frontally. Instead, he tried to capitalize on the president's abolitionist impulse to achieve massive reductions in nuclear arms. As he put it delicately in a September 19, 1985, memorandum to the president, "We want SDI positioned in the agreement as the key to implementation of the offensive nuclear reductions, all of which would be consistent with the continuation of a vigorous research program within the terms of the ABM Treaty. We would want to clarify the development and testing of SDI permitted by the treaty."[27]

To Ronald Reagan, nuclear abolitionist, SDI was "the means of rendering these nuclear weapons impotent and obsolete."[28] To the unilateralists in his administration, Congress, and the Republican Party, SDI was a defense against cooperation with the Soviet Union. To the nuclear conservatives, SDI was a threat to nuclear deterrence and to arms control. To a few others, SDI was leverage for deep cuts. These sharp differences over SDI would impede arms control negotiations throughout President Reagan's first term in office and much of his second and prohibit more extensive cooperation with the Soviet Union.

So would the conflict in priority between an unconstrained arms buildup and radical reductions. In the 1980 campaign, Reagan had criticized the SALT II treaty for two seemingly contradictory reasons: it had inhibited American arming and it had not led to disarming. "As president," he pledged, "I will make immediate preparations for negotiations on a SALT III treaty. My goal is to begin arms reductions."[29] Yet Reagan had ridden to the White House on the contention that Soviet power was on the rise and that the United States had let down its defenses. He sounded dire warnings of a nuclear "window of vulnerability." Nightly coverage of the Iranian hostage crisis had traumatized the nation, and he, along with other critics of Jimmy Carter, seized on the incident as a symbol of American weakness. Although it was unclear how a conventional and nuclear buildup could have rescued the hostages or deterred Iranian fundamentalists from occupying the American embassy, the 1980 Republican platform called for reestablishing American military superiority. Peace through strength alone was the new administration's watchword.

Within two years of the inception of the Reagan presidency, however, the public mood shifted. All the rhetoric about rearming seemed to convince many Americans that the military buildup was already an accomplished fact, and public support for further hikes in defense spending dissipated.[30] In reaction to the administration's outspoken antipathy to negotiations and loose talk of nuclear war fighting, fears of superpower conflict quickly overtook worries about

American weakness.[31] Demonstrations in Europe against the deployment of Pershing and cruise missiles drew protesters by the hundreds of thousands, and the nuclear freeze movement in the United States attracted both a mass base and backing in Congress. A pastoral letter by the Conference of American Bishops urged "accelerated work for arms control, reduction, and disarmament." The Reagan administration found itself in dire need of an anti-freeze.

If the freeze movement called for a halt to the arms race, the administration could come out for reversing it. By crafting arms reduction proposals attractive to the American people but disadvantageous to Moscow, the administration could capture the public fancy for disarming and counter the freeze. At the same time it could rebut criticism of its arms buildup with the claim that a freeze now would deny negotiators bargaining leverage and dash hopes for disarmament.[32] Under pressure from Congress and the NATO allies, the administration resumed negotiations with the Soviets but with radically new aims: the elimination of all intermediate-range missiles and deep cuts in strategic arms. In talks on intermediate-range forces (INF), Reagan reversed NATO's two-track decision of 1979 requiring INF deployment regardless of Soviet reductions and backed the zero option invented by West Germany's Social Democrats. "The United States," he declared on November 18, 1981, "is prepared to cancel its deployment of Pershing II and ground-launched cruise missiles if the Soviets will dismantle their SS-20, SS-4, and SS-5 missiles."[33] It was an offer to give up 572 missiles, which then existed only on paper, in return for some 500 missiles already fielded by the Soviet Union.

Reducing strategic arms was the administration's answer to the freeze, too. Having pronounced the unratified SALT II Treaty "fatally flawed," it reached the reluctant conclusion that it was better off adhering to SALT limits for the moment than renouncing the treaty. In its determination to do things differently, it was quick to coin a new name for SALT, strategic arms reduction talks (START), but it took sixteen months to come up with a new negotiating position. The president announced it at his alma mater, Eureka College, on May 9, 1982.[34] It sought ceilings of 5,000 warheads and 850 missiles a side, with subceilings of 2,500 on land-based warheads and 210 on heavy and medium missiles, of which 110 could be heavies. The proposal would cut the heart out of the Soviets' strategic arsenal, their land-based missile force, reducing it to 2,500 warheads from 6,000, but allow the United States to add land-based warheads and carry out the planned deployment of new and more accurate MX and Trident missiles. More perniciously, it would exacerbate the incentive to shoot first in a crisis by reducing the number of land-based missiles per side while arming each missile with up to ten warheads, with the accuracy to target the other side's missiles.

Another way for Reagan to outflank the freeze movement was to change the subject from offense to defense. A freeze would not do away with deterrence based on nuclear retaliation. To those who believed that threat to be morally repugnant, Reagan offered a superficially appealing alternative, SDI, "to give us the means of rendering these nuclear weapons impotent and obsolete."[35] Missile defense had always been popular because it held out hope that America's vaunted technological prowess could somehow offer a way out of its nuclear predicament.[36]

Reagan put up a third line of defense against the freeze movement: American moral superiority over communism. In a speech to evangelical Christians on March 8, 1983, in Orlando, he preached a new gospel, "Let us pray for the salvation of all of those who live in the totalitarian darkness—pray they will discover the joys of knowing God. But until they do, let us be aware that while they preach the supremacy of the state, declare its omnipotence over individual man, and predict its eventual domination of all peoples on earth, they are the focus of evil in the modern world." He was determined to have might and right on his side against the freeze movement:

> So I urge you to speak out against those who would place the United States in a position of military and moral inferiority. . . . In your discussions of the nuclear freeze proposals, I urge you to beware the temptation of pride—the temptation of blithely declaring yourselves above it all and labeling both sides equally at fault, to ignore the facts of history and the aggressive impulses of an evil empire, to simply call the arms race a giant misunderstanding and thereby remove yourself from the struggle between right and wrong and good and evil.[37]

Beyond demonizing Moscow and accusing the freeze movement of impiety, he implied that cooperating with the "evil empire" was blasphemy. His moral absolutism stimulated apocalyptic fears of an unbridled arms race and, worse, of nuclear war.

These fears may have contributed to Soviet hypervigilance, leading to its shootdown of KAL 007, a Korean civilian airliner that strayed over Soviet territory on September 1, 1983.[38] Shultz and Gromyko had an acrimonious meeting in Madrid a week later. Fears intensified on November 23, 1983, the hottest moment in the cold war since the Cuban missile crisis, when deployment of Pershing and cruise missiles began in Europe and the Soviets walked out of all nuclear arms talks.[39] The Pershing II's accuracy and brief flight time made it suitable for targeting Soviet command and control installations in a first strike. As a May 1984 national intelligence assessment conceded, the Pershing II deployment "could not but have created apprehension" in Moscow of reduced warning time and increased vulnerability.[40] It aroused apprehension in the United States as well. Prominent scientists reported on the possibility of "nuclear winter," catastrophic changes in climate that could result from nuclear detonations. *The Day After*, a dramatic portrayal of a nuclear attack on Lawrence, Kansas, and its aftermath was televised on Sunday evening, November 20.[41]

What few Americans in or out of government realized at the time was that the war scare in Moscow was not just a propaganda ploy aimed at antinuclear protesters. Nor was Ronald Reagan's response. "While we in American intelligence certainly saw the tension in the U.S.-U.S.S.R. relationship firsthand," wrote Robert Gates, then deputy director of central intelligence, "we did not really grasp just how much the Soviet leadership felt increasingly threatened by the United States and by the course of events."[42] The catalyst was Able Archer, a regular command post exercise carried out by NATO simulating the release of nuclear weapons in wartime, which took place November 2–11, 1983. Although it involved no movement of troops or nuclear forces, it was otherwise an unusually true-to-life war game that went through all the stages of alert up to general alert. Since 1981, when Yuri Andropov became alarmed at what he believed to be U.S. preparations for nuclear war, K.G.B. "residents" in NATO capitals and Japan were alerted to maintain "close observation of all political, military and intelligence activities that might indicate preparations for mobilization." Now, Able Archer prompted a flash request from the G.R.U., Soviet military intelligence, for all information about American preparations for "a real-life nuclear strike."[43] It also led to the alerting of nuclear-capable Soviet fighter planes in East Germany and Poland and the suspension of all combat flight operations. Oleg Gordievsky, a double agent who spied for Britain while serving as intelligence chief in the Soviet embassy in London, sent word of Moscow's over-reaction. His report was initially discounted. Director of Central Intelligence Casey briefed President Reagan on December 22 that Gordievsky's report "seems to reflect a Soviet perception of an increased threat of war."[44] A British assessment shared with the president in March 1984 confirmed the gravity of the war scare and had a sobering effect on Reagan. "I don't see how they could believe that—but it's something to think about," he told National Security Adviser McFarlane.[45] A subsequent national intelligence estimate played down the impact of Able Archer in Moscow, but the incident made President Reagan aware of the peril of peace through strength and the value of reassurance.[46] That buttressed his conviction about abolishing nuclear arms. It also prompted him to use personal diplomacy to edge away from confrontation toward cooperation.[47]

NUCLEAR RADICALS AGAINST NUCLEAR CONSERVATIVES

Insider histories of the Reagan administration all trumpet the importance of the American defense buildup and especially of SDI with bankrupting the Soviet Union and forcing it to reform. That version of events is mostly a post hoc rationalization. Driving the Soviet Union to ruin was not even a consideration in the 1981 budget deliberations that hiked defense spending; countering assumed Soviet military superiority and constraining domestic spending were.[48] U.S. defense spending peaked in 1985, well before Gorbachev began the most radical phase of his reform program. SDI aroused such intense opposition in Congress and the armed services, especially after its most zealous enthusiasts threatened to breach the ABM Treaty, that the program was reined in. Moreover, the Soviet Union did not try to outbid the United States in defense spending or strategic defenses. Top officials in the Soviet military-industrial complex did try to convince Gorbachev to accelerate development of Soviet defenses. Roald Sagdeev, director of the Space Research Institute, recalled, "If Americans oversold SDI, we Russians overbought it."[49] Technical objections from scientists like Sagdeev, Evgeny Velikov, and Andrei Sakharov reinforced the political proclivities of reformers like Andrei Kokoshin not to spend much more on Soviet defenses. At first, however, SDI did lead Gorbachev, at the urging of military leaders and against the advice of these scientists, to hold up deep cuts in offenses until he got curbs on U.S. defenses.[50] That was precisely what some SDI proponents in the Pentagon wanted—but not Ronald Reagan.

Volumes have been written about the bureaucratic warfare in Washington over arms control, mostly from the perspective of the officials in the trenches, but it was policymaking at the very top of the administration, and especially Secretary of State Shultz's ability to turn the president's abolitionist convictions to his own ends, that opened the way to agreement with Moscow. The key channel of communication was not the formal START talks but the direct one that Reagan had opened up with his Soviet counterparts through personal correspondence and later through one-on-one meetings with Gorbachev, a channel to which only a few senior officials were privy.[51]

Reagan told Shultz on December 17, 1983, that he wanted to make a major speech on Soviet relations affirming his desire to get rid of nuclear arms. "Every meeting I go to," Shultz told his top aides, "the president talks about abolishing nuclear weapons. I cannot get it through your heads that the man is serious. We either have to convince him he is barking up the wrong tree or reply to his interests with some specific suggestions."[52] At first Shultz tried to dissuade the president from emphasizing abolition and instead to adopt policies more acceptable to the allies: "The present structure of deterrence and of our alliances depends on nuclear weapons, and the best approach is to work for large reductions in nuclear arsenals." Reagan could not be deflected from his goal, but he was more amenable to Shultz's means of attaining it. "Strength and dialogue go hand in hand. We are determined to deal with our differences peacefully, through negotiations," the president declared in his January 16, 1984, speech in the East Room of the White House. "I support a zero option for all nuclear arms. As I have said before, my dream is to see the day when nuclear weapons will be banished from the face of the earth." With Shultz due to meet Soviet foreign minister Andrei Gromyko in Stockholm two days later, the president adopted a much less strident tone: "We could establish a basis for greater mutual understanding and constructive cooperation, and there's no better time to make that good-faith effort than now." He spoke repeatedly of the two sides' common interests. Mindful that tensions had been dangerously exacerbated by what he called "dangerous misunderstandings," he went out of his way to reassure the Soviet side. "Our challenge is peaceful. We do not threaten the Soviet Union," he said. "Our countries have never fought each other; there is no reason why we ever should." Without bothering to seek interagency agreement, Shultz also won Reagan's approval for "greater flexibility in our approach to the START talks."[53]

Twelve days later, Andropov sent a scathing letter replying to the president's speech, but two sentences in the letter caught Reagan's eye, "We are prepared to accept very deep reductions both of the strategic and European nuclear weapons. With regard to the latter, even to the point of ridding Europe entirely of medium-range and tactical-range nuclear weapons."[54] The president sent a hand-written note to his national security adviser, Robert McFarlane. "He suggests that they want an elimination of nuclear weapons. In Europe, that is. Let's take him up on that."[55]

Inflexibility was the rule instead, as Washington remained immobilized by bureaucratic infighting and Moscow became bogged down in a prolonged succession struggle set off by the death of Andropov on February 9, 1984, and his replacement by an ailing representative of the truly old guard, Konstantin Chernenko.

Change was coming, however. In December 1984, three months before he took power in Moscow, heir apparent Mikhail Gorbachev made his mark in a visit to London. While his main theme, common security, was largely lost on Reagan administration officials, a sentence in one of his speeches again caught the president's eye. "The Soviet Union is prepared," he told guests at a December 17 luncheon hosted by Britain's foreign minister, Geoffrey Howe, "to advance towards the complete prohibition and eventual elimination of nuclear weapons."[56]

Gorbachev's words may have appealed to Reagan, but they alarmed Britain's prime minister, Margaret Thatcher. When it came to nuclear arms, Thatcher was no radical. She was determined to rein in Reagan's quest for military superiority, strategic defenses, and nuclear abolition. She was particularly upset about the implications of strategic defenses and nuclear abolition for Britain's deterrent, the Trident missiles it was buying from the United States.[57] Fresh from Gorbachev's visit, she hastened to Washington on December 22 and secured the president's agreement to a four-point statement:

(1) the US, and Western, aim is not to achieve superiority but to maintain balance, taking account of Soviet developments;

(2) SDI-related deployment would, in view of treaty obligations, have to be a matter for negotiation; (3) the overall
aim is to enhance, not undercut, deterrence; (4) East-West
negotiation should aim to achieve security with reduced levels of offensive systems on both sides.[58]

In her own words, it was a "good day's work."

The points were affirmed in NSDD-153, dated January 1, 1985.
"The overriding importance of SDI to the United States is that it
offers the possibility of radically altering the dangerous trends [of
ever-growing offensive arsenals] by moving to a better, more stable
basis for deterrence, and by providing new and more compelling
incentives to the Soviet Union for seriously negotiating reductions in
existing nuclear arsenals."[59] It would not be the last attempt to put
limits on Reagan's vision.

A week later, on January 7, Shultz met with Gromyko to try to
revive U.S.-Soviet arms talks. Knowing the strength of the president's
commitment to SDI, Shultz sensed that if he would ever accept any
limits on defenses, it would be in return for a 50 percent cut in
offenses. Shultz's problem was how to show his Soviet interlocutors
that SDI was "open for discussion" without explicitly turning it into a
bargaining chip. His chief adviser on arms control, Paul Nitze, devised
a solution, a "strategic concept," that won the acceptance of the joint
chiefs of staff. McFarlane "took the responsibility of clearing it with
Reagan. And I don't believe that Bud [McFarlane] ever really did it,"
Nitze later recalled. "He talked to Reagan about it, but he never made
it clear to him what we had in mind."[60] Over the intense opposition of
Defense Secretary Weinberger, who wanted to prevent Shultz from
even discussing SDI in Geneva, it became the crux of Shultz's opening
statement to Gromyko: "For the next ten years, we should seek a radical reduction in the number and power of existing and planned
offensive and defensive nuclear arms, whether land-based, space-
based, or otherwise. We should even now be looking forward to a
period of transition, beginning possibly ten years from now, to effective non-nuclear defensive forces, including defenses against offensive nuclear arms. This period of transition should lead to the eventual
elimination of nuclear arms, both offensive and defensive."[61] Within
two days, Shultz and Gromyko agreed to talks on "space and nuclear
arms, both strategic and intermediate range, with all the questions
considered and resolved in their interrelationship."[62]

Shultz managed to inch forward in a June 17 meeting with Ambassador Anatoly Dobrynin. Drawing on a paper by Nitze that had been "run past" the president, he outlined a "package approach":

> Its essence is an agreement of indefinite duration provid-
> ing for deep and continuing cuts in offensive nuclear arms,
> both strategic and [INF], and agreement by the sides not to
> develop, test or deploy ABM systems or components in con-
> travention of an agreed, strict interpretation of the provi-
> sions of the ABM Treaty as it currently stands . . . as long as
> both sides complied with the reduction schedules spelled
> out below for strategic and [INF] arms. . . . In order to facil-
> itate the above, the sides would reach a mutual under-
> standing of the demarcation between research which is
> permitted, and development and testing which is prohib-
> ited under the ABM Treaty.[63]

The paper spelled out various formulas for annual reductions that would amount to 50 percent cuts in ballistic missile warheads over ten years and an additional 50 percent in the following decade. Starting in 1986, the 9,000 ballistic missile warheads would come down to 4,500 by 1995 and 2,250 by 2005. Comparable cuts would be made in the 3,000 air-launched cruise missiles. Dobrynin did not take up Shultz's offer, but Max Kampelman, the American negotiator in Geneva, soon learned informally from Yuli Kvitsinsky that Moscow's aim was "to make certain you will stay with the [ABM] treaty for at least ten years."[64]

On July 3 a summit meeting in Geneva was announced. That same day, Gorbachev named Shevardnadze to replace Gromyko. He told the surprised Shevardnadze that with Gromyko and his people in charge of the foreign ministry, the arms race would go on unabated. Shevardnadze took that as a license to change personnel and set a radical new course.[65]

One of the most important innovations was a restructuring of the Soviet policy process on arms control, widening the circle of par-ticipants and reducing the weight of the military-industrial complex. Ever since the early days of SALT, Soviet arms control policy had been set by a commission of the politburo. Known to insiders as the Big Five, it consisted of the defense minister, the foreign minister, the chairman of the Military Industrial Commission (VPK), and the

K.G.B. chief and was chaired by the party secretary for national defense. "The commission's decisions," recalled two participants, Aleksandr Savel'yev and General Nikolai Detinov, "went to the politburo which, in most cases, simply rubber-stamped them."[66] Within the commission, "all the agencies involved were virtually equal," said Savel'yev and Detinov, but some were more equal than others. Dmitri Ustinov, the chairman from its inception in November 1969 until his death in 1984, "nominally represented the Central Committee but, in fact, he represented the interests of the defense industries," his purview in the Central Committee secretariat, which "united him with [Leonid] Smirnov, the official representatives of the VPK on the panel." That gave the military-industrial managers two votes on the commission. Moreover, the ministry of defense "had a monopoly on the information concerning the state of the state's armed forces and its weapons," confining the foreign ministry's role to that of "ideologist and propagandist" rather than policy formulator. The K.G.B. was "mostly concerned with showing its flag" and "was not especially active." The expert community was largely excluded. The president of the Academy of Sciences served on the commission briefly, but his tenure was short-lived and his role a mere formality since the Academy "was not included among the agencies that received copies of the negotiations record."[67] Ustinov convened few meetings of the Big Five and ran it like a fiefdom of the military-industrial complex. In 1974 the politburo informally established a group of experts, the Small Five, which drafted instructions for the negotiators, often without clearing them with the Big Five, further tipping the scales in favor of the military-industrial complex.[68]

The scales were rebalanced in 1985. Under its new chief, Anatoly Dobrynin, the international relations department of the Central Committee secretariat, long excluded from Big Five deliberations, was now brought in as a counterweight to the military-industrial managers. In another break with the past, "it then became the rule for the Big Five to conduct preliminary discussions on practically all questions that would become the subject of politburo approval." Other top officials were invited, including Aleksandr Yakovlev and the chief of the general staff, Sergei Akhromeyev. The expert-level group gradually expanded, making more officials privy to arms control matters. Shevardnadze also expanded his influence by establishing a department on arms limitations and disarmament under veteran negotiator Viktor Karpov and by inviting leading scientists, engineers, and arms control experts to participate in its discussions. In some cases the foreign ministry presented its own proposals directly to Gorbachev, "bypassing the mechanism of the Fives."[69] Above all, instead of having the politburo rubber-stamp decisions of the Big Five, "the most important political problems were now usually solved at a higher level."[70]

The first shift stemming from the new procedures came in the run-up to the summit, when Gorbachev matched Reagan's proposed 50 percent cut with one of his own. Predictably it protected Soviet advantages in land-based missiles while forcing drastic cuts in sea-based missiles, where the United States had the edge. In a much more significant move, Gorbachev broke Gromyko's linkage between cuts in offenses and limits on defenses.[71] In unveiling new thinking in Paris on October 3, Gorbachev told French deputies a stand-alone INF agreement could be concluded "separately, outside of direct connection with the problem of space and strategic arms." But Gorbachev kept the linkage on strategic arms, saying that the Soviet Union would be willing to get rid of all nuclear forces on condition that the United States prevent the militarization of space by curbing SDI. On November 4 when Shultz and McFarlane spoke to him of a cooperative transition from offenses to defenses, Gorbachev was uninterested. "If you want superiority through your SDI, we will not help you. We will let you bankrupt yourselves. But also we will not reduce our offensive missiles. We will engage in a buildup that will break your shield."[72]

On November 20–21, 1985, Reagan and Gorbachev held the first U.S.-Soviet summit since 1979. The Geneva meeting did little to narrow the distance between the two sides. SDI was a key point of contention in the plenary sessions. Gorbachev tried to persuade Reagan to abandon the program. SDI, he said, "will only foment mistrust and suspicion, with each side fearing the other is overtaking it." While noting that "we have already developed a response," Gorbachev emphasized the need to ease mistrust.[73] According to close aide Anatoly Chernyaev, "There would be, certainly, a backlash in the Soviet Union; and he knew that he would have to explain this to the Soviet . . . people."[74] One plenary ended with a long and passionate appeal by Reagan, expressing abhorrence at continued reliance on the ability to "wipe each other out" to keep the peace. "We must do better, and we can." After a long silence, Gorbachev said, "Mr. President, I don't agree with you, but I can see that you really mean what you say."[75] Gorbachev's failure to curb SDI would later spark criticism from Marshal Akhromeyev and Vladimir Scherbitsky, one of the old guard in the politburo.[76]

The agreed statement called for "early progress" toward "an interim INF agreement," the strongest indication yet that Soviet negotiators were preparing to separate the issue of INF from START and SDI and resolve it first. The statement endorsed a 50 percent cut in strategic arms, "appropriately applied," a reference to the vast disparity between the two sides' force structures. The United States had advantages in accuracy, air-delivered weapons, sea-based missiles, and cruise missiles, while the Soviet Union had the edge in payload and land-based missiles. Quoting Reagan's words to the Japanese Diet, it noted, "The sides . . . have agreed that a nuclear war cannot be won and must never be fought." It added that "they have emphasized the importance of preventing any war between them, whether nuclear or conventional. They will not seek to achieve military superiority."[77]

Although the communiqué did not say so, and most of the U.S. delegation was unaware of it, a breakthrough of sorts came in an hour-long, one-on-one fireside chat during the summit when Reagan told Gorbachev, "If there were an agreement that there would be no need for nuclear missiles, then one might agree that there would also be no need for defenses against them." Reagan then acknowledged, "SDI is still years away from reality. Why then should we sit here in the meanwhile with mountains of weapons on each side?"[78] It was a variation on a theme that McFarlane had repeatedly sounded in urging the president to trade in SDI for deep cuts.[79]

Alarmed at the enthusiasm for arms control in high places, the Soviet general staff, acting on the axiom that "the best is the enemy of the good," drafted a proposal of its own for "general and complete disarmament" over a fifteen-year period. Like Soviet ploys of the 1950s, it made the military appear eager to get rid of nuclear arms while making sure that START would not "lead to any practical results in the foreseeable future," said General Nikolai Detinov, a member of the Small Five.[80] Gorbachev took advantage of the military initiative to call for elimination of all nuclear weapons by the year 2000. The sharpest dispute came over INF. The armed forces were reluctant to accept the zero option but "unwittingly" became "entrapped by their own gambit." At Gorbachev's behest, Lev Zaikov, Central Committee secretary for defense, got them to go along.[81] In an "interim" agreement, the Soviet Union would eliminate all its intermediate-range nuclear forces from Europe but leave a residual SS-20 force in Asia—a break with its long-held position that British and French nuclear forces had to be taken into account. In a more significant break with the past, Soviet negotiators proclaimed themselves open to intrusive verification. On January 15, 1986, shortly after Ambassador Dobrynin passed the offer to Secretary of State Shultz, Gorbachev made it public. The timetable in the proposal impressed Shultz, who used the intervening hours to persuade the president to respond favorably. "This is our first indication that the Soviets are interested in a staged program toward zero," he told Reagan. "We should not simply reject their proposal, since it contains certain steps which we earlier set forth." The president agreed but had one question, "Why wait until the end of the century for a world without nuclear weapons?" At a press conference the next day, Reagan was generous, "We're grateful for the offer. . . . It's just about the first time that anyone has ever proposed actually eliminating nuclear weapons."[82] Most Western commentary dismissed the Soviet proposal as propaganda, but it was not the last time that a bureaucratic ploy would prompt Reagan and Gorbachev to talk seriously about nuclear abolition.

On May 14 Shultz tried to coax Reagan into using limits on SDI as leverage for deeper cuts: "Your successor should be able to decide whether to deploy a defensive system. Keeping an SDI research program alive is important but difficult. To keep it alive, we have to be willing to give up something in SDI. An agreement for massive reductions in strategic missiles can use SDI research and potential deployment of a strategic defense as a means to win Soviet compliance on continuing reductions." After saying he liked the approach, the president reversed himself on June 3. Reflecting the suspicions of Weinberger and Perle at the Pentagon, "he was afraid that *any* discussion with the Soviets about strategic defense would be used as a way to scuttle SDI."[83]

Yet funding for SDI was in deep trouble in Congress, trouble of the administration's own making. It had been unable to make a convincing case for the technical feasibility of the president's vision. Instead, on this issue, as on others, it seldom spoke with one voice. Every official seemed to have his own idea of SDI and said so. SDI's most zealous supporter, the secretary of defense, was its own worst enemy. "Cap Weinberger's contemptuous attitude toward the Congress made his dealings with that body fractious and troublesome at all times," recalled McFarlane.[84] Then the unilateralists in the Pentagon overreached. On May 27, 1986, they persuaded the president to reject the advice of the joint chiefs of staff and the secretary of state and abandon SALT II. While approving the decommissioning of two missile-carrying submarines, as required by the "fatally flawed" treaty, he announced that the United States would no longer abide by its limits. That sparked an uprising in Congress and in NATO. "I am not sure the president and Weinberger were prepared for the magnitude of what hit them," commented George Shultz.[85] One likely casualty was full funding for SDI. Another was underground nuclear testing, which ran smack into a congressionally mandated moratorium.

To quell the uprising, much as the Soviet general staff had done, civilians in the Pentagon came up with a deep cuts ploy of their own. On May 29 Moscow had edged away from the attempt to prohibit research, development, and testing of SDI with a new proposal in Geneva to confine research to the laboratory.[86] On June 12 the president convened top officials to consider a reply. Defense Secretary Weinberger proposed a ban on all ballistic missiles.[87] That appealed to Reagan's abolitionist impulses. It also appealed to his belief that "slow-flyers" were preferable to "fast-flyers"—that bombers and cruise missiles were better for stability than ballistic missiles because they were not first-strike weapons. Their flight time was too long to catch the other sides' missiles in their silos before they could be launched. A ban might help counter criticism that the administration was intent on exploiting the synergy between offense and defense to achieve a first-strike capability. Of course, getting rid of all ballistic missiles would still leave the United States in an advantageous position because of its strength in bombers and its advances in cruise missile technology. Although Admiral William Crowe, Jr., chairman of the joint chiefs of staff, was opposed to the idea, he did not object vehemently in the expectation that the Soviet side would reject it.[88]

The ballistic missile ban was transmitted to Gorbachev in a July 25, 1986, letter, which also incorporated a State Department proposal that the two sides continue to abide by the ABM Treaty for seven and a half years. For five years, each side would confine itself to research, development, and testing consistent with the treaty. After that, if either side decided to deploy strategic defenses, it would be obliged to offer and negotiate a plan for sharing "the benefits of strategic defense" and for eliminating all ballistic missiles. If no agreement were reached by the end of the seven-and-a-half-year period, either side would be free to deploy defenses after six months' notice.[89] Gorbachev was unhappy with the reply prepared by the bureaucracy. "It was a short, routine statement, and as I was reading it, I suddenly realized that I was gradually being forced into accepting a logic that was alien to me—a logic that was in open contradiction to our new attitude, to the process we had started in Geneva," he recalled. "In the end, I decided to take a strong stand, suggesting an immediate summit meeting with President Reagan to unblock the strategic talks in Geneva, which were in danger of becoming an empty rite."[90] On September 19 Foreign Minister Shevardnadze called on the White House with Gorbachev's reply.[91]

Arms control was still a competition in propaganda for most administration officials. Robert Gates, the C.I.A.'s deputy director for intelligence, offered an insider's perspective. "Everyone knew by the end of 1985 that Gorbachev desperately needed improved relations with the West, especially with the United States," he wrote. "Domestic crises compelled Soviet initiatives to relax tensions." He dismissed Gorbachev's efforts to cooperate without even considering the possibility of American reciprocity: "Throughout 1985 and 1986, Gorbachev tried to achieve that change in atmosphere on the cheap—without paying anything for it. He changed the tone and the face of Soviet foreign policy but not the substance." That posed a public relations problem: "How to respond to Gorbachev and counter the public image of a Soviet Union leaning far forward to reduce the nuclear threat dominated debate in the Reagan administration in 1986," Gates recalled. "From this distant perspective, there was little difference in the administration on the basic response: don't budge, and keep the pressure on the Soviets everywhere." The only difference was over tactics. "Weinberger and Casey, because of their suspicion of Shultz and negotiators in general, were very leery of engaging with the Soviets at all. Shultz, no less yielding on basic strategy, was convinced that Gorbachev had to move in our direction at some point and believed the United States could accelerate that process by engaging the Soviets on nearly every subject at nearly every opportunity. I think he believed that flexibility and modest concessions on our part would result in major, fundamental concessions on the part of an increasingly desperate Soviet Union."[92] That may have been what some senior administration officials thought, but the president had a different idea: cooperating with the Soviet Union to eliminate the risk of nuclear Armageddon. It turned out that he was not alone.

REYKJAVIK: THE ABOLITIONISTS TRY TO DEFUSE THE DOOMSDAY MACHINE

The Reykjavik summit was held over the weekend of October 11–12, 1986. In a one-on-one session on Saturday morning, Reagan quoted his favorite Russian maxim, *doveryai no proveryai* (trust but verify), and Gorbachev agreed to intrusive verification, including on-site inspection. The new openness had come about as a result of "pressure from Gorbachev and Shevardnadze," said Savel'yev and Detinov.[93] Reagan presented the U.S. proposal on START, to reduce ballistic missile warheads to 4,500, below the 6,400–6,800 in the most recent Soviet proposal.[94] On INF, the United States would set limits of 200 INF missile warheads per side, 100 in Europe and 100 in Soviet Asia and the United States.[95] Reagan and Gorbachev then reaffirmed their objective of eliminating all nuclear arms.

Later, when Shultz and Shevardnadze joined the two leaders, Gorbachev presented the Soviet proposal, directing the foreign ministers to prepare the texts of accords for a summit meeting in Washington with the following provisions: a 50 percent reduction in strategic offensive weapons and limits on the deployments of sea-launched cruise missiles; the complete elimination of INF missiles in Europe, without taking British and French forces into account; and negotiations on missiles with ranges of less than 1,000 kilometers and on U.S. and Soviet Asian INF systems. He was agreeing to the radical reductions Reagan wanted—but on one condition: that the two sides agree "to strictly abide" by the ABM Treaty for ten years and prohibit "the testing of all space-based elements" of ABM defenses.[96] The duration was down from fifteen years, bringing the Soviet position closer to the seven and a half years proposed by Reagan in July.

"This is the best Soviet proposal we have received in twenty-five years," Paul Nitze exulted when the U.S. delegation was briefed on the morning's discussion in its "security bubble" at the embassy. "Never mind that we came with nothing to offer and had offered nothing; we merely sat there while the Soviets unwrapped their gifts," recalled Kenneth Adelman.[97]

That afternoon, President Reagan outlined the U.S position, which Gorbachev dismissed as "shopworn goods."[98] The president then made a long plea for the need to proceed with SDI. Any testing of SDI, he said, could be witnessed by observers from the other side. If tests showed that the system worked, then an agreement could be negotiated on the elimination of all ballistic missiles and on sharing SDI. Gorbachev responded with irritation, "You will take the arms race into space, and could be tempted to launch a first strike from space." He scoffed at Reagan's offer to share SDI: "If you will not share oil-drilling equipment or even milk-processing factories, I do not believe that you will share SDI." Tempers flared as Gorbachev called the ABM Treaty the one agreement that had kept the world from nuclear war and Reagan responded that the treaty kept vast populations hostage to a balance of terror.[99]

A joint working group was set up to put in writing what had been agreed to in INF and START and to try to narrow the remaining differences. Heading the Soviet delegation, much to the surprise of the Americans, was the chief of the Soviet general staff, Marshal Akhromeyev.[100] The U.S. delegation had no high-ranking military representative. On START, Moscow proposed 50 percent cuts that would still leave it with a numerical advantage. The United States responded by proposing equal limits of 6,000 warheads and 1,600 delivery vehicles a side, and the Soviets agreed.[101] Akhromeyev specified that Soviet heavy missiles would be cut by 50 percent. Gorbachev was also amenable to a counting rule for bombers advantageous to the United States: so long as it did not carry cruise missiles, a strategic bomber would count as one, no matter how many gravity bombs or short-range attack missiles it carried.

On Sunday morning, Reagan and Gorbachev agreed on zero INF missiles in Europe and 100 warheads a side in the United States and Soviet Asia and on 50 percent cuts in START over a five-year period. To Reagan, "a miracle was taking place." Then Gorbachev "threw the curve": no cuts in offenses were acceptable without limits on defenses.[102] In Paris Gorbachev had severed the link between offenses and defenses when it came to INF. Relinking them now was done at the behest of the ministry of defense in return for dropping its insistence on including British and French forces, although the politburo had given Gorbachev the authority to decide whether or not to accept separate agreements.[103] Reagan suggested recording the agreements on START and INF and leaving the disagreements on defenses for negotiators in Geneva to resolve, but Gorbachev muttered dismissively, "Kasha forever," and refused. "No, let's go home. We've accomplished nothing."[104] Instead, they recessed for lunch and let Shultz and Shevardnadze try to break the deadlock that afternoon.

The feeling was, said Shultz, that "something bold from us might be called for."[105] Over dinner with the president, White House chief of staff Donald Regan, and Secretary of State Shultz the previous evening, National Security Adviser John Poindexter had argued that unless the administration came up with something dramatic, it could be placed in the difficult position of having turned down large-scale Soviet concessions for the sake of SDI. He suggested resurrecting Weinberger's zero-ballistic-missile proposal. As the afternoon session began, Air Force Colonel Robert Linhard, with Richard Perle at his side, began jotting down a version of that proposal. Poindexter passed it to Shultz, who told Shevardnadze, "I would like to explore with you an idea that I have not discussed with the president, but please hear me out."[106] He then read Linhard's draft:

> Both sides would agree to confine [themselves] to research, development and testing which is permitted by the ABM Treaty, for a period of five years, through 1991, during which time a 50 percent reduction of strategic nuclear arsenals would be achieved. This being done, both sides will continue the pace of reductions with respect to the remaining ballistic missiles, with the goal of the total elimination of all offensive ballistic missiles by the end of the second five-year period. As long as these reductions continue at the appropriate pace, the same restrictions will continue to apply. At the end of the ten-year period, with all offensive ballistic missiles eliminated, either side would be free to deploy defenses.[107]

The two sides caucused, and the president asked General John Moellering, the joint chiefs of staff representative, if the chiefs would support the proposal. Lacking instructions, Moellering was noncommittal. Reagan then approved what Shultz had read to Shevardnadze.

When the talks resumed, Gorbachev made a counterproposal that went well beyond banning ballistic missiles. He offered to eliminate all strategic nuclear arms. Reagan agreed. Gorbachev then spelled out the Soviet proposal:

> The U.S.S.R. and the United States undertake for ten years not to exercise their existing right of withdrawal from the ABM Treaty, which is of unlimited duration, and during that

period strictly to observe all its provisions. The testing in space of all space components of ABM defense is prohibited, except research and testing conducted in laboratories. Within the first five years of the ten-year period (and thus by the end of 1991), the strategic offensive arms of the two sides shall be reduced by 50 percent. During the following five years of that period, the remaining 50 percent of the two sides' strategic offensive arms shall be reduced. Thus by the end of 1996, the strategic offensive arms of the U.S.S.R. and the United States will have been totally eliminated.[108]

Gorbachev was forcing Reagan to choose between nuclear abolition and strategic defenses. Just how much of SDI would be ready for testing in the next ten years was an open question, but Gorbachev was betting that, with reductions under way, the steam behind SDI would dissipate.

After more back and forth over SDI, they recessed again. During the break, according to Kenneth Adelman, "We tried to explain to the president and those around him the differences on the offensive side between scrapping all ballistic missiles (as we proposed) and all strategic arms (as they wished)."[109] They argued that some nuclear arms were needed to counter Soviet conventional forces, but the president was unpersuaded. "The last thing we advisors wished to do on nuclear matters at Reykjavik," said Adelman, "was to 'let Reagan be Reagan.'"[110] Having failed to coax Reagan away from abolition, aides tried to toughen his stance on SDI by rewording the U.S. proposal to reaffirm that tests of defenses could proceed in the ten-year interim. They also succeeded in blurring the scope of abolition.[111] After the break, the president offered the new version:

> The U.S.S.R. and the United States undertake for ten years not to exercise their existing right of withdrawal from the ABM Treaty, which is of unlimited duration, and during that period strictly to observe all its provisions while continuing research, development and testing, which are permitted by the ABM Treaty. Within the first five years of the ten-year period (and thus through 1991), the strategic offensive arms of the two sides shall be reduced by 50 percent. During the following five years of that period, all remaining offensive ballistic missiles of the two sides shall

be reduced. Thus by the end of 1996, all offensive ballistic missiles of the USSR and the United States will have been totally eliminated. At the end of the ten-year period, either side could deploy defenses if it so chose unless the parties agreed otherwise.[112]

Gorbachev picked up the discrepancy in the U.S. proposal: in the first five years "the strategic offensive arms of the two sides" would be reduced by half, but in the second five years only "offensive ballistic missiles" would be eliminated. Why? "I thought you were interested in missiles," replied Reagan. "No," said Gorbachev, "we're interested in weapons." The Soviet Union wanted to include bombers, where the United States had an advantage. Reagan then suggested taking out the word strategic. "That way we would also be eliminating all ballistic missiles." The issue of intermediate-range ballistic missiles was being dealt with in separate talks, Shultz interjected. "In fact, maybe here is the place to deal with it decisively." After some back-and-forth on shorter-range missiles, Gorbachev returned to the distinction between getting rid of ballistic missiles and getting rid of all strategic arms, and Reagan said, "It would be fine with me if we eliminated all nuclear weapons." Gorbachev immediately agreed, "We can do that. Let's eliminate them. We can eliminate them."[113]

Gorbachev then resumed sparring over SDI: "The Soviet side is for strict observance of the [ABM] treaty and only laboratory testing. I cannot do without the word, laboratory." That dismayed Reagan, "You're asking me to give up SDI."[114] Having broken the linkage between INF and SDI, Gorbachev, on advice of the armed forces, now reforged it.[115] He was under injunction from the politburo not to relax the ABM Treaty restriction on testing.[116] He told Reagan, "If I go back [to Moscow] and say that research and testing and development can go ahead outside the laboratory and the system can go ahead [and be deployed] in ten years, I will be called a dummy and not a leader."[117] Reagan would not relent. "Do I understand this is your final position—you will not confine work to the laboratory?" asked Gorbachev. "Yes," replied Reagan. The summit meeting broke up over that difference. Administration apologists would later contend that SDI was a lever for prying loose a better deal from Moscow. It was not. Instead, it was a barrier to an agreement, at least for a time.

GETTING OVER THE SUMMIT

The stricken looks on the faces of the departing Reagan and Shultz, telecast around the world, left a lasting impression of failure.[118] That impression was misleading. Reykjavik laid the groundwork for deep reductions, both in INF and in strategic arms. The question was how long it would take both sides to regroup and draft detailed treaties fleshing out the agreements reached in principle at Reykjavik. To do that, Reagan and Gorbachev had to surmount opposition from both left and right.

To nuclear disarmers, Reykjavik was a near miss. To nuclear conservatives, both in Europe and the United States, it was a near catastrophe, and they assailed it with a vengeance. To cloak its exposure, the administration initially tried to obscure what was said at the summit, but the facts soon seeped out.[119] On October 28 Britain's defense minister, George Younger, denounced the "hastily patched together and superficially attractive deal . . . which would have been disastrous for us all."[120] Appalled at the zero-ballistic-missile proposal, Prime Minister Thatcher at a November 15 meeting at Camp David urged Reagan to drop it.[121] Henry Kissinger warned portentously of neutralism in Europe: "The Western Europeans, unable to rely on an instant U.S. nuclear response on their behalf, will make their political accommodation with the Soviet Union."[122] James Schlesinger, secretary of defense in the Ford administration, wondered whether "the existing structure of Western security" is to be "cast aside before we are assured that an alternative truly exists?" Schlesinger was especially caustic about the president's enthusiasm for SDI "as if it were a reality (the 'key to a world without nuclear weapons') instead of a collection of technical experiments and distant hopes" and his willingness "almost heedlessly" to negotiate away the American nuclear deterrent.[123] "A love affair with the status quo has started," Assistant Secretary of State Rozanne Ridgway told Secretary of State Shultz. "A lot of people are starting to love the bomb."[124] Nuclear conservatives were not alone in opposing what happened at Reykjavik. After the Democrats recaptured the Senate on November 4 and the Iran-contra scandal broke into the open, they renewed efforts to rein in SDI.

In Moscow, Gorbachev also found himself on the defensive. Conservative critics charged that he had given away too much and gotten nothing in return.[125] In a sign of dissension, the politburo downgraded its praise of Gorbachev's performance at Reykjavik from "fully approved" to "approved."[126]

On October 27, 1986, at a meeting of top officials to review arms control policy, Admiral Crowe, chairman of the joint chiefs of staff, registered the chiefs' objection to giving up ballistic missiles without a significant improvement in the conventional military balance.[127] Shultz was instructed to back away from the zero-ballistic-missile proposal and to try to pocket the Soviets' summit concessions when he met Shevardnadze in Vienna, November 5–6. Shevardnadze, meanwhile, was attaching new strings to those concessions and trying to get Shultz to reaffirm the goal of abolition. As a result, Shultz's attempt to revive Reykjavik failed.[128]

On November 3, 1986, Shultz's hand would be strengthened by the Iran-contra scandal. By the time it receded, William Casey was gone from the C.I.A., replaced by William Webster. Frank Carlucci was the new national security adviser, and General Colin Powell, his deputy. Soon thereafter, former senator Howard Baker became White House chief of staff.

Yet Weinberger was still at the Pentagon doing his best to bury any chance for a revival of Reykjavik. At a National Security Planning Group meeting on February 3, the defense secretary tried to convince the president to embrace a loose interpretation of the ABM Treaty as "the legally correct interpretation" and to begin deploying defenses immediately. He was opposed by Admiral Crowe, who said that abandoning the ABM Treaty would be advantageous to the Soviet side. Warning that the reinterpretation would cause trouble in the Senate, Shultz urged, instead, that a study of the negotiating record and legislative history be undertaken to counter opponents.[129] Reagan's first instinct was to dismiss any need to cooperate with Moscow in the transition from offense to defense: "Why don't we just go ahead on the assumption that this is what we're doing and it's right. . . . Don't ask the Soviets. Tell them."[130] In the end, however, he sided with Shultz and signed National Security Decision Directive 261 authorizing the study. Yet Reagan's offhand comment became policy. On that Sunday's "Meet the Press," National Security Adviser McFarlane, much to the surprise of other top officials, announced that the president accepted the broad interpretation as the legally correct one but would confine SDI research to the narrow interpretation until further notice. Not consulted in advance, influential senators reacted vehemently. Eight days later, Shultz testified before the House Appropriations Committee that "we don't think any further negotiations are necessary" to interpret the ABM Treaty and the administration intended to proceed on the basis of "what we think it says."[131]

The Soviets, meanwhile, were doing a study of their own, starting in late 1986. Under Shevardnadze's direction, a major review of policy toward Washington recommended that concluding an INF agreement while Reagan was president would open the way to more far-reaching arms control arrangements with his successor.[132] Demands for change were coming from outside as well. Before a large audience attending an international disarmament conference in Moscow in mid-February 1987, dissident nuclear physicist Andrei Sakharov told Gorbachev in public what Roald Sagdeyev, Evgeny Velikov, Andrei Kokoshin, and other experts had been telling him in private: that SDI was technologically infeasible and had been oversold by the United States and overbought by the Soviet Union. At the urging of Jeremy Stone and Frank von Hippel of the Federation of American Scientists, Sakharov called for "untying the package," dropping insistence on linking deep cuts to limits on SDI and instead negotiating reductions as soon as possible. Stone and von Hippel also put the case to Gorbachev at a banquet concluding the conference.[133] Less than two weeks later, Gorbachev yielded to their entreaties by again untying SDI from INF but not from START. On February 28 he announced that the Soviet Union now wanted to reach "a separate agreement" on INF "without delay."[134] It was no longer linking limits on offensive weapons in START to limits on SDI testing but instead to "prevention of *deployment* of weapons in outer space."[135]

Nuclear conservatives mounted a concerted attack on the zero option. General Bernard Rogers, retiring as NATO commander, fired the first salvo on February 24. An agreement to ban INF "in isolation" without balanced levels of both battlefield nuclear arms and conventional forces "makes our deterrence noncredible," he said in an interview with the *Financial Times*, and "impacts unfavorably upon the security of the West." Brent Scowcroft, John Deutch, and James Woolsey echoed Rogers's criticism in a March 31 op-ed in the *Washington Post*. They argued for 100 warheads a side in Europe, not zero.[136] Not to be outdone, Henry Kissinger wrote an op-ed saying that the zero option "reduces the Soviet nuclear threat to Europe only very slightly," while eliminating "the American capacity to retaliate from Europe." Having overlooked the U.S. air-delivered warheads that remained, he suddenly rediscovered them a few paragraphs later: "Indeed," he warned, "it may well be a big step towards the eventual denuclearization of Germany."[137]

That March negotiations in Geneva began in earnest on how to verify the INF accord. A ban on intermediate-range-missiles made verification less complex. The United States proposed very intrusive monitoring, including on-site inspections of missile production facilities and missile destruction and challenge inspections anytime, anywhere. This was asking a lot of Soviet officials, who had even invented special designations for their missiles to avoid using their actual names in exchanging data for SALT II.[138] Reversing decades of secrecy, the Soviet Union agreed—only to have the United States withdraw its own proposal when the arrangements proved too costly and the challenge inspections too intrusive. In the end, the treaty did provide for unprecedented intrusiveness, a measure of Soviet willingness to cooperate on verification.

Shultz took an inflexible stance when he met with Gorbachev and Shevardnadze on April 13–14, 1987. "The U.S. position on many issues seemed to amount to a continuing escalation of demands, many of them not unreasonable, but with little understanding that Gorbachev's and Shevardnadze's freedom to maneuver was limited and that opening them to criticism by conservatives at home was a dangerous tactic," Pavel Palazchenko, Shevardnadze's interpreter, recalled. Shultz's recollection was comparable: "I was given tight instructions, almost as if to assure that I would not come back from Moscow with any progress toward an agreement."[139] On SDI, Shultz had to backtrack from the U.S. offer at Reykjavik not to withdraw from the ABM Treaty for ten years and to propose a seven-year period instead. He also was precluded from discussing what was permitted and not permitted under the treaty. On INF missiles, Gorbachev asked, "At Reykjavik you agreed to 100 on each side globally and none in Europe—do you still agree?" Shultz said, "Yes, we agree." But he added, "That is not what we want; we want zero globally, but we agree to that as a step in the right direction."

When Gorbachev proposed a freeze on shorter-range missiles in Europe, Shultz objected, "We must have equality and the right to match your deployments." Gorbachev then proposed treating shorter-range missiles like INF missiles: zero in Europe and 100 per side in Soviet Asia and the United States. When Shultz objected that "these weapons are easily moved," Gorbachev offered to eliminate

all shorter-range missiles on a global basis. Shultz said he would take
the offer to the NATO allies. That step had been worked out in
advance with Bonn, where the coalition government was divided over
the issue, with some Christian Democrats against zero and Hans-
Dietrich Genscher's Free Democrats for it.[140]

The double-zero proposal set off heated debate in NATO.
Chancellor Kohl, anticipating public opposition to new missile
deployments in Germany, sided with Genscher in favor of zero. Prime
Minister Thatcher was adamantly opposed. On July 16 she flew to
Washington and urged President Reagan to assign F-111 aircraft and
sea-based cruise missiles to NATO and to deploy a replacement for
the Lance missile and a new tactical air-to-surface missile (TASM).[141]
The Pentagon came up with the idea of reserving the right to convert
the Pershing II missiles to be banned under the INF accord into
shorter-range Pershing I-Bs. When the United States proposed that in
Geneva, Soviet negotiators countered with a demand that the United
States dismantle its warheads for the 72 Pershing I-As assigned to
West Germany.

On July 23 Gorbachev broke the impasse by publicly offering a
global ban on both INF and shorter-range missiles, including the SS-
23. That eased the complications of monitoring production and
deployment, but the decision took its toll in Moscow. Inclusion of
the SS-23 was "an unpleasant surprise to the military leadership as
well as to the Five's members," said Savel'yev and Detinov. The military raised vehement objections and blamed Shevardnadze for circumventing the Big Five.[142]

On August 26 Kohl, acting at Washington's suggestion,
announced his willingness to scrap West Germany's Pershing I-As
after all U.S. and Soviet INF and shorter-range missiles were eliminated.[143] To appease nuclear conservatives on both sides of the
Atlantic, the administration instead pledged to modernize its short-
range nuclear missiles. That further inflamed passions in Moscow.

It also would exacerbate the new nuclear dangers. On July 6, 1987,
Crimean Tatars had held a demonstration in Red Square to protest
their mass deportation by Stalin in 1944 and to demand restoration of
their autonomous republic in the Crimea. It was the most significant evidence to date that democratization was leading to a possible breakup of
the Soviet Union, leaving control over Soviet nuclear stocks in a parlous
state. The appropriate response was to speed up arms reductions, especially of the 30,000 short-range warheads most susceptible to theft or

misuse. Yet some nuclear conservatives in the West drew the opposite conclusion and sought to deploy new short-range warheads. That was a sign of how much nuclear weapons had become a totem of power, irrespective of security requirements. Thatcher was an exemplar of this misguided view. "Events now increasingly suggested that a far-reaching political crisis in the USSR might soon be reached," she recalled. "The implications of this for control over nuclear weapons and indeed the whole arsenal which the Soviet military machine had accumulated could not be ignored even by the most enthusiastic Western disarmers. In short, the world of the 'new world order' was turning out to be a dangerous and uncertain place in which the conservative virtues of hardened cold warriors were again in demand."[144] Cooperating with the Soviet Union in reciprocal steps to dismantle nuclear arms and secure the warheads and material that remained would hardly count as one of the "conservative virtues of hardened cold warriors." It is difficult to fathom how deploying new warheads for the sake of deterrence would prevent the Soviet nuclear infrastructure from collapsing, or dissuade the guardians of the Soviet arsenal from spiriting away a few warheads or a few pounds of nuclear material for sale abroad, or keep renegade commanders from seizing some warheads in the midst of civil war.

Yet negotiations to reduce arms made little headway in three days of talks in Washington in September. Shultz and Shevardnadze did announce an "agreement in principle to conclude a treaty" to eliminate all INF missiles for signing at a late fall summit meeting in Washington but did nothing else of substance on arms.

By the time Shultz went to Moscow on October 21–23 to try to wrap up the INF accord and set a date for a summit meeting, the political climate in Washington had improved. Caspar Weinberger had resigned. Frank Carlucci, who accompanied Shultz to Moscow, was chosen as Weinberger's successor, and Colin Powell was named to replace Carlucci as national security adviser. The political climate was not as propitious in Moscow, however. The day of Shultz's arrival, unbeknownst to the Americans, Boris Yeltsin opened a rift in the collective leadership by attacking Yegor Ligachev at a Central Committee meeting. That led to Yeltsin's ouster from the politburo, leaving Gorbachev without a powerful politician on his left to play off against Ligachev and others on his right so that he could occupy the middle ground. Moreover, Gorbachev's political base in the Communist Party shrank as reformers resigned by the thousands.

No progress was made on the technical issues remaining in INF. Gorbachev offered a somewhat less restrictive version of linkage than at Reykjavik: 50 percent cuts tied to a ten-year period of nonwithdrawal from the ABM Treaty "as we both interpreted it and observed it before 1983" and talks on "what could be in space and what could not be in space."[145] Shultz turned him down. Gorbachev no longer insisted on completing agreements on START and on space weapons before holding a summit, but he said he would be satisfied with an agreement on "key provisions." He proposed sublimits for the 6,000-warhead limit: 3,000–3,500 ICBM warheads, 1,800–2,000 SLBM warheads, and 800–900 air-launched cruise missile warheads. The ICBM warhead sublimit bracketed Washington's proposal of 3,300, but the submarine-launched warhead sublimit was too low for American tastes. Shultz countered with a subceiling on ballistic missile warheads of 4,800. Without agreement on these critical provisions, Gorbachev abruptly balked at setting a date for the summit. "The agenda," he complained, "does not seem to measure up to what would be necessary at a summit." Shultz parried that thrust, suggesting that a delay in signing the treaty might not leave time for ratifying it while Reagan was in office and that the signing could go ahead without a summit.[146]

Within the week, Shevardnadze was back in Washington to set a summit date. On November 23–24 he and Shultz resolved most of the remaining INF differences.

By December 5 the INF Treaty was done. It banned all ballistic missiles with ranges from 500 to 3,000 kilometers, requiring the Soviet Union to scrap 1,836 missiles and the United States 859 missiles, though not the warheads they carried. By eliminating the Pershing II missiles that could target Soviet command and control facilities, the treaty enhanced crisis stability. It also provided for the most intrusive verification in the history of nuclear arms control.

The Washington summit was held December 7–10, 1987. It made little progress on strategic arms. The joint communiqué finessed the differences over SDI with convoluted prose: "the leaders of the two countries also instructed their delegations in Geneva to work out an agreement that would commit the sides to observe the ABM Treaty, as signed in 1972, while conducting their research, development, and testing as required, which are permitted by the ABM Treaty, and not to withdraw from the ABM Treaty for a specified period of time."

The high point of the summit came on December 8, the signing of the INF Treaty. Ratification would take six months more. In the meantime, strategic arms reduction talks languished. "The air did not completely go out of the START balloon," said Shultz. "I just couldn't keep pumping the necessary air into it."[147] Nor did talks on reducing short-range warheads get under way. At the NATO summit in March 1988, Prime Minister Thatcher insisted that such talks "should only take place after parity on conventional weapons and a ban on chemical weapons had been achieved." She won President Reagan's assent.[148]

On May 27, 1988, two days before President Reagan arrived in Moscow for his last summit meeting with Gorbachev, the Senate finally voted its consent to the INF Treaty, 93 to 5. On June 1 the treaty entered into force.

Criticism of the president's abolitionism by the nuclear conservatives was unrelieved. So was the despair in right-wing circles about his cooperation with the communists. Columnist George Will's farewell to Reagan was typical: "How wildly wrong he is about what is happening in Moscow. Reagan has accelerated the moral disarmament of the West—actual disarmament will follow—by elevating wishful thinking to the status of political philosophy."[149]

In his own retrospective on the Reagan era, Secretary of State Shultz defended cooperation with the Soviet Union on arms control. He also recognized that nuclear radicalism made sense for American security in the post–cold war era. "In light of the subsequent dissolution of the Soviet Union and the attendant concerns about the location and control of strategic and other nuclear weapons, I am even more convinced of the wisdom of Ronald Reagan's objectives. How much safer we would all have been if those arsenals had been declining in magnitude in a manner where we could have seen firsthand just what was taking place."[150]

Nuclear abolition had been Ronald Reagan's fondest wish, but it required far more extensive cooperation than either he or his advisers were willing to contemplate. His other wish, to build a defense against ballistic missiles, aroused Moscow's suspicions, impeding cooperative security. Yet U.S.-Soviet collaboration in the form of arms control had survived the unilateralists' determination to stifle it. That seemed to confirm Gorbachev's admonition to Reagan on survival in the nuclear age, "We're doomed to cooperate."[151]

6

An Imprudent Excess
of Caution

It was easy to see what was wrong. What is harder is to find out what works. But I need a long period of peace.

—Mikhail Gorbachev to
Henry Kissinger, January 1989[1]

I don't want to make the wrong mistakes.

—President George Bush,
quoting Yogi Berra[2]

As the Gorbachev revolution progressed, cooperative security with the Soviet Union became politically easier to pursue in the United States. It also became more imperative for American security. If the revolution was likely to trigger a reactionary coup by orthodox Communists and restoration of authoritarian rule, as some U.S. officials believed, then it made sense for President Bush to lock in agreements on nuclear and conventional force cuts that would constrain Soviet arming well into the future. If, on the other hand, as some Soviet experts believed, the revolution was dissolving the Soviet regime and the union itself, that could pose a grave risk of loss of nuclear control, which made it all the more urgent to negotiate and implement arms reductions and move on to more radical forms of cooperative security. The Bush administration was slow to recognize the danger and even slower to cope with it.

The administration could hardly be faulted if disunion was obvious only with 20-20 hindsight. Yet the nuclear dangers were increasingly evident as the Soviet Union unraveled in 1989–90. In 1988 nationalists in the "prison of nations" began rattling their cages, starting in the Caucasus. On February 13 Armenians rioted in Nagorno-Karabakh, an Armenian enclave in Azerbaijan. On February 28 several people died in anti-Armenian pogroms in Sumgait, Azerbaijan. On July 23 mass demonstrations in Tallinn, Riga, and Vilnius, Lithuania, protested the Soviet annexation of the Baltic republics in 1940. On November 16 Estonia's Supreme Soviet declared sovereign control over state property, an act annulled by the U.S.S.R. Supreme Soviet ten days later. On November 22 anti-Armenian riots ripped Baku, Azerbaijan. On April 9, 1989, Soviet troops suppressed a peaceful demonstration in Tbilisi, Georgia, killing twenty people and wounding hundreds.

An April 1989 C.I.A. assessment warned of Soviet disunion. The resurgence of nationalism, the agency concluded, made it "far from certain that Gorbachev will be able to control the process he has set in motion." Perestroika, it said, "could unleash centrifugal forces that will pull the Soviet Union apart or create such serious tensions among nationalities that the ensuing social and political chaos will undermine Gorbachev's reforms."[3]

Based on C.I.A. reporting and assessments, on July 18, 1989, Deputy National Security Adviser Robert Gates sent the president a memorandum, "Thinking about the Unthinkable: Instability and Political Turbulence in the U.S.S.R." It recommended "contingency planning" for Soviet "leadership or internal policy changes or widespread ethnic violence and repression." The president gave his approval in September 1989, and Gates asked N.S.C. staffer Condoleezza Rice to gather an interagency group and "in very great secrecy" commission a number of studies by the C.I.A.[4] Among the obvious subjects for study were the potential risks that political instability posed for nuclear control.

Yet the Bush administration was reluctant to negotiate deep nuclear cuts with the Soviet Union or to cooperate more comprehensively to reduce nuclear risks. That owed largely to top officials' deeply ingrained realism.

GEORGE BUSH, NUCLEAR CONSERVATIVE

If Ronald Reagan was a nuclear radical, George Bush was a nuclear conservative. He thought Reagan had gone too far in questioning deterrence, in valuing defense over offense, and in contemplating nuclear abolition.[5] He wanted to restore the old nuclear verities, and he was in no hurry to negotiate with Mikhail Gorbachev, who, like

Reagan, seemed all too eager to call those verities into question. The most widely accepted of those verities, however untrue, was that American nuclear arms offset a Soviet advantage in conventional forces. That was the administration's motive for its ill-timed campaign for a new short-range missile to replace the nuclear-armed Lance in Europe. It was also the rationale for seeking to cut Soviet conventional forces first while slowing START to a standstill.[6]

When it did negotiate on arms, the administration pressed Moscow for every advantage, in the words of Ambassador Jack Matlock, trying to get "120 percent of what it wanted."[7] Sometimes more is less, however. "Unfortunately," concluded two Soviet analysts at the C.I.A., "Washington contributed to Shevardnadze's demise by pushing the foreign minister to the limit on each and every issue, without realizing the cost in terms of his loss of influence."[8] It also weakened Gorbachev.

President Bush's top advisers, Secretary of State James Baker and his deputy, Lawrence Eagleburger, National Security Adviser Brent Scowcroft and his deputy, Robert Gates, and Secretary of Defense Dick Cheney all had deep doubts about Gorbachev's commitment to transform the Soviet system and his likelihood of success. They disagreed about how to respond: to hold the line against cooperation in the belief that Gorbachev did not mean what he said or would soon be ousted, to treat his proposals as public relations problems requiring public relations solutions, to "lock in" whatever concessions he might make, or to reciprocate on arms and cooperate with him to reform the Soviet Union. Scowcroft was inclined to err on the side of caution. "I believe," he wrote, "that one should try to change the direction of the great Ship of State only with care, because changes, once made, are inordinately hard to reverse."[9] His view was seconded by Gates and Cheney. Baker was more inclined to accommodate change, as was General Colin Powell, soon to be chairman of the joint chiefs of staff. "My sense," said Baker, "was that Gorbachev might actually be prepared to usher in far-reaching, fundamental change—but we would be able to find out how far he was willing to go only by moving forward ourselves."[10]

The administration's initial response was to stand still—the *pauza*, or pause, Gorbachev called it.[11] Then it set a series of "tests," hurdles for Gorbachev to surmount before it would enter into sustained give-and-take on arms or cooperate more comprehensively. As political pressures mounted at home and in Europe to meet Gorbachev halfway, the president tried soothing words. When they failed to relieve the stress, Secretary of State Baker convinced the president to take advantage of

Gorbachev's goodwill and lock in American arms control gains. Yet the administration made few compromises and stopped far short of the thoroughgoing reciprocity required for cooperative security.

The administration was cross-pressured from the outset in dealing with Gorbachev. Fifteen days before Bush was sworn in, William Safire launched a preemptive strike from his right flank, accusing Secretary of State-designate Baker of being "eager for a first-year START treaty."[12] Far from it, the president and his top advisers already had decided to buy time by commissioning a study on what to do about the Soviet Union and to hold up START in the meantime.[13]

Scowcroft expressed the administration's skepticism about new thinking in Soviet foreign policy on January 22, two days after taking office. Gorbachev, he contended on ABC's "This Week with David Brinkley," seemed "interested in making trouble within the Western alliance. And I think he believes that the best way to do it is a peace offensive, rather than to bluster, the way some of his predecessors have." He dismissed new thinking as a mere expedient to secure breathing space for Gorbachev to revive his economy and restore Soviet military strength before resuming the offensive.[14] It was the same line that Robert Gates, then deputy director of the C.I.A., had been taking throughout 1988.[15]

That line proved politically untenable. Even Gates soon conceded that Gorbachev was a genuine reformer. Instead, he and other antagonists of U.S.-Soviet cooperation began to argue that Gorbachev was an aberration, "an exception that would prove the rule," and would not be around for long. "Bear in mind that the guy who's running the Soviet Union now may not be running the Soviet Union ten years from now."[16] Defense Secretary Cheney took the same line on Gorbachev in an April 29 interview on CNN, "If I had to guess today, I would guess that he would ultimately fail; that is to say, that he will not be able to reform the Soviet economy to turn it into an efficient, modern society. And when that happens, he's likely to be replaced by somebody who will be far more hostile than he's been . . . towards the West."[17] It sounded like his wish was father to that thought. After Secretary of State Baker telephoned Bush, the White House disassociated the president from Cheney's remarks.[18]

While right-wing Republicans in Congress shared Safire's suspicions, most of the pressure on the administration came from Democrats and Republicans alike, including former presidents Nixon and Reagan, who wanted the Bush administration to try reciprocity with Gorbachev and to expedite arms cuts. Some career officials and foreign leaders also sought to sustain the momentum in U.S.-Soviet relations. As early as January 28–29, 1989, Matlock, the U.S. ambassador in Moscow, drafted three cables questioning the reigning wisdom in the administration. To him, Gorbachev was intent on cooperating "since good relations with the West were essential if perestroika was to succeed." Nor was Gorbachev in imminent danger of losing power. "I was aware that some in Washington were now predicting that Gorbachev would not last and therefore the administration should not waste time and effort dealing with him," he recalled. "I thought that this attitude was totally mistaken and pointed out that Gorbachev had demonstrated his ability to outmaneuver his critics and was likely to continue to do so in the foreseeable future." If events proved him wrong, that was all the more reason to deal with Moscow and lock in agreements now: "Even if the doubters turned out to be right, we would lose nothing by solving as many problems as possible while Gorbachev was in office."[19] On March 3, Matlock met with the president and urged him to continue the practice of regular summit meetings and to hold one before too many months passed. Bush was unpersuaded. "Our marching orders are clear," Matlock told State Department colleagues afterward. "Don't just do something. *Stand there!*"[20] Prime Minister Margaret Thatcher also grew restless at Washington's inaction. When Secretary of State Baker made his first official visit to London in February, she cautioned him on the pause and its consequences for world opinion. "Don't let things linger. Don't let them lie fallow."[21]

The political difficulty that the Bush administration was experiencing in trying to hold the line against cooperation with Moscow stemmed in part from what Gorbachev did just a month before President Bush took office: his dramatic announcement to the United Nations General Assembly of unilateral cuts in Soviet conventional strength.

GORBACHEV REMOVES THE SOVIET THREAT

The idea of a massive troop withdrawal originated in 1987. In Geneva NATO and the Warsaw Pact were preparing new negotiations on conventional forces in Europe (CFE) to replace the long-moribund talks on Mutual and Balanced Force Reductions (MBFR). Eager to get on with perestroika, Gorbachev needed substantial cuts in the armed forces to enable him to redirect resources from defense to domestic needs. He also had been discreetly told by some Eastern European leaders that the Soviet troop presence posed problems for them.[22] In the fall of 1986 Marshal Sergei Akhromeyev and General Nikolai Chervov, the chief arms controller on the general staff, had set out the main tenets of a new military doctrine, defensive sufficiency, which was formally adopted by the Defense Council by the end of the year.[23] In 1987 Gorbachev commissioned studies not only by the general staff and the defense ministry but also by civilian experts in IMEMO and other institutes on how to implement the new doctrine by reducing and restructuring conventional forces. On May 30, 1988, the second day of his Moscow summit with Reagan, he made a three-part proposal: first, to exchange and verify data on troops and some categories of weapons, then to eliminate asymmetries in the forces of the two sides, and finally to reduce troops on each side by 500,000. The troop drawdown implied that the United States would withdraw from Central Europe, which Washington was unwilling to do. The only public hint of the proposal was Gorbachev's complaint at the conclusion of the summit that "it did not prove possible to reach agreement on the subject of talks on conventional weapons in Europe."[24]

Approval in principle by the Soviet general staff of a negotiating proposal for drastic cuts in conventional forces opened the way to a much more radical move by Gorbachev at the United Nations in December that did not have general staff endorsement.[25] In July 1988 he ordered the general staff to plan for unilateral cuts ranging from 300,000 up to 700,000 troops, as well as larger negotiated reductions.[26] Unilateral reductions were pushed by civilian experts, led by Alexei Arbatov and Andrei Kokoshin, who would become Russia's deputy defense minister under Yeltsin.[27] With these plans in hand, Gorbachev opted for a unilateral cut, over the objections of the armed services, who were concerned that many officers would be retired early, without jobs, housing, or adequate benefits. His choice surfaced publicly in September when Andrei Kozyrev, deputy chief of the foreign ministry's international organizations administration and later foreign minister of Russia, published an article in the journal *International Affairs* in favor of unilateral reductions, or "eliminating asymmetries in order to set an example."[28] On November 3 Gorbachev won politburo approval for the cuts.

Gorbachev made his stunning announcement at the United Nations General Assembly on December 7, 1988: the Soviet Union would unilaterally reduce its armed forces by 500,000 troops by the end of 1990. Where all the reductions would come from was not immediately clear, but he did specify that six tank divisions, numbering 5,000 tanks and 50,000 troops, would be withdrawn from Central Europe and disbanded and that Soviet forces in Europe would be reduced by a total of 10,000 tanks, 8,000 artillery pieces, and 800 combat aircraft—one-fifth of all the Soviet planes then based in Eastern Europe. River-crossing units would be removed along with their bridging equipment. So would air assault units. Six weeks later he told a delegation from the Trilateral Commission that of the 500,000 troop reduction, 240,000 would come from the European part of the Soviet Union and that half of the tanks would be "physically liquidated" and the rest converted to civilian purposes or used for training. The military budget, he said, would be reduced by 14.2 percent and production of arms and military technology by 19.5 percent.[29] When carried out, these force and budget cuts would eviscerate the Red Army and end the Soviet threat of sudden attack in Europe or, as a November 1989 intelligence estimate put it, "virtually eliminate the Soviets' already limited short warning attack capability."[30] That, in turn, minimized the need for large arsenals of nuclear arms to deter such an attack.

It was in that context that the Bush administration drew the line on further nuclear cuts and reaffirmed the retention of a substantial American troop presence in Europe. President Bush tried to minimize Gorbachev's unilateral reduction: a cut of 500,000 in Soviet forces, "given their total size, was small but a good start."[31] If Gorbachev wanted to make drastic cuts, Bush was not eager to cooperate, especially on nuclear arms.

TILTING AT WINDMILLS WITH LANCE

President Bush's nuclear conservatism was nowhere more evident than in his ill-fated campaign to replace the Lance missile. The idea of deploying a new short-range missile in Europe was the Reagan administration's sop to opponents of the INF Treaty. Known as the "follow-on to Lance," or FOTL, the new missile may have been technically up-to-date, but it was a strategic and political anachronism. FOTL's range, while longer than Lance's, was just below 500 kilometers, too short to be covered by the INF Treaty. Its range would make it capable of striking targets only as far as East Germany and Czechoslovakia from bases in West Germany. That made little strategic sense when Gorbachev was withdrawing enough of the Red Army from Eastern Europe to close off any chance of a surprise attack and to open up the possibility that the Warsaw Pact might break up. Deployment of FOTL made even less political sense when Germans were warmly welcoming Gorbachev's troop cuts and when it could feed discontent with Gorbachev's unilateral cuts in the Red Army. "Why must we destroy our SS-23 missiles," some were asking, "while the other side is developing and deploying missiles similar to the Lance?"[32] Yet Robert Blackwill of the N.S.C. staff echoed the sentiments of top U.S. officials when he called FOTL the "defining security issue of the next couple of years."[33] The question it raised for one top official in Bonn was, "Has America fallen off the planet?"[34]

Prime Minister Thatcher, even more of a nuclear conservative than President Bush, staunchly supported FOTL.[35] President François Mitterrand of France, while less outspoken than Thatcher, was just as eager to avoid stigmatizing nuclear arms. Yet Chancellor Helmut Kohl was not about to rekindle public passions in Germany over new nuclear deployments, especially after the strong showing by vocally antinuclear Social Democrats in West Berlin elections in January 1989. He raised the Lance issue with Bush when the newly installed president first telephoned him on January 23. On February 10, two days before Secretary of State Baker was due in Bonn, the chancellor, in an interview in the *Financial Times*, called on NATO to postpone a decision on Lance modernization.[36] Kohl made his objections clear to Baker. He was dismissive of enthusiasm for FOTL and opposition to arms talks in London: "Mrs. Thatcher is rid of *her* missiles." He asked Baker to defer a decision until after the December 1990 German elections, saying his government would fall if Washington pressed to replace the Lance now.[37] "We let up on modernization then," said an adviser to Baker.[38] NATO's Nuclear Planning Group met on April 20–21 and, bowing to Bonn, deferred a decision to deploy FOTL.

That did not satisfy political demands in Bonn, where even Alfred Dregger, an archconservative and leader of the Christian Democrats in the Bundestag, threw his support behind talks on short-range nuclear forces (SNF). In an acrimonious meeting on April 18,

Dregger, Foreign Minister Hans-Dietrich Genscher, and other barons in West Germany's ruling coalition—Kohl was absent—endorsed talks "soon" and leaked their decision to the press. Genscher and Defense Minister Gerhard Stoltenberg were dispatched on a high-profile mission to Washington to push for talks.[39]

"We were received coolly," said Genscher. Bush was opposed to talks out of concern that Gorbachev would seize the occasion to propose a ban on short-range missiles. Cheney left the meeting abruptly to deliver a speech, calling talks a "dangerous trap" and warning that NATO "must maintain the will to resist the call for a third zero"—eliminating short-range in addition to INF and Pershing IA missiles.[40] Administration officials were bitter. "The Germans have not been straight with us," said one. "They promised to continue engaging in a discussion to sort out our differences, and then they turned around and presented us with a *fait accompli*. They staked out a public position without consultations with us."[41] President Bush chided Kohl by telephone the next day. "I told Helmut I understood his situation and I did not wish to meddle, but he should have discussed SNF with us before such decisions were made—and were made public. I did not want Bonn to present us with a *fait accompli*. 'It also means no leaks, which only tend to lock one into a position,' I added firmly."[42]

A day later, Bush telephoned Thatcher, who tried to use the issue to revive the special relationship at German expense: "What is important is agreement between the U.S. and Britain, because without those two countries there would be no NATO." Bush demurred. "I preferred to wait until after the talks with the Germans in Washington before we said anything. We would deal privately and in good faith with the Germans when they came."[43]

Those talks "got nowhere," said Scowcroft, and "the mood was anything but conciliatory."[44] Thatcher, believing Kohl had "gone wobbly," upbraided him: "I had acrimonious discussions with Chancellor Kohl behind the staged-managed friendliness of our meeting at Deidesheim at the end of April."[45]

Some in Washington began muttering, "no nukes, no troops," an admonition to Bonn last invoked in the 1950s when nuclear arms were thought to offset Soviet conventional superiority. Yet saying so could put the administration on slippery ground when some members of Congress were finding that calling for U.S. troops to return home from Europe was the best applause line of all in their districts. At the same time, nuclear conservatives like Henry Kissinger feared that negotiations would inevitably lead to elimination of all U.S. nuclear arms from Europe and that denuclearization would "institutionalize Soviet hegemony over Western Europe." Such fears in Washington were derided in Bonn. "At a time when their empire is collapsing and the economy with it, and the regime is trying to stave off disaster by imitating us," said one German official, "the idea is laughable."[46]

Elimination also made sense for American security. Not only would Moscow be giving up some 1,400 launchers in return for just 88 Lance missiles, but also removing them would strengthen NATO's defenses by reducing the vulnerability of its air bases to attack by missiles armed with conventional or chemical warheads. Talks also could lead to removal of the Soviet warheads most vulnerable to theft and misuse in peacetime and least controllable in a crisis—nuclear artillery shells, atomic demolition munitions, and other battlefield nuclear weapons that constituted the bulk of the 20,000 tactical warheads in the Soviet arsenal.[47] At a time when disintegration of the Warsaw Pact and of the Soviet Union itself seemed possible, the withdrawal of all battlefield nuclear warheads to secure storage sites in Russia would reduce the risks of both unauthorized use and nuclear proliferation. Those risks had not yet blipped onto the radar screen of the Bush administration, but they had crossed the minds of some experts in Moscow and in American nongovernmental organizations.

What worried many more people in Washington was the prospect of a divisive fight in NATO just when the need for the alliance was coming under question at home and abroad. In a May 2 interview, Paul Nitze attacked the Bush administration for pressing for FOTL while resisting talks. "I cannot think of a German who would agree to that," he said. "Many of the allies think it is a crazy proposition."[48] Other Nixon, Carter, and Ford administration officials endorsed a report obliquely critical of White House policy: "Wiser strategic thinking, the intra-NATO political benefits of a reduction and the fact that the very justification of these weapons is disappearing all point to an opportunity for removing a substantial number of these systems."[49] Senator Sam Nunn (D-GA), chairman of the Senate Armed Services Committee, told Defense Secretary Cheney at a May 3 hearing that NATO was "shooting itself in the foot" by rejecting negotiations on short-range missiles while insisting on deploying new ones. Nunn proposed that Washington tell Bonn, "You agree to modernize; we'll agree to negotiate, with a limit, not going to zero. But we'll make the negotiation dependent on the conventional arms control outcomes. . . ." Cheney countered, "If you can't resist the pressure to get into the negotiations, how do you resist the pressure" to accept zero, which would mean "the denuclearization of Europe"? Holding up agreement on short-range missiles until an accord on conventional arms was concluded, Admiral Crowe added, "would be very difficult to sell."[50]

Deploying the FOTL was intended to show the administration's resolve not to end reliance on nuclear arms. That risked bringing down a government in Bonn that it wanted to keep in power. Washington would belatedly relent on FOTL. Yet, if it were up to the administration, there would be no talks on short-range forces in Europe.

INSISTING ON INEQUALITY

To forestall talks, the Bush administration changed the subject. "The key to solving this nuclear dilemma," Baker concluded after visiting Bonn, "lay in conventional arms control." The dispute over short-range nuclear forces could be finessed by proposing to reduce troops and tanks in talks on conventional forces in Europe. "A bold CFE proposal," he argued on his return, "would make SNF basically irrelevant, allowing us to resolve the issue and ensure alliance unity."[51] Focusing on CFE was also a flanking maneuver, intended to put off the prompt conclusion of a START agreement. Scowcroft agreed. "I thought that this changing atmosphere warranted a shift in the priority of U.S. attention away from our relations with the Soviet Union, which were focused almost entirely on [strategic] arms control, to Eastern Europe," he wrote. "Emphasizing Eastern Europe would also remind everyone that the fundamental structure of the cold war was still in place and Soviet troops still occupied Eastern Europe." One way to do that was to disparage Soviet unilateral cuts and seek "agreements on conventional force reductions to get the Soviet Army out, or at least reduce its stifling presence."[52]

Talks on conventional force cuts were a political necessity for domestic as well as alliance reasons. With the start of the Red Army's withdrawal from Europe, calls to "bring the boys home" rang louder. The administration also expected demands in Germany to remove all foreign troops or, as Secretary of State Baker delicately put it, "a barely conscious and growing resentment" of "what was perceived to be an overly intrusive American military presence."[53] To head off such demands, the Bush administration adopted a strategy used successfully by the Nixon administration two decades earlier: open new conventional arms talks and use the prospect of negotiated cuts to head off unilateral cuts by Congress. For President Nixon to deal with the stodgy and slow-moving Leonid Brezhnev when most NATO allies wanted to prevent any American drawdown in Europe was relatively easy. The Nixon administration could get away with tabling proposals that had little chance of acceptance. Now, faced with a nimble Gorbachev determined to reduce Soviet forces and many allied leaders eager to accommodate him and slash their own defense spending, President Bush did not have that luxury. With the unilateral Soviet withdrawal on the verge of freeing Eastern Europe and calling into question the need for NATO, the issue of retaining a firm American foothold in Europe, militarily as well as politically, came to the fore, and the Bush administration turned its attention to holding the line against pressure for a precipitous American withdrawal.

One way to hold the line was to adopt a decidedly one-sided negotiating position, making a conventional force accord more difficult to reach. That was the Bush administration's strategy. Once again, it was being uncooperative when cooperation might have done more for American security.

The need to rethink the American negotiating position was also driven by the start of new talks on Conventional Forces in Europe. Gorbachev had opened the way to the CFE talks in April 1986 by proposing a phased reduction in ground and air forces deployed from the Atlantic to the Urals. This encompassed far more than the area covered by MBFR, which had excluded Soviet territory and most of NATO Europe. Extending the reach of CFE into Soviet territory meant that, to satisfy any agreed ceilings, the Soviet Union would have to demobilize forces or withdraw them east of the Urals. An agreement would thus codify an end to the threat of surprise attack since any attempt to remobilize these forces or move them westward would provide ample warning. In another break with the past, Gorbachev acknowledged force asymmetries that NATO could well regard as threatening and suggested that the side with the quantitative advantage make larger reductions. He also accepted on-site inspections. Gorbachev's offer was formally adopted by the Warsaw Pact in June 1986 in Budapest. In what became known as the "Budapest appeal," the Pact proposed new bloc-to-bloc negotiations to supplant

MBFR, with all seven of its members on one side and all sixteen members of NATO on the other. In December 1986, NATO agreed and began discussions with the Warsaw Pact on a mandate for the talks.[54]

On May 29, 1988, the first day of the Moscow summit, after President Reagan had spoken of Soviet superiority in conventional forces, Gorbachev had come back with a three-stage proposal: "As a first stage, we would define and eliminate existing imbalances and asymmetries," he said. "Let us verify the data which will serve as a basis for negotiations by way of on-site inspection right at the start." Having eliminated the asymmetries, "both sides would reduce their conventional forces by approximately half a million men each. In the third stage, conventional forces on both sides would be restructured to become purely defensive and unsuited for offensive warfare. At all stages of the negotiations, we are prepared to reduce offensive weapons on both sides—tactical nuclear weapons, strike aircraft and tanks."[55] Equal ceilings would deprive NATO of its long-held nuclear rationale, the Warsaw Pact's quantitative advantage in conventional forces. That is why the proposal was closely held in Washington. Prompted by Gorbachev's unilateral cut seven months later, the sides signed a mandate for talks on January 19, 1989, in Vienna.

CFE talks began on March 9, 1989, just as the Warsaw Pact was starting to unravel. At the opening session Baker defended NATO's proposal for modest cuts, but Shevardnadze upstaged him with a variant of Gorbachev's three-stage proposal: that the Warsaw Pact make 10–15 percent cuts to reach equal ceilings on military equipment and manpower in phase one, that NATO and the Warsaw Pact agree to dramatically deeper cuts of 25 percent in phase two, and then that both sides reduce and restructure their remaining forces, including navies, into defensive postures in phase three. Baker expressed concern about the public impact to his aide, Dennis Ross. "Look who's getting the big cheers. Then look who's getting the big yawns."[56] Baker's critics were blunter. "We look like a bunch of bean counters and Gorbachev looks like a guy who wants a different relationship in Europe," commented Les Aspin (D-WI), chairman of the House Armed Services Committee. "Public opinion is just going to come down the mountain and rip the NATO position out from under us."[57]

In a meeting in the Oval Office on March 30 with Baker, Scowcroft, Cheney, Eagleburger, Gates, Vice President Dan Quayle, and John Sununu, the White House chief of staff, President Bush requested "a bold proposal for force reductions" to regain the political initiative in

Europe. To counter what Scowcroft derided as Gorbachev's "proposal-a-day" strategy, the national security adviser, in a move prearranged with the president, proposed putting Eastern Europe front and center and adopting a new aim, getting the Red Army out. "I introduced a version of an initiative I had first made to the president during the transition," said Scowcroft, "the withdrawal of both U.S. and Soviet ground forces in Central Europe. It made military sense because NATO, minus most of its U.S. troops, was better off than the Warsaw Pact without Soviet troops. But, primarily, such a move would reduce the smothering presence of Soviet forces in Central Europe—one of our goals." Robert Blackwill, an aide of Scowcroft's, later quipped that the retired air force general had come up with "the fly-boy's answer to arms control: Bring the army home so you guys can provide air cover for those folks who stay behind."[58] Scowcroft had a larger purpose in mind. For an administration skeptical of Gorbachev's intentions and unaware that the Soviet leader had already prepared for further troop withdrawals, the new proposal was designed to temper talk of an end to the cold war and relieve the pressure to meet Gorbachev halfway.[59] President Bush recalled, "My own thoughts were focused on putting the United States back out in front, leading the West as we tackled the challenges in Eastern Europe and the Soviet Union."[60] Yet Defense Secretary Cheney was resistant, arguing that it was too early to get out in front on withdrawals from Europe because of uncertainty about what was going to happen in the Soviet Union. Scowcroft reported, "Jim Baker chimed in with his own proposal, also first raised during the transition, for the elimination of all tanks on both sides" in Central Europe.[61] As the inconclusive meeting drew to a close, Bush said grumpily, "If we don't regain the lead, things will fall apart."[62]

Baker would be upstaged again on his first visit to Moscow in May. He arrived a week after Cheney had put on the record the administration's opposition to talks on short-range nuclear arms, and he himself had spoken publicly of having to "test the application of Soviet 'new thinking,'" especially in regional conflicts. En route to Moscow, he told reporters, "*If* we find that the Soviet Union is serious about new global behavior, *then* we will seek diplomatic engagement in an effort to reach mutually beneficial results."[63] In his May 10 meeting with Shevardnadze, Baker denied that the administration wanted to "sidetrack" arms control. It wanted "a more creative approach" instead, "by taking unilateral steps (such as . . . publishing a real defense budget); by addressing sources of war, such as regional disputes, rather than just the means of war, such as weapons; and by focusing on 'strategic stability' rather than just numbers." The intention, Baker recalled, was a sharp break with Reagan's approach: "Given Soviet massive advantages in almost every type of weapons system, we felt the numbers game was a losing game; we preferred the concept of arms 'control' to arms 'reduction.'"[64]

The next day, Gorbachev began his meeting with Baker by saying, "I know you're being given a lot of advice, and that some of this advice is that the United States should not hurry and should wait until the Soviet Union has become destabilized and disintegrated. It would then be like a ripe apple that will fall to the ground by itself. But things are not that simple."[65]

Gorbachev then previewed the position that the Soviet Union would take in conventional force talks. Going well beyond the unilateral cuts of 500,000 he had announced at the United Nations in December, he said that the Warsaw Pact was prepared to reduce or retire 40,000 tanks out of 59,740 (the Pact's total according to Moscow), 47,000 of its 71,560 artillery pieces, 42,000 of its 70,330 armored vehicles, and 1 million of 3.6 million troops. At the same time, he sought a 55 percent reduction in NATO attack aircraft and other cuts to bring NATO and the Warsaw Pact down to equal levels of 1,350,000 troops, 1,500 strike aircraft, 1,700 helicopters, 20,000 tanks, 24,000 artillery pieces, and 28,000 armored personnel carriers.[66]

Then, "in an almost off-handed sort of way," Gorbachev said that the Soviet Union would withdraw 500 tactical nuclear weapons from Eastern Europe that year and would consider removing the rest by 1991 if the United States was prepared to reciprocate. In his memoirs, Baker dismissed the move as a ploy to generate pressure for the elimination of short-range nuclear forces. "It was a patently one-sided offer," he wrote, to "score public relations points with European publics."[67] Yet Baker himself disclosed the offer to reporters en route to Brussels, inspiring many of them to lead their stories with the nuclear withdrawal and to play down Gorbachev's more significant proposal to reduce conventional forces. Moreover, Gorbachev might have had a more important motive for the nuclear arms cut than scoring public relations points. The unilateral withdrawal of ground forces already under way would leave fewer troops to guard Soviet nuclear arms against theft or terrorism. If the withdrawal uncorked political unrest in Eastern Europe, the warheads would be safer in Russia. Similar concerns were leading Moscow to remove warheads from restive republics in the Soviet Union.

Baker responded to Gorbachev by noting Soviet quantitative and qualitative advantages in short-range nuclear force (SNF) launchers. "'The Soviet Union also has a large advantage in conventional forces, notwithstanding your good intentions,' I added somewhat sarcastically. 'So the fact remains, until we actually reach agreement, there is a major imbalance in SNF and conventional forces favoring the Warsaw Pact.'"[68]

Having flashed his irritation at being upstaged, Baker headed home determined to "come up with a bold and politically imaginative proposal for the NATO summit." The American riposte was to defer talks on short-range nuclear arms until a treaty reducing Soviet conventional forces in Europe was concluded.

Upon receipt of Gorbachev's CFE proposal, the president had Scowcroft ask Defense Secretary Cheney and Admiral William Crowe, Jr., chairman of the joint chiefs of staff, to confect a proposal to unveil at the May 29–30 NATO summit. At a meeting of top advisers on May 15, Bush emphasized the need "to seize the offensive." He spoke of cutting U.S. forces in half if the Soviet side would agree to come down to the same level. Cheney warned that the troop proposal would "unhinge the Alliance" and that the "British and French would go crazy."[69] Over lunch at the White House on May 17, Baker told Bush, "You need to get ahead of the power curve." Preoccupied with the effect on public opinion, at home and in Europe, Baker pushed for the largest cuts possible in U.S. troops: "Twenty five percent would, I thought, generate the kind of political effect we were looking for, while not endangering us militarily." In meetings of top officials over the ensuing week, Baker, with Scowcroft's backing, insisted that cutting NATO troops was not good enough; a significant cut in U.S. troops was essential. They also wanted to meet Gorbachev partway by including aircraft and armor as well as troops in the cuts. The Pentagon was united in opposition. "Crowe acted as though Leonid Brezhnev were still running the Kremlin, and he fought virtually every proposal tooth and nail," remembered Baker. "Cheney was far less dogmatic, but Dick felt Gorbachev was going to come our way anyway, so why move?"[70]

President Bush was due to host President Mitterrand of France at Kennebunkport over the weekend of May 20–21, 1989. Bush, Baker, Scowcroft, Cheney, and Crowe met there on May 19 to discuss what to do at the NATO summit. The pressures on them were palpable. Bush was warned that resisting a short-range missile ban and instead leaning on the West Germans to replace the Lance would risk a blowup in Brussels. The sense that Gorbachev had caught the public's fancy was brought home by that Sunday's *New York Times* editorial: "Imagine that an alien spaceship approached earth and sent the message: 'Take me to your leader.' Who would that be? Without doubt, Mikhail Sergeyevich Gorbachev."[71] Bush expressed his exasperation. He was "sick and tired of getting beat up day after day for having no vision and letting Gorbachev run the show," he confided to Scowcroft. "There's real danger in jumping ahead. Can't people *see* that?"[72]

In Kennebunkport Admiral Crowe recoiled at a 25 percent cut, which he argued would "make a mockery of forward defense" and require "a whole new strategy" for NATO, but he did concede that reductions of 5 to 10 percent were "doable."[73] "After a long debate," President Bush recounted, "I asked him to go back to the joint chiefs of staff to figure out just how deeply we could slash without disrupting the alliance."[74] At a May 22 meeting in the White House, Baker renewed his appeal for a CFE initiative with "impact" and "punch" and again proposed a 25 percent cut. When Cheney and Crowe resisted, President Bush was annoyed. "I want this done. Don't keep telling me why it can't be done. Tell me how it can be done."[75] Crowe then acquiesced to a cut of 30,000 in troop strength. "That did not seem to me to be much of a reduction," Bush noted, "but I was reluctant to ignore the unanimous advice of the joint chiefs."[76] When Cheney asked that the cut be taken from NATO as a whole, not just from U.S. forces, however, the president overruled him. "I want something that the U.S. can do alone, by itself, on its own."[77] In the end, "Crowe did agree that the reductions would be taken in combat forces (as opposed to support troops)," said Bush. "That allowed us to recast the arithmetic to claim a more respectable 20 percent reduction, by virtue of excluding the noncombat element."[78] The administration would seek a ceiling of 275,000 on the number of Soviet and U.S. troops that could be stationed in the center of Europe. The United States would have to withdraw just 30,000 troops and the Soviet Union 325,000, a cut of roughly 10 percent for the Americans compared to more than 50 percent for the Soviet Union.

The reductions were smaller than the president originally sought. They were also far smaller than Gorbachev was willing to make, but they were intended to leave the Soviet leader little choice. "It also made it plain," said N.S.C. staffer Robert Hutchings, "what the alternative was: a united NATO, fully prepared to maintain and continue modernizing its forces into the indefinite future, leaving Moscow to cope on its own with an eroding empire and bankrupt economy."[79]

The conventional force proposal won approval in NATO capitals, but Kohl and Thatcher were still at odds over Lance. Kohl was willing to accept modernization only if it was tied to negotiations on short-range nuclear arms. Thatcher was insistent that the opening of arms talks be made "dependent upon a decision to deploy a successor to Lance."[80] Trying to steer a path between the two, Bush sought to delay but not abandon modernization, to negotiate on short-range nuclear forces in Europe eventually but not now, and to reduce but not eliminate short-range warheads.[81] Bush did not consult Thatcher. "The truth of the matter was that we knew what Thatcher's reaction would be and had decided not to say anything ahead of time," commented National Security Adviser Scowcroft. "Had we consulted the British, it would have been very awkward to proceed over their strong objections." The stratagem worked. Thatcher was isolated and forced to yield. NATO endorsed Washington's language that the United States was prepared to enter into negotiations to achieve a "partial reduction"—underlining the word "partial"—in short-range nuclear arms.[82]

"Here we go now, on the offensive, with a proposal that is bold," exulted Bush in unveiling it to the press in Brussels. The administration proclaimed the May 29–30 NATO summit a triumph of Bush's "vision." Many observers were unimpressed. His stance on short-range nuclear forces was backward-looking, and his CFE proposal was not nearly as forthcoming as Gorbachev's. By fall, the criticism was telling, and so was the administration's defensiveness. Calling the administration "almost nostalgic about the cold war," Senate Majority Leader George Mitchell (D-ME) urged the president to "reach beyond the status-quo thinking that appears to dominate administration policy" and embrace "a more energetic and engaged policy" toward Eastern Europe. Secretary of State Baker snapped back, if "the president of the United States is rocking along with a 70 percent approval rating on his handling of foreign policy and I were the leader of the opposition party I might have something similar to say."[83]

Baker, just back from his Jackson Hole ranch, where he had heard Shevardnadze's frank account of the deepening disorder in the Soviet Union, now went out of his way to try to change public perceptions of the administration's "status quo plus" policy and make the best of its own dour assessments of Gorbachev's reforms that were impeding cooperation with Moscow. In an October 16 speech to the

Foreign Policy Association, he declared, "Our task is to find enduring points of *mutual* advantage that serve the interests of both the United States and the Soviet Union." He went on, "It would be a mistake to conclude that the challenges are too daunting or that the impediments to success are too great. So far, Gorbachev has secured greater power over the years, and he reveals every intention to 'stay the course.'"[84] A week later in San Francisco, he argued for locking in agreement with Moscow. "Any uncertainty about the fate of reform in the Soviet Union, however, is all the more reason, not less, for us to seize the present opportunity. For the works of our labor—a diminished Soviet threat and effectively verifiable agreements—can endure even if perestroika does not."[85] When Deputy National Security Adviser Gates circulated a draft speech calling Gorbachev's chances for survival into question, Baker called Scowcroft to quash it and leaked the fact that he had done so to the press.[86]

Yet Baker and other top officials shared Gates's pessimism. "My position was: 'Let's get what we can now and lock in as much change as possible," the secretary of state wrote in his memoirs. "I didn't want anyone in the future to be able to look back and say, 'If only . . . '"[87] Pessimism about Gorbachev's future remained the highest hurdle to cooperation. As Scowcroft said privately on October 23, "It would be dumb if we decided the cold war is over, or that the Soviets aren't a threat anymore, or that we don't need NATO and we can use our defense budget to straighten out our domestic economic order."[88]

As Moscow began unilaterally withdrawing forces from Germany and negotiating their withdrawal from Czechoslovakia and Hungary, pressures mounted from both left and right in Washington to draw down U.S. troops. Liberals who had long sought to lighten the country's defense burden were joined by unilateralists on the right who saw no reason to remain in Europe after the Red Army had departed. If there was a consensus among outside critics, it was that 100,000 U.S. troops in Europe would be ample to show that the United States would remain, in Bush's words, "a European power." Again, the administration reacted by seeking to negotiate reductions but proposing a troop ceiling much higher than needed.

The president's new military adviser was willing to go lower than either the secretary of defense or the chiefs of staff. More than any other top official in the Bush administration, General Colin Powell, who took over as chairman of the joint chiefs on October 1, 1989, realized how much of a revolutionary Gorbachev was and what that implied for the defense budget. On November 4, 1989, four days before the Berlin Wall was breached, he jotted down what he foresaw for the Soviet Union by 1994: "Rise of opposition parties, Western investment, market pricing, and Gorbachev still supreme authority." Other expectations came even closer to the mark: "No Soviet forces in Eastern Europe," "Warsaw Pact replaced," "East Germany gone," Germany "reunified" and the rest of the Warsaw Pact "neutral states with multiparty systems," Soviet defense budget cuts of 40 percent, manpower cuts of 50 percent, and a cap on shipbuilding—in short, a force structure intended for a "defensive posture." Anticipating a "stampede" by members of Congress to slash defense spending and declare a peace dividend, he decided, "We had to get in front of them if we were to control our own destiny." He came up with a strategy for doing that: reduce the U.S. force structure to levels low enough to hold the line against deeper cuts. "These levels would be tough to sell to Cheney," he found. "He was still a hardliner and not ready to bet on a 'kinder and gentler' Soviet Union."[89] They proved an even tougher sell to the chiefs of staff of the army and the other armed services.

On January 4, 1990, the president convened his top advisers to consider force cuts in Europe. "There were rumors that the Soviets were about to make fresh proposals for additional conventional reductions," recalled Scowcroft, "and the president wanted to announce a new U.S. position in his State of the Union address on January 31."[90] The national security adviser stressed the need to take the lead in proposing troop cuts: "We can get ahead of the Congress and establish a sustainable level." He suggested negotiating a bilateral cut in manpower to 200,000. When Cheney warned that deep troop cuts would spell trouble in NATO and on Capitol Hill, the president intervened decisively.

> Why do we always need the same number of troops and bombs? We should test the Soviets. Ask them to do something we think they'll never do [make asymmetrical cuts]. Otherwise, we'll pass up the opportunity, be cut unilaterally by the Congress, and get nothing for it. We shouldn't be seen as begrudging change, but acting boldly. We have an enormous opportunity to do something dramatically different.[91]

On January 16, 1990, President Bush was given three options. The Pentagon wanted to retain 275,000 troops. "Why negotiate for further reductions?" wondered Cheney. "It just creates problems for the allies." When Baker agreed, Scowcroft rejoined, "Why not find out instead of pontificating about it?"[92] Fearing deeper cuts were politically unavoidable, Scowcroft and the president wanted to set a floor of 200,000. The State Department sought to retain 275,000 until a CFE Treaty was signed, then promise a unilateral cut to 200,000. On January 22 the group reconvened, and Powell, just back from Europe, reported that the Germans would support further cuts, the British would oppose them, and the French would be uneasy, but all of them expected levels significantly lower than the current one. "I can feel the sand easing out of my position," remarked Cheney.[93] The president directed the Pentagon to choose a ceiling for U.S. troop strength close to 200,000. It settled on 195,000.[94] After speaking to Kohl, Mitterrand, and Thatcher by telephone, Bush dispatched Eagleburger and Gates to London, where they won Thatcher's grudging acquiescence.[95] Then Bush called Gorbachev before announcing the figure in his State of the Union address on January 31, 1990.

To get under that ceiling, the United States would have to remove 60,000 troops and the Soviet Union 370,000. What Bush neglected to say in his speech was that the ceiling would apply to U.S. and Soviet forces in the central region but that the United States would retain the right to deploy an additional 30,000 troops elsewhere in Europe. Beyond rejecting reciprocity, the Bush proposal also reversed a long-standing American position calling for equal ceilings on conventional forces. Now that Gorbachev had finally acknowledged Soviet quantitative advantages and accepted equal ceilings, Bush upped the ante.

The purpose, said Robert Hutchings of the N.S.C. staff, was "to place a floor on U.S. reductions and to begin 'delinking' U.S. and Soviet troop withdrawals, lest the principle of reciprocity be taken to mean that if all Soviet forces eventually left Europe then all U.S. forces should do so as well."[96] The point was not lost on Gorbachev. "You have emphasized that the United States will maintain its military presence in Europe after the negotiations are complete. If I understand you, this is regardless of what the Soviet Union does," he told Bush in their January 31 telephone conversation. He wanted limits on German forces in return: "We'll need to talk not just about U.S. and Soviet forces but other forces."[97]

With the Warsaw Pact and the Red Army in a shambles, the Soviet threat was gone. In its place were new nuclear dangers posed by Soviet disunion. These dangers were best headed off by a co-operative security approach, adopting a more equitable stance on troop cuts and negotiating deep reductions or elimination of all short-range nuclear arms. Equal manpower and equipment limits would have been politically more acceptable in Moscow, hastening an accord and legitimating Gorbachev's policy of common security at home. Instead, the unequal limits armed the hard-liners in the Soviet military and parliament with a potent grievance against co-operation, that the United States was taking advantage of the Soviet Union's weakness brought about by the Gorbachev reforms to tilt the balance of power in Europe in its favor. Conservative opposition would force Shevardnadze's ouster and help fuel the resurgence of the ultranationalists. An agreement to make deep cuts in short-range nuclear arms could have expedited removal of the very warheads that posed the greatest peril of proliferation and misuse if the Warsaw Pact, the Red Army, and the Soviet Union itself were to come apart.

Why did Bush administration officials and much of the American foreign policy establishment reject equal limits on conventional forces and deep cuts in American short-range nuclear arms? Many had doubts that the retrenchment of Soviet military power was irreversible and believed that a substantial American military and nuclear presence was essential to hedge against Soviet revival. Lower conventional force ceilings and a treaty to eliminate nuclear arms from Europe would limit future American freedom of action. Another reason for the administration's stance was that the American presence was a form of insurance against what some called the "renationalization of foreign policy"—renewed national rivalry in Europe, perhaps leading to the further spread of nuclear arms. Yet Germany had forsworn such arms. These grounds were less influential than a third, less tenable reason: to demonstrate that the United States was now the sole superpower, whose military and nuclear forces were indispensable for European security. As General Powell put it, "We have to put a shingle outside our door saying, 'Superpower Lives Here,' no matter what the Soviets do, even if they evacuate from Europe."[98] All three reasons were steeped in the shared images of realism prevalent in policymaking circles. Officials discounted, as realists do, the effect of internal developments: the Soviet Union was breaking up, with potentially grave consequences for Soviet nuclear control.

THE RED ARMY REACTS

By now, the Warsaw Pact was moribund. Some of its members were openly siding with the West and privately seeking to join NATO. Yet negotiators on Conventional Forces in Europe decided to proceed as if the Warsaw Pact were still intact lest they end up with no limits at all. They sought parity between the two alliances, postponing for the moment the more demanding task of apportioning the quotas among putative allies. The CFE negotiations would outlast the Warsaw Pact, and the resulting ceilings would survive the Soviet Union itself.[99]

With the disintegration of the Soviet bloc, the Red Army had become a wasting asset in Eastern Europe. Gorbachev needed to conclude a CFE accord before all his troops were withdrawn, leaving him little leverage for a more equitable deal. In a meeting with Baker on February 9, 1990, he offered to set a troop ceiling at 195,000 or 225,000, so long as it was the same for both sides. Just four days later in Ottawa, Shevardnadze accepted the American proposal of 195,000 troops a side in the central region and an additional 30,000 for the United States elsewhere in Europe. "I was stunned," said Baker.[100]

With that concession in hand, Washington began to reverse course on CFE. By the time of the Washington summit in late May 1991, the administration was moving to expedite negotiations and lock in limits. One reason was that Bonn might prefer fewer U.S. troops in Germany. "We did not want to approach the final stages of unification with the question of future agreed force levels in Europe left undetermined, particularly in light of ongoing discussions between Bonn and Moscow on limiting the size of future German armed forces," according to Hutchings. "With so much in flux, a few fixed points of reference were needed." Senior administration officials were gratified when Soviet officials accepted a joint communiqué that committed them "to intensifying the pace of the negotiations in Vienna and to reaching rapid agreement on all outstanding issues."[101]

One way to expedite agreement was to defer personnel limits. At its July 1990 summit, NATO pledged follow-on talks on CFE. That left three major issues to be settled: definitions for each category of weapons, quotas for each country, and detailed verification arrangements. In September 1990, reflecting the rising influence of the military in Moscow, Soviet negotiators proposed that if a country abandoned its alliance, the remaining members could absorb its quota, which would have permitted the Soviet Union to fill the Warsaw Pact's entire allotment of treaty-limited equipment. Needless to say, the Soviet Union's presumed allies opposed this as strenuously as its onetime foes. In bilateral talks with the United States in October, Moscow relented and agreed to a sufficiency rule, limiting any country's entitlement to about one-third of the equipment that its alliance as a whole could retain in each of the treaty zones. These talks also narrowed or resolved other differences.

The CFE Treaty was signed on November 19, 1990, at a summit meeting of the Conference on Security and Cooperation in Europe. The treaty mandated the largest reduction of ground forces in arms control history, mostly the Soviet Union's. It set much lower limits on five categories of conventional arms: tanks, artillery, armored combat vehicles, helicopters, and aircraft. It also imposed sublimits on three categories of equipment stationed within four geographic zones: a central zone embracing Germany and its immediate surroundings, a separate zone covering the western military districts of the Soviet Union and Hungary to prevent the massing of follow-on forces, and two zones to cover the flanks—one in the north that encompassed Norway and Kaliningrad and another in the south that included Turkey and the Caucasus. It covered equipment assigned to naval aviation units but based on land, which was soon to become a matter of dispute.

The treaty's verification provisions were far more extensive and intrusive than previous conventional arms accords. They called for sharing data on force levels and on the organization and location of forces. They also called for three sorts of inspections: mandatory inspections to verify the reduction of treaty-limited equipment; a quota of inspections of sites where brigades or regiments were stationed to verify that the ceilings were being observed; and challenge inspections at other sites.

The verification provisions in the CFE Treaty were supplemented by confidence-building measures negotiated in other forums. By themselves, such measures cannot preclude premeditated attack, but they can reduce the likelihood of inadvertent war and can ease suspicions and promote cooperation among countries that have no intention of attacking one another. The first of these confidence-building measures, and the most modest, were part of the Helsinki Final Act concluded in 1975. The act's only obligatory measure required CSCE members to notify others three weeks in advance of any exercise involving at least 25,000 troops. It applied only to Soviet exercises conducted within seventy-five miles of the border, and an exception was made for exercises arranged on short notice. The other measures were purely voluntary: advanced notification of smaller exercises and of major movements of armed forces not engaged in exercises and the exchange of military personnel to visit bases and participate in training. The Stockholm Conference, which began in January 1984 and concluded in September 1986, yielded more substantial measures: notification six weeks prior to any military activities involving 13,000 troops or 300 tanks, 200 combat aircraft sorties, a parachute drop, or an amphibious landing by 3,000 or more troops; two observers from each CSCE member at maneuvers involving 17,000 troops; an annual calendar specifying the date of regular exercises at least a year in advance; and on-site aerial and/or ground inspections. Talks in Vienna yielded agreement on additional measures in time for the November 1990 CSCE summit meeting in Paris: a detailed annual accounting of each state's military organization, manpower, equipment, and expenditures; mandatory visits to evaluate the accuracy of the data; risk reduction provisions, obliging CSCE members to consult and cooperate in the event of unusual military activities; and establishment of a CSCE Center for Conflict Prevention.[102]

Foreign Minister Shevardnadze had pushed for the concessions that made the CFE Treaty possible, often over the objections of the armed services. As Defense Minister Dmitri Yazov later told Richard Nixon, he and many of his fellow officers thought the treaty was "one-sided and unfair."[103] They were incensed by the asymmetric cuts in troop strength and the refusal of the United States to agree to any offsetting limits on navies.

Two weeks after the CSCE summit in Paris, the Red Army struck back. It reopened some provisions of the treaty and reneged on another. Even worse, conservative opponents of common security in the Congress of People's Deputies began hounding Shevardnadze out of office. Just weeks before the treaty was signed, the Red Army had redeployed more than 16,000 tanks from Eastern Europe and the western military districts to areas east of the Urals, where they would not be covered by the treaty and hence spared from destruction. Upon signing the treaty, Moscow underreported the artillery pieces in its inventory and the military sites to be subject to inspection—895 sites instead of the 1,500 it had originally designated.[104] It also reassigned some aircraft and armor to naval infantry or to newly formed "coastal defense" units at Kaliningrad, Murmansk, and Sevastopol in order to avoid destroying them under the treaty. In December 1990, just before Shevardnadze was due to meet Baker in Houston, the army gained defense council approval to exempt unilaterally three motorized rifle divisions from reductions to be taken under the treaty. Shevardnadze protested the defense council's decision to Gorbachev, denouncing its circumvention of the spirit, if not the letter, of the treaty as "dishonest behavior on our side."[105]

Early in December 1990, American negotiator R. James Woolsey went to Moscow and confronted Defense Minister Yazov and General Mikhail Moiseyev, chief of the Soviet general staff, on the one clear violation of the treaty, the Soviet attempt to exempt some armored combat vehicles by reassigning them to naval infantry and coastal defense units. Waving his finger at Woolsey, Yazov insisted that naval infantry would have to be limited in a future agreement that covered U.S. aircraft carriers and submarines as well. Pushing Yazov's hand away, Woolsey said, "Marshal, over *my* dead body!" The defense minister replied, "Yes, Mr. Ambassador, perhaps so."[106]

The acrimony had not dissipated by December 10, when Baker met Shevardnadze in Houston to seek Soviet cooperation with the U.S. stance against Iraqi aggression. To Baker's dismay, Woolsey objected to redeployments east of the Urals and insisted to Shevardnadze that the armor had to be destroyed instead. Even the joint chiefs were unconcerned about the problem, Baker later complained to an aide, saying that he had been told by one chief, "They're dumping the stuff there in order to let it rust."[107] The treaty limits, and the Soviet obligation to live up to them, would outlast the rusting tanks.

Baker was unaware that Shevardnadze had drafted a compromise offer to deal with problem, but when he sought approval from Moscow, Gorbachev turned him down. It was the first time that Gorbachev had overruled Shevardnadze on an arms control issue, a sign of the growing strength of conservatives in the politburo. The foreign minister expressed his frustration to his aide, Sergei Tarasenko: "I can't do this anymore."[108]

In his memoirs, Shevardnadze is critical of Gorbachev: "The threats to unseat the foreign minister were heard not somewhere out on the streets, but in the corridors of power. Worse, they were not challenged by those whose business it was to respond."[109]

Instead of defending Shevardnadze, Gorbachev proposed kicking him upstairs from the foreign ministry to the vice presidency.[110] Gorbachev's tactical shift from alliance with the reformers to alliance with the conservatives also made Shevardnadze uneasy: "He has constantly to choose among constituencies, and if one of them turned out to be weak and unreliable, then, willingly or not, he had to cast his lot with another that could guarantee him more stability. Some of his backers really were unreliable; others he himself alienated, and as a result, the old standbys . . . rushed to fill the vacuum. But I fear they are not as reliable as they seem to Gorbachev."[111]

Joining Baker on a flight back to Washington from Houston, Shevardnadze confided that it was a "very difficult period" for him. The generals were staging a "counteroffensive" to retaliate for all the times he had gone over their heads to get Gorbachev's approval for arms control concessions. Moscow's reformers were "vanishing," he added, and Gorbachev, who was now deferring to the conservatives, "always thinks he is the master of events."[112] It was a rehearsal of themes Shevardnadze would repeat in a speech to the Congress of People's Deputies just ten days later, on December 20, 1990, when he shocked Moscow and Washington by denouncing a creeping coup by hard-liners, warning of "the onset of dictatorship" and abruptly announcing his resignation.[113]

His successor, Aleksandr Bessmertnykh, was a career diplomat who lacked the influence to stand up to opponents of cooperation in Moscow even if he had wanted to. He shared the career Soviet foreign service officers' faith in realism and disdain for outsiders.[114] Bessmertnykh's mentor and longtime ambassador in Washington, Anatoly Dobrynin, was typical. When Shevardnadze was appointed foreign minister, Secretary of State Shultz had asked Dobrynin about him. Dobrynin's reply was disdainful: an "agricultural type," he said.[115] Dobrynin's disdain was undiminished after Shevardnadze's departure, contending that he was "outwitted and outflanked" by the Americans and the Europeans and went "further than necessary in concessions . . . on arms control, Eastern Europe, German unification, and the Persian Gulf."[116]

Shevardnadze's resignation coincided with the revival of the realists in the Soviet foreign ministry and the temporary eclipse of common security in Moscow. It also marked the beginning of the end of Gorbachev's rule and of the Soviet Union itself.

START to Finish

In Washington, Shevardnadze's resignation ignited the slow-burning dispute over backing for Gorbachev and his government. Since summer, Americans sympathetic to the plight of the Baltic republics and Ukraine and their allies on the Republican right had been urging the Bush administration to push for dismemberment of the Soviet Union. Others were recommending that Bush distance himself from Gorbachev and cultivate Boris Yeltsin and the government of the Russian Federation, the core of any post-Soviet commonwealth. Arrayed on the other side were those who urged the administration to back Gorbachev unconditionally in order to head off a hard-line coup and possible civil war. Still others recommended a "grand bargain," conditional support for Gorbachev, using aid to induce him to undertake radical economic and political reform. Preoccupation with the appropriate political relations between the United States and the Soviet republics obscured a more important concern for American security: the risk that Soviet disintegration would loosen central control over Soviet nuclear arms. One solution consonant with cooperative security was to negotiate and implement deep cuts in those arms.

In the last year of the Reagan administration, a START treaty had been within reach. Secretary of State Shultz had tried to keep alive the chances of concluding the treaty but to no avail. The protracted struggle to ratify the INF Treaty absorbed what little time and attention he and other top officials gave to nuclear matters, and START stalled. The Bush administration took office determined to put off START until a conventional force treaty was negotiated. Indeed, the Geneva talks did not resume until July 1989, more than a year after the previous round had ended.

In Moscow, Washington, and around the globe, strategic arms talks had become the touchstone of U.S.-Soviet cooperation during the cold war. Gorbachev and Shevardnadze were eager to conclude a START treaty to have something to show for their policy of common security. The Bush administration was uncooperative. In a portent that he intended to retrace steps in START already taken by his predecessor, President Bush announced on June 19, 1989, that the United States would "reaffirm much of the treaty text negotiated with the Soviets by the previous administration," but it "reserves the right to introduce new initiatives."

As with short-range nuclear arms, the administration was interested in deploying new weapons, which it wanted to protect in START. One was a pet project of National Security Adviser Scowcroft's, a single-warhead ballistic missile small enough to be mounted on a truck. He liked its mobility because that made it less vulnerable to missile attack, which was good for stability. The Air Force did not want to spend money for a mobile missile, especially one that carried just a single warhead compared to ten on the MX, and gave it the dubious name of Midgetman, implying that it was too diminutive for real men. The other weapons that the administration sought to shield from START were air-launched and sea-launched cruise missiles. The Pentagon was particularly eager to protect the Tacit Rainbow cruise missile, which, thanks to technological breakthroughs in guidance systems, was accurate enough to be conventionally armed. The small size of such cruise missiles and the difficulty of distinguishing the nuclear from the conventional versions made them a verification nightmare.

Yet, more than any particular weapon, the administration was eager to protect nuclear arms in general from elimination. Reagan's rush to disarm, in Scowcroft's view, had been a "mighty dubious objective for grown-ups in this business," and START had turned into "seeing how much you can shave from deterrence and still keep it in effect. I think this is playing with fire."[117]

The long pause in START negotiations had contradictory effects in Moscow. It led Gorbachev and Shevardnadze to press the bureaucracy for new proposals by April, "so that whenever the Bush administration was ready we could hit the ground running," but it reinforced doubts in other quarters. "The fact that the administration took so long to reassess its Soviet policy created an opening for the conservatives and 'the agencies' in Moscow" like the defense ministry and K.G.B., recalled Pavel Palazchenko, a strong supporter of START. "They had their own interpretation of the pause and the debate, which they were putting into cables and memorandums sent to Gorbachev . . . 'Mikhail Sergeyevich, they don't like you, they don't trust you, and they want you out.'"[118]

Soviet suspicions were heightened by the administration's strategy of "testing" Gorbachev, erecting higher and higher hurdles for him to surmount. One such "test" was the START proposal that President Bush sent to Gorbachev before tabling it in Geneva in July. The Soviet leader found it so one-sided that he refused to dignify it with a direct reply. His response did not come until September, a nine-page letter that Shevardnadze hand-delivered.

Shevardnadze's visit was intended to move the U.S.-Soviet relationship to a "new level," up from "understanding to interaction, and perhaps partnership."[119] Gorbachev was willing to pay the price of partnership. Bush was not.

Shevardnadze brought with him several significant START concessions. He received nothing in return. In a September 21 meeting at the White House, he affirmed that the Soviet Union would dismantle the radar at Krasnoyarsk. Long a bone of contention, the large phased-array radar was designed to fill a hole in the Soviet early-warning system, but its location, deep in Siberia, violated the ABM Treaty, which confined deployment of such radars to the periphery of each side's national territory. Since 1987, at the insistence of the Soviet general staff, Moscow had linked resolution of the issue to similar U.S. radars at Thule, Greenland, and Fylingdales Moor, England. Acting on his own, without obtaining clearance from the defense minister or the four other pivotal members of the defense council, Shevardnadze obtained Gorbachev's assent to break the linkage.[120]

In his letter to Bush, Gorbachev had written, "Let us set aside, for the time being, our conceptual argument about whether the placing of weapons in space . . . will strengthen strategic stability or have the opposite effect. Let us not allow this issue to make the already complex talks more difficult."[121] Later, at Secretary of State Baker's ranch in Jackson Hole, Shevardnadze confirmed what the letter implied, that the Soviet Union was willing to sign START even if agreement were not reached on SDI. "This was a dramatic breakthrough," admitted Baker.[122] Stating that any violation of the treaty would be grounds for withdrawal from a START treaty, Shevardnadze called for talks to clarify limits on testing and deployment under the ABM Treaty. Baker refused.

Shevardnadze's other concession dealt with sea-launched cruise missiles (SLCMs). The Soviet Union had insisted that START impose limits on SLCMs, where the Americans had a technological edge. The United States wanted the right to deploy 880 nuclear-armed SLCMs, even though it had fielded only 350 and had no plans to deploy more than 758. The Soviet Union had proposed a ceiling of 760, high enough to accommodate the entire planned deployment, but Washington insisted on 880.[123] Shevardnadze now dropped the Soviet demand that SLCMs be covered in START. He proposed a side agreement on SLCMs instead. Anticipating objections from the Pentagon, Baker turned him down.[124] Shevardnadze would later come under harsh criticism from Marshal Akhromeyev and former deputy foreign minister Georgy Korniyenko for failing to get anything from Washington in return for making this concession.[125]

The thrust of Baker's brief was to change the subject again, from START to controlling chemical arms. He proposed a bilateral accord with the Soviet Union to reduce chemical weapons stockpiles by 80 percent. Shevardnadze accepted. Two days later, President Bush announced another initiative to give impetus to a global treaty to ban such weapons, proposing to reduce U.S. and Soviet chemical weapons stocks by 98 percent in advance of a global ban. The next day, Shevardnadze expressed willingness to eliminate Soviet stocks altogether.

Shevardnadze's cooperation on arms control and his candor on Soviet domestic difficulties gave Baker confidence to move in a more cooperative direction, at least rhetorically. In testimony before the Senate Finance Committee on October 4, he went beyond the policy of seeking to lock in agreements that served U.S. interests and cited the Jackson Hole talks as an example of the "search for points of *mutual* advantage."[126] One point of mutual advantage was to scrap as many Soviet nuclear arms as soon as possible. "Any uncertainty about the fate of reform in the Soviet Union is all the more reason, not less, for us to seize the present opportunity," Baker said in a speech to the Commonwealth Club in San Francisco. "If the Soviets have already destroyed weapons, it will be difficult, costly, and time-consuming for any future Kremlin leadership to reverse the process and to assert military superiority."[127]

Unfortunately, the secretary of state's words were meant mainly for public consumption and had little immediate bearing on administration policy. In anticipation of a December summit in Malta, President Bush asked Robert Gates, deputy national security adviser, what Gorbachev wanted most out of the meeting. "He wants added momentum for the relationship as a whole and for arms control in particular," Gates replied. "He hopes for a START agreement and summit in the U.S. in late spring or early summer of 1990 and a conventional-forces agreement later in the year." He could reallocate more money from defense to the civilian sector than he could ever get in aid from the West, Gates added. "Let's really get going on this," Bush told his top aides.[128]

The president did what most new presidents do: try to put his own stamp on strategic arms talks. It had the usual result, prolonging the talks and delaying a treaty. In Bush's case, the delay was deliberate.

His proposal was to limit missiles armed with more than one warhead, each of which could be aimed at a separate target. Known as MIRVs, which stood for multiple, independently targeted reentry vehicles, they made the nuclear balance more precarious. A land-based MX carried ten MIRVs, a sea-based Trident eight, and a Soviet SS-18 ten apiece. By rule of thumb, two warheads were targeted against a single Soviet silo, so that a single MX missile, with its pin-point accuracy, could destroy five Soviet missiles if it caught them on the ground before they could be launched. That gave both sides an incentive to shoot first as a last resort in the event that nuclear war seemed imminent. The Reagan buildup had done nothing to alleviate this problem, and his proposals for deep cuts would have made the predicament all the more pernicious by reducing the number of Soviet missiles to be targeted while permitting the United States to deploy all the accurate warheads it planned to and more. One way to reduce the vulnerability of the MX was to make it mobile, and the Reagan administration had adopted the idea of basing the MX on rail cars in the West. Nearby residents would be a potential target, hardly an appealing prospect, and the resulting political friction had all but stopped mobile basing in its tracks. That led State Department officials to favor a ban on MIRVed mobile missiles, in effect, to trade away MX in return for an equivalent Soviet missile, the SS-24.

In the run-up to the December 1989 Malta summit, START negotiator Richard Burt and Reginald Bartholomew, under secretary of state for politico-military affairs, renewed that effort. They were aware that Brent Scowcroft had long favored "de-MIRVing." So did the chairmen of both armed services committees, Senator Sam Nunn and Representative Les Aspin. Secretary of State Baker was persuaded that the offer was a "real twofer," putting a "Bush stamp" on START and attracting bipartisan support.[129] Scowcroft had a better idea. "Why limit de-MIRVing to mobiles?" he told the president. "Let's go all the way." He convinced Bush to propose a ban on all MIRVed missiles based on land, not just mobiles. Bush was willing to go along, but Defense Secretary Cheney demurred, fearing that an offer to ban the MX would only discourage congressional funding for the missile. The Air Force belittled Scowcroft's substitute for MX, the single-warhead Midgetman, for yielding much less bang for a buck. Air Force plans to take preemptive action in a crisis required at least one hundred MXs, each armed with ten accurate MIRVs. To some in the Pentagon, giving up the fifty MXs already being built and the fifty remaining Minuteman missiles in hopes of deploying the new Midgetman seemed like trading away two stars for a future draft pick, and a light-hitting one at that. Baker and Scowcroft backed off. "It turned out to be more than the traffic could bear," Baker told aides.[130]

Had Washington proposed a ban on land-based MIRVs at Malta, it might have been more than the traffic could bear in Moscow as well. Although Scowcroft found Marshal Akhromeyev open to de-MIRVing when the two met in July, Gorbachev was sure to encounter resistance from the Soviet general staff, which had invested heavily in MIRVed, land-based missiles and had nothing to match the Americans' highly accurate, MIRVed Trident missiles at sea.

Gorbachev, meanwhile, was preparing no new arms control initiatives of his own. He was preoccupied with persuading Bush of the American stake in the success of perestroika and of his own determination to cooperate. A briefing paper by Georgi Arbatov and Andrei Kokoshin of the Institute for the Study of the U.S.A. and Canada, based on conversations with administration officials and members of Congress, portrayed the doubts and divisions in Washington. While no longer questioning Gorbachev's sincerity, the paper concluded, administration officials doubted his ability to succeed or survive and expected a period of "consolidation" in Soviet foreign policy. The administration was divided between officials like Gates and Cheney who wanted to exploit Soviet weakness to extract as many concessions as they could and others like Baker who worried that excessive demands by Washington could lead to Gorbachev's downfall. Arbatov and Kokoshin counseled Gorbachev not to make any dramatic new arms control proposals, both because administration officials they had talked to had expressed concerns about "another Reykjavik" and because they feared it could cause a backlash from Moscow's hard-liners.[131]

Neither side, in short, made any effort at Malta to propel START to a conclusion. Gorbachev pressed for "meaningful naval arms control" to limit sea-launched cruise missiles: "How can we really have a big START agreement that does not restrict an entire category of nuclear weapons?" Small and easy to hide, cruise missiles were difficult to monitor, and the U.S. Navy was opposed to shipboard inspections as an infringement on its autonomy. It was long-standing policy "neither to confirm nor deny" the presence of nuclear arms aboard U.S. vessels, easing access to ports in Japan and other antinuclear countries willing to go along with the pretense. Inspections would have thrown that policy overboard. President Bush deflected Gorbachev and instead suggested that Baker and Shevardnadze meet in Moscow in January 1990 to discuss how to limit sea-launched cruise missiles, how to count and limit nondeployed ballistic missiles, and how to assure that telemetry encryption, encoded data transmissions from missile tests, not impede treaty verification. There was still disagreement within his own administration on these issues, Bush acknowledged, but he promised that "we'll have our own position resolved" by the time Baker saw Shevardnadze. On conventional arms, Bush proposed a CFE summit for all the nations involved before the end of 1990. "If we impose a sense of deadline," he said, "it'll help move the negotiations forward."[132] He expressed no equivalent urgency about completing a START accord.

On January 4 the president and his top advisers again took up de-MIRVing. "The question," said Scowcroft, "was whether we should stick to the now three-year-old proposal we had inherited and get it signed as fast as possible, or modify it to reflect recent developments. Add-ons would slow it down and potentially interfere with strategic programs in the defense budget. Moreover, the Soviets might get upset and could derail things." Cheney was still opposed to a proposal to ban MX, fearing that would jeopardize its funding by Congress. "We should take what's on the table and run," he argued. "We can do the rest in START II." Baker agreed with Cheney: "We've gone too far to reopen START I now." The president differed. "What's stopping us?" he asked. "The Soviets are open. Let's talk to them." He worried that Congress would cut off funding for MX if the administration did not try to deal it away. "The Congress is going to take this and screw us up," he said. "This is the opportunity to get something from the Soviets."[133]

In 1990, as German unification and conflict in the Baltic republics took center stage, START was left in the wings. Baker did not get around to holding a serious discussion of strategic arms with Shevardnadze until mid-March. By then, Scowcroft told the president, the Soviet Union was in a "prerevolutionary" condition. "The situation . . . is so bad that it is hard to believe that an explosion can be avoided," Scowcroft warned him on March 7. "The more visible and aggressive posture of the K.G.B., the police, and the army could spark violence at any time. The already dysfunctional economy is likely to get worse in the next few months and it is not clear how much longer Soviet citizens can muddle through and feed themselves. No one knows for sure where the army stands."[134] The president was preoccupied with how to deal with the republics, not with the nuclear dangers entailed in disunion. His diary entry of March 17 is one indication: "My view is, you dance with who is on the dance floor—you don't try to influence this succession, and you especially don't do something that would [give the] blatant appearance [of encouraging] destabilization. We meet with the republic leaders but we don't overdo it."[135] Another indication of how remote the nuclear risks of disunion seemed was an attempt by Robert Blackwill of the N.S.C. staff to arouse action on arms control. He cast it as a way to "help Gorbachev deal with his domestic situation" and gain acceptance for a united Germany in NATO. He recommended "Christmas in June" for Gorbachev at the summit in Washington: "He could address a joint meeting of Congress. We'll have agreements on START, CFE, CSCE, chemical weapons, a commercial trade agreement, so that he can go back to Moscow and show his own people what he's gotten from his relationship with the West."[136] With the administration under Republican pressure to distance itself from Gorbachev, Blackwill's idea did not get far. "While we needed to get arms control straightened out," Bush recalled, "I would go in a minute if there was some way that he could announce that the Baltic states were being set free."[137]

Baker and Shevardnadze neared agreement on sea-launched cruise missiles in Moscow on February 7–9. Instead of setting treaty limits, Shevardnadze conceded each side could declare the number of SLCMs it planned to deploy. Baker agreed to treat the declarations as "politically binding." The Soviet negotiators wanted all nuclear and conventionally armed SLCMs with ranges of more than 600 kilometers covered, however, while the Americans wanted coverage confined to nuclear-armed SLCMs with ranges beyond 300 kilometers. They reached agreement on telemetry encryption and on nondeployed missiles. Moscow tentatively accepted a "counting rule" for air-launched cruise missiles (ALCMs) that attributed a number to each type of heavy bomber instead of trying to determine by on-site inspection the number that each bomber actually carried. The provision was very advantageous to the United States: current U.S. bombers were counted as carrying ten ALCMs even though they were permitted to carry up to twenty. Soviet bombers were counted as carrying eight ALCMs and permitted to carry up to twelve. Some Soviet bombers carried six ALCMs and others sixteen. The counting rule had been proposed without getting the Big Five to agree in advance, and representatives of the general staff and military-industrial complex were sharply critical, arguing that, if the offer were accepted, "the Soviet Union would have to modernize its entire ALCM bomber fleet."[138]

Instead of trying to resolve the few remaining issues and expedite an agreement on START, Baker took up the issue of de-MIRVing with Shevardnadze at Windhoek, Namibia, on March 19. He proposed a two-stage solution: they would ban MIRVed mobile missiles in START and then go on in START II to ban all land-based missiles armed with more than one warhead. "We were doubtful," Baker admits, "that Gorbachev would be interested in the proposal, since he was under such pressure from hard-liners." The military and Supreme Soviet, Shevardnadze confirmed, were "scrutinizing everything that we are doing, and they tend to get emotional." To him de-MIRVing meant delay. "Our first objective is to complete the START agreement." That was enough to convince Baker that "de-MIRVing would have to wait for another day."[139]

When Shevardnadze came to Washington on April 4–6, he brought a response to Baker's Windhoek initiative: de-MIRVing should be deferred to START II. Under pressure from the Soviet general staff, he backtracked on his concession on sea-launched cruise missiles by calling for "legally binding" ceilings.[140]

In May 1990, ten days before his trip to Moscow, Baker secretly gave Shevardnadze new START proposals. In Moscow, while managing to resolve two outstanding issues, he also glimpsed the growing power of opposition to further concessions there. On May 18 he won Gorbachev's assent to exempt the Tacit Rainbow from START limits and from a START provision that conventionally armed cruise missiles be distinguishable from nuclear versions, only to have Soviet negotiators reverse themselves later that day. Baker remained in Moscow an extra day to resolve the dispute by means of a side letter detailing Tacit Rainbow's capabilities and the number the Air Force planned to deploy without agreeing to any limits.[141] The two sides also concurred on a "politically binding" side agreement to deploy no more than 880 SLCMs with ranges in excess of 600 kilometers. The United States proposed a 800-warhead sublimit on mobile missiles, and the Soviet Union countered with 1,200.

With de-MIRVing yet to be resolved, a START treaty could not be ready in time for signing at the Washington summit at the end of May. The Bush administration was content to let it slip until after a CFE Treaty was signed. Then, having slowed START for three years, the administration at last turned its attention to completing the treaty. By the time it did, those opposed to cooperative security had gained ascendancy in Moscow.

In a violation of the CFE Treaty, the Soviet military sought to exempt some armored combat vehicles by reassigning them to naval infantry and coastal defense units. Shevardnadze had tried and failed to resolve the dispute in Moscow, and he made little headway on it with Baker in Houston on December 10, 1990. On December 20 Shevardnadze resigned.

Just as hard-liners in Moscow used the naval infantry and coastal defense equipment to impede Soviet-American cooperation, opponents of cooperation in Congress, most of them Republicans, seized on the dispute as evidence of Soviet cheating. American negotiators had become accustomed to getting their way. As Under Secretary of State Bartholomew put it, "We've been spoiled by Shevardnadze."[142] As a result, the Bush administration took an unyielding stance on the issue. On January 28 in Washington, Baker told Foreign Minister Bessmertnykh that the dispute over CFE put the credibility of arms control in jeopardy. "We feel that we've been deceived. I will not be able to recommend that the treaty be sent for ratification unless this problem is resolved."[143] Under mounting pressure from conservatives, who castigated the CFE Treaty as a surrender to the West, Gorbachev ceded the issue to top military officials, who were just as unyielding. So long as CFE remained unresolved, efforts to conclude a START treaty stalled.

A summit meeting scheduled for February 1991 was postponed after the crackdown in Lithuania. By spring, Gorbachev was seeking to reschedule it. Bush tried to use the Soviet leader's desire for the summit as leverage on CFE compliance and START.

General Mikhail Moiseyev, chief of the Soviet general staff, was spearheading military resistance to complying with CFE.[144] During a mid-March trip to Moscow, after making little progress with Moiseyev, Baker raised the issue with Gorbachev. The next day Baker told Foreign Minister Bessmertnykh, "It doesn't matter how you reach the limits. If you have to maintain naval infantry units, then do so. But you've got to take forces from some other category." Baker came to the conclusion that Gorbachev was the key to resolving the issue. "I really hit him over the head," he told Bush on his return to Washington. "We've to keep Gorbachev himself involved."[145]

In a letter to Gorbachev, the president reiterated the Baker formula, but the most that Gorbachev would do was to freeze the number of armored combat vehicles assigned to coastal defense and naval infantry units. At Bessmertnykh's suggestion, he put Moiseyev in charge of the next round of talks, so that the military would have responsibility if the talks broke down and the treaty was not implemented. At the suggestion of Robert Gates and Arnold Kanter, Bush wrote Gorbachev again to invite Moiseyev to see him. "That way," said Gates, "we can give him a firsthand look at how dug-in the president himself is on this issue."[146]

At issue were just 753 armored combat vehicles. The Americans offered to let the Soviet military convert them from troop carriers to ammunition carriers, which were permitted by the treaty. Bush repeated the offer in a letter to Gorbachev, who accepted it on June 1. On June 14, 1991, the Soviet Union presented a "legally binding" statement on how it would comply with the treaty that was formally accepted by all the CFE signatories at a conference in Vienna.

With CFE out of the way and Gorbachev in trouble, there was a new sense of urgency in the Bush administration about finishing START. De-MIRVing was a major sticking point. By now the idea of replacing MIRVed missiles with new single-warhead missiles was seen as too costly in both capitals, and proposals to ban MIRVed, land-based missiles had been put off until START II. A cheap and easy way to de-MIRV had first been broached in 1987 by the Reagan administration to get under START's lower ceilings without having to scrap the Minuteman III—"downloading," removing warheads from deployed missiles. Verifiable procedures to dismantle the downloaded warheads would have been a quick fix for de-MIRVing, but neither side was ready to negotiate such procedures.

If the warheads were not dismantled, however, downloading was reversible, raising fears of "breakout"—that some future, revisionist Soviet regime could evade treaty restraints by abruptly reinserting the warheads. Brent Scowcroft had objected to the Reagan administration's de-MIRVing proposal on precisely those grounds. As national security adviser, Scowcroft reluctantly yielded to the Pentagon on a proposal to allow each side to download one missile type: the U.S. Minuteman III from three warheads to one and the

Soviet submarine-launched SS-N-18 from seven warheads to three. Scowcroft was adamantly opposed to letting Moscow download two other missile types in order to accommodate newer models of the SS-24 and the SS-N-20, which carried fewer warheads than earlier models. That meant twice as many warheads would be downloaded, doubling the breakout risk. A far greater risk, however, was that differences over de-MIRVing would endanger START.

That concerned U.S. negotiator Richard Burt, who floated a compromise to let the Soviet Union download the types of missiles it wanted to but limit the number of warheads downloaded. The issue came to a head in spring of 1991. Baker was worried that a START treaty and a June summit in Moscow would be jeopardized by such an "absurd and trivial" issue. Defense Secretary Cheney favored downloading on grounds of cost. So did the chairman of the joint chiefs of staff, General Powell. "I'm not as exercised about it as Brent," he told Cheney. "The situation is changing so fast and so profoundly that someday we'll wonder why we ever argued over this. With everything that's going on over there, I have a hard time convincing myself I should stay awake worrying about the Sovs' future breakout capability."[147] When Baker suggested Bush write Gorbachev indicating some willingness to be flexible, Scowcroft relented. Baker handed the letter to Bessmertnykh in Geneva on June 6. In reply, Gorbachev went along with the compromise Burt had floated, holding fast on missile types to be downloaded but offering to halve the number of warheads. Scowcroft remained unmoved.[148] So did the Soviet Union.

Bessmertnykh, accompanied by General Moiseyev, came to Washington on July 12 to try to resolve the differences over de-MIRVing. Yielding to military objections, he turned down a U.S. proposal to ease restrictions on the new Soviet missiles. He appealed to Baker, "You must understand, Jim, there are certain limits in my freedom to maneuver." Baker set up a conference call with Bush, Scowcroft, Cheney, and Powell. He had tried and failed to get the Soviets to accept Scowcroft's position on downloading, Baker said, but he saw no point in "trying to squeeze every last drop of blood out of this stone." He proposed that Moscow be permitted to download the SS-N-18 and two other missile types, so long as the number of warheads downloaded did not exceed 1,250. Cheney and Powell agreed. Scowcroft acceded. The president sounded relieved, "Well, it sounds like we've finally wrapped this thing up."[149]

He spoke too soon. No lacuna was too trivial to delay the START treaty. Some C.I.A. and Pentagon experts believed that the Soviet SS-25, a single-warhead mobile missile, had the potential throw weight to carry three warheads. Soviet officials denied that. To resolve the issue, the Americans proposed that the Soviet military test the latest model of the SS-25 at 11,000 kilometers instead of the usual 10,000. The proposal was rejected. The issue was not settled until July 17, just before Bush and Gorbachev met for lunch at the G-7 talks in London. Bessmertnykh hurried to tell Bush, "This is the end of a ten-year-long journey, Mr. President."[150] The START Treaty was signed in Moscow on July 31, 1991.

It was too late. By then the prospects for ratification and implementation of the treaty—indeed the very existence of the Soviet Union—were in doubt. "The Soviet Union as we have known it is finished," a November 1990 national intelligence estimate had warned. "The Soviet Union is, *at a minimum*, headed toward a smaller and looser union." The estimate did not rule out "a period of anarchy."[151]

The centrifugal forces unleashed in the Soviet Union were already loosening central control over its vast and dispersed nuclear infrastructure. In late June, three authorities on nuclear matters, Hans Bethe, Kurt Gottfried, and Robert McNamara, warned of "a new danger" that "a disintegrating Soviet Union might lose control over its immense nuclear arsenal." They also recognized the risk that a "chaotic breakup of the Soviet government could cause the officials who run the Soviet nuclear command system to take actions that would have catastrophic results, especially if the breakup were to occur during an international crisis that threatens Soviet security." They urged adoption of a policy of minimum deterrence, no longer threatening nuclear retaliation for conventional attack and no longer preparing to launch on warning or to target the Soviet leadership. They also recommended a ban on production of fissile materials, uranium and plutonium for use in weapons; verified destruction of warheads; monitoring of all nuclear weapons production facilities; and an eventual ban on nuclear tests. As a critical first step, they recommended deep and swift cuts in arms, from 50,000 warheads down to 2,000.[152] A *New York Times* editorial on July 19, 1991, echoed their plea: "Chaotic conditions in the Soviet Union raise fears in both countries that its tight controls over nuclear weapons could loosen, allowing lethal warheads to fall into hands of renegade groups or nations. Reducing the number of Soviet warheads would reduce that risk."[153]

If Moscow's nuclear control were not to unravel, nuclear conservatives in the Bush administration would have needed to adopt a
more radical solution—cooperative security with the Soviet Union
and its successor republics. They did not prove equal to the task. Nor
did their successors in the Clinton administration.

AMERICAN AID FOR SOVIET REFORM

What does George Bush want from me? If my colleagues
among the "Seven" tell me, when we meet later, that they
like what I am doing and they want to support me but
first I have to stew in my own soup for a while, I must tell
them that we are all in that soup.

—Mikhail Gorbachev to George Bush
at the G-7 summit, July 17, 1991[1]

By 1989 Mikhail Gorbachev and his reform-minded allies were revo-
lutionizing the Soviet state and the Communist Party from above.
Perestroika, said Aleksandr Yakovlev, "was launched by a very small
group of Party and government leaders."[2] Not even the general secretary of the Communist Party could dictate that the Soviet Union
embrace democracy or markets, however. Gorbachev had to get the
party and the bureaucracy to go along.

Democracy and markets threatened the bureaucracy's power
and perquisites. When it resisted reform, Gorbachev began dismantling it. Personnel in the economic ministries totaled 2.4 million in
1986. By 1989 that workforce was slashed to 1.6 million, too few to
run a command economy, especially a malfunctioning one.[3] He also
put an end to the party's practice of issuing directives to the ministries and cut the Central Committee departments by half.[4] Without
central direction, the economy went into a tailspin.[5]

When Gorbachev attempted to renew the Communist Party by
subjecting apparatchiks to competitive elections, they manipulated
the nominating process, leaving diehard Communists in power in
most localities. In the meantime, the intelligentsia was abandoning
the party by the thousands, weakening Gorbachev's political base
and emboldening his opponents. As he tried to overcome opposition from party conservatives, he tacked to and fro, sometimes slowing, sometimes accelerating, reform. His aim remained relentlessly

radical. Perestroika was, in his own words, "revolutionary in its essence but evolutionary in its tempo."[6]

In 1989 Gorbachev stepped up the tempo. By then the economic crisis had intensified. So had popular displeasure with the Communist Party. Output was falling precipitously—from a growth rate of 4 percent in 1986 to minus 1 percent in 1989—and shortages were making life miserable for Soviet consumers.[7] As wages shot up, the Soviet state kept enterprises afloat with subsidies, and the budget deficit ballooned, to 80 billion rubles or 8.6 percent of GDP in 1989, up from 13.9 billion or 1.8 percent of GDP in 1985.[8] As the world market price of oil plunged, the value of Soviet exports failed to keep pace with imports; foreign debt exploded to $60 billion by the end of 1989, more than double that of five years before.[9] In the March 1989 elections for the Congress of People's Deputies, the party hacks were routed. On November 26 *Pravda* ran a page-one article by Gorbachev that was nothing short of revolutionary. "We have begun to see many things differently," it read. "Whereas at first we thought it was basically a question of . . . perfecting the system that had developed, we are now saying we must radically remodel our entire social system from the economic foundation to the superstructure." That included "reform of property relations, the economic mechanism, and the political system, along with changes in the spiritual and moral atmosphere of society." Even though he deemed it "expedient" to maintain the Communist Party's leading role for the time being, he wanted the party to abandon its management of the economy and to accept pluralism.[10]

Gorbachev continued to espouse faith in socialism right up to his dramatic encounter with Yeltsin in the Duma after the August 1991 coup. Yet he gradually emptied it of Marxist-Leninist content by redefining it as European-style social democracy. "By conviction," he told his aide Georgy Shakhnazarov in December 1989, "I am close to social democracy."[11]

High-level U.S. Soviet-watchers did not take notice of Gorbachev's radicalism until the release of the "theses" for discussion at the Communist Party conference just before the Moscow summit in May 1988. "What had passed for 'socialism' in Soviet parlance had dropped from sight," recalled the American ambassador in Moscow, Jack Matlock, who briefed President Reagan on the development in Helsinki en route to the summit. "What the 'theses' described was something closer to European social democracy." If they were implemented, Matlock told Reagan, the Soviet Union could never again be what it was. What Matlock did not know at the time was that Gorbachev had tried and failed to obtain politburo endorsement of a constitutional amendment to drop the party's "leading role" and permit a multiparty system.[12]

In the end Gorbachev's reforms caused the Communist Party to fall apart but put nothing in its place. He rejected the advice of Yakovlev and others to set up a party organization of his own, and he delayed establishing a popularly elected presidency independent of the party apparatus until it was too late. His reforms caused the ministries in command of the economy to lose control of it, but, again, nothing took their place. He stopped short of introducing markets. Rather, the economy collapsed. He did not undertake large-scale privatization. Rather, factory managers seized the moment to enrich themselves at public expense by unlawfully selling off state assets or using state-owned plant and equipment to manufacture products "off the books." Obtaining hard currency for transactions, especially overseas, they deposited the proceeds in banks abroad instead of investing them at home. Gorbachev pushed democratization, loosing the centrifugal forces of nationalism, but he was slow to placate separatist sentiment by a devolution of power from Moscow that might have bound the union loosely together. Instead, it fell apart. The revolution wrought by Gorbachev was, in short, one of creative destruction. Yeltsin carried the revolution one step further by dissolving the union altogether.

Whatever followed, the old Soviet Union could never again be resurrected. That was of incalculable benefit to the United States, which no longer had to allocate billions of dollars and thousands of troops or risk its very existence to deter a Soviet threat to Western Europe.

Under these circumstances, whether to give American aid to the Soviet Union, and later to Russia, was a political question in economic guise. One critical issue was whether aid would help the reformers around Gorbachev, and later Yeltsin, keep their hold on power. Another was whether aid would make it easier for democratization and glasnost to take root. Although the Bush administration gave priority to a market economy, democratic values were more essential for cooperative security than freer markets. Andrei Sakharov put it best in his Nobel Prize acceptance speech. "I am convinced that international trust, mutual understanding, disarmament, and international security are inconceivable without an open society with freedom of information, freedom of conscience, the right to publish, and the right to travel and choose the country in which one wants to live."[13]

For doctrinaire free-marketeers in the United States, reforming the Soviet economy came first, but the primacy of politics over economics was evident in calls for a Marshall Plan for Eastern Europe and the Soviet Union. These advocates of Soviet aid did not treat the Marshall Plan as a model for economic reconstruction but as a measure of political commitment to the reformers in Moscow. Eastern Europe after 1989 differed in fundamental respects from Western Europe after 1945, which mostly had functioning market economies and democratic governments. Eastern Europe's problems were more comparable to those faced during the occupation of Germany and Japan.

Some economists urged "shock therapy," using aid as the impetus for radical reform, to take advantage of the window opened by the discrediting of state socialism. Others, doubtful that the political base in Russia was resilient enough to support radical reform or that the institutional underpinnings were in place, urged more incremental or sectoral approaches. While economists debated how aid could contribute to moving the Soviet Union from a command to a market economy, that consideration was seldom decisive in Washington, either inside or outside the bureaucracy. Of greater importance was whether the administration would be blamed more for failing to help, as proponents of aid believed, or for "pouring money down a rat hole," as critics contended. For many right-wing Republicans, habituated to embargoing trade and investment in order to contain communism and weaken the Soviet threat, aid was simply out of the question. They reinforced President Bush's reluctance to offer assistance. Once the Soviet Union disintegrated and posed no threat, Russia no longer mattered as much to the conservative realists in the Bush administration, who came to view aid as irrelevant.

The idea that Soviet aid could strengthen Gorbachev and his allies and enable them to adopt more far-reaching cooperative security measures that would benefit the United States did not receive the attention it deserved.

A PITTANCE FOR POLAND

Washington viewed Soviet aid not as a capitalist tool or a means of cooperative threat reduction but as foreign aid, and foreign aid was controversial in Congress. With two exceptions—aid to Israel, which had a strong domestic constituency not only among American Jews but also in Christian fundamentalist circles, and food aid, which was a form of price supports for American farmers—administration requests for foreign assistance have rarely emerged from Capitol Hill intact in recent years.

Like Israel, Poland had an influential constituency in the United States. Nonetheless, the Bush administration was not very forthcoming on aid to Poland. The question is why.

To satisfy the domestic constituency for aid to Poland, the president resorted to time-tested stratagems: give speeches on aid without pledging much money and name a high-level coordinator for aid without empowering him to do much. President Bush gave the first of several such speeches on April 17, 1989. His venue was Hamtramck, Michigan, an ethnic enclave of Detroit that was home to thousands of Polish-Americans. It was "a natural," said Brent Scowcroft.[14] Deputy Secretary of State Eagleburger was named high-level coordinator for aid to Eastern Europe in late 1989. "After Eagleburger's appointment," noted Robert Hutchings, who became his special adviser for Eastern European aid in 1991, "not a single meeting of the National Security Council . . . nor even of the N.S.C. Deputies Committee, was devoted to Eastern European assistance strategy."[15]

In preparation for the Hamtramck speech, the issue of how much aid to provide Poland was joined at an April 4, 1989, National Security Council meeting. It was Treasury Secretary Nicholas Brady's contention that only economic, not political, reform was worthy of help. He recalled the experience of the 1970s, when the United States poured aid into an economically unreconstructed Poland only to see it squandered and have Poland fall deeper into debt. It was different now, countered Secretary of State Baker and National Security Adviser Scowcroft. Poland was distancing itself from the Soviet Union and making significant political strides to an open society, including economic reform. "Nick properly put forward the argument for being cautious and not throwing good money after bad," President Bush wrote in his memoirs. "On the other hand, Brent and Jim recognized that, while Poland's credit was not good, we had to help the dramatic changes underway there. I was convinced we simply had to encourage Poland with substance; rhetoric would do little to guarantee [its] movement toward greater political change and openness."[16] That was also the premise for using aid as inducement for political reform and cooperative security in the Soviet Union.

Yet the president approved just a token amount of aid to Poland. He decided, instead, to provide tariff relief, propose that the G-7 help Poland reschedule its $39 billion debt, seek authority from Congress to have the Overseas Private Investment Corporation provide loan guarantees, and otherwise encourage U.S. private investment. "Funds were tight, and the deficit tied our hands," Bush explained. That was the president's own doing, though. At the urging of the Office of Management and Budget (O.M.B.) he had imposed a rule barring any new commitments of funds without offsetting cuts elsewhere in the budget. "The long shopping list of incentives for reform laid out in the speech," Bush and Scowcroft claimed, "made embarrassingly obvious our lack of resources to provide real rewards for Eastern Europe."[17] To the contrary, a rich country like the United States was not short of resources; the Bush administration lacked the vision and will to reallocate them. "The expenditure of an additional $500 or $600 million" in aid, noted Robert Hutchings, N.S.C. director for Europe at the time, "was a modest sum relative to a defense budget running in the hundreds of *billions* of dollars."[18]

The Hamtramck speech paid lip service to Soviet aid, nothing more. President Bush himself had words inserted denying that the administration wanted to see perestroika fail: "Let no one doubt the sincerity of the American people and their government to see reform succeed inside the Soviet Union."[19] That would become a standard refrain in American official discourse with the Soviet Union, in private as well as in public.

With President Bush about to visit Poland on July 9, Warsaw asked informally for $10 billion in assistance over three years. In response, the administration repackaged its Hamtramck offer, throwing in a request to the World Bank for $325 million in loans and another $100 million in U.S. loans to Poland's private sector.[20]

That fall, under attack by Democrats in Congress who were eager to court Polish-Americans, the administration came up with $50 million in emergency food aid for Poland. On September 15 it announced another $50 million in longer-term, nonemergency food aid, only to have Senate Majority Leader George Mitchell criticize the sum as inadequate. On September 20 the Democratic majority on the Senate Foreign Relations Committee authorized a $1.2 billion, three-year aid package to Poland and Hungary. To underscore that the problem was not lack of resources but their allocation, it paid for the assistance by taking funds from the Defense Department's research and development budget. Fearing further demands in Congress for a "peace dividend" that would eat into defense spending, the White House opposed breaching the budget walls. Approval came in a straight party-line vote after all but one of the Republican members walked out in protest.

The vote put the administration in a political predicament. "It would be extremely awkward if the president had to veto Polish assistance. The question was what we could do about it," recalled Scowcroft. "Within the administration the acrimonious battle reopened over whether we should send aid to Poland at all." The battle was joined just before the president was due to address the annual joint meeting of the International Monetary Fund and the World Bank on September 27. "Treasury," according to Scowcroft, "was still adamantly opposed to doing anything until Poland adopted economic reforms. The Office of Management and Budget, while not so obstructionist, insisted that any funds provided had to be fully offset. I do not recall any enthusiasm on its part for finding a way around the problem or locating suitable offsets."[21] On the eve of the president's speech, Poland's finance minister, Leszek Balcerowicz, presented a package of reforms to Scowcroft and asked for $500 million to cover Poland's current payments deficit and $1 billion for a currency stabilization fund. "His program seemed to meet any reasonable preconditions for aid," said Scowcroft, "but it was too late to include a response in the president's address the next day, and we still could not agree upon aid policy."[22] Treasury wanted the International Monetary Fund (I.M.F.) and World Bank to approve Poland's reform program and provide loans before the United States considered lending of its own. O.M.B. insisted that aid for Poland come from the foreign assistance budget. That meant it would be a claim against the accounts of other countries. In the end, the financial and budgetary interests of the Treasury and O.M.B. prevailed. The administration settled on a contribution to the stabilization fund of $200 million, to be delayed until Poland had reached agreement with the I.M.F. The bulk of the $1 billion fund came from Western Europe, especially Germany.

That was the Bush administration's intention. "Our view from the beginning was that the West Europeans should assume the principal financial assistance burden," said Robert Hutchings. "We were unwilling to come up with a significant U.S. financial commitment." He acknowledged, though, that "absent such an American commitment, the European Community never rose to the challenge."

Hutchings, who made several attempts to secure $1 billion in aid in 1991–92 without success, saw "no satisfactory explanation for Western failure to provide adequate resources for Eastern Europe." Instead, he offered only "a partial explanation": the administration treated the question as one of "foreign assistance rather than national security."[23]

LIP SERVICE AT MALTA

The future of the Soviet Union was much more critical to the national security of the United States and its allies than Poland's. Unlike Poland, however, the Soviet Union lacked a constituency in the United States, and aiding it was much more controversial in Congress. Most proponents of Soviet aid saw it as inherently political, a tangible commitment to reformers in Moscow. Opponents of aid inside the American government succeeded in framing the issue as a bailout for a failed economy and a failing state, deflecting attention from how to strengthen support for security cooperation with the United States or for democracy and the rule of law, or even from how to direct aid where it would most help ordinary Russians, not American contractors.

For instance, humanitarian assistance in the form of food or medicine benefited those Russians it reached, but some of it was siphoned off for sale by corrupt bureaucrats, and much more—half of the food by some estimates—spoiled before it could reach those in need because of gross inefficiencies in the wholesale and retail distribution system. An alternative way to help the Soviet people was project aid, transfer of American goods and services or technical know-how intended to remedy some structural deficiency in the Soviet economy. One project promoted by the U.S. ambassador to Moscow, Jack Matlock, would eventually have reduced Soviet dependence on American providers but never made much headway: instead of continuing to offer credit guarantees for loans to finance imports of grain, much of which never reached Soviet consumers, the idea was to have the United States government "sell agricultural products in the Soviet Union for rubles and then invest the rubles in an investment bank, run under American supervision, to finance farmers and entrepreneurs in the food-processing industry."[24] Though compensating American farmers for their produce out of the federal budget would run up the deficit, American taxpayers would end up footing the bill for the loan guarantees in any event. A third way to help was macroeconomic assistance, like contributing to a currency stabilization fund. A fourth was to offer inducements for economic reform. Inducements could take the form of relaxing trade sanctions, allowing the Soviet Union to import technology and food. That would break down the walls of protectionism for Soviet monopolies and satisfy consumer demand for quality products while keeping domestic prices from soaring. Yet Moscow lacked hard currency to buy the consumer goods it needed. One way for it to obtain hard currency was to sell its goods abroad, including in the United States, but that met with resistance from American producers. The alternative to freer trade, aid in the form of credits to import foreign goods, did have some political support.

Alternatively, Washington could offer to provide substantial aid, contingent on reform by Moscow. Such a "grand bargain," as it came to be called, gained some support in autumn 1989, once Gorbachev had consolidated his power in the politburo and turned his attention from political to economic reform.

In September, after the economy had taken a sharp downturn and a strike by coal miners over living and working conditions had spread like wildfire, Gorbachev immersed himself deeply in economic reform for the first time.[25] In December he asked Nikolai Petrakov to become his economic adviser. "The very fact that he had offered me the job demonstrates that Gorbachev had realized the need to go over to the market economy, because everyone knows me as an economist who believes in the market," said Petrakov. "I never made a secret of it and of course he was aware of that."[26]

Without Gorbachev's active involvement, radical reform did not stand a chance. Even with it, radicalism would be tempered. Reformers made up half the politburo, and radical reformers just a third, by one reckoning.[27] The Soviet government was even less hospitable. While Prime Minister Nikolai Ryzhkov favored modest market reform, even that was more than other ministers could stomach. Given Gorbachev's political style, it was likely that whatever reform program did emerge would be a compromise.[28] Holding out a firm promise of American aid, contingent on Soviet introduction of a comprehensive reform package, might have tilted the political balance in favor of more radical reform. That was the premise of a grand bargain.

Instead of offering aid as inducement, the policy preferred by top administration officials was to withhold aid as "pressure to push

Gorbachev more rapidly toward disarmament and market reforms."[29] Withholding aid was antithetical to cooperative security. It inhibited the attainment of American security aims: accused of yielding to economic pressure, Gorbachev and Yeltsin had to back away from concessions on arms.

Using aid as pressure reflected the administration's shared beliefs in realism and in economic liberalism. As realists, most U.S. officials did not believe that Gorbachev was serious about common security. Any concession he made, in their view, was a response to force majeure—the disintegration of the Warsaw Pact, the command economy, and the union—not deliberate action designed to alter the rules of international politics. As liberals, most officials believed that aid would work only when markets were in place. More doctrinaire liberals took a hands-off approach to the economy in the belief that "that government is best which governs least." To them, a "regulated market economy," a "social market," or a "third way" common to various European economies was unworthy of aid.

The issue of Soviet aid first came to a head just before the December 1989 Malta summit. By then, the U.S. intelligence community was uncertain whether Gorbachev could survive the unrest stirred up by perestroika without reverting to repression. "Reforms are fueling expectations for improvements in the quality of life," the C.I.A. estimated in April 1989, "but, from the standpoint of the Soviet workers, Gorbachev's economic program has been a near disaster, and there is a widespread popular perception that conditions have deteriorated." Radical reform could result "in economic chaos and a sharp drop in production." Political reform was even more dangerous, in the C.I.A.'s view. "Under the banner of glasnost, Soviet citizens are organizing groups that could form the basis of a political opposition and are advancing a wide range of demands that challenge central authority. The most dangerous of these are the nationalist movements that have blossomed in many republics, unleashing centrifugal forces that, if unchecked, could tear the system apart." Even Gorbachev realized, said the C.I.A. assessment, "it is far from certain that he will be able to control the process he has set in motion."[30] Such analysis provided the rationale for the do-nothing approach favored by most top officials.

In September 1989, two months before Bush and Gorbachev met at Malta, a national intelligence estimate predicted that while Gorbachev might have to resort to repression to curb secessionist strife, he would stay on his reform course and remain in power "for the long haul." The policy implication was that Gorbachev deserved American support.

The C.I.A.'s Office of Soviet Analysis (SOVA) disputed that judgment. In a paper that same month on "Gorbachev's Domestic Gambles and Instability," SOVA noted that Gorbachev had backed away from price reform out of fear of "possibly violent popular response to price increases" and hope that conditions "would be more propitious later, once financial 'stabilization' had been achieved and hyperinflation averted" and steps had been taken to deal with monopolies. Reform would lead to "revolution, a hard-line takeover, or Ottomanization," SOVA predicted. As one republic after another threatened to break away, hard-liners would seize power in Moscow, or else Gorbachev would save himself by reverting to harsh repression.[31]

Either way, top administration officials reasoned, the policy implication was that economic assistance should be withheld from Moscow.[32] Words, not deeds, were mostly what Bush would offer Gorbachev on aid.

During his first visit to Moscow, Baker repeated the refrain of Hamtramck. "We have no interest in seeing perestroika fail," he told Foreign Minister Shevardnadze on May 10. Later, after Shevardnadze cited Defense Secretary Cheney's comment that Gorbachev "would ultimately fail," Baker returned to this theme: "While there is a body of opinion in the United States that believes it would be good for the United States if perestroika were to fail, because it would mean a weaker U.S.S.R., no one in the administration subscribes to that view. Everyone is anxious for perestroika to succeed."[33] That was too sweeping a statement; upon his departure, his public endorsement was more limited: "The president has said and I have said that we have no wish to see perestroika fail. To the contrary: we would very much like it to succeed." In private, the secretary of state was liberal in dispensing advice but not aid. When Baker urged that price reform be adopted quickly, Gorbachev worried aloud that price hikes would take "money out of the pockets of people." Baker offered no inducements.[34]

A month later, an interagency task force recommended that the United States offer technical assistance on market economics, in short, free advice.[35] The administration did not relax cold war restrictions on trade, investment, and technology transfers. It was also wary of inviting Gorbachev to participate in the Group of Seven summit meeting in July, although the Germans wanted his presence.[36] Gorbachev had written to the host of the G-7 summit, President Mitterrand of France, saying that the Soviet Union wanted to be part of the world economy and would be changing its economic system to make it compatible with the market economy of the West. "We want to play by the rules," he said. "The letter was not a request to be invited," contended Pavel Palazchenko.[37] In the end, Gorbachev was left out. Ambassador Matlock recalled urging Baker that June to promote economic engagement with Moscow: "Baker seemed to suspect that Gorbachev was mainly interested in worming his way into international organizations, such as the General Agreement on Tariffs and Trade (GATT), in which he could play a spoiler role." In Matlock's view, policy was being driven by American politics, namely, "concern that any talk of expanded trade would stimulate right-wing opposition."[38]

When Shevardnadze came to the White House on September 21, 1989, he provided what Scowcroft called "a graphic description of the internal situation in the Soviet Union."[39] Economist Nikolai Shmelyov, an advocate of market reforms, accompanied the foreign minister to Baker's ranch in Wyoming. There, Baker was again free with his advice, recommending rapid price reform, privatization, and steps to soak up excess rubles in the hands of consumers and to keep the prices of goods from being bid up. "It is up to you to make the specific decisions," he kept saying. "We can only suggest."[40] Baker could have done more, like offering inducements for reform. He did not.

That was a foretaste of Malta. When Bush first agreed to a get-together with Gorbachev, he had sought an "informal meeting in the interim before a real summit," but the revolutionary changes in Eastern Europe convinced some officials that the president could no longer afford to seem standoffish. Robert Blackwill told colleagues on the N.S.C. staff, "The question now is how to satisfy the wild beast of public opinion."[41]

The president's own perceptions of the politics of Soviet aid were driven less by a need to demonstrate responsiveness or by fear of being blamed if Gorbachev was overthrown than by concern about attacks by right-wing Republicans for propping up a Soviet Union on the verge of collapse. That undercurrent surfaced in late October during lunch with Zbigniew Brzezinski, formerly President Carter's staunchly anti-Soviet national security adviser, who was just back from Moscow. President Bush said he might consider aid for environmental cleanup and public health, which "couldn't be used against us if Gorbachev is overthrown." He asked, "Will the Europeans consider me miserly if that's all I do?" Brzezinski said yes. White House chief of staff John Sununu intervened, "Are you proposing a *bailout* for the Soviet Union?" Brzezinski had something else in mind, that the president "dangle something in front of Gorbachev" as inducement for reform.[42] That was the crux of the grand bargain.

Around the same time, Shevardnadze sent Gorbachev a note marked "confidential personal" urging him to seek Bush's "public commitment to the reform program" at Malta.[43]

At Malta, Bush tried to look forthcoming from the start, especially on trade. The Jackson-Vanik amendment, enacted by Congress in 1974, conditioned most-favored-nation (MFN) status on the easing of Soviet emigration law. "I want to waive Jackson-Vanik, which prohibits MFN," Bush told Gorbachev, but first "two things have to happen," enactment of a new Soviet emigration law and conclusion of a trade agreement. "Let's begin trade negotiations immediately. I will push the American side to move," Bush pledged. "I would like to wrap up an agreement by the 1990 summit."[44] He also committed himself to "explore with Congress" the removal of legal impediments to U.S. Export-Import Bank loans and to seek observer status for Moscow in GATT. Bush stopped short on aid, however. He offered "technical cooperation"—more advice—on how to establish a banking system, a stock exchange, and other market mechanisms. Later, the president tacked on a key condition to all such assistance, an end to Soviet aid for Cuba and Nicaragua. During a discussion of the Baltic republics, Bush put down another marker on aid: use of force there "would create a firestorm" of anti-Soviet feeling in the United States.[45]

After lunch, when discussion turned to the economy, Gorbachev said the Soviet Union was moving from state ownership to "collective ownership." He had the "Swedish model" in mind because it was fairer than American capitalism. "But it's still the *private sector* in Sweden that makes the money, not the public [sector]," Bush interjected. Gorbachev went on to exclude anything owned collectively by more than one person from the category of private property. "I know and you know there is almost no private property in the United States," he said. "Why some of your firms have as many as twenty thousand shareholders."

In the weeks to come, Bush would justify his opposition to aid by telling others in private how "absolutely blown away" he had been by Gorbachev's "ignorance" of economics, adding that he was eager to "help educate the guy" but relieved that he had not been put in the position of having to turn down a request from Gorbachev for a "bailout" of the Soviet economy.[46] Bush missed the point. Gorbachev was not being obtuse about economics but subtle about politics by "redefining the meaning of 'socialist' property," commented Jack Matlock. "Though he still gagged on the term 'private property,' he was prepared to consider corporations owned by stockholders an acceptable form of 'collective' property. If he could make this definition stick, it would open an avenue to privatization of large state enterprises."[47]

Some Democrats criticized President Bush for not doing more to help Soviet reform at Malta, but his stance on aid averted an open split in the Republican Party and his own administration.

"TOUGH LOVE"

Trade, not aid, now became the watchword of American economic engagement with the Soviet Union. Talks on relaxing cold war restrictions on the transfer of technology began in February in the seventeen-nation Coordinating Committee for Multilateral Export Controls (COCOM). Expert-level talks on an agreement to normalize trade relations opened on February 12 and had resolved all the technical issues by late May, in time for the Washington summit. The politics remained unsettled. In March, when Lithuania declared independence and Moscow responded with military maneuvers and economic pressure, the president came under intense fire from right-wing Republicans for failing to call off the summit and apply counterpressure.

"Tough love" was White House spokesman Marlin Fitzwater's characterization of the administration's response. On April 23 Bush decided not to impose sanctions but instead to hold up new economic initiatives with Moscow. He wrote Gorbachev on April 29 to warn that "there is no way we will be able to conclude our trade agreement, and thus MFN, unless dialogue with Lithuania begins."[48] Two days later, the Senate voted 73 to 24 to instruct the president not to submit a trade pact to Congress as long as Moscow was blockading Lithuania.

On May 31, 1990, at a state dinner capping the first day of the Washington summit, Gorbachev buttonholed Bush and said that a trade agreement "would make or break the summit for him."[49] The next day, after Gorbachev had appealed to members of Congress for MFN over breakfast, the two leaders resumed their discussion. "I understand why you can't have us in your internal affairs and I don't want to be," Bush told Gorbachev, but "I know I can't get it through Congress in the present situation." Gorbachev bridled, "You have chosen the Baltics over me, and let's leave it at that." Bush began groping for a compromise. "We want a trade deal. I don't want to publicize any conditions because that makes it look like I'm dictating to you. But there is no point in sending up legislation and having the hell kicked out of it." It was the basis of a deal he had Secretary of State Baker arrange: "While we would sign the grain and trade agreements, we would not send the package to Congress until the Soviets completed the conditions we had publicly laid out for granting them MFN status: they had to pass legislation on emigration." To that he added a secret condition: he would not submit the package "until negotiations with the Lithuanians had begun and Moscow lifted the economic embargo." That satisfied domestic imperatives in Moscow and Washington. "We could hand Gorbachev a tangible success in the form of a signed agreement with public stipulations he had a chance of meeting," Bush later wrote, "but . . . we would get the conditions we wanted."[50] It was a modest step toward cooperative security. The president would be accused of a sellout, but he could live with criticism of the public deal so long as trade remained secretly linked to dialogue between Moscow and Vilnius.

The administration repeatedly rejected pleas for Soviet aid, however. A new European Bank for Reconstruction and Development (E.B.R.D.) was being set up to lend money to Eastern Europe. Most of the European allies were in favor of extending loans to the Soviet Union as well, but the United States insisted on conditions for Soviet aid.[51] Gorbachev had raised the E.B.R.D. conditions with Baker on May 18 in Moscow, citing his own critics "who say the Soviet Union is conceding everything unilaterally. There's a lot of resistance but we are moving forward and we expect you to move forward as well, and not just wait for the apples to fall into the barrel." The Soviet Union was moving to a "regulated market economy," Shevardnadze told Baker on May 15. "To cushion the impact and expedite the transition," Gorbachev sought $20 billion in loans and credits "to buy consumer goods and to invest in the conversion of defense plants to civilian output," Baker recalled. "He said he needed the symbol of our involvement in the loan effort—in large part, I suspected, so he could demonstrate how his policies were succeeding in getting the United States to contribute to Soviet needs." Baker demurred, noting "it was difficult for us to justify using U.S. taxpayer money to help finance loans through the E.B.R.D. when the Soviets were still subsidizing countries such as Cuba, Vietnam, and Cambodia to the tune of ten to fifteen billion dollars a year, while maintaining very high defense expenditures. Moreover, Moscow still had not come forward with a credible economic reform program."[52] To Baker, the phrase "regulated market economy" sounded like a hybrid of free market and socialism, allowing Gorbachev to insist he was not abandoning communism. Gorbachev, he complained on his return, was unable "to fish or cut bait on economic reform."[53]

The administration was just as unwilling to bait the hook with aid as inducement for Soviet reform. Its list of excuses was seemingly inexhaustible. By contrast, in return for going along with German unification, Chancellor Helmut Kohl was willing to supply aid to the Soviet Union. In mid-May Kohl told Bush and Scowcroft of Gorbachev's request for credits to make timely payments on his country's existing debt and to purchase goods abroad. In the expectation that Gorbachev would make a comparable request to Washington, Kohl said he would be willing to guarantee a loan of $3 billion. Bush was unwilling to follow suit. He blamed Moscow's actions in Lithuania. He also disapproved of adding to Soviet debt without putting economic reform in place.[54] At Camp David in June, Gorbachev took Bush aside. Explaining that he did not want to ask for money in front of the Soviet delegation, he made a plea for aid. Bush turned him down, citing "difficult political problems to overcome, problems he was aware of, such as aid to Cuba and progress on Germany. There were also issues of economic reform."[55]

Gorbachev renewed his plea in letters to Bush, Thatcher, and others before the Group of Seven summit meeting in Houston. Without aid, he wrote, "a further renewal of our society would be impossible." At Houston on July 9–10, Kohl and Mitterrand lobbied their colleagues on Gorbachev's behalf, but Bush balked. Until the Soviet economy was restructured, he argued, and military spending and foreign aid reduced, Gorbachev would not use the money wisely. If Gorbachev were "chucked out" of office, retorted Canada's prime minister, Brian Mulroney, "we would be in an infinitely worse position than we are today."[56] In the end, the G-7 agreed to send Gorbachev a letter expressing support for perestroika and promising an expedited study of the Soviet economy. It was a polite way of turning down his aid request.

Although the administration was loath to provide aid, even to benefit U.S. security, it made a partial exception that fall. On September 13, 1990, four days after a hastily convened summit meeting to coordinate a riposte to Iraqi aggression in Kuwait and one day after a two-plus-four ministerial meeting in Moscow removed the legal impediments to German unification, Gorbachev renewed his appeal for aid. "We need help now. We have to meet the people's needs during this period of transition," he told Baker in the Kremlin. "I understand there's a limit to what you can do, but can you help get some money from the Saudis for us?" He cited a figure of $4–5 billion.

Two weeks later, the secretary of state told Prince Saud and Prince Bandar in New York of the appeal for aid. "I can't tell you what to do, but Gorbachev's situation is difficult," Baker told them. "He's under a lot of pressure from the old guard, and it's important to sustain him in the face of that pressure." The Saudis extended a $4 billion line of credit, not conditioned on economic reform, to help the Soviet Union survive the winter.[57] The Bush administration made an exception and indirectly supported Soviet aid on cooperative security grounds: Soviet acquiescence in the Persian Gulf War. It did not put up any American money, however.

THE MARKET AND THE UNION

Preparation of a market reform program began in earnest in 1990. From the outset, a market economy was inextricably linked to devolution of power from Moscow. As the ministries' control over economic activity loosened, their resistance to radical reform hardened. That resistance was felt most strongly in the Soviet council of ministers chaired by Prime Minister Nikolai Ryzhkov. Two rival centers of radical reform emerged, one in the presidential council established by Gorbachev after his election as president of the Soviet Union in March and the other around Boris Yeltsin after he was elected chairman of Russia's Supreme Soviet in May and began asserting the supremacy of Russian laws over the economy.

Most other republics, as well as some of the regions within the Russian Federation, seized the moment to assert control over economic activity, ostensibly to protect local consumers against shortages by restricting the outflow of goods but in practice to enhance local officials' power over distribution and to line their own pockets. As the Communist Party and Soviet state fell apart, trade within and between republics was disrupted and economic growth ground to a halt. Breaking up was hard to do.

The Soviet and the Russian parliaments instructed their respective governments to draw up new economic programs by September 1990. Nikolai Petrakov and Stanislav Shatalin of Gorbachev's presidential council collaborated in preparing the Soviet Union's transition to a market economy. Russia's reform team included Grigory Yavlinsky, a thirty-eight-year-old deputy prime minister for economic reform, Boris Fedorov, a thirty-two-year-old minister of finance, and Yegor Gaidar, a thirty-six-year-old journalist who would be named deputy prime minister in November. Concluding that the republics were too closely linked economically to prepare Russia's reform plan in isolation from the union's, Yavlinsky approached Petrakov, who invited him to prepare a paper for Gorbachev.[58] On reading it, Petrakov says, Gorbachev became "very excited" and asked to see Yavlinsky. The Soviet leader wanted Russia's reform team to cooperate with Soviet economists in drawing up a single program for market reform. He met with Yeltsin on August 1 and proposed setting up a joint team. Yeltsin agreed. Gorbachev had trouble getting Prime Minister Ryzhkov's acquiescence. Ryzhkov had commissioned Leonid Abalkin to draw up a reform program, one that the ministries could live with, and he did not want a more radical alternative. Ryzhkov reluctantly went along in the end, lest he be blamed for opening a rift with Russia.[59]

The origins of the Shatalin group and its 500-day program exposed the underlying tensions in Moscow. With the Soviet government in open revolt against Gorbachev over economic reform and Yeltsin determined to build up Russia's authority, the move to markets and disunion went hand in hand.[60]

In Washington, Moscow's struggle to reform raised the question of whether to offer aid and, if so, to whom. On July 13, three days after the G-7 had rejected Gorbachev's plea, Deputy National Security Adviser Gates advised President Bush to distance himself from Gorbachev, who "remains, in his heart of hearts, a Communist—and continues to say so." Gates disparaged Gorbachev's idea of economic reform: "His effort to meld state socialism and 'regulated' markets . . .

and the incoherent mishmash of reform measures all have produced economic catastrophe. And, there is no indication that, in fact, he has the faintest way out." Taking the measure of Gorbachev's shrunken stature at home, Gates contended that "as more reform leaders emerge in the USSR as a result of elections, he is becoming more and more a symbol of the old way of doing business." Gates ruled out a grand bargain. "Gorbachev has earned his place in history but history now seems to be moving beyond him. It would be a pity for you . . . to be seen in the Soviet Union as wagering everything on a man whose vision at the end of the day does not reach far enough." The president's reaction to the memorandum was noncommittal: "Brent/Bob—Good thought paper. The advice . . . is sound, however, Gorby seems, at least so far, to be a survivor."[61]

Gorbachev established a joint working group by presidential decree in August. Its mandate was to prepare a concept "for the transition to a market economy as a foundation of a union treaty." It drew on an earlier reform program of Yavlinsky's. In February 1990, while working for the reform commission of the Soviet government under Leonid Abalkin, Yavlinsky and two other young economists had put together a so-called 400-day program. Inspired by "shock therapy" in Poland, it combined an extensive sell-off of state assets, rapid marketization and price liberalization, and monetary stabilization to slow runaway inflation. In April 1990 the presidential council rejected the program. Instead, the Ryzhkov government elaborated a plan of its own, which did not involve large-scale privatization or rapid marketization but did recommend a sharp rise in retail prices. When the price hike was made public on May 24, people rushed to withdraw their savings from banks, empty the store shelves of goods, and hoard whatever they could buy. The price hike was retracted. Yavlinsky resigned from the Soviet reform commission to become deputy prime minister of Russia, and the 400-day proposal became the basis of the 500-day program of the joint Soviet-Russian working group headed by Shatalin.[62]

Working nonstop for three weeks, the "Shatalin group" produced a "Transition to the Market: Conception and Program" by September 1. No doubt, the 238-page document was the first in Soviet economic history never to mention the word "socialism." The Shatalin program would free prices for 70–80 percent of retail sales within 400 days, but for political reasons it kept controls on the prices of 150 essentials. It would privatize quickly and use the proceeds from sales of state property to finance the transition to markets. It would balance the budget by 1991 by slashing development aid 70–80 percent, subsidies to unprofitable state enterprises 30–50 percent, and administrative personnel costs 5–10 percent. In a frontal assault on the military-industrial complex, it proposed cutting the K.G.B. budget by 20 percent and defense spending by 10 percent.

Meanwhile, the rival team of Ryzhkov, Abalkin, and Valentin Pavlov, the Soviet minister of finance, put together "The Government Program for Formation of Structures and Mechanism of a Regulated Market Economy." The government plan spoke of gradual decontrol of most retail prices but was vague about the timing. Instead, it proposed price hikes and promised to compensate fully for them with offsetting wage increases. It aimed at reducing the budget deficit to 2.5 percent of GDP.[63]

The differences went well beyond market reform. The Ryzhkov government envisaged a state budget based on continued central control of tax collection, while the Shatalin group spoke of compiling the center's budget "through the transfer of financial means by the republics for the accomplishment of tasks delegated to the Union." The Ryzhkov plan had the central government coordinate mutual assistance, reallocating resources from richer to poorer republics; the Shatalin program did not. Ryzhkov, but not Shatalin, wanted the central government to control all foreign aid. Ryzhkov asserted central government ownership of all state property, which the republics were claiming as theirs; the Shatalin program privatized most state property, and what was left became the common property of the republics. Most important to the Soviet government, participation in the reform plan and in the union was mandatory, or, as it said, "powers delegated to the Union cannot be changed without agreement of the parties to the treaty." To the Shatalin group, membership in the Union was strictly voluntary: "Members of the Union preserve their right to leave it freely." So was participation in the reform program. "The main thesis on the mutual relationship between the republics and the center constitutes that nobody governs or commands anybody."[64] In short, the Shatalin program rewrote the Union Treaty, devolving power to the republics and turning the Soviet Union into a confederation.

Caught between Soviet bureaucrats who wanted to preserve as much of the centralized state as possible and leaders of the republics who wanted to grab power from the center, Gorbachev temporized and scrambled for a middle ground. He commissioned a compromise plan, which ended up coinciding largely with the Shatalin program. He then postponed a vote on reform by the Supreme Soviet scheduled for September 24, 1990, in order to draft a new compromise that watered down the Shatalin program to a set of vague principles. By then Gorbachev had come under increasing pressure from reactionary forces in the Communist Party and state ministries and had begun tacking to the right. The "Basic Guidelines on Economic Stabilization and Transition to a Market Economy" emerged in mid-October. "What was submitted for consideration by the U.S.S.R. Supreme Soviet does not even constitute a program," economist Oleg Bogomolov said at the time, "rather a set of unfounded postulates, intentions, and statements which are often contradictory."[65]

In the midst of Gorbachev's attempts to reconcile the irreconcilable, President Bush dispatched a trade mission of fifteen corporate executives to Moscow led by Commerce Secretary Robert Mosbacher to discuss trade and investment possibilities. When Gorbachev met with the Mosbacher mission in September, he had Shatalin and Abalkin join them. "It was bizarre," remarked Pavel Palazchenko, "to see the two men, gloomy and obviously hostile to each other, on Gorbachev's side of the table while he was making a pitch for U.S. help in the Soviet Union's transition to a market economy."[66] Worse yet, recalled Ambassador Matlock, Gorbachev turned the group over to the head of Gosplan, who "dismissed the Shatalin program as visionary and destructive. To my consternation, when the group met with Ryzhkov the following day, several commented that he had been right not to listen to 'those radicals.'"[67] Much more damaging to reform, the Mosbacher mission hardened President Bush's conviction against aid.

THE G-7 FINESSES THE GRAND BARGAIN

Some outsiders came to a different conclusion: that the United States had to offer a substantial, multiyear aid package, amounting to billions of dollars, contingent on Gorbachev's commitment to implement the 500-day program. These advocates of a grand bargain wanted the aid for three purposes: a rescheduling of the Soviet Union's foreign debt, a hard-currency reserve for it to forestall a balance of payments crisis in the future, and credits for it to import technology to retool its economy and food and consumer goods to forestall shortages and keep prices from soaring. Others, like Harvard economist Jeffrey Sachs, also wanted to provide for a new social welfare system independent of the state enterprises. In Soviet-style communism, employees received health care, housing, even recreation through their workplace. The company cafeteria and commissary supplied them with food. In company towns across the Soviet Union layoffs from state enterprises would risk popular unrest unless the government put a social safety net in place. Pensioners were especially hard hit. Pensions were paid late, if at all, and did not keep up with the rapidly rising cost of living. People used to eking out a mean existence now plunged into penury.

Yet prospects for a grand bargain were dim in Washington, where the issue in 1991 remained whom to aid in Moscow. Some wanted to help Gorbachev. To right-wing Republicans, that was out of the question. To the president, it was important to keep up appearances and "dance with who is on the dance floor."[68]

The C.I.A.'s Division of Soviet Affairs made the case for a hands-off approach in a paper, "The Soviet Cauldron," which was sent to the N.S.C. on April 25, 1991: "The centrally-planned economy has broken down irretrievably and is being replaced by a mixture of republic and local barter arrangements, some of whose aspects resemble a market, but which do not constitute a coherent system," it said. "Only luck can prevent the decline in GNP from going into double digits this year." The political system was also disintegrating. "Economic crisis, independence aspirations, and anti-communist forces are breaking down the Soviet empire and system of governance," it concluded. "In the midst of this chaos, Gorbachev has gone from ardent reformer to consolidator."[69]

Gorbachev not only lurched rightward from reform but also reversed alliances, turning away from Yeltsin and the radicals and embracing conservative statists who called for a crackdown to "restore order." In December Shevardnadze, Yakovlev, Shatalin, and Petrakov all left the government. Then the right overreached. Soviet security forces staged a deadly assault on a radio station in Vilnius on January 13, "Bloody Sunday," but Gorbachev recoiled from a crackdown and Yeltsin sided openly with Lithuania, further eroding support for the union.

Faith in communism also ebbed. In January 1991 Valentin Pavlov replaced Ryzhkov as prime minister. He promptly announced a surprise currency "reform," withdrawing all 50- and 100-ruble notes from circulation. The response was predictably Pavlovian. People rushed out to buy goods and convert rubles into dollars and deutsche marks. In the panic, few banknotes were confiscated, but public confidence in the ruble plunged. So did the exchange rate. More egregious economic mismanagement followed in April, when Pavlov announced price increases in many retail goods and an offsetting increase in wages. A poll conducted that month found only 20 percent still believed that "socialism should be our goal," while 38 percent said that "socialism has shown that it is bankrupt."[70]

That was literally true. As production slowed and revenues fell, state enterprises bartered products or sold them under the table. Fearful of social unrest, they did not lay off employees but demanded massive subsidies and credit from the state to pay them or provide for their benefits. The budget deficit exploded, kindling hyperinflation. Real wages shrank.

All the elements were now in place for what has been called a "virtual economy." In Soviet times, the saying went, the workers pretended to work and the state pretended to pay them. As the command system unraveled, that saying had a new corollary: the state ordered goods it pretended to need, state enterprises pretended to fulfill them, and the state pretended to tax the transactions. Most transactions among enterprises and between enterprises and the state were done on a barter or IOU basis, without cash, and a substantial portion were fictitious. The cash economy was rather small, confined mostly to exports and imports, much of it conducted in dollars and deutsche marks rather than rubles. Many transactions remained "off the books" to avoid taxation. The economy's main cash cow was the natural resources sector, especially oil and natural gas, which was ruthlessly exploited by managers, often for personal gain, despite gross inefficiencies in extraction and leaky pipelines that wasted much of the country's natural inheritance. In 1997 the Karpov commission would describe the situation this way: "An economy is emerging where prices are charged which no one pays in cash; where no one pays anything on time; where huge mutual debts are created that also can't be paid off in reasonable periods of time; where wages are declared and not paid; and so on." The bottom line was bottomless: "illusory, or 'virtual' earnings, which in turn lead to unpaid, or 'virtual' fiscal obligations," with business conducted at "nonmarket or 'virtual' prices."[71] This shell game did have one important political advantage: it kept the ranks of the unemployed from swelling explosively.

The disintegration of the economy and rapidly rising prices polarized Soviet politics. When democrats scheduled a mass rally in Moscow on March 28 to protest a Communist effort to oust Yeltsin from office, Gorbachev imposed a ban on demonstrations and readied troops to enforce the ban. Russia's Congress of People's Deputies voted to override the ban, and 100,000 protesters defied it. The rally proceeded without bloodshed, but the whiff of civil war chastened both sides. In a conversation with Ambassador Matlock on April 6, Andrei Kozyrev, the Russian Federation's designated "foreign minister," compared the threat to take to the streets to the threat of nuclear weapons: "Once we understand the danger, we realize we have to cooperate to prevent their use."[72]

On April 23 Gorbachev sat down with Yeltsin and the leaders of eight other republics at his dacha in Novo-Ogaryovo, just outside Moscow, and agreed to renegotiate the Union Treaty and to adopt a program of economic stabilization. At a plenary meeting of the Central Committee two days later, he faced down a challenge from party conservatives to oust him as general secretary by threatening to resign. It was another opening for radical reform.

Washington, meanwhile, was still debating whether to take sides between Gorbachev and Yeltsin. In April former president Richard Nixon, just back from seeing Gorbachev, wrote off the Soviet leader as an unreconstructed Communist who was now on a retrograde course. Nixon's report was "an influential factor in changing Bush's and Scowcroft's approach toward Yeltsin," according to Deputy National Security Adviser Robert Gates.[73] On April 18 Matlock related Kozyrev's remark to President Bush in the Oval Office and advised him that "we should talk to all parties and not be drawn into the internal political struggle." Matlock also discussed aid and technical assistance. "I felt we should finesse the center-republic issue and deal with localities—municipalities and regions—that favored development of a private sector. I also thought that aid should be directed at the private sector, rather than being funneled through the central government, as Gorbachev was urging." The president also asked Matlock about a request from Gorbachev in late March for another $1.5 billion in credit guarantees to buy food from the United States. "I told him I would consider this primarily a domestic issue," wrote Matlock. "Congress had approved the program to support U.S. agricultural exports. If he thought it would serve that purpose, he should approve it, provided we were convinced the USSR could repay the loan. He should not approve the request, however, as assistance to economic reform in the Soviet Union because the loan would not have that effect. The Soviet Union might in fact face food shortages that following winter, but Gorbachev's policies were making matters worse."[74]

In a late April meeting with Baker, Scowcroft, and Treasury Secretary Brady, Bush sided with the Treasury: "The guy doesn't seem to get it. He seems to think that we *owe* him economic help because we support him politically. We've got to give him a lesson in basic economics. Business is business. Loans have to be made for sound financial and commercial reasons."[75]

On April 29 the president told a group of farm-state broadcasters that the Soviet Union "regrettably" had not yet begun market reforms "that I think Gorbachev aspires to" and "that I know . . . Mr. Yeltsin aspires to."[76] His comment about Soviet creditworthiness, which Gorbachev misinterpreted to mean trustworthiness, prompted a cri de coeur from the Soviet leader to Ambassador Matlock in Moscow that Bush was "reassessing" their relationship.[77] In late May, with Yeltsin's election as president of Russia just two weeks away, Kozyrev, on a visit to Washington, urged State Department officials to do just that: "Any money you give to the center will not only be wasted, but worse than that, it will keep afloat a system that should be allowed to sink."[78]

On May 11 Bush telephoned Gorbachev to reassure him. The Soviet leader told him that Grigory Yavlinsky was drafting a new reform program and would be coming to Washington with Yevgeny Primakov to discuss reform and seek aid. He asked Bush to receive them. He also renewed his request for grain credits. Stalling for time, Bush said he would send an agricultural delegation to Moscow to assess Soviet needs. On May 25 the delegation asked for more information. Upset at the delay, Gorbachev replied testily, "We have always paid off these credits punctually. I have given you my word. To ask for more is an insult!"[79] On their return to Washington, the delegation recommended extending the credits. Gorbachev got word of Bush's approval on June 11. Jack Matlock, who accompanied the delegation at the session with Gorbachev, observed, "Governments and the public alike needed to understand that a humanitarian aid program is no substitute for a well-organized, well-planned, cooperative effort to assist a country that requires fundamental change in its political and economic system. . . . But Washington had never done a serious study of the transition options available to the Soviet Union."[80]

Despite the grim economic prognosis in Moscow and the even grimmer political prognosis in Washington, a group of Russians and Americans tried to fill the void and broker a "grand bargain." It was "track II diplomacy" by outside experts with ties to officials inside governments and by officials acting in their unofficial capacity. They formed a Joint Working Group on Western Cooperation in the Soviet Transition to Democracy and the Market Economy, cochaired by Grigory Yavlinsky and Graham Allison, dean of the Kennedy School of Government at Harvard. Among the group's members were economists Jeffrey Sachs of Harvard and Stanley Fischer of M.I.T., and Robert Blackwill, who had just left the N.S.C. staff for a professorship at the Kennedy School.

In mid-May Ambassador Matlock spoke to Yavlinsky, who told him about attending "a recent cabinet meeting in which Gorbachev had made stinging comments about Pavlov's 'anti-crisis program' on five different occasions." Yavlinsky said that he was going to Harvard on May 19 to work on a revision of the 500-day program. "He said Gorbachev had personally assured him of his support; for his part, Yavlinsky had made it clear that he would withdraw from the effort if his ideas were not eventually accepted." Matlock then conferred separately with Allison, who was also in Moscow, and suggested that instead of economic conversion "the group consider something like a G.I. Bill for the defense industry: unemployment benefits and a program of retraining, to ease the transition. While expensive, it would cost less than keeping unneeded defense plants open."[81]

The group proposed various stages of economic aid, starting with humanitarian and technical assistance, then a stabilization fund, rescheduling of foreign debt, provision for a state-run system of social security, and eventually large-scale financing for reconstruction of the country's infrastructure. They estimated the total cost at $15–20 billion a year for three years—all of it contingent on various steps toward reform, like the freeing of prices, privatization, and tougher controls of the money supply that would phase out subsidies to industry. The aid would come from Western Europe and Japan as well as the United States.[82] Mounting a campaign aimed toward the G-7 summit meeting in July, they began circulating their conclusions even before they completed their report in mid-June.

A prime target was Robert Zoellick, now under secretary of state for economic affairs, who had worked closely with Blackwill on German unification. Allison took Yavlinsky to see Zoellick unofficially about the grand bargain on May 21. Zoellick was cautious, noting that Jeffrey Sachs had publicly put the cost of the aid package as high as $300 billion. He told Yavlinsky, "You've got to avoid looking like you're holding out a tin cup." Yavlinsky tried to disabuse Zoellick of his misimpression of the grand bargain: "Do not give us any money up front. You'd only be putting my children in debt. You have to use the *promise* of money *in the future* to make us do what we must do *now*."[83]

Meanwhile, Gorbachev, tin cup in hand, stepped up lobbying for a stabilization fund to ease the transition to a convertible ruble. With dwindling reserves of hard currency, the Soviet Union could not peg its exchange rate unless it received international credits. He also wanted the Soviet foreign debt renegotiated and asked for Western aid for major investment projects to stimulate the economy. In private he cited a figure of $100 billion in aid. He made a convert of Margaret Thatcher when the former prime minister visited Moscow in late May. "Please get a message to my friend George," she asked Ambassador Matlock. "We've got to help Mikhail. Of course, you Americans can't and shouldn't have to do it all yourselves, but George will have to lead the effort, just as he did with Kuwait." She also urged that Gorbachev be invited to the G-7 summit and not be sent home empty-handed. Now that he had helped end the cold war and set a course of real reform, "history will not forgive us" if the West failed to rally to his support. Matlock agreed about "the stake we all had in Soviet reform" but observed that "Gorbachev had not yet adopted policies that made foreign assistance relevant: the budget deficit was out of control, there were as yet no effective plans to separate social services from state industry, private enterprise was not yet protected, most of the economy was still in the grip of monopolies, and there was still no strategy for building the institutions necessary for a market system. To pour money into the country at this time would do no good and might do a lot of harm." Thatcher bristled, "You're talking like a diplomat! Just finding excuses for doing nothing. Why can't you think like a statesman? We need a political decision to support this process, which is so much in everyone's interest."[84] One way to meet Matlock's objections and still achieve Thatcher's aim was the grand bargain, offering aid conditioned on reform. As Matlock noted in his diary, "Aid, of course, should be contingent, and should be tied to specific projects or objectives. But we should organize a very substantial program to support and help guide the reform effort here."[85]

The administration, however, rejected the grand bargain out of hand. "When I first heard of the idea from Bob Zoellick, I was openly skeptical," recalled Secretary of State Baker. "I doubted Gorbachev had either the political will or capability to push through such a plan. Moreover, there was no Western consensus behind massive sums of assistance, and I didn't see one developing on the horizon."[86] Baker managed to obscure the guiding idea of the grand bargain, that a promise of aid was needed for Gorbachev to risk radical reform. Making good on the promise would depend on Gorbachev's ability and will to deliver. Other officials openly dismissed the grand bargain as beyond U.S. means. Pleading poverty was a lame enough excuse. To blame America's own inaction on a lack of Western consensus, instead of taking the lead as the United States had just done in mobilizing a coalition to wage the Persian Gulf War, was inexcusable.

Others offered more defensible grounds for opposing a grand bargain. Economists warned that, without the necessary financial, legal, and regulatory institutions in place, rapid liberalization was premature. Soviet experts contended that comprehensive liberalization and macroeconomic stabilization were too much to ask of Gorbachev under the straitened political and economic circumstances. Many believed, perhaps wrongly, that the Soviet people, long conditioned to believe that private property and the accumulation of wealth were morally objectionable, would prove inhospitable to capitalism and that dependence on Western aid would be an affront to Soviet pride. Members of Congress, like Senator Sam Nunn, worried about aggravating U.S.-Soviet relations if economic reform "made in the U.S.A." failed, or impoverished millions of Russians before it succeeded. These were not the administration's reasons for opposing the grand bargain, however.

In mid-May the Moscow bureaucrats struck back. They arranged for the high-level mission of Primakov and Yavlinsky to be led by a ranking member of the Pavlov government, Deputy Prime Minister Vladimir Shcherbakov. When Ambassador Matlock learned of this he called Primakov to say that President Bush was "mainly interested in hearing Yavlinsky's ideas." Gorbachev would not approve any program that his government could not stomach, replied Primakov. Bush himself then called Gorbachev to repeat that he was looking forward to hear what Yavlinsky had to say, to no avail.[87] On May 31, when the delegation met with the president in the White House, Bush went out of his way to solicit Yavlinsky's views. After Yavlinsky argued for sweeping price reform and privatization, Primakov dismissed the recommendations as "too radical." He later told Bush that Yavlinsky was a "smart young man" with "interesting views" but "not always practical."[88]

Most administration officials blamed the messenger. "Unfortunately, the whole notion of any bargain was stillborn when Gorbachev decided to send Primakov to Washington in late May to discuss economic issues. Politically, Primakov's Gulf meddling had severely undermined his credibility in the administration, and economically, he was a neophyte," said Secretary of State Baker.[89] "Why Gorbachev ever dreamed that Primakov could sell the Bush administration anything is a puzzle," echoed Deputy National Security Adviser Gates. "It was a measure of Bush's continuing respect for Gorbachev, and his bottomless well of courtesy, that he agreed to see Primakov at all."[90]

The president himself blamed the message. "Gorbachev had sent us ahead of time a detailed document outlining his economic and social reform programs." It arrived in mid-June. "He was vague on details, and the language still stressed a mixed economy and socialist goals, but he did commit himself to the broad principles that were necessary to construct a market-based economy, such as privatization. My feeling at the time was that Gorbachev and the Soviets were crawling before they walked." Bush had other objections: "We were still concerned by their spending on defense and foreign aid to Cuba, and told Gorbachev so."[91]

The administration gave no serious consideration to a contingent offer of inducements to reform, the essence of the grand bargain. It wanted Gorbachev to reform first. In early June Vice President Dan Quayle buried the grand bargain. Calling large-scale aid a nonstarter, he told reporters that the administration would not subsidize an "inefficient, bankrupt economic system." Glossing over the key point of a contingent offer of aid, he insisted Gorbachev had to move first. "Until the Soviet Union makes some of the systematic reforms that are necessary, you can put as much money as you want in there, but it's not going to help." He went on to trash the grand bargain: "Harvard has got more ideas out there than there are problems."[92] Quayle was speaking for the administration, Secretary of State Baker made clear in his memoirs. "Gorbachev continued to equivocate," he wrote, "and while he made the political case for Western assistance quite convincingly, he never established the economic reforms to get such an effort off the ground."[93]

Even inviting Gorbachev to London was a problem because "we had to make sure the summit was a political success for him," wrote President Bush. "I had told Primakov we had to work it out so that Gorbachev did not ask for money and then go away empty-handed. Primakov assured me that Gorbachev would not come to London and push for a gigantic check."[94] Bush also ruled out support for full membership for the Soviet Union in the G-7, the World Bank, and the International Monetary Fund.

On July 6, just before the departure of both leaders for the G-7 meeting, Bush wrote to Gorbachev to tell him what assistance he would provide: a pilot project to privatize wholesale food distribution in one locale and survey missions to study defense conversion and the energy sector. He warned that assistance would be more difficult if the administrative controls of Pavlov's anticrisis program were retained. He also discouraged any rescheduling of the Soviet debt, which was essential to any reform program. "As it turned out," Matlock commented, "the debts had to be rescheduled anyway, but without any reform quid pro quo."[95]

Although the issue had long been decided, public debate raged until July 15, when the Group of Seven convened in London. "The question of what to do about, or rather for, the Soviet Union at the G-7 summit hung over our heads the rest of June and the beginning of July," recalled Scowcroft. "The temptation among some of the G-7 would be to promise too much."[96] He need not have worried. Only Mitterrand and Kohl were willing to promise anything, while Toshiki Kaifu of Japan and John Major of Britain were every bit as opposed to aid as George Bush. The tone of the discussion even made Bush uncomfortable:

> Jacques Delors, the head of the European Community, interrogated Gorbachev like a professor questioning a student. The implication was, if you don't pass, beware. Others, such as [Canada's] Brian Mulroney, made equally important points, but in a more collegial tone, without the lecture and the scolding. I was always careful to avoid the appearance of haranguing Gorbachev. I knew the enormous problems he was facing. He deserved to be treated as a peer and a friend.

Gorbachev, for his part, tried not to offend Soviet pride by looking like a supplicant. According to Bush, "He made only one reference to financial assistance during a presentation, when he said that if we could find $100 billion for a war, there ought to be some way to help the Soviet Union."[97] His basic message, in a July 11 letter to the seven leaders, was the need for "reciprocal movement" by the G-7 to "integrate the Soviet economy" into the global economy.[98]

Gorbachev made Bush more uncomfortable over lunch on July 17. "What does the United States want the Soviet Union to be like?" he asked pointedly. "Until we get an answer to this question, many issues in our relations cannot be clarified. And time is running out." Bush grimaced, but Gorbachev plunged ahead undeterred. "Isn't it strange: a hundred billion dollars were scraped up to solve a regional conflict. Money can be found for other programs. But what we have here is a project to transform the Soviet Union, to give a totally new quality, to bring it into the world economy so that it will not be a disruptive force and a source of threats. There has never been a task so great and so important!"[99]

The G-7 agreed to support "special associate status" for the Soviet Union, not full membership, in the International Monetary Fund. No aid was forthcoming.

On June 17 Prime Minister Pavlov attacked the grand bargain as a threat to the Soviet way of life. By taking aid, the Soviet Union would have to "stand in line with Israel and Nicaragua," he told the Supreme Soviet. "Whoever wants to do that is welcome to, but not me!" K.G.B. chief Vladimir Kryuchkov saw the grand bargain as part of a sinister American plot to destabilize, "demilitarize and even occupy" the Soviet Union. "Among the conditions," he warned, "is the implementation of fundamental reforms in the country, not as they are envisioned by us but as they are dreamed up across the ocean." Shevardnadze, at his new foreign policy think tank, viewed aid in a different light. He told American visitors, even as the Supreme Soviet debate was still raging, that the Bush administration had precipitated the reaction by "provocatively" linking assistance to concessions on reform and cuts in Soviet foreign aid and defense spending: "Just as I feared, such pressure tactics have played into the hands of those who have the power to get rid of democracy, which is still young and fragile in this country. If you say, 'Let the Baltics go and we'll give you fifty billion dollars,' the reactionary forces and the military will say, 'That's it! Let's finish with this whole political experiment.'"[100]

Two months later, hard-liners tried to topple Gorbachev. As the coup was unfolding, President Bush conferred by telephone with

Prime Minister Mulroney of Canada. "George, one point where you
might get some criticism on behalf of all of us," Mulroney began.
"They may say, well, if you people had been more generous in
London, maybe this wouldn't have happened." Mulroney reminded
Bush of his own exchange with Helmut Kohl over lunch at the G-7,
"'If a month from now, Gorbachev is overthrown and people are
complaining that we haven't done enough, is what we're proposing
the kind of thing we should do?' He said absolutely; there was no
second-guessing the nature of the decision in London." Bush had
not forgotten Mulroney's exchange with Kohl, but he was worried
about criticism from the opposite direction, his right: "I'll get hit for
holding the country too close to Gorbachev."[101] The president's
domestic political preoccupation precluded American aid for Soviet
reform. It all but precluded American aid for cooperative security.

No Aid for Russian Reform Either

The collapse of the August coup opened a window for radical reform.
In a note to President Bush on his first visit to Moscow after the coup,
Secretary of State Baker sensed the opportunity and the challenge:
"The simple fact is we have a tremendous stake in the success of the
democrats here. Their success will change the world in a way that
reflects both our values and our hopes. What may be at stake is the
equivalent of the postwar recovery of Germany and Japan as democratic allies. . . ." Baker was still cautious about an offer of aid conditioned on reform: "At this point, the onus is still on them [Russia's
reformers] to step up to the plate and prove that they are prepared
to carry out an economic revolution that matches their political revolution. But if they do that—indeed if they really do work with the
IMF and the World Bank to shape a very credible program for moving to a market economy, the onus will be on us, especially if we hang
back."[102] Washington did hang back, waiting for Moscow to sort out
center-republic relations.

     When the Soviet Union came to an end in 1991, so did the strug-
gle over whom to aid, Gorbachev or Yeltsin. The answer was neither.
The administration remained just as reluctant to offer Yeltsin aid for
Russian reform as it had been to help Gorbachev. Secretary of State
Baker, wrote Anders Åslund, a Swedish economist who was advising

Russia's reformers, "saw the post-Soviet dilemma as a humanitarian emergency. This obscured the real nature of the problem, which was a need for systematic transformation and macroeconomic stabilization." Baker convened an international conference on aid in Washington on January 22, 1992. It was "tightly organized" around the subject of humanitarian aid, said Åslund. "Strangely, the intended recipients of this aid were not invited to participate in the Washington meeting. There was no humanitarian emergency in most of the FSRs [former Soviet republics], but humanitarian aid is cheap and generates good publicity. The real issue of providing substantial financial support to help Russia move to a market economy was avoided."[103] A follow-up conference in Lisbon in May with more than sixty nations would take a similar course.

At Camp David in early February 1992, Secretary of State Baker recalled, President Yeltsin asked President Bush for American aid for Russian reform: "The Russian government, Yeltsin said, was committed to tightening credit, cutting the deficit, restricting the money supply, and privatizing state enterprises." Yeltsin specifically wanted a stabilization fund to bolster confidence in the ruble. Baker assured him, "I personally will push for a stabilization fund."[104]

Baker had three political concerns: "I didn't want to leave it to the 'green eyeshades,' my term for officials who looked at questions like these in technical and accounting terms, without factoring in the broader geostrategic and political context that mattered most of all." A second was Capitol Hill, where "in the midst of a slow economy, few members of Congress were interested in voting for more foreign aid." By mid-March the administration had prepared a "Freedom Support Act," combining the lifting of trade sanctions with aid. Timing its submittal was critical both in Washington and in Moscow. "We didn't want to do it before March 31, the deadline for a continuing resolution in the Congress regarding foreign assistance. If we moved before that date, the Freedom Support Act would be held hostage to other assistance issues; moreover, the act would be labeled as 'just more foreign aid,' which would put it in a hole politically." Communists in the Congress of People's Deputies were mobilizing, and Yeltsin needed "to show that the West was truly supporting the democrats in Russia." Hence, Baker concluded, "we needed to move *after* March 31, but *before* April 6, the date for the opening of the Congress of People's Deputies." Baker's third political concern was George Bush: "The president had always agreed what was at stake geopolitically, but now electoral considerations had to be taken into account." Bush was running for reelection in 1992. Polls were registering disaffection with his interest in global concerns at the expense of domestic ones, and by spring Bush was trying to downplay foreign policy. The "come home America" sentiment was attracting some voters to third-party candidate Ross Perot. It was especially salient on the right wing of the Republican Party, boosting Bush's challenger in the Republican primaries, Patrick Buchanan, a unilateralist and America-firster who believed that the primary purpose of U.S. engagement abroad had disappeared with the demise of the Soviet Union and the retreat of communism. At the same time Bush had to fend off the Democrats pushing for aid. Baker's appeal to Bush on March 25 was couched to close off the Democrats' line of attack: "The best way to help, and ensure that we won't bear responsibility for having 'lost Russia,' is to do everything we can to help reform succeed, and that means going forward with this omnibus, stand-alone legislation."[105] That required the appearance of a response to Russia's request for aid, not necessarily an adequate or appropriate package for reform. Bush's main fear remained the reaction of the right wing of the Republican Party, not the Democrats. His definition of doing "everything we can" ruled out much new money from Washington.

On April 1 Bush and German Chancellor Kohl announced that the G-7 would provide $24 billion in aid in 1992. That was, said Robert Hutchings, "a wildly misleading figure that mixed together old and new, U.S. and non-U.S., bilateral and multilateral, loans and grants, all in an understandable but ill-advised effort to impress."[106] The I.M.F. and World Bank were to provide $4.5 billion according to a U.S. statement, $5.5 billion according to a German statement. Washington spoke of a multilateral fund for currency stabilization of just $6 billion, plus $2.5 billion for deferral of Russia's debt payments, but Japan, a key contributor, protested that it had not given its approval. (By comparison, Washington put up a sizable share of the $57 billion for a similar stabilization fund for South Korea in 1998.) The bulk of the package—a U.S. statement put the figure at $11 billion, a German statement said $13 billion—consisted of bilateral credits, mostly for food. For Russia to import large quantities of food it could not afford was deleterious to reform. That would add to its budget deficit and to claims against the ruble, leading the I.M.F. to disqualify Russia for stabilization funds subsequently. "Western governments," argued Åslund, "did not want to finance Russian financial stabilization; on the contrary, they provided financing that undermined Russia's finances and did so for the benefit of their domestic farm lobbies."[107]

Had President Bush wanted to take the lead, he could have mustered a bipartisan coalition in Congress for substantial aid for Russian reform. He did not. Once again, assistance fell victim to Bush's fear of the Republican right wing. In the end, American aid never measured up to Russia's need. In 1948–49, at the peak of the Marshall Plan, aid totaled 2.1 percent of U.S. GDP. In 1995, the total aid requested for the former Soviet republics amounted to 0.01 percent of GDP, with only part of that dedicated to Russia.

The main effect was to dishearten America's reform-minded allies in Moscow. "Not only the Communist opposition," observed Åslund, "but also representatives of the reform government started to ridicule the small amounts proffered in the much-publicized Western humanitarian aid. It was all too evident that the Western governments did not take the Russian attempt at economic transformation seriously."[108] Hutchings, who was coordinating the aid effort in the State Department, concurred. "Because the objectives were so extravagant, participating countries, beginning with the United States, wildly inflated their projected levels of assistance and disguised the conditions under which their assistance would be offered. When the levels of assistance actually extended fell far short of what seemed to have been promised, Russians increasingly believed that they had been misled by a Western community bent on weakening, not assisting, their country."[109]

The larger question was obscured by the focus on economic reform by proponents of the grand bargain outside the government and was never joined inside the Bush administration: could targeted American aid strengthen security cooperation between the Soviet Union and the United States and nurture an open society that is the foundation of long-term peace?

Nuclear Roulette

If the atomic bomb were merely another though more devastating military weapon to be assimilated into our pattern of international relations, it would be one thing. . . . But I think the bomb instead constitutes merely a first step in a new control by man over the forces of nature too revolutionary and dangerous to fit into the old concepts.

—Secretary of War Henry Stimson to
President Truman, September 11, 1945[1]

From the dawn of the nuclear age, officials responsible for the development of nuclear arms recognized the fundamental problem that their advent posed for mankind: how to control such a destructive force, both domestically and internationally. Just a month after the atomic bombings of Hiroshima and Nagasaki, Secretary of War Henry Stimson highlighted the issue of control for the president. That issue already had been a matter of high-level concern for months, even before the atomic bomb was tested and used. Control remains the central predicament of the nuclear age, but that predicament took new forms with the demise of the Soviet Union.

Democratization had loosed nationalism throughout the Soviet Union, even within the Russian Federation. Regional resentment of Moscow's misrule intensified as the central planning apparatus unraveled and the economy went into free fall, impoverishing millions. As state power over the economy devolved from the center or simply evaporated, secessionist sentiments spread, and republic after republic asserted its own sovereignty. Gorbachev belatedly tried to forestall disunion by patching together a "renewed federation." On April 23, 1991, he and leaders of nine of the republics—the Baltics, Armenia, Georgia, and Moldova boycotted the proceedings—gathered near Moscow to renegotiate the Union Treaty, granting substantial powers to the republics. The proposed devolution of power outraged those in the party, K.G.B., armed forces, and military-industrial complex who were determined to preserve a unitary state. Many assailed Gorbachev bitterly at an April 24–25 plenary session of the Communist Party's Central Committee. A few others began planning a putsch. The plotting began in earnest on August 5, the day after Gorbachev left Moscow on vacation.

The Union Treaty was due to be signed on August 20, 1991. The plotters struck on August 19. When Yeltsin rallied units of the army and the K.G.B. to the side of the Russian government, the coup collapsed. It was a close call. Many Russians remained on the sidelines, thinking the coup would succeed. Even President Bush hesitated before issuing a statement opposing the plot.[2]

The August coup had a major, unintended effect: it shattered the Soviet Union. The withering away of the state, desirable as that may have been for other reasons, unleashed several new dangers for nuclear security.

Anxiety about the whereabouts of the "nuclear suitcase" during the coup symbolized the most immediate danger: who had control over Soviet nuclear-armed missiles capable of striking the United States and its allies? Could command-and-control arrangements after the coup assure reliable "negative control," precluding use of the weapons without an authentic order?

A second danger was a takeover of these missiles by Russia and the three other republics where they were stationed, or by renegade groups within them. Disunion left Ukraine with a total of 1,656 warheads, the third-largest strategic arsenal in the world. It had 130 six-warhead SS-19s and 46 ten-warhead SS-24s, as well as 30 long-range bombers armed with air-launched cruise missiles. Kazakhstan had 1,400 warheads on 104 ten-warhead SS-18s and 40 nuclear-capable Bear H long-range bombers. Belarus had 81 single-warhead SS-25s. Proliferation by inheritance was the object of considerable congressional and public attention because of the START Treaty. It was not an urgent security concern, however, because as a precaution the Russians already had removed the computer instructions for targeting the missiles. While officers loyal to the other republics may have possessed the know-how to retarget the missiles, it would have taken them months to accomplish that feat. The weapons also were a wasting asset: the tritium in the warheads would decay over time, and the missiles would eventually become inoperative as well.

While Americans focused attention on the long-range missiles and bombers in Russia, Ukraine, Belarus, and Kazakhstan, the most proliferation-prone part of the Soviet nuclear legacy was the arsenal of 20,000 tactical warheads that were more liable to misuse—gravity bombs and cruise missiles designed to be released from aircraft and artillery shells, atomic demolition munitions, and nuclear-tipped surface-to-air missiles.[3] As of August 1991 most had quietly been withdrawn to Russia, but 2,300 remained in Ukraine, 725 in Belarus, and an unknown quantity was scattered throughout the rest of the Soviet Union. Most were fitted with electronic "locks" preventing immediate use, but over time these locks and other impediments to their use could be circumvented. The warheads were vulnerable to seizure not only by the eight republics that had them on their territory but also by dissident groups within Russia and the other republics, especially in the Caucasus. They also could be smuggled out of the Soviet Union.

While the nightmare of nuclear terrorists getting their hands on a warhead gripped the public imagination, it was mainly grist for moviemakers. The principal proliferation specter for officials who lived in the nasty world of nonfiction was the plutonium and highly enriched uranium at military and civilian sites throughout the Soviet Union—1,500 metric tons of fissile material in 1991, or enough to make 64,000 warheads—a total that would mount in time.[4] With the decay of law and order and with organized and disorganized crime rampant, how to prevent the seepage of Soviet nuclear material to would-be nuclear states like Iraq was a danger that would persist for years.

With thousands of knowledgeable technicians and scientists in the nuclear establishment underpaid and underemployed, a fifth danger was and continues to be a "brain drain" of those with nuclear know-how to countries trying to develop nuclear arms.

A sixth danger persists to this day: nuclear forces in the United States and Russia remain at high levels of alert, ready to shoot first in the last resort. Holes in the Soviet early warning system, the deterioration of missiles and warheads, and Russia's inclination to rely on nuclear arms with the disintegration of the Red Army all place undue stress on remnants of the Soviet nuclear infrastructure. The risk of a grave crisis is low, but if one should occur, the chance of unauthorized or accidental nuclear use would be unacceptably high. Keeping nuclear forces at high levels of alert increases the risk of accidental launch, even in the absence of a crisis.

From 1989 until 1991, the Bush administration did little to head off these new nuclear dangers.

It had plenty of advanced warning. The breakup of the Soviet Union hardly came as a surprise to those who followed events there closely. By 1990 a "war of laws" had broken out across the Soviet Union as republic after republic tried to supersede Union laws and take control of Union property. Russia declared its sovereignty on June 12, followed by Uzbekistan on June 20, Moldova on June 23, Ukraine on July 16, and Belarus on July 27. On October 24 Russia and Ukraine both asserted supremacy of their laws over the Soviet Union's, and the U.S.S.R. responded by affirming the supremacy of Soviet laws. On November 24, 1990, Gorbachev proposed a new Union Treaty devolving powers to the republics. Reactionaries in the party, K.G.B., and military-industrial complex responded by launching a creeping coup, gradually undermining Gorbachev.

Soviet reformers provided timely warning of trouble. "Destabilization in such a huge country with enormous military and economic potential would be a grave thing for the Soviet Union and the world," Foreign Minister Shevardnadze told Secretary of State Baker in Paris in July 1989. Shevardnadze candidly described the labor unrest and seething nationalities.[5]

On June 20, 1991, with Boris Yeltsin in Washington, Gavriil Popov, the mayor of Moscow, slipped a note to Ambassador Jack Matlock warning that "a coup is being organized to remove Gorbachev." Asked who was behind it, Popov scrawled, "Pavlov, Kryuchkov, Yazov, Lukyanov," four key functionaries in the "gang of eight," plotters who would take part in the August coup. Matlock passed the warning to Gorbachev and to Bush, who informed Yeltsin.[6] The June plot proved abortive, but the conspirators continued to aggravate relations with the republics, including the Russian Federation.

The warnings from Shevardnadze and other reform-minded officials did not go unheeded. The C.I.A.'s Office of Soviet Analysis prepared an April 25, 1991, assessment ominously entitled, "The Soviet Cauldron." It concluded, "Economic crisis, independence aspirations, and anti-communist forces are breaking down the Soviet Empire and system of governance." The analysts noted "preparations for a broad use of force" by the military and K.G.B. and warned of a putsch by hard-line elements in the Soviet government, but they judged that "the long-term prospects of such an enterprise are poor, and even short-term success is far from assured." The assessment recommended shoring up Boris Yeltsin to deter the plotters.[7] Weeks later, the C.I.A. raised another alarm: "The Soviet Union is now in a revolutionary situation in the sense that it is in a transition from the old order to an as yet undefined new order. Although the transition might occur peaceably, the current center-dominated political system is doomed. As happened in Eastern Europe over the past two years, the ingredients are now present in the USSR that could lead not only to a rapid change in the regime, but in the political system as well." Gorbachev's powers "will not be restored," the assessment noted. "Whether or not he is in office a year from now, a major shift of power to the republics will have occurred unless it has been blocked by a traditionalist coup."[8]

In response, the Bush administration, under prodding from Congress and especially from right-wing Republicans, began to distance itself from Gorbachev in 1990, but it did little to address the serious risks that Soviet disunion would pose for nuclear control. Baker says his July 1989 conversation with Shevardnadze reinforced his own inclination to "do as much as we could to make progress with Gorbachev—to 'lock in' change, as Bob Zoellick put—while he was still in power."[9] Baker drew the same conclusion from a January 1991 briefing by Soviet specialists at the C.I.A.: "to get as much as we could out of the Soviets before there was an even greater turn to the right or shift into disintegration."[10] Yet the president's political preoccupation is reflected in his diary entry for August 19, 1991, the day of the Moscow coup: "I'm trying to figure out where the critics'll be hitting us. And it's hard to tell whether they'll be coming at me from the right. I don't think they can come at us from the left. By 'right' I mean what are we going to do now about the Baltics?"[11] As he campaigned for reelection, responsiveness to the right inclined him to pay more attention to freeing the Baltics than to controlling the nuclear risks of Soviet disunion. As a result, the administration was in no hurry to complete START and implement deep cuts in strategic arms. It was slower still to address the risks associated with Soviet short-range warheads. It also failed to face up to the adverse consequences of not requiring dismantlement of warheads, in addition to missiles, under START and the safe disposal of the extracted nuclear material. When Moscow offered to ship much of its fissile material to the United States in return for cash, Washington was slow to take up the offer.

In a mockery of the very idea of "national security," the government abandoned public purposes to private initiative. Early in 1991, as the result of talks with Soviet officials, the National Resources Defense Council (N.R.D.C.) and the Federation of Atomic Scientists proposed a joint program to locate, identify, and tag all warheads in Russia and the United States. The Bush administration rejected the idea. The guardians of the American nuclear arsenal, fearing any intrusion on their turf, opposed reciprocity. "We busted our chops to try to get the administration interested back then," recalled Thomas B. Cochran of the N.R.D.C. "But there wasn't a flicker."[12]

In October 1991 Thomas Neff, an M.I.T. physicist, proposed that the United States purchase excess uranium extracted from Soviet arms.[13] The Bush administration showed no interest. When the Soviet Union offered to sell the uranium to the United States, the administration took ten months to begin negotiations. After a deal was finally struck in November 1992, implementation was impeded by uranium mining interests in the United States out of fear that the bottom would drop out of the world market for uranium. Instead of having the U.S. government buy the uranium, the administration turned the responsibility over to a quasi-private corporation, which had little interest in acquiring as much Russian uranium as it could. As a result, very little of that uranium is now in American possession. A lot of it remains at large in Russia.

In December 1991 financier George Soros announced that his foundation would provide $100 million over the next two years for research grants to keep scientists gainfully employed on civilian projects in Russia and other former Soviet republics instead of marketing their nuclear know-how abroad. The reaction of the acting chief of mission at the U.S. embassy in Moscow said it all: "I certainly think he has given the U.S. government a standard to live by."[14] It would take the U.S. government more than two years to begin meeting that standard by providing research grants to scientists from the former Soviet Union. By that time Soros's International Science Foundation had disbursed $20 million in $500 grants to 40,000 scientists and awarded another $120 million in grants for research projects. "I wanted to demonstrate that foreign aid could be successful," Soros later recalled, "but the mechanics of the emergency aid distribution could have been made to work for pensioners as well as scientists."[15] Or, he might have added, as severance pay for demobilized Red Army officers.[16] Soros's motives were political in the largest sense. "During the Soviet regime many of the best brains had joined research institutes where independent thinking was more tolerated than in the rest of Soviet society," he reflected, and scientists were "in the forefront of political reform."

To sound out Soviet officials on the possibility of disposing of excess warheads and the nuclear material in them, the Natural Resources Defense Council and the Federation of Atomic Scientists held track II discussions in Moscow in October 1991 and in Kiev in December 1991. Among those participating in Moscow in an unofficial capacity were scientists from Los Alamos and Livermore national laboratories, representatives of the Soviet and Russian foreign ministries, the scientific directors of the two Soviet weapons labs, and senior officials from the Ministry of Atomic Power and Industry. "It was clear in Moscow that Russian officials believe that cooperative verification measures covering the nuclear warhead elimination process and fissile material storage are both desirable and achievable," according to two of the participants, Christopher Paine and Thomas B. Cochran. "If the Bush administration presented a reasonable proposal for implementing these measures, Russian participants assured us it would be accepted."[17] The administration never did. Nor did its successor.

NGOs helped call administration attention to the danger of Soviet loose nukes. So did editorials in the *New York Times* from 1989 on. The *Times*'s concern was exemplified by an editorial on August 1, 1991, three weeks before the coup, "Now, Reduce the 'Renegade' Risk," calling for further arms cuts to reduce "the risk of renegade nationalists or military officers in the Soviet Union gaining access to some of its huge stockpile of weapons." It recommended unilaterally removing all short-range nuclear missiles and artillery, as well as warheads aboard ships, and installing electronic locks on all submarine-launched ballistic missiles.[18] "By early 1991," Robert Gates recalled, there was "a growing worry that any fragmentation of the Soviet Union other than whatever might be worked out politically and by agreement would provoke civil war and dangerous instability in a country with tens of thousands of nuclear warheads."[19] Coping with the new nuclear dangers would require leadership to overcome more parochial concerns. That leadership was lacking.

By the summer of 1991, experts at Harvard University's Center for Science and International Affairs, with funding from the Carnegie Corporation, were completing a study warning of the risk that nuclear warheads could fall into unauthorized hands through "desertion or mutiny of military custodians, seizure by political groups or terrorists, sale, or smuggling." The study recommended American government cooperation and aid for transport and safe storage of warheads, dismantlement, and conversion of weapons facilities to civilian use.[20]

The Bush administration again was slow to respond. Instead, on November 19, at the initiative of Carnegie's president, David Hamburg, one of the study's authors, Ashton Carter, along with William Perry, then at Stanford University, and John Steinbruner of the Brookings Institution briefed the Senate Armed Services Committee chairman, Sam Nunn, and a ranking member of the Senate Foreign Relations Committee, Richard Lugar (R-IN), on the findings. That day the senators' staffs completed drafting legislation to set aside $1 billion in defense appropriations for aid to safeguard and dismantle Soviet arms cooperatively. Over breakfast two days later, they mustered bipartisan support.[21] Nunn and House Armed Services Committee chairman Les Aspin introduced the legislation. Without backing from the White House, though, the measure was set aside. Then Senate minority leader Robert Dole (R-KS) threw his weight behind legislation to transfer $500 million from the Defense Department budget to Soviet aid, $400 million of it to help dismantle Soviet nuclear and chemical arms. After enactment of the Cooperative Threat Reduction Act, usually called Nunn-Lugar in recognition of its cosponsors, the Bush and Clinton administrations took many months to implement it.

Even when Washington did act, it was loath to embrace the overall strategy needed to cope with Soviet nuclear dangers—cooperative security. Unilateral action was politically out of the question for fledgling governments in the former Soviet Union, all dominated by Communists and former Communists who were desperate to establish their nationalist credentials. Nuclear disarming, nuclear transparency, and nuclear accountability in the Soviet Union all demanded reciprocity by the United States and more: they necessitated thoroughgoing political and economic engagement to overcome years of enmity and estrangement. In Washington, however, nuclear conservatism and nuclear autonomy took priority over nuclear cooperation. The United States still lives with the consequences of inaction today.

Unilateral Withdrawal of Tactical Nuclear Arms

Skeptical of deep nuclear arms cuts, the Bush administration had delayed completion of the START treaty until a month before the coup. It was even more reluctant to negotiate on tactical nuclear warheads, a critical part of the "loose nukes" problem.

The administration's desire to maintain an American nuclear presence in Europe and to preserve the possibility of upgrading that presence had kept it from offering deep cuts in short-range nuclear arms in return for equivalent Soviet cuts. Yet time was running out on the possibility of a negotiated solution. Soviet officials with operational responsibility for nuclear arms were already taking matters into their own hands and quietly transporting as many warheads as they could back to Russia from exposed positions in Eastern Europe and the restive Soviet republics. A reciprocal step by the United States, American experts began suggesting, might make it politically possible to expedite Soviet nuclear demobilization. The U.S. armed services had their own organizational interests in cutting back nuclear forces, which imposed budgetary and personnel costs without the promise of much practical military utility. In early 1990 General Colin Powell had ordered a joint staff study on tactical nuclear weapons. It recommended removing all the nuclear artillery based overseas.[22]

Instead of facing the future, the Bush administration was still looking backward. Its principal preoccupation was what to do with the Lance missile. A decision on a follow-on to Lance had been postponed. When Bush met with Helmut Kohl at Camp David on February 24–25, 1990, the president assured the chancellor, "FOTL is dead as a doornail." Yet Congress was about to take up its budget request to modernize nuclear arms, wrote Philip Zelikow and Condoleezza Rice, and the administration "wanted to bury FOTL in a way that would not touch off a wider debate questioning the presence of U.S. nuclear forces in Europe or rule out some possible modernization of air-delivered systems later in the 1990s."[23] A plan drawn up by the National Security Council staff won the concurrence of Baker, Dick Cheney, Brent Scowcroft, and Powell in early April. It would cancel FOTL as well as scrap plans to replace obsolescent nuclear artillery shells and outline an approach to new talks on short-range nuclear arms reductions. The plan was disclosed in mid-April.[24] Prime Minister Thatcher, who had not been consulted in advance, insisted that Washington first get firm assurances from Bonn about future stationing of nuclear weapons in Germany, in particular, the new tactical air-to-surface missile (TASM).[25]

By 1990 the fissures in the Soviet Union were wide enough for anyone to see. "I think they are going to have a revolution," a senior C.I.A. official predicted in mid-May.[26] The Red Army, riven by national discord, was falling apart. For more than two years, officials from Ukraine had been quietly recruiting officers of Ukrainian descent to desert and join a Ukrainian army.[27] As glasnost exposed the hazing and brutality of army life, some republics resisted conscription. Crack divisions in Eastern Europe, their morale shattered, retreated to Russia. Officers, unpaid and ill housed, grumbled in their beer or plotted revenge, draft calls went unheeded, equipment was left out in the open to rust or put up for sale on the black market. The economy was also in a shambles. Plant managers began selling off machinery or producing goods "off the books," unlawfully exploiting state assets for private gain. Members were leaving the Communist Party in droves. The state was unable to collect taxes or govern. As the Red Army and the Soviet Union came apart, any need for American tactical nuclear arms all but vanished. Fear of Soviet loss of nuclear control, however, had yet to take precedence over the administration's anachronistic preoccupation with Lance.

How to treat short-range nuclear arms became part of a package of incentives to induce Moscow to acquiesce to membership of a united Germany in NATO. In mid-May Arnold Kanter of the National Security Council staff proposed replacing NATO's doctrine of flexible response with no first use of nuclear arms. His colleagues, Robert Blackwill and Philip Zelikow, stopped short of no first use. Abandoning early reliance on nuclear arms, they proposed withdrawing all but the air-delivered warheads from Europe and asking Moscow to reciprocate. They also wanted to negotiate a phased elimination of nuclear artillery and short-range missiles worldwide but excluding air-delivered warheads. Europeanists in the State Department objected, fearing that talks would feed popular enthusiasm in Germany to withdraw all nuclear arms. Civilians in the Pentagon opposed any change in NATO doctrine but settled for a rhetorical flourish: "Nuclear weapons in this new Europe will truly become weapons of last resort." Hardly a novel idea, it was contradicted by leaving air-delivered weapons on vulnerable air bases. By the time the interagency process was finished, little was left of the N.S.C. initiative.[28] Included in the nine-point package that Robert Zoellick disclosed to the Soviets at a working-level meeting on June 18 were a speedup in the start of new arms control talks on short-range arms and a review of NATO strategy to reduce reliance on such arms.[29]

At the NATO summit in London on July 6, 1990, Prime Minister Thatcher insisted on having the communiqué reaffirm that nuclear weapons still played "an essential role," and that it foresaw "no circumstances in which nuclear retaliation in response to military action might be discounted."[30] President Mitterrand of France went a step further and publicly disavowed the communiqué language on "last resort."[31]

In a bow to Bonn, Washington committed itself to talks on short-range arms but not anytime soon. According to the London communiqué, "New negotiations between the United States and the Soviet Union on the reduction of short-range nuclear forces should begin shortly after a CFE agreement is signed." Making a virtue out of necessity, Washington included in its incentive package to Moscow a pledge to move up the talks, but it was in no hurry to carry out that pledge. Among the reasons officials gave for their reluctance were the complexity of negotiating a formal treaty on short-range arms and the difficulty of verifying it. "If we leave it to the lawyers," said one U.S. official, with the INF Treaty in mind, "we'll be in Vienna for another three years and end up with another 600 pages of running treaty text."[32] To administration officials, however, the most compelling reasons not to negotiate remained a refusal to foreclose the option to deploy new nuclear arms in the future and a fear of public pressure in Europe to ban short-range nuclear arms.

The administration decided to avoid any detailed offer on short-range arms and instead to withdraw the nuclear artillery shells unilaterally. The assumption was that a partial withdrawal would head off pressure for an across-the-board withdrawal and keep open the possibility of future deployments. The withdrawal was scheduled for August 2, 1990, but was shelved after Iraq invaded Kuwait.[33]

Reconsideration of a unilateral withdrawal began at the end of the Persian Gulf War. Nothing came of it until the immediate aftermath of the Moscow coup, when loose nukes finally became a high priority. On September 4, 1991, Baker discussed the agenda for his pending trip to the Soviet Union with President Bush. "Far more important than either politics or economics to the president," Baker recalled, "was the question of nuclear weapons. During the coup, U.S. intelligence had picked up several anomalous indicators involving the strategic rocket forces (SRF), the nuclear arm of the Soviet military."[34] The Soviet general staff had remained loyal to Gorbachev and decided not to activate the nuclear suitcase held in reserve for his legal successor, Vice President Gennadi Yanayev, when he unlawfully took over as president. In a counterconspiracy, those in command of nuclear forces in the army, navy, and the strategic rocket forces pledged to disobey any nuclear orders from the plotters. They could "severely impede if not completely block the dissemination of launch orders from the general staff through the normal channels of communication down the chain of command," said Bruce Blair, a close student of such arrangements.[35] Bush asked Baker "to pay particular attention to nuclear command-and-control questions when [he] talked to Gorbachev, Yeltsin, and the military leadership."

The growing worry about Soviet loose nukes did not drive President Bush's decision to draw down nuclear forces, however. Nor did the prospect of reciprocal action by Moscow motivate most top administration officials. Had that been the case, the administration would have tried to consult with Moscow in advance about the need to follow suit and tighten control over its vast nuclear stockpile. It did not. Instead, loose nukes became the public rationale for a decision taken on other grounds. The main motives were the political interest of the president in deflecting criticism at home and abroad that he was unresponsive to changes in the Soviet Union and the organizational interests of the army, navy, and air force. The army was getting out of the nuclear business. To generals who had commanded nuclear units in Europe, like Colin Powell, nuclear artillery diverted scarce resources from the army's primary mission, waging a ground war with firepower and mobility.[36] They believed they would never get timely authorization to use such warheads and had to allocate otherwise useful manpower to secure them against theft and attack. The navy increasingly regarded nuclear arms on board surface ships as detracting from its ability to perform its other missions, impeding port calls in countries like New Zealand and Japan where antinuclear sentiment ran strong, and wasting scarce resources. "The Navy really wanted to take them off ships," said a top official who took part in the decision. "But they were reluctant to take that step [on their own]."[37] The air force, too, while still the most strongly pronuclear of the armed services, was undergoing a change of heart at the top. Since its inception, it had had an interest in strategic bombing, striking targets other than those on the battlefield, especially urban industrial areas that it believed would affect the enemy's ability and will to resist. During the cold war, the air force had regarded strategic nuclear roles and missions as its organizational essence, but it had come to view conventional bombing as increasingly essential since the collapse of the Soviet threat. That shift is evident in the promotion of aviators in the Tactical

Air Command to top posts in the service, including leadership of the Strategic Air Command, its intraservice rival. Aided by advances in guidance technology, this organizational interest inclined the air force to stress precision bombing of strategic targets without resorting to nuclear arms.

A week before seeing Baker, the president had had informal discussions with National Security Adviser Scowcroft at his summer retreat in Kennebunkport about undertaking a unilateral initiative on nuclear arms, but after Defense Secretary Cheney expressed reservations, Bush convened his top advisers in the Oval Office on September 5, 1991. Discussion focused initially on whether to try to encourage a new post-Soviet confederation or deal separately with the republics. "The breakup of the Soviet Union is in our interest," asserted Defense Secretary Cheney. "If democracy fails, we're better off if the remaining pieces of the U.S.S.R. are small." Scowcroft agreed, although he did not say so. Baker disagreed. "*Peaceful* breakup is in our interest, not another Yugoslavia." The chairman of the joint chiefs of staff, General Powell, was of two minds, but control of loose nukes took top priority: "Some confederation is in our interest, and then seek bilateral relationships." When Powell was asked about Soviet nuclear control, Gates recollected, he focused on the tactical arms: "I'm comfortable with *where* they are. *Who* has them is more important. The Red Army has them now. If they are moved back to Russia, who will control them?"[38] His response was more relaxed than was warranted. Aware of Cheney's opposition to a unilateral cut in arms, Powell had to tread carefully. Another reason for his seemingly sanguine stance was the president's attitude. "It is important not to alarm people on this," Bush told the group.[39] Doing so could trigger radical changes in the American nuclear policy and posture.

It was in this context that Bush requested "some new ideas on nuclear disarmament."[40] The ideas he had in mind included the most sweeping unilateral cuts in nuclear arms ever, a worldwide withdrawal of tactical nuclear weapons, and deactivation of some strategic nuclear forces. "A handful of such proposals would put us on the offense," said the president.[41] Yet this and other steps were easier for some senior administration officials to support, among them Powell, Scowcroft, and Under Secretary of State Kanter, because they believed that tactical nuclear arms were not worth the risks with which they burdened their possessors. As a top Bush aide put it, "They did not confer any great military advantage. The implication of tactical nuclear weapons was that this was a useful military weapon and I didn't see any reason to perpetuate that. I'm not for the use of nuclear weapons."[42]

On September 27, 1991, President Bush made the announcement. All tactical nuclear warheads based on land overseas or on board aircraft carriers and other surface ships would be redeployed to storage sites in the United States or dismantled. Ground-launched warheads and naval depth charges, some three thousand in all, would be scrapped. The other warheads would be withdrawn and stored.[43] All the Navy's air-delivered warheads and all air-delivered warheads in South Korea would be withdrawn, but some air-delivered warheads would be left in Europe. Strategic nuclear warheads on long-range ballistic missiles that were slated for dismantling under the pending START Treaty would be deactivated. So would nuclear-armed strategic bombers. Deactivation, by removing the 2,700 warheads from their means of delivery, reduced the risk that they could be used without authorization. Still, most strategic missiles remained on alert.

In a gesture that acknowledged the devolution of central control in Moscow, the president telephoned both Gorbachev and Yeltsin later that day to inform them of the moves. Gorbachev promised to reciprocate. In a sign of the post-Soviet succession struggle already under way among the republics, a top aide to Yeltsin, Gennadi Burbulis, staked the Russian Federation's claim to a "greater responsibility" for nuclear arms on the entire territory of the Soviet Union.[44]

The first Soviet reaction was decidedly mixed. Gorbachev's closest aide, Anatoly Chernyaev, chaired a meeting of General Vladimir Lobov, the new chief of the Soviet general staff; General Fyodor Ladygin, chief arms controller in the defense ministry; Viktor Karpov, the foreign ministry's veteran arms negotiator; and Pavel Palazchenko of the president's staff. The generals were unenthusiastic. Lobov was critical of the proposal to dismantle nuclear artillery. Ladygin said that accepting the proposal on strategic arms and defense would end "strategic parity as we know it." Chernyaev lost patience. "Tell me, do you think these U.S. proposals are intended to lead us into some kind of trap, or are they an earnest attempt to start a process of reducing arms?" After an awkward silence, Karpov spoke up: "I believe it's the second thing." The generals remained noncommittal. "We'll have to study it all very carefully," said Lobov. Moments after their departure, Marshal Yevgeny Shaposhnikov arrived, and Palazchenko briefed him on the Bush initiative. Shaposhnikov, who had been commander of strategic rocket forces during the coup and was now Soviet defense minister and soon to be Russia's defense minister, was receptive. "Well, it's okay," he said. "As for tactical weapons, it's practically all acceptable. On strategic arms it's mostly old stuff, but there are some new things—and we must take a fresh look at the whole subject."[45] His reaction cleared the way for the Soviet Union to reciprocate.

On October 5 Gorbachev matched Bush and raised him. He promised to scrap all ground-launched tactical warheads, withdraw all anti-aircraft warheads and scrap some, and remove all nuclear arms from surface ship and attack submarines, scrapping some and storing the rest. He proposed a mutual ban on all sea-based tactical nuclear arms, which was intended to eliminate the cruise missiles that Bush was putting in storage. He offered to dealert all warheads from tactical aircraft on a mutual basis, inviting the removal of the remaining U.S. air-delivered weapons in Europe. He pledged to take out of operation the 500 ICBMs slated for dismantling under START, including 134 armed with multiple warheads. He also promised to reduce his strategic nuclear arsenal to 5,000 warheads, 1,000 below the level agreed to in START. He announced a one-year moratorium on nuclear testing and invited other nuclear powers to join in it. Finally, he said he would reduce the Red Army by another 700,000 troops.[46]

President Bush's reference to the remaining warheads in his September 27 announcement revealed one of the deficiencies in the reasoning of his decision. "We will, of course, insure that we preserve an effective air-delivered nuclear capability in Europe," he declared. "That's essential to NATO's security." Arguably much more essential to NATO's security, and America's, was the need to get rid of as many Soviet nuclear arms as possible and to take the remaining warheads off alert. By continuing to base the deterrent posture of the United States on the first use of nuclear arms, the Bush administration ensured that far too few Soviet nuclear warheads would be scrapped and that far too many missiles on both sides would remain on hair-trigger alert.

The reciprocal unilateral withdrawal also sidestepped talks and kept open the option of eventual redeployment. In the absence of a negotiated equivalent of the INF Treaty to cover short-range nuclear forces, no provision was made for an accurate accounting of existing warheads, for verifying their removal, or for dismantling them under international monitoring, as would have been done under a cooperative security approach. Moscow was unwilling to accept such provisions unless they were reciprocal. The guardians of the American nuclear arsenal opposed reciprocity as an unwarranted intrusion on their autonomy.

Nine months later, the C.I.A. told Congress it had only a "highly uncertain estimate" of the number of warheads in Russia's tactical nuclear arsenal and put the overall warhead count at 30,000, plus or minus 5,000 warheads.[47] The whereabouts of every last one of the warheads in the arsenal remains a concern today.

PREVENTING PROLIFERATION BY INHERITANCE

Coping with this and other nuclear dangers resulting from Soviet disintegration required urgent attention and cooperation from Washington. Cooperation with whom? That was the immediate question that gripped policymakers. Leaders in Moscow soon showed they were ready to cooperate with the United States. But what about the other republics with nuclear arms on their territory?

Baker's September 10–18 visit to Moscow and the capitals of five other republics enabled him to gauge the current state of Soviet disunion. His talks with Mikhail Gorbachev and Boris Yeltsin left him more reassured than he ought to have been: "I asked both of them, 'Who will have control of nuclear weapons? We have said publicly that we want to see one central command authority. We do not want to see more nuclear states.' Both agreed that the center must retain control of all nuclear weapons, strategic and tactical, and Gorbachev indicated that the chain of command ran through him."[48] What Gorbachev and Yeltsin did not agree on was who controlled the center. Leaders in the other nuclear republics also would have a say on that.

Reforging the union was out of the question after a December 1, 1991, referendum in Ukraine, when ethnic Ukrainians and Russians alike had voted overwhelmingly in favor of independence. A loose confederation was the most that could be expected. On December 8 the leaders of Russia, Ukraine, and Belarus met near Brest to dissolve the Soviet Union and establish the Commonwealth of Independent States (CIS). They also agreed to a unified command of nuclear forces. It was a countercoup by Yeltsin and other leaders of the republics, disbanding the state over which Gorbachev was presiding. Yeltsin called President Bush from the conference to inform him of the developments and assure him, "We are also for the unitary control of nuclear weapons and non-proliferation."[49]

On December 12 Secretary of State Baker spelled out American goals in a speech at Princeton University: "We do not want to see new nuclear weapons states emerge as a result" of the breakup of the Soviet Union. A "single unified authority" had to control Soviet nuclear arms, although "a single authority could, of course, be based on collective decision-making on the use of nuclear weapons." Independent republics would have "to adhere to the Non-Proliferation Treaty as nonnuclear weapons states, to agree to full-scope IAEA safeguards, and to implement effective export controls on nuclear materials and related technologies. As long as any such independent states retain nuclear weapons on their territory, those states should take part in unified command arrangements that exclude the possibility of independent control."[50]

On December 15 Baker asked for Yeltsin's public commitment to work with the other republics on command, control, and safe storage of nuclear arms, to cooperate in taking nuclear arms off alert, to expedite ratification of the START and CFE treaties, and to curb proliferation. Yeltsin told Baker that, in Baker's words, "there would be a single, highly unified command-and-control structure in the new Commonwealth. Joint management of the 'button' would not be possible, Yeltsin continued, and Russia would end up being the only nuclear power in the CIS after nuclear force reductions were implemented." Later, in a remarkable demonstration of cooperative security in action, Yeltsin briefed Baker on current launch procedures, how he, Gorbachev, and Marshal Shaposhnikov, the newly named defense minister, "each had a briefcase with the launch codes, and all had to agree to push the button. The CIS system, he explained, would work similarly, but only he and Shaposhnikov would have briefcases." The other nuclear republics would have to make do with a telephone hot line. "'The leaders of Ukraine, Kazakhstan, and Byelorussia do not understand how these things work, that's why I'm telling only you,' he said. 'They'll be satisfied with having telephones.'"[51]

Yet Yeltsin was in no position to speak on behalf of the other republics. What constituted "strategic nuclear forces" was in dispute. Moreover, the entire discussion of the "button" had an air of unreality. Control of nuclear arms is no mechanical matter but inherently political. With the national loyalty of commanders up for grabs and the arms in question in the physical possession of other republics, lines of authority were under enormous stress in the post-Soviet armed forces. It remains a subject of speculation whether nuclear command and control was predisposed to fail disastrously or "fail safe" under these conditions.

Baker then saw Gorbachev, whose mood kept shifting between defiance and resignation. In one breath, he was denouncing the leaders of the republics. "They met in the woods of Brest, and they closed down the Soviet Union," he fumed. "This is a kind of coup. I was only told about this agreement after President Bush was told." In the next breath, he vowed to help establish the CIS and arrange for an orderly succession.[52] Nevertheless, in weeks to come, Gorbachev would demonstrate statesmanship by arranging for the transfer of the "nuclear suitcase" to Yeltsin.[53]

Baker next spoke to Defense Minister Shaposhnikov, commander of the strategic forces, who confirmed that he was still taking orders from Gorbachev, but he would not say how that would change once the CIS came into being on December 21. He did assure Baker that, despite problems in Ukraine, the understanding between Bush and Gorbachev on tactical nuclear arms was being fulfilled: "We are in the process of withdrawing all tactical nuclear systems from the other republics to Russia," and the withdrawal would be completed by early 1992. President Leonid Kravchuk's takeover of all Soviet forces in Ukraine had caused a problem, said Shaposhnikov, but they had arranged a workable solution.[54] Baker broached the question of Nunn-Lugar funding and other American help for dismantling Soviet nuclear and chemical arms. "It is up to you to decide whether you want us to help you, and if so, where."[55] Shaposhnikov welcomed the offer, but he was not ready to discuss details.

On December 15 Baker flew to Almaty, the capital of Kazakhstan, another of the nuclear republics. Kazakhstan's president, Nursultan Nazarbaev, was still seething about being left out of the founding meeting of the CIS. "Now the fact is the three of them held a meeting and the three of them signed a deal," he told Baker. "Why should you have three nuclear powers meet and leave out the fourth? There was never any reason given to me why I was excluded." Nazarbaev was moved by more than personal pique. Soviet disunion threatened the integrity of Kazakhstan, which had experienced communal tensions between its Kazakh majority and its sizable minority of ethnic Russians. Yet the three Slavic republics had abolished the Soviet Union without deigning to invite him. Nazarbaev told Baker that he intended to convene a meeting of republic leaders in Almaty and to extend the commonwealth pact to the Central Asian republics. He also wanted the four nuclear republics to spell out command-and-control arrangements in a treaty. Nazarbaev sidestepped Baker's request to have Kazakhstan sign the nuclear Nonproliferation Treaty (NPT) as a nonnuclear state. "If the international community recognizes and accepts Kazakhstan," Nazarbaev said, "we will declare ourselves a nonnuclear state. This is the best way that our territorial integrity will be assured."[56]

On December 18 Baker met with the presidents of the two other nuclear republics, Stanislav Shushkevich of Belarus and Leonid Kravchuk of Ukraine. Downwind from Chernobyl, Belarus had developed an intense nuclear allergy, and Shushkevich was eager to get rid of nuclear arms. He welcomed U.S. aid for dismantling. Ukraine, the site of Chernobyl, also was strongly antinuclear, and Kravchuk had already invited the International Atomic Energy Agency to Kiev to begin preparing Ukraine for accession to the NPT. He assured Baker that Ukraine would abide by all existing U.S.-Soviet nuclear agreements and would deactivate the strategic arms, pending their removal.[57]

Their reassurances counted for little. Political winds in these fledgling republics were mercurial, while nationalism was a hurricane force, especially in Ukraine. Politicians were uninformed about details of nuclear operations, but they knew nuclear arms were potent symbols of nationhood. That unstable mix of ignorance and knowledge proved to be highly combustible in the months to come. Even before Ukraine voted for statehood on December 1, politicians there began posturing on nuclear arms. Some regarded the arms as anathema after Chernobyl, others as a valuable bargaining chip, and still others as a counterweight to Russia or a way to attract attention and aid from the West.[58]

On December 21 Nazarbaev telephoned Baker with the results of the Almaty meeting. The CIS was expanded to eleven republics; Georgia and the Baltic republics did not join. The four nuclear republics signed an Agreement on Joint Measures on Nuclear Arms obliging them to return all tactical nuclear warheads to Russia by July 1, 1992, and to open their nuclear facilities to inspections by the International Atomic Energy Agency. Ukraine and Belarus also pledged to join the Nonproliferation Treaty as nonnuclear weapons states. Kazakhstan did not. "We are determined," Nazarbaev said, "that there will only be four nuclear republics, but that control of nuclear weapons will be handed over to Russia." By 1998 Ukraine and Belarus would transfer their nuclear weapons to Russia, where destruction of all tactical nuclear weapons would take place. "Strategic nuclear weapons will remain in Russia and Kazakhstan; however, Kazakhstan will declare itself a non-nuclear zone when it is admitted to the United Nations."[59] Although Baker put the best face he could on the agreement, claiming it was "definitely a positive step forward," the news was decidedly mixed. Missiles and bombers capable of reaching the United States would remain in four of the republics for six years, perhaps longer in Kazakhstan. Had the START Treaty been completed earlier, much of the problem could have been averted.

On December 25 Gorbachev placed a "final call" to President Bush and then went on television to announce, "I am ceasing my activity in the post of president of the USSR." When he returned to his office, he was greeted by Marshal Shaposhnikov, who took possession of his nuclear briefcase.[60] With this gesture, the Soviet state ceased to exist. For weeks Gorbachev had lacked the authority to command the Soviet nuclear arsenal. The question remained, who, if anyone, was in control of it?

The United States could do little to resolve that question for now. That was up to the newly independent states themselves. Washington could eventually facilitate control, however, by helping to disarm the nuclear republics. The Bush administration belatedly came to the conclusion that deeper reductions in Russia would enhance American security and that reductions required reciprocity. In his State of the Union address on January 28, 1992, President Bush proposed a START II Treaty to cut strategic arms by another 50 percent, to about 4,700 warheads from 9,500. He also proposed further de-MIRVing, banning all land-based MIRVed missiles.[61]

That level was not low enough for Yeltsin. Maintaining and modernizing that large a nuclear force was beyond Moscow's means and, especially in the case of its submarine-based missiles, potentially beyond its control. Moreover, the Bush proposal would eliminate all SS-18s, which had the accuracy to attack U.S. land-based missiles in their silos, while allowing the United States to retain much of its Trident sea-based missile force, which had even greater accuracy. In a letter to Bush, Yeltsin proposed reductions to a level of 2,000 to 2,500 warheads and elimination of all MIRVed missiles, sea based as well as land based.

The fewer nuclear warheads that remained in Russia, the more controllable they would be and the more secure that would make the United States. Yet, once again, the Bush administration was not prepared to reciprocate if that required deeper cuts.

It focused on disarming the new nuclear republics instead. "While I discussed ways to bridge the gaps between the two proposals on my visits to Moscow in January and February," said Baker, "my sense was that we were not going to make much progress on START II until we first resolved the proliferation problem with Ukraine, Kazakhstan, and Belarus."[62] As Russia's ambassador to Washington, Vladimir Lukin, told Baker on March 18, "Yeltsin cannot give the impression that he is dismantling everything."[63] Disarming the other nuclear republics would give Yeltsin cover.

The administration gave primacy to getting the four Soviet successor states to sign a protocol to the START Treaty that would allow Russia to assume the Soviet Union's obligations under START and commit the three other nuclear republics to join the nuclear Nonproliferation Treaty as nonnuclear weapons states. In taking this legalistic approach, the administration deferred the urgent practical need to help store, transport, and dismantle their nuclear arsenals. It treated such help as a reward for disarming. It was also slow to engage in more extensive cooperation. This was especially evident in its dealings with Ukraine.

COERCION FAILS, THEN COOPERATION SUCCEEDS WITH UKRAINE

When the United States cooperated, it made headway. The trouble was, it was not always as cooperative as it should have been. To some in Washington the question was whom to cooperate with, Russia or Ukraine. The answer was both, but it took time for the United States to come to that conclusion. It first tried coercing Ukraine and failed. Then it tried cooperation and succeeded.

When Ukraine's parliament, the Rada, asserted the republic's sovereignty on July 16, 1990, it pledged permanent neutrality, eschewing all military blocs, and it laid down three nonnuclear principles, "not to accept, not to produce, and not to acquire nuclear weapons." The Rada reiterated the nonnuclear assurances in October 1991, two months after the failed coup in Moscow and a month before the republic voted overwhelmingly for independence.

Despite the results of the referendum, the Ukrainian nation was fragile. Nationalism was stronger in the western part of the republic, which had been forcibly incorporated into the Soviet Union a generation ago during World War II, weaker in eastern Ukraine, where ethnic Russians predominated, and strongest among the Ukrainian diaspora in the United States and Canada. Antipathy to Moscow's misrule was a potent rallying cry throughout Ukraine, but nationalists had to take care not to open an east-west rift in the country by alienating the ethnic Russians, a majority of whom had voted for independence.

Boris Yeltsin and his allies had been instrumental in shattering the Soviet Union, but many Russians harbored hopes of reuniting it. Although reunion would burden Russia with the ruins of Ukraine's economy, dashing any hope for Russian reform, even Russia's radicals could hardly reconcile themselves to living with an independent Ukraine. It was unimaginable to more conservative Russian elites. High-handedly asserting control over the Soviet nuclear legacy, they turned the Bomb into a popular symbol of Ukrainian nationalism and resistance to Moscow.

Some in the United States took sides. Ukraine had its partisans among ethnic Ukrainians and among Russophobes on the American right wing, while many in the American foreign policy establishment gave primacy to cooperation with Russia. A secure Ukraine, in the view of the Russia-firsters, depended on a peaceful and prosperous Russia.

The Bush administration was caught in the middle—and deeply divided as well. A priority of the joint chiefs of staff was to prevent proliferation. Russia, with thousands of warheads and thousands of tons of fissile material, posed the principal problem, and strengthening control in Moscow seemed the key to any solution. Civilians in the Pentagon, while worried about an adverse reaction in Germany and Poland, saw a nuclear-armed Ukraine as a counterweight to Russian expansionism. Instead of an exclusive focus on the nuclear issue, they favored economic and political engagement with Ukraine. The State Department was institutionally predisposed to take Moscow's perspective. Few American diplomats had ever been posted to Ukraine, and even fewer spoke Ukrainian, but if the department was Russocentric, it was hardly Russophile. Sensing Kiev's eagerness for recognition and aid, officials at State wanted to withhold political and economic support until Ukraine fulfilled its nuclear commit-ments. They worried that a nuclear Ukraine would sow instability, even would provoke an encircled and insecure Russia to lash out.[64] With Secretary of State Baker in the lead on the issue, the State Department prevailed over the Pentagon.

Of two minds about whether to discourage the breakup of the Soviet Union and unwilling to be seen encouraging it, President Bush, against Gorbachev's wishes, had decided to lend support to Ukraine's aspirations by visiting Kiev on August 1, 1991, but he went out of his way to placate Moscow while he was there.[65] What *New York Times* columnist William Safire labeled the "chicken Kiev" speech had had the unintended consequence of alienating Ukraine. "Freedom is not the same as independence," Bush told the Rada. "Americans will not support those who seek independence in order to replace a far-off tyranny with a local despotism. They will not aid those who promote a suicidal nationalism based on ethnic hatred." Fear of virulent nationalism was understandable when communal hatred was tearing apart Yugoslavia, but Ukraine's nationalists took umbrage. The visit left them with lingering suspicions, hampering subsequent efforts by Washington to have Kiev turn over the nuclear arms on its territory to Moscow.

Those suspicions deepened at a NATO summit in mid-November when Canada, home to a substantial number of ethnic Ukrainians, pressed for early recognition of Ukraine. The Bush administration was opposed. One reason was uncertainty about the outcome of the December 1 referendum on independence in Ukraine. During a visit to Washington in late September, President Leonid Kravchuk had told President Bush that Ukraine wanted total independence.[66] Yet the American embassy in Moscow highlighted the uncertainty in a late October cable, noting that a majority in Ukraine, including most ethnic Russians, had voted for union in March 1991. Fear of arousing nationalist passions that might lead to a breakup of Ukraine, espe-cially after the bloodbath in Bosnia, reinforced the doubts. Bush and Baker did not want to be seen openly advocating disunion and pre-ferred some form of confederation to emerge from the wreckage of the Soviet Union. They were initially encouraged by the founding of the CIS at Almaty on December 21.

Ukraine's actions also were reassuring at first. At Almaty Ukraine had pledged to return its tactical nuclear arms to Russia for disman-tling by July 1, 1992, a date set by the Russian military, based on its logistical capacity. On December 30, at a CIS summit in Minsk, Ukraine promised to dismantle the strategic nuclear arms on its soil by December 31, 1994. That timetable was set by the Russian military. Immediately after the summit, Moscow began transporting the 2,300 tactical nuclear warheads from Ukraine.[67]

The summit failed to stop the squabbling between the two republics over how to divide up another Soviet legacy, the 350-ship Black Sea Fleet based at Sevastopol in the Crimea. The fleet was more the symbol than the substance of national power. Neither Ukraine nor Russia could afford to man and maintain a large navy, but they could profit from the sale of the ships to China or others. Another source of tension was Crimea itself, handed over to Ukraine during the Khrushchev years. Separatists were demonstrating for reunion with Russia, egged on by Yeltsin's opponents in Moscow. Further aggravating relations, Russia had temporarily stopped supplying oil and natural gas until Ukraine paid its bills and assumed its share of the Soviet national debt.

On March 12 Ukraine reneged on its nuclear commitments. Assailed by nationalists in the Rada, who realized that Ukraine was getting nothing in return for handing over the nuclear arms to Russia, President Kravchuk announced that he would "suspend" further shipment of tactical nuclear warheads to Russia. He expressed doubt that Russia was destroying the warheads, but that was a pretext. A backlog was causing delay at dismantling plants. Kiev began demanding compensation for giving up the warheads. Some in the Rada wanted this as a ploy to get Ukraine's share of Nunn-Lugar aid for dismantling. Russia had been promised $400 million; Ukraine as yet had none. It was receiving some U.S. humanitarian assistance, and it had high hopes for more. Others wanted compensation for the highly enriched uranium Russia could extract from the warheads. Still others like General Volodymyr Tolubko, a legislator who had commanded a division in the Strategic Rocket Forces, feared that, bereft of its nuclear inheritance, Ukraine would be left alone with its collapsing economy to fend off its overbearing neighbor. Regardless of their stance, almost all of Ukraine's politicians had one thing in common: they knew next to nothing about nuclear arms. Military leaders, some of whom were knowledgeable, lobbied against nuclear arming because it would divert resources from more urgent needs like paying the troops and maintaining land, sea, and air forces.[68]

With President Kravchuk due to meet President Bush on May 5, haggling intensified over the language of a draft START protocol and a legally binding side letter. Kravchuk was unwilling to make a firm commitment to denuclearization or to abide by the December 31, 1994, deadline he had accepted at Minsk for removing all the warheads from Ukraine. That, he said, depended on ratification by the Rada. He insisted that dismantling be done under international supervision. He also wanted security assurances, including a guarantee of Ukraine's "territorial integrity," which could embroil the United States in the dispute over Crimea. Between April 28 and May 4, Secretary of State Baker spoke to Ukraine's foreign minister, Anatoly Zlenko, eight times by telephone. Baker was willing to grant Ukraine the same security assurances given to any other state that renounced nuclear arms and signed the nuclear Nonproliferation Treaty, but no more. On May 2 Baker dropped his insistence on a specified date and agreed to let Ukraine accede to the NPT "in the shortest possible time." On May 4 he turned down Ukraine's demand for international supervision of dismantling on the grounds that the START Treaty contained no such provision. He then read Zlenko that day's editorial in the *New York Times,* headlined "Nuclear Backsliding in Ukraine." President Kravchuk, it said, "needs to be told that toying with nuclear arms is no way to protect Ukraine's hard-earned independence, boost its prestige, or win America's favor. Washington is prepared to work directly with Kiev on disarming, thereby acknowledging that Ukraine is a sovereign state, not an appendage of Russia. But Washington may have to withhold political and economic support to keep nuclear arms in Ukraine from endangering regional security."[69] It was a deft way for Baker to apply pressure. Kravchuk accepted the protocol and a side letter promising to eliminate "all nuclear weapons" on its territory within "the seven-year period as provided by the START Treaty."

Disarming went ahead even without a firm commitment by Kiev. Tight secrecy and security shield the shipment of nuclear arms even in normal times and places, and post-Soviet Ukraine was hardly normal. Russia's nuclear guardians ignored Kravchuk's order to suspend the shipments and, unbeknownst to their hosts, kept spiriting tactical arms out of Ukraine.[70] Washington, meanwhile, continued to put pressure on Kiev. On April 7 Secretary of State Baker threatened to reduce aid and cancel a Bush-Kravchuk meeting if Ukraine did not return the tactical nuclear warheads to Russia. At the same time he urged Moscow to satisfy Kiev on monitoring the removal and dismantlement of the arms.[71] On April 16 Kravchuk and Yeltsin reached agreement on joint monitoring, and the warhead withdrawal, never actually suspended, officially resumed. On May 6 the last of the tactical nuclear warheads reached Russia. Later that morning, Marshal Shaposhnikov made that fact public, much to the surprise and embarrassment of Kravchuk, who had just arrived in Washington on his official visit.[72]

Russia's high-handedness fanned nationalism in Ukraine. The main impediment to denuclearization, however, was the haphazard policy process in Kiev. The president, the defense minister, the foreign minister, and influential members of the Rada each seemed to have their own nuclear strategy. Even the top officials who wanted to get rid of Ukraine's nuclear inheritance found it expedient to talk tough before meeting with American officials, sowing further confusion about Ukraine's nuclear intentions.

On May 19 President Nazarbaev announced Kazakhstan's accession to the START protocol in Washington after obtaining a pledge of aid from President Bush. A signing ceremony was set for May 23 in Lisbon. Learning en route that Ukraine was balking once again, Baker telephoned Foreign Minister Zlenko in exasperation. "Within a minute of the conversation," he recounted, "it became clear he was backing away from minor issues we had already resolved. That infuriated me; there's nothing worse in a negotiation than to have an interlocutor who you feel can't be trusted. Finally, I had enough and slammed down the receiver."[73] In Lisbon, after Baker, Zlenko, and Andrei Kozyrev, Russia's foreign minister, had negotiated a last-minute agreement, Ukraine joined Belarus, Kazakhstan, and Russia in signing the Lisbon Protocol.

That removed the main impediment to deeper arms cuts by Russia. Later in Lisbon Kozyrev proposed a phased approach to START. In phase one, the seven-year period covered by START I, the two sides would reduce to 4,500–4,700 warheads. In phase two, between 1998 and 2005, the sides would reduce further to 2,500 warheads. Baker said 2,500 was unacceptably low. He proposed, instead, a written commitment to pursue further reductions in phase two. Kozyrev was amenable, but he lacked room for maneuver in Moscow.

On June 4 Baker met with Scowcroft, Cheney, and Powell to discuss the Russian offer. He made an election-year appeal. "De-MIRVing will be a major substantive and political triumph for the president, something he needs. This is his issue. This is not old-style arms control, in form or substance." He then made the case for accepting the Russians' proposal. "They have offered us what we want, and what no else has ever come close to: zero MIRVed ICBMs, and without eliminating MIRVed SLBMs. We can't let this slip through our fingers because we think we need a *higher* total number. That is not sustainable with the public or the Congress."[74] Yet Pentagon civilians balked at reciprocal cuts, preferring to keep more warheads.

Baker invited Kozyrev to Washington. They quickly agreed to reduce to 4,700 warheads, but they differed over sublimits on land-based, submarine-launched, and bomber warheads under the overall 4,700-warhead limit. Experiencing bottlenecks in dismantling, the Russians also wanted more time to scrap their arms. Baker offered to travel to Moscow to settle the issue. Kozyrev rejected that on grounds of appearances: it would look as though Russia was making concessions for cash. "That just won't work," he said. "We're accepting $24 billion in aid, and the U.S. secretary of state comes to Moscow to get what he wants." Kozyrev was worried about carrying the day in Yeltsin's security council. "I've been outvoted seven to two on many issues," he noted. "We have some hard-line thinkers who say moderate things to Westerners, but in private, there is no change."[75] On June 11 in London the two managed to narrow the differences further.

Four days later, President Yeltsin arrived in Washington for his first summit meeting with President Bush. After an evening of negotiating with Kozyrev, said Baker, "I was beginning to lose patience with our side. The Russians had moved as far as they were going to, and the arms control theologians at the Pentagon seemed to prefer no agreement [to] one that got us 'only' ninety percent of what we wanted."[76] Yeltsin then introduced the idea of a range instead of a single number for the ceiling. Each side would reduce to between 3,800 and 4,250 warheads by the year 2000, and to between 3,000 and 3,500 warheads by 2003. "It would allow the Russians to go to lower limits (which they wanted to for economic reasons) and it would allow us to have slightly higher numbers (which were consistent with our force structure)," Baker explained. "Above all, Yeltsin's approach recognized that in the realm of nuclear weapons, a few-hundred-warhead advantage, when both sides had over three thousand warheads, was not all that important."[77] That afternoon, the two presidents announced the basic terms of the START II accord that would be signed on January 3, 1993.

There were three shortcomings in Baker's reasoning, however. START II would not be that good for stability. By banning SS-18 missiles, which Russia could use to attack U.S. land-based missiles in their silos, it would reduce the American incentive to shoot first in a crisis. Yet the United States, by retaining its Trident D-5 missiles with the accuracy to strike Russia's land-based missiles and command and control, left Moscow with reason to shoot first in a crisis. That was bad for American security. The United States also would have been better off with deeper cuts. Russia was prepared to accept a lower ceiling, below 2,000 warheads. Given its parlous economy, it could ill afford to maintain the missiles and warheads it had, let alone replace those that outlasted their expected service lives. Given its disintegrating nuclear infrastructure, fewer warheads would be easier for it to control. Finally, by insisting on a higher limit for its own warheads, the United States undermined political support in Russia for cooperative security. Unequal ceilings were unfair, an indignity that members of the Duma could use against ratification, much as hard-line opponents had done against SALT II in the U.S. Senate. Since a few hundred warheads did not matter militarily, why insist on retaining more than Russia?

A track II initiative in Moscow on June 24–25 sponsored by the W. Alton Jones Foundation picked up disturbing signs of discontent from Russian officials who were sympathetic to cooperative security. "The participants stated that the agreement addressed the central U.S. concern of the SS-18 but did not dispel longstanding Russian concerns about the Trident D-5 and SDI. This visceral sense of asymmetry seemed to dominate Russian reactions," according to an American trip report. "They made it clear that Russian unease with the agreement will express itself in the form of delaying the process of turning the framework agreement into a written treaty." The Americans also came away with a firsthand impression of "tension between Russia and Ukraine," highlighted by "a remarkably insensitive speech" by a Russian usually noted for his moderation and an equally blunt retort by a senior Ukrainian official "hedging" on denuclearization.[78] Over dinner, a Ukrainian official spoke of U.S. officials coming through Kiev and alluding to possible aid but not delivering any, of Americans berating Ukraine to give up its nuclear weapons as if Ukraine were a wild and untrustworthy nation. "Why do you Americans trust the Russians, and not us?" he asked. "Why do you press us so hard about nuclear weapons, but accept the fact that the

Russians will keep thousands of them?" To one American the heart of the matter for the Ukrainians was respect.[79] Among the officials participating in their unofficial capacity were Robert Einhorn of the State Department's policy planning staff, Sergei Kortunov and Oleg Shagov of Russia's foreign ministry, and Colonel Valentin Astakhov of Ukraine's defense ministry. Among the nonofficials was Ashton Carter, who as assistant secretary of defense for counterproliferation in the Clinton administration would soon play a part in reversing U.S. policy and adopting a cooperative, "problem-solving" approach to both Kiev and Moscow.

Bush administration efforts to disarm the nuclear republics slowed appreciably by late summer. Baker, who had spearheaded these efforts, left the administration on August 13 to help manage the president's campaign for reelection. Bill Clinton's message, "It's the economy stupid," had struck home, and Bush was reluctant to be seen engaging in foreign policy. Later, as Bush's defeat seemed likely, unemployment displaced nuclear policy as a concern of top officials. They were updating their resumes and looking for jobs. Without high-level attention, it was difficult to spur the American government to corral loose nukes, especially when that required putting up inducements for nuclear cooperation with Russia and the other republics.

The Bush administration, on autopilot, stayed on a coercive course with Ukraine, but it did not get far by withholding aid and threatening isolation. In September, when an N.S.C. official in Washington told Ivan Plyusch, chairman of the Rada, that "you have to give up your nuclear weapons or else U.S.-Ukrainian relations will be endangered," he retorted, "What relations?"[80]

In the meantime, Russian assertiveness in the countries of the former Soviet Union it called "near abroad" made nationalists in Kiev anxious and stirred opposition to U.S.-Russian cooperation in Washington. Russian moves on the nuclear front also were seen as ominous in Kiev. In June 1993 the joint military command of the CIS was dissolved, leaving all nuclear arms under the command of the Russian strategic rocket forces.[81] To justify their get-tough posture, Russian officials put out alarming reports that Ukraine was trying to get operational control of the nuclear arms. There were dark hints of a military clash.[82] In July the Russian parliament, in contravention of the provisions of the treaty establishing the CIS that it had earlier ratified, approved a resolution asserting that Sevastopol, the capital of Crimea and home port of the Black Sea Fleet, "was and remains

part of the territory of the Russian Federation."[83] Even the high official in Moscow most committed to cooperative security, Foreign
Minister Kozyrev, unsettled Ukraine with a speech to the UN General
Assembly in September. Under intense pressure from nationalists in
the Duma who were antagonized by the prospect of NATO's eastward expansion, he asserted a special role for Russia as peacekeeper
in the "near abroad," in effect, incorporating the successor states to
the Soviet Union into a Russian sphere of influence, and he opposed
Ukraine's membership in NATO's Partnership for Peace. "We would
not like NATO to protect Ukraine from Russia. We ourselves can
defend Ukraine from anyone."[84]

Politicians in Ukraine began to talk about holding onto its
nuclear inheritance to secure independence, gain international
respect, and deter Russian aggrandizement.[85] A leading realist theo-
retician in the United States, John Mearsheimer, even criticized U.S.
attempts to disarm Ukraine as misguided and advocated a strategy of
"controlled proliferation." He rested his case on a contention and a
prediction: "Ukraine cannot defend itself against a nuclear-armed
Russia with conventional weapons, and no state, including the United
States, is going to extend to it a meaningful security guarantee."
Further, "it is unlikely that Ukraine will transfer its remaining nuclear
weapons to Russia, the state it fears most."[86]

That prediction soon appeared to be right on the mark. On April
5, 1992, President Kravchuk decreed that the ministry of defense would
take administrative control over all armed forces on Ukraine's soil,
including nuclear forces. On April 10 nuclear personnel were ordered
to take an oath of allegiance to Ukraine. In June the defense ministry
set up a unit for administrative control of the strategic nuclear forces.
In November Ukraine claimed legal title to the warheads, missiles, and
bombers.[87] Yet physical possession, legal title, and administrative control did not mean operational control. Ukraine could not use air-
launched cruise missiles without circumventing their electronic codes,
which would take many months, and the bombers themselves were
not fully operational. It could not launch missiles without replacing the
computerized targeting instructions removed by the Russians, and it
lacked the means to retarget them against Russia or to keep them
operationally reliable, safe, and secure. Nor could Ukraine be sure of
the loyalty of officers in command of nuclear forces: in February 1992
six strategic bombers took off on a routine training flight to Belarus
and never returned.[88] Ukraine had a nuclear arsenal in name only.

Nuclear arming also would have antagonized its neighbors and alienated its allies. The true threat to Ukraine was not external but internal: that its imploding economy and spiraling inflation might rend its social fabric, loosing separatism among indigenous Russians. Nuclear posturing would not put food on the table or hold the country together.

Ukraine was desperately in need of reassurance, however. That was just what the Bush administration was determined to withhold until Ukraine gave up its nuclear arms. Washington's uncooperative approach, denying aid and threatening to isolate Ukraine to pressure it into disarming, was playing badly in Kiev, leading Ukrainians to conclude that the Americans would lose interest in Ukraine once it disarmed.

The fledgling Clinton administration, under attack from its inception for weakness on national security, picked up where the Bush administration had left off, talking tough to Ukraine. With its appointees yet to be confirmed by the Senate and holdovers from the Bush administration still occupying many senior positions, inertia propelled policy.

In Washington on March 25, 1993, Foreign Minister Anatoly Zlenko complained that the United States had yet to make good on any of the $175 million in Nunn-Lugar aid pledged to Ukraine in 1992. He put the cost of dismantling at an exorbitant $2.8 billion. The American reply was blunt, that signing START I "is a precondition to a long-term successful relationship."[89] Zlenko was told Clinton would "not necessarily" be available for a meeting in May, when Ukraine's new prime minister, Leonid Kuchma, was due in Washington. Appointed by President Kravchuk in October, Kuchma was a mechanical engineer who had risen through the ranks to run the largest missile production plant in the world, at Dnepropetrovsk. More than any other politician in Ukraine, Kuchma appreciated the limitation of its nuclear arms as deterrents and their value as bargaining chips. He was someone in Kiev with whom Washington could do business.

Realizing by now that its use of threats instead of promises was backfiring, swelling the pronuclear ranks in Kiev, the Clinton administration reversed course and turned to cooperative security. An interagency review chaired by Rose Gottemoeller of the N.S.C. staff redefined both the ends and means of Washington's Ukraine policy. Aid would no longer be conditioned on ratification of START and accession to the nuclear Nonproliferation Treaty but on practical steps toward denuclearization. The administration announced on April 23 reciprocal steps for "early deactivation" of missiles covered by START I, in advance of ratification. As applied to Ukraine, the aim was to separate the warheads from the missiles but let them remain temporarily on Ukrainian territory under international supervision.[90] The administration held out three inducements in return: Nunn-Lugar aid for dismantlement, economic assistance, and security assurances. To reassure Kiev, it offered to extend relations beyond nuclear arms, to open talks on political, economic, and military matters—including advice on effective restructuring of Ukrainian conventional forces— and to hold out the prospect of a "defense partnership" and broader political and economic engagement. In the first of series of high-level visits, Strobe Talbott, friend of Bill Clinton and ambassador at large to the CIS, went to Kiev on May 10 to sketch out the new policy.[91] He was followed on June 6 by Defense Secretary Les Aspin, who laid out the details of deactivation, removing the nuclear warheads from their launchers, and offered Ukraine a share of proceeds from the purchase and eventual resale of the highly enriched uranium extracted from the warheads, once they were shipped to Russia. Russia's defense minister, General Pavel Grachev, who had not been told in advance, criticized the offer.[92] Some in Moscow harbored suspicion of a plot to discover Russian weapons secrets and resentment at American interference in a strictly Russian-Ukrainian affair.

Cooperation soon bore fruit. The SS-19s were nearing the end of their service life, and their liquid fuel posed environmental hazards. President Kravchuk publicly acknowledged on June 18 that they would have to be dismantled within a few months.[93] Without seeking Rada approval in advance, the defense ministry on July 15 began to deactivate them.[94] Defense Minister Konstantin Morozov confirmed this in a July 27 meeting with Defense Secretary Aspin. In return, Washington released the $175 million in Nunn-Lugar aid, dropping its precondition that Kiev first ratify the NPT.

On September 4 Yeltsin and Kravchuk met at Massandra, near Yalta, to try to settle the festering disputes between Russia and Ukraine. They nearly succeeded, but the Massandra summit ended in a fiasco when the deals were assailed in Kiev and Moscow.[95] It was an inauspicious time in both capitals. Nationalists were riding high in Kiev, and the feud between Yeltsin and the Duma was escalating in Moscow. Massandra was subsequently subject to widely disparate interpretations that deepened the mistrust and eventually led both sides to revive American mediation efforts.

Yeltsin announced a "breakthrough" on nuclear arms. Russia would compensate Ukraine for the highly enriched uranium in its warheads with an equal amount of low-enriched uranium for use as nuclear fuel in power plants. An agreement initialed by the prime ministers, Viktor Chernomyrdin and Leonid Kuchma, was leaked to the press the next week. Ukraine agreed to "provide for, no later than twenty-four months from the date of ratification, the withdrawal of all nuclear warheads of the strategic nuclear forces deployed in Ukraine to the Russian Federation for dismantling and destruction." After both sides initialed the text, President Kravchuk's national security adviser, Anton Buteiko, crossed out the word "all" and inserted the phrase "subject to the treaty" after "the strategic nuclear forces deployed in Ukraine." That limited Ukraine's obligations because START I did not require dismantling of the SS-19s, which the Ukrainians were getting rid of in any case, or the SS-24s, which they wanted to retain. Buteiko neglected to have both parties initial the changes, however, and the Russians, after insisting that the original text was binding, annulled the accord.[96]

An agreement to compensate Ukraine for the tactical nuclear warheads already shipped to Russia also fell apart. After the prime ministers agreed orally that a bilateral commission would determine how much Ukraine should be reimbursed for the fissile material extracted from the warheads, the deal was never put in writing, and Yeltsin scotched it.[97]

According to Yeltsin, Ukraine also agreed to hand over its share of the Black Sea Fleet in exchange for Russia's forgiveness of its debt. Nationalists in the Rada promptly denounced the deal as a "national betrayal," and Kravchuk backed away from it. In Kiev's version of events, the offer on the Black Sea Fleet was an ultimatum: if it rejected the deal, Russia threatened to cut off its oil and gas supplies and seize the fleet.[98]

Within the month the political feuding in Moscow turned violent. On October 3–4 Yeltsin prorogued the parliament and sent in tanks to put down an attempted coup. Politics in Ukraine were almost as parlous as inflation accelerated to 70 percent a month and people faced the grim prospect of an early winter on short rations of heating oil. Ukrainian nationalists, fearful that a "red-brown" tide of Communists and ultranationalists would soon swamp Russia, clung to nuclear arms like a life raft.

With Belarus and Kazakhstan well on their way to disarming, Ukraine was now the lone holdout. On October 19, six days before Secretary of State Warren Christopher was due in Kiev, President Kravchuk raised doubts about Ukraine's intention to remove all nuclear arms from its territory within seven years, as he had pledged in a May 7, 1992, side letter to the United States at Lisbon. "A shot across the bow," one administration official called it.[99] The Ukrainians also began asking for $5 billion in compensation for the uranium contained in their warheads, in addition to $2.8 billion in Nunn-Lugar aid. After Christopher promised another $155 million in economic aid for Ukraine in fiscal year 1994 and emphasized engagement across a broad front, Kravchuk reaffirmed his intention to seek ratification of START I and total elimination of Ukraine's nuclear arms. The two signed an agreement that provided $175 million in previously announced Nunn-Lugar aid for dismantling the SS-19s. Kravchuk nearly agreed to deactivate the SS-24 missiles in Ukraine in return for U.S. security assurances, but Ambassador Talbott and Under Secretary of State Lynn Davis wanted to withhold the security pledges as inducement for Kiev to ratify START, the Lisbon Protocol that required it to give up all nuclear arms, and the NPT, while Foreign Minister Zlenko wanted the assurances given at the time Ukraine made its deactivation pledge.[100]

In what was looking more and more to Kiev like a tough-cop soft-cop routine, Russia turned up the pressure. On November 3 Defense Minister Grachev announced adoption of a new military doctrine abandoning the 1982 pledge of no first use of nuclear weapons. It forswore the use of nuclear weapons against any non-nuclear state that signed the nuclear Nonproliferation Treaty and was not allied with a nuclear state.[101] Although this echoed the nuclear assurance given by the United States to states that adhered to the NPT, many in Kiev took it for a threat. Two days later, Foreign Minister Kozyrev warned that Ukraine's warheads were unsafe. Their deterioration, he said pointedly, "could lead to a tragedy much worse than Chernobyl."[102] Maintenance of the warheads required some help from Russia.

On November 18, 1993, the Rada took one step forward and one step back. It finally brought itself to ratify START I, but it resolved that START ceilings covered only 42 percent of the warheads and 36 percent of the launchers in Ukraine. It reasserted ownership and administrative control of the strategic nuclear arms on its territory and imposed thirteen conditions for implementing the treaty, most notably, international guarantees of its security and compensation for the fissile material in the warheads that Ukraine turned over to Russia. The Rada also refused to be bound by Article 5 of the Lisbon Protocol, which obliged it to join the NPT as soon as possible, as well as the side letter of May 7, 1992, committing it to eliminate all nuclear weapons from its territory within seven years.[103] This apparent repudiation of Ukraine's commitment to become a nonnuclear state stirred unease in Washington because Russia's Supreme Soviet had ratified START on condition that the other three nuclear republics also ratify it and join the NPT. On November 29 President Clinton telephoned President Kravchuk to complain. He elicited a promise to resubmit START and NPT ratification to the new parliament to be elected in March.[104]

Deactivation went ahead nevertheless. By year's end, the warheads were off 41 of 130 SS-19 missiles, and the government, interpreting the Rada's resolution of ratification as permission to proceed with START I's schedule for dismantling, deactivated 20 of its 46 SS-24 missiles as well.[105]

On December 12, 1993, parliamentary elections took place in Russia. In a sharp rebuff to reformers, the ultranationalist party of Vladimir Zhirinovsky was the top vote-getter with about one-third of the total. The resistible rise of Zhirinovsky, with his rabble-rousing calls to defend the Russians living in the "near abroad" by force if necessary and reincorporate Ukraine into a Russia-led union, shocked Washington and Kiev into action. The Clinton administration, which had just offered to mediate security disputes between Russia and Ukraine, began brokering a tripartite accord on nuclear arms.

During meetings on December 15 and 16 in Moscow, Prime Minister Chernomyrdin accepted Vice President Al Gore's suggestion that a senior Russian official accompany Deputy Secretary of Defense William Perry to Kiev.[106] The Kiev meeting laid the groundwork for a meeting of all three sides in Washington on January 3–5, 1994, where they worked out a detailed trilateral agreement, an annex, and six secret letters. As details began to seep out and officials in Kiev expressed reservations, Kravchuk remained noncommittal. After President Clinton stumped for the accord during an airport stopover in Kiev on January 12, Kravchuk climbed off the fence and joined Clinton and Yeltsin at a signing ceremony in Moscow on January 14, 1994. Russia and Ukraine pledged to deactivate all their SS-24s within ten months. Ukraine promised to transfer all warheads to Russia "in the shortest possible time," within three years, according to a secret letter from Kravchuk to Clinton setting out the withdrawal schedule. In a transaction to be completed in ten months, Ukraine promised to deliver at least two hundred SS-19 and SS-24 warheads to Russia for dismantling under Ukrainian monitoring. In return, Russia pledged to compensate Ukraine for the highly enriched uranium in its strategic warheads with 100 tons of nuclear fuel. The United States would give Russia a $60 million advance to defray the cost of transporting and dismantling the warheads and producing the nuclear fuel. That sum would be deducted from U.S. payments for purchases of highly enriched uranium from Russia and would be spent on environmental cleanup and nuclear safety. In a formula devised by Washington to compensate Ukraine for the tactical warheads it had already shipped to Russia, Moscow agreed to forgive Kiev's unpaid oil and gas bills.[107] The United States also assembled an international consortium to provide funds for dismantling.[108]

The agreement had intangibles intended to reassure Ukraine. In the trilateral accord, the three presidents "reiterated that they will deal with one another as full and equal partners and that relations among their countries must be conducted on the basis of the respect for the independence, sovereignty, and territorial integrity of each nation." The United States and Russia also enumerated the security assurances they would give once START I entered into force and Ukraine renounced nuclear weapons and became a party to the NPT: reaffirmation of their respect for Ukraine's borders, their obligation not to use or threaten military force or economic coercion against Ukraine, a pledge not to use nuclear arms against Ukraine, and a commitment to seek immediate action by the UN Security Council in the event of aggression or a nuclear threat against Ukraine.

The signatures were barely dry before nationalists in Kiev cried foul. Vyacheslav Chornovil, leader of the nationalist party Rukh, accused Kravchuk of "shameful capitulation" and "betrayal" of the nation. Kravchuk lobbied strenuously for the agreement. So did the United States, which promised to double economic aid to $310 million if the Rada voted favorably and threw in personal blandishments like junkets to Washington for wavering legislators. On February 3 the Rada passed a two-part resolution, unconditionally ratifying START I and acknowledging Ukraine's obligation under the Lisbon Protocol to accede to the NPT. It also voted 193-27 in favor of immediate accession to the NPT, but that vote fell short of the necessary majority in the 450-member body because of absences and abstentions.[109]

By November Ukraine had turned over 360 warheads to Russia for dismantling, but the Rada had yet to ratify the NPT. Although Defense Secretary Perry had pledged $100 million in Nunn-Lugar aid for dismantling and conversion during a March 21–22 visit to an SS-24 missile base at Pervomaisk and the missile factory at Dnepropetrovsk, bringing total U.S. aid pledges to $700 million, Ukraine had yet to receive one-tenth of the funds. The Rada was also seeking firmer security assurances from the United States, Russia, and Britain. American officials paraded to Kiev promising to expedite aid, and the three nuclear powers put the finishing touches on a list of security guarantees by early November. It added a pledge to consult one another in the event of a problem.[110] On November 16, the Rada voted overwhelmingly for Ukraine to join the NPT as a nonnuclear weapons state. That cleared the way for START I's entry into force. As of June 1, 1996, the last of the warheads on Ukrainian soil crossed the border into Russia. Ukraine was a nuclear-free state.

U.S. nuclear diplomacy with Ukraine was a clear success for cooperative security. Washington initially made little headway by focusing exclusively on Ukraine's nuclear inheritance and pressuring the new state to disarm by withholding aid and threatening to isolate it. Only when Washington changed course and tried cooperation, offering inducements for disarming and reassurances in the form of high-level contacts and broader political and economic engagement, did Kiev relent and relinquish its warheads.

COOPERATIVE THREAT REDUCTION WITH RUSSIA

Unlike Ukraine, which had nuclear arms in name only, Russia had a vast nuclear arsenal. In the minds of many in its defense establishment, that arsenal was a lingering source of pride in the Soviet system and the bedrock of Russia's security, now that the Red Army had crumbled and the navy was rusting away. For the United States to help Russia control and dismantle its nuclear arms under these circumstances was not just a technically complicated task but a politically delicate one as well. More than an end to enmity, it would require mutual accommodation and, in particular, cooperation with Russia's nuclear establishment.

Washington tried accommodating Moscow at first but later relapsed into coercion, which proved self-defeating. It was slow to provide the token economic aid that it did offer. Nor did Washington further its own cause by describing aid to Moscow in ways that were psychologically demeaning to the Russians—as a helping hand to the fallen or downtrodden, as an act of charity, not as self-interest. In the end, the United States stopped far short of the thoroughgoing polit-ical and economic engagement that nuclear cooperation required. Even worse, it let disputes over Moscow's export of rocket engines to India and a nuclear reactor to Iran get in the way of collaboration to reduce the new nuclear dangers in Russia. Worst of all, it alienated even its closest allies in Moscow by embarking on NATO's eastward expansion.

Having put in place a legalistic approach to arms control that combined lower START ceilings with the extension of START I and the NPT to the other ex-Soviet nuclear republics, Washington at last began taking more immediate practical steps to control loose nukes. The United States provided millions of dollars to help Russia dis-mantle its missiles and bombers—refurbishing rail cars to transport warheads and liquid rocket propellant safely, improving the security of storage sites for fissile material extracted from its dismantled war-heads, supplying computers for its nuclear guardians to keep track of their deadly stockpiles, and expanding its plant capacity for destroying missiles. It also provided training and technical assistance to improve Russia's export controls to impede nuclear contraband from seeping across its borders. It began buying highly enriched uranium extracted from Russia's warheads. It funded research projects by Russian scien-tists to keep them from selling their nuclear know-how abroad.[111]

These efforts fell far short of what was needed to cope with the nuclear dangers in Russia. Competing priorities and parochial concerns partly account for the failure, but the larger reason was attitudinal—American reluctance to cooperate.

The purchase of Russia's highly enriched uranium showed how easy it was for private interests to subvert the public good in the absence of sustained attention and determined effort by top offi-cials. Uranium-235 was the main explosive ingredient in most of Russia's nuclear warheads. U-235 constitutes just 1 percent of the various isotopes of uranium found in nature. To obtain the 90 percent concentration needed to power a warhead, U-235 is separated from other uranium isotopes by a process known as enrichment, hence the term highly enriched uranium (HEU). When blended down with other isotopes, reducing the concentration of U-235 to 4–5 percent, it can be used to fuel nuclear power plants but not to make bombs. In a track II initiative, M.I.T. physicist Thomas Neff met with Viktor Mikhailov, the Soviet minister of atomic energy, on October 18, 1991, to propose that the United States purchase the HEU the ministry was extracting from Soviet warheads and blending down in order to keep would-be proliferators from obtaining it.[112] Mikhailov was amenable, but the Bush administration showed no interest. On October 24, 1991, Neff surfaced the proposal in a *New York Times* op-ed.

It took months for the Bush administration to open talks. In the meantime, the Soviet Union disintegrated, intensifying worry about the fate of its fissile material. On August 31, 1992, President Bush announced a government-to-government agreement to purchase HEU, but his announcement proved premature. It was not until January 14, 1994, that the United States signed a contract to buy 500 metric tons of HEU, enough for up to 25,000 bombs, for some $11.9 billion over the next twenty years. Twenty years was a long time to live with doubts about the whereabouts of the HEU, and the amount to be purchased represented less than half of Russia's stock of fissile material.

A year later, with very little Russian uranium in American hands, the HEU deal was near collapse. The main reason was that the Bush administration designated a quasi-private entity, the U.S. Enrichment Corporation, to buy the Russian uranium instead of having the U.S. government make the purchases. Congress had authorized creation of the U.S.E.C. in 1992 as a wholly owned government corporation to take over operation of two uranium enrichment plants from the Department of Energy and eventually privatize them. The two plants fabricated fuel rods for nuclear reactors, supplying 80–90 percent of the nation's nuclear fuel for generating power. In an obvious conflict of interest, the Department of Energy officials who were about to take over as managers of the U.S.E.C. secured for the soon to be privatized corporation the exclusive right to purchase Russian HEU.[113]

Russia expected to be compensated for the value of the uranium and the enrichment services it provided, but the U.S.E.C. had little incentive of its own to implement the HEU deal.[114] It was not about to let Russia sell uranium directly to American utilities, which would reduce its market share and shrink its profit margins. It also was cheaper for the U.S.E.C. to enrich natural uranium for fabrication into fuel rods itself than to buy blended-down HEU from Russia because the Department of Energy was subsidizing its costs of production by charging below-market electricity rates. That subsidy also made it unprofitable for the U.S.E.C. to use more uranium in the enrichment process in order to reduce its consumption of electricity, a technique called overfeeding.[115]

The HEU deal was further impeded by an "antidumping" petition filed in November 1992 by thirteen uranium mining firms, the Department of Energy, and the Oil, Chemical, and Atomic Workers' Union. That petition was precipitated by a sharp drop in uranium prices after the Soviet Ministry of Atomic Energy (Minatom) began marketing uranium to the United States in 1988.

Minatom's call to arms had become "export or die." Desperate to stay in business and no longer able to count on government subsidies, Minatom ventured abroad in search of revenues. Its aggressive marketing of everything from uranium to nuclear reactors went largely unchecked by Soviet officials responsible for preventing proliferation.[116] The disintegration of the Soviet state and Moscow's need for hard currency led to a relaxation of export controls. Minatom gave exclusive rights to Soviet uranium exports to a Colorado-based uranium mining and trading firm, which, without anyone's knowledge, manipulated the market by borrowing uranium from U.S. firms and repaying them with its Soviet imports.[117] By 1991 the price of uranium had halved.

Although there was no evidence that Minatom was deliberately driving down uranium prices, congressional relaxation of antidumping rules had made it easier for U.S. firms to obtain tariff protection against foreign competition. It also gave the Commerce Department the leverage to get other governments to limit imports in return for suspending antidumping proceedings. On May 29, 1992, the Commerce Department ruled in favor of the petitioners and ordered a duty imposed on all uranium imports from Russia.[118]

At the G-7 summit meeting on July 8, 1992, President Yeltsin complained that the denial of access to the U.S. market was costing Russia millions of dollars in much-needed hard-currency earnings. In response, the Bush administration opened talks to suspend the antidumping proceedings. At the same time it began negotiating in earnest to purchase Russian uranium extracted from warheads. The suspension agreement negotiated by the Commerce Department all but precluded the U.S.E.C. from reselling Russian uranium, thereby foreclosing the most expeditious way to compensate Minatom for its HEU shipments.[119] On August 31, 1992, the United States initialed a government-to-government agreement with Russia to purchase uranium extracted from its warheads. An agreement to purchase 500 metric tons of HEU over twenty years, at least ten tons of it in each of the first five years and thirty metric tons a year thereafter, was signed on February 18, 1993. In May the U.S.E.C. initialed a long-term contract with Minatom giving it the option, but not the obligation, to buy HEU extracted from Russian warheads. Minatom refused to sign the contract, however, until the suspension agreement was relaxed to permit it to export other Russian uranium to the United States.

For a year the Commerce Department did little to satisfy Minatom. The lack of movement, said Richard Falkenrath in his definitive study, was attributable to "the low level of attention that the HEU deal and the suspension agreement received from the Clinton administration's senior national security officials, and pressure from the domestic uranium industry, U.S.E.C., and Congress not to relax the suspension agreement."[120] The U.S.E.C. also made effective use of lobbying by a lawyer well connected to the Clinton White House.

On November 18, 1993, the Rada voted to make Ukraine's implementation of START contingent on compensation for the HEU in its warheads. That prompted Vice President Gore to broker the trilateral accord providing for Russia to compensate Ukraine with nuclear fuel to keep its power plants running. The need to secure Minatom's cooperation in implementing the trilateral accord galvanized Washington into amending the suspension agreement to mandate "matched sales," permitting the importation of uranium from Russia so long as the amount imported was matched by equal amounts of U.S.-produced uranium. Minatom and the U.S.E.C. signed the HEU contract on January 14, 1994, the day that the trilateral accord was signed. Yet amendment of the suspension agreement did little to meet Russia's hard currency needs or to expedite the shipment of HEU out of Russia. Minatom even offered to form a joint venture and let the HEU be blended down in the United States in order to speed the flow of hard currency into Russia and HEU out, but to no avail.[121] As a consequence, Russia was slow to ship out HEU to the United States.

This outcome could have been avoided by having the American government, instead of the U.S.E.C., purchase the Russian HEU. In a model for how the HEU deal should have worked, the Clinton administration spirited 600 kilograms of HEU out of Kazakhstan and flew it to the United States for safekeeping. That was just fifty bombs' worth. By comparison, Russia has enough HEU for tens of thousands of warheads.

The covert operation, code-named Project Sapphire, began when President Nazarbaev telephoned President Clinton in summer 1993 to say Kazakhstan had HEU at a fuel fabrication plant and lacked a secure means of storing or disposing of it. After months of secret negotiations conducted by Ambassador William Courtney, the United States agreed to buy the HEU for an estimated tens of millions of dollars, much of it in the form of humanitarian aid. Russia also agreed to the arrangement. It took several months more to satisfy U.S. environmental and legal requirements for transporting nuclear material before a thirty-one-member U.S. team packed the HEU into containers, loaded it aboard three C-5 aircraft on November 23, 1994, and flew it to the United States, where it was stored at Oak Ridge, Tennessee, under International Atomic Energy Agency safeguards.[122]

By and large, however, the Bush and Clinton administrations did not give nuclear cooperation with Moscow the high priority it deserved, making it difficult to overcome bureaucratic impediments in Washington. Perhaps the main impediment was that the Department of Defense had been assigned responsibility for Nunn-Lugar programs. In the beginning that seemed to make sense for the same reason that Willy "the Actor" Sutton robbed banks: that's where the money was. Career officials in the Pentagon, however, resented congressional reprogramming of funds as a diversion from their traditional roles and missions and a distraction from their customary way of thinking about security. They were slow to obligate the funds. Pentagon procurement practices were also hamstrung by "buy American" provisions enacted by Congress. As a result, a significant share of Nunn-Lugar money ended up lining the pockets of "Beltway bandits," Pentagonese for the consultants and contractors around Washington. That did little for the livelihood of the Russians whose cooperation was essential to keep nuclear know-how and material from going abroad.

Congress proved even more of an impediment in other ways. Despite legislators like Nunn and Lugar who recognized the risks to

American security posed by loose nukes in Russia and the need for cooperative threat reduction, Congress was unwilling to appropriate much more than $400 million a year for Nunn-Lugar, a pittance by Pentagon standards. It also attached stipulations to funding that impeded cooperation with Russia at every turn. The result was that, as of February 1995, the United States had committed just $300 million in Nunn-Lugar aid to Russia and $142 million to Ukraine.[123] The Russian share did not measure up to the magnitude of the new nuclear dangers there, as compared to Ukraine. Domestic politics may help account for the way the money was allocated. Ukraine had a small but passionate constituency in the United States; Russia had nothing like that. In this and other respects, Nunn-Lugar expenditures were treated like foreign aid, which is viewed in Congress as an unpopular giveaway. Yet foreign aid can be a very cost-effective form of cooperative security and enjoys much wider public support than members of Congress think it does, especially compared to military intervention overseas.[124]

Congress also construed the scope of cooperative threat reduction quite narrowly, confining funds to helping with the destruction of Russia's warheads and missiles while blocking aid to convert Russia's defense industries to civilian use, to house officers demobilized from the strategic rocket forces, or even to improve security at Russia's far-flung network of nuclear facilities. Such aid may have seemed more difficult to justify when Congress was unwilling to spend much on conversion of defense industries at home and was cutting back public housing appropriations, but the pinched financing for Nunn-Lugar did not advance the nation's security.

One Nunn-Lugar program that Congress did support was the effort to impede diversion of fissile material from Russia's nuclear facilities. Getting Moscow's cooperation proved more difficult without appropriate inducements, inducements that Washington was slow to offer in part because of Pentagon procurement practices. Minatom, unwilling to appear as if it were dependent on outside help to secure its own facilities, drove a hard bargain. It took more than a year to sign a government-to-government agreement for $10 million in Nunn-Lugar aid to develop a model system of material protection, control, and accounting (MPC&A) for the Electrostat fuel fabrication plant near Moscow. At Russian insistence, however, the agreement covered only the production line for low-enriched uranium at the plant. It took another year to extend coverage to its production line for HEU intended for military use. That and five other facilities were part of a $20 million, government-to-government agreement signed on January 20, 1995, but work commenced only after the United States agreed to make an advanced payment of $100 million to Minatom for HEU purchases.[125]

A similar effort initiated by the national laboratories at Los Alamos and Livermore made much more rapid progress. The lab-to-lab programs dated from a February 1992 meeting of laboratory directors with their Russian counterparts at Arzamas-16 and Chelyabinsk-70, which led the Department of Energy to sponsor collaborative research projects in metallurgy, lasers and optics, and internal confinement fusion. As of April 1994, it had signed more than two hundred contracts with some forty institutes in Russia and Ukraine for a total of $5 million.[126] That, in turn, helped cement working relationships between the labs and attracted funding from the Russian government, keeping Russian scientists gainfully employed. In April 1994, in response to increased anxiety about nuclear smuggling, lab-to-lab cooperation was extended to encompass MPC&A at the direction of Under Secretary of Energy Charles Curtis.[127] By December, at a cost of less than $1 million, the lab-to-lab program had installed an improved security system using indigenous technology at the Kurchatov Institute, a leading nuclear research establishment in Moscow that housed more than three hundred pounds of HEU, and had completed the first accounting of nuclear materials there.[128]

The MPC&A program was eventually transferred from the Pentagon to the Department of Energy. That made sense because D.O.E. officials already had responsibility for fissile material protection and accounting at U.S. nuclear installations and were more experienced at it than Pentagon officials. The Department of Energy also was less constrained by "buy American" provisions than the Pentagon, enabling it to finance Russian initiatives, which helped create a constituency for cooperation in Russia's labs.[129] With the collapse of the ruble, the dollar went a long way in Russia, making it more cost-effective to pay Russian scientists and technicians to do the work.

The low standard of living of the estimated 60,000 people in the Soviet Union with technical know-how to work on nuclear, chemical, and biological weapons and missiles was very worrisome. About 20,000 of them did nuclear work, of whom 200 had the ability to design a warhead.[130] With salaries running at between $50 and $100 *a month* in 1991, if they were paid at all, some experts began consulting abroad.

Enticed by salaries of $25,000 a year, a group of twenty-five Russians from the Machine Building Research Institute in Miass, which specialized in designing submarine-launched ballistic missiles, tried to go to North Korea, only to be turned back at the airport by Russian security officials.[131]

The International Science and Technology Center was set up to keep such specialists gainfully employed at home by providing project grants for research that paid them salaries of $200 to $300 a month.[132] Impetus for the center came from Germany's foreign minister, Hans-Dietrich Genscher, in late 1991. The United States, Japan, and the European Union each pledged $67 million. By contrast, George Soros alone had spent $140 million. Moreover, it took nearly a year to negotiate an international agreement to establish the center. The agreement was delayed four months while France and other European Union signatories insisted on having the agreement translated into their own languages.[133] By that time ratification became embroiled in the struggle between Yeltsin and the Duma, Russia's parliament. Most Russian government officials avoided taking sides, but Minatom, bowing to pressure from scientists at Arzamas-16, spearheaded the lobbying for ratification. "The West's archenemies of years past and the center's chief antagonists of recent months had suddenly become our allies," said Glenn Schweitzer, the center's first executive director.[134] It took until March 18, 1994, for the first projects to be approved, more than two years after Soros had first provided funding for scientists set adrift by the collapse of the Soviet Union.

While this and other forms of cooperation encountered resistance in Moscow, the more significant problem was the dearth of support for cooperative security in Washington. Top officials paid only intermittent attention, and Congress was fitful in its support. As a consequence, the United States did too little, too late to cope with the new nuclear dangers.

Washington also went out of its way to antagonize Moscow by applying sanctions to punish it for cryogenic rocket exports to India and other sanctions to try to overturn its nuclear reactor deal with Iran. Sanctions angered the very players in Russia whose cooperation Washington most needed, the missile manufacturers and Minatom.

In January 1991 Glavkosmos, a marketing arm of the Soviet missile industry, agreed to sell India cryogenic rocket engines, which used supercooled oxygen and hydrogen as their propellant. Even more troubling, Glavkosmos agreed to transfer technology that would enable the Indian Space Research Organization to build cryogenic rockets of its own. The Bush administration charged that the deal violated the Missile Technology Control Regime (MTCR), the international compact to impede proliferation by regulating missile technology exports that could be used to deliver nuclear warheads. Under a 1990 law, a violation would require imposition of sanctions on government agencies or firms involved in the transaction. Moscow responded that the engines had no conceivable military application because of the time it took to fuel them and that they were intended for peaceful use in India's space program. Unpersuaded, Washington went ahead on May 6, 1992, and slapped sanctions on imports from and exports to Glavkosmos, as well as the Indian Space Research Organization, for two years. The largely symbolic sanctions did not dissuade Glavkosmos from proceeding with the sale, but the symbolism damaged American interests in Russia, where it was portrayed as an American attempt to bar Russia from the supposedly lucrative market for space launches. "The backlash triggered by US sanctions," conclude the authors of an authoritative study of the incident, "provided a rallying-point for anti-Western political factions and consolidated their political base."[135]

Sanctions failed to move Moscow. In February 1993 the Clinton administration turned to inducements instead. An interagency task force identified projects for cooperating with Russia in space, like joint development of a new space station, but the White House was adamant about avoiding any appearance of an explicit quid pro quo. Instead, the Clinton administration asked Moscow to demonstrate restraint in missile exports. At his first summit meeting with Yeltsin in Vancouver on April 3–4, 1993, Clinton proposed that if Russia pledged to observe the MTCR guidelines and amended its agreement with India to exclude a transfer of technology to produce cryogenic rocket engines, the United States would no longer oppose the sale of the engines themselves. That was the basis of agreements concluded on July 15–16 in Washington and signed on December 16.[136]

The American response to Russia's nuclear deal with Iran was even more detrimental to U.S. interests. In 1995 Minatom signed an $800 million contract with the Atomic Energy Agency of Iran to complete an unfinished nuclear reactor at Bushehr. Construction of the reactor, begun by a West German firm during the Shah's rule, was halted after the Iranian revolution. Minatom agreed to provide the necessary nuclear fuel and to train Iranian nuclear specialists as well.

Most alarming of all were reports that Minatom was willing to sell Iran gas centrifuge technology equipment, which could be used to enrich uranium. Suspecting that Iran's civilian nuclear program was a cloak for bomb making, Washington tried to get Moscow to cancel the deal. At the May 1995 summit in Moscow, President Yeltsin pledged not to go ahead with the gas centrifuge sale, but Russia refused to back away from the reactor deal, noting that Iran, as a signatory in good standing of the nuclear Nonproliferation Treaty, was entitled to help in building reactors, that the light-water reactor resembled the reactor to be supplied to North Korea under the October 1994 Agreed Framework between that country and the United States, and that Iran had agreed to have Russia reprocess the spent fuel produced in the reactor, reducing the risk of proliferation. Congress reacted by threatening to cut off Nunn-Lugar funding for Russia.

The move manifested the confusion in Congress about American security interests. Russia had 24,000 warheads and enough nuclear material—plutonium and highly enriched uranium—to make tens of thousands more. By comparison, Iran had none and would not be able to produce a bomb on its own for at least seven years—five years for Russia to build a reactor at Bushehr plus at least two more years to generate a bomb's worth of plutonium from the reactor's spent fuel and fabricate it into a warhead.[137] In the meantime, instead of imposing sanctions, the United States would have been better off trying to persuade Russia to insist on further safeguards against any diversion of nuclear equipment or material from civilian or military uses, or trying to coax Iran into verifiably abandoning its nuclear weapons program.

Much of the blame for America's unwillingness to cooperate with Russia rests with Capitol Hill. In the November 1994 elections, Republicans took control of both houses of Congress. Many of the newly elected members came from the unilateralist wing of the GOP. The dominant trend, in the words of one proliferation expert, was "anti-foreign, anti-aid, anti-Russian, and anti-Clinton," in a word, anti-cooperation.[138] The new Congress moved to curtail the scope of the Nunn-Lugar program and to cut its funding. At the same time it moved to increase spending on ballistic missile defenses. It seemed as if some Republicans preferred to spend tens of billions to defend against the new nuclear dangers instead of spending hundreds of millions to get rid of them.

Congress was not the only problem in Washington, however. The administration was exhibiting its own ambivalence about cooperative threat reduction. In remarks to a Carnegie Endowment conference on nonproliferation on January 31, 1994, Jane Wales, a senior director at the N.S.C., characterized the administration's policy on fissile material in Russia: "The fundamental principles of our approach are *cooperation* and *reciprocity*. Only by genuine cooperation can we solve these problems." She spoke of "a shift from a strategy of containment to one of engagement."[139] Yet the more powerful pull of policy was in the opposite direction. In a September 21, 1993, speech in Washington, Wales's boss, National Security Adviser Anthony Lake, had proclaimed a "successor" strategy to containment, "a strategy of enlargement—enlargement of the world's free community of market democracies." It marked the start of a campaign for NATO expansion.[140] Lake saw enlargement as a way to unite the left and right wings of the Democratic Party on foreign policy, keep Poles and other ethnic constituents in the Democratic fold, and head off Republican attacks on Clinton's leadership.[141] In a bow to the GOP, some of Lake's rhetoric was suggested by House minority leader Newt Gingrich (R-GA).[142] Lake got the president to move beyond the Partnership for Peace and commit himself to add new members to the alliance in a January 11, 1994, speech in Prague: "While the Partnership is not NATO membership, neither is it a permanent holding room. It changes the entire NATO dialogue so that the question is no longer whether NATO will take on new members but when and how."[143] With its echo of a Kantian community of like-minded nations, Lake's rhetoric and reasoning were rooted more in liberalism than in realism. As a consequence, expanding the alliance attracted support from some realists who still regarded Russia as a threat to Eastern Europe but opposition from others who did not. NATO expansion had become a partisan issue, with support from influential Republicans like Senator Richard Lugar of Indiana and Representative Benjamin Gilman of New York and inclusion in the "Contract with America," the GOP platform for the 1994 election campaign. That intensified the competition for votes among Eastern European ethnic groups. Once the Republicans captured control of Congress, expansion became an issue of presidential leadership in the eyes of White House political advisers.[144]

As the drive to expand NATO gained momentum in Washington, however, it made nuclear cooperation politically more difficult in Moscow. In December 1994, after NATO announced its intention to expand, reformers in Moscow saw it as a sign of Washington's doubts about their success. "It's too early to bury democracy in Russia!" was

Boris Yeltsin's reaction. He warned that Europe "runs the risk of plunging into a cold peace." After Secretary of Defense Perry's last-ditch effort to slow the momentum for NATO expansion at a cabinet-level meeting on December 21 was thwarted, nuclear cooperation with Russia suffered.[145]

Reducing the new nuclear dangers in Russia became a matter of urgency for Washington after the August 1991 coup in Moscow. That was decidedly in the national security interest of the United States. The only way to reduce those dangers was to engage in cooperative security with Russia. Yet competing priorities, parochial interests, and sheer inattentiveness kept the Bush and Clinton administrations from doing what was needed. It was a failure that Americans will live to regret.

9

AMERICA'S SECURITY AGENDA
WITH RUSSIA

Whoever heard of a military alliance begging with a weakened adversary?

—Henry Kissinger[1]

Today the United States is drifting toward benign neglect of Russia in the belief that its former rival is too weak to pose much danger to American security. That course is shortsighted so long as Russia has not disposed of its nuclear warheads by the thousands and nuclear material by the tons. It is misguided also because Russia will eventually recover, and, when it does, the security of Europe will depend on whether it seeks to regain its lost sway or to get along with its neighbors. Contrary to the view of realists like Henry Kissinger, Russia's interests should not be ignored because it is too weak to defend them. Nor should it be treated as a potential adversary, as other realists want to do, out of concerns about a renewed threat to its neighbors.

By opposing cooperation with Russia, these realists fuel Russian ultranationalists who cast Russia as the victim of a punitive settlement of the cold war and want to avenge its loss. Yet today's Russia is not Weimar Germany. The Soviet Union was not defeated in war and forced to accept a punitive peace. Its leaders chose to transform it, shedding its empire and pursuing common security with its neighbors. They did so with substantial support from the Russian people, who continue to back the nation's westernizers over its ultranationalists. Even if the ultranationalists eventually were to seize power, it would take them more than a decade to restore Russia's military might.

If Russia is not Weimar Germany, neither is China like Japan in the 1930s. Some realists regard China as a rising power and want to contain, not accommodate, it. Even if some Chinese leaders have a hostile intent, it will take fifteen years or more before China begins to acquire the forces needed to mount a credible threat, even against Taiwan. In the meantime, it may undergo an internal transformation as profound as the Soviet Union's. More worrisome than China's capabilities is the conviction of some influential Chinese that war with the United States is inevitable. Belief in the inevitability of war would doom cooperative security. A policy of containment would surely reinforce that conviction in China today. So could erecting missile defenses.

Notwithstanding the worst fears of some well-publicized threat-mongers, there are good reasons for thinking that the current conditions conducive to cooperative security will outlast the next decade. Americans are living in a world remarkably free of foes. Of the handful of countries whose intentions are inimical, none has the capability to defeat the United States in war. Indeed, no major power now has the intention and the capability to challenge the structure of peace by taking on any other major power, as Germany and Japan did in the 1930s. An economic catastrophe like the Great Depression, which could exacerbate tensions and foster the rise of aggressive nationalism in the great powers, does not appear in the offing.

If there is a clear and present danger to the United States, it comes not from hostile states with the potential to do great harm to this country but from the proliferation of weapons of mass destruction. That has been the assessment of the American intelligence community since 1993. Yet American attempts to prevent the spread of nuclear arms have been impeded by shared images that the main proliferation menace comes from so-called rogue states like North Korea, Iran, and Iraq and that the way to get states to abandon their nuclear ambitions is to demonize them as outlaws and force them to disarm—the crime-and-punishment approach to preventing proliferation. Russia, China, Israel, India, and Pakistan are not considered rogue states. Some of them pose even greater proliferation risks by stimulating their neighbors to acquire nuclear arms and by serving as sources for nuclear know-how and technology.[2] Above all, that is the case with Russia. That is why Russia rightly remains the principal focus of American security concerns for now. That is also why the United States needs to cooperate with Russia.

WAYS TO DEAL WITH THE NEW NUCLEAR DANGERS

With the disintegration of the Soviet Union, the threat that nuclear war could arise out of a superpower conflict in Europe or elsewhere has evaporated. Instead, new nuclear dangers came to the fore. Four of them persist to this day. First and foremost is the danger of nuclear leakage: that a few bombs' worth of nuclear material, neither fully accounted for nor thoroughly secured, could be smuggled out of Russia to would-be proliferators. A second is the danger of nuclear accident because Russia lacks the capacity to maintain the thousands of warheads and launchers it has, especially its tactical warheads. Third is the danger of unauthorized nuclear use if Russia increasingly relies on nuclear forces to counter threats along its borders and maintains excessive nuclear forces on hair-trigger alert. Fourth is the danger of a nuclear brain drain: with hundreds of nuclear scientists and technicians at the mercy of the market, some may be tempted to sell their know-how to the highest bidder.

Dealing with the new nuclear dangers in Russia should be the overriding international objective of the United States. It has not been, to judge from Washington's dealings with Moscow from 1985 until 1994. A number of steps are long overdue.

NUCLEAR MATERIALS

The riskiest cold war legacy is the vast stockpile of fissile material at military and civilian installations spread across Russia—1,000 metric tons of highly enriched uranium (HEU) and 120 metric tons of plutonium, or 100,000 bombs' worth.[3] Accounting for and securing this material is a matter of great urgency.

The stockpile of fissile material in Russia and the United States is so vast that neither side has been able to account for all of it. The best estimate of the total amount of plutonium produced or acquired by the United States since 1945 is 2.8 tons more than the 99.5 tons now believed to be in its stockpile. (This does not count another 9.1 tons removed by tests, waste, decay, use as reactor fuel, accidents, or transfers.)[4] The amount unaccounted for is enough to make more warheads than China, Great Britain, France, India, Pakistan, and Israel combined now have in their arsenals. The amount of fissile material unaccounted for in Russia is far greater—5 to 10 percent of its stockpile, according to U.S. intelligence. Even the number of war-heads is subject to considerable uncertainty: in 1992 a C.I.A. official testified that Russia had 30,000 warheads "plus or minus 5,000."[5] In 1997, after substantial reductions, the estimate was 20,000 to 25,000 still in its possession.[6]

A nuclear inventory is needed to bound this uncertainty. The sooner it is taken, the better. As elaborated by former Pentagon offi-cial Steve Fetter, a comprehensive accounting would cover the mass, and the chemical and isotopic composition of all fissile material and its location and status, whether it is in warheads or their compo-nents or in reactors, storage, or waste; the production and materials records of all fissile material acquired and removed from inventory and of all facilities used to produce such material; the location, type, status, serial number, and historical record of all warheads; a list and operating history of all facilities where nuclear devices have been designed, tested, assembled, stored, deployed, modified, repaired, and disassembled and where key components such as detonators, high-explosive packages, and all special nuclear materials have been produced.[7] It is in the national interest of the United States to help Russia finance this accounting. It is also in the American interest to cooperate in exchanging data with Russia on its own nuclear mate-rial and warheads.

Beyond accounting, a comprehensive system for safeguarding fissile material is needed. The United States could do much more to help consolidate Russia's weapons-usable stocks at a few highly secure locations—the fewer, the better. It could provide Russia with the equipment, techniques, and inducements to maintain security at all such sites and to set up monitoring systems to track fissile mate-rial and warheads from the cradle to the grave. And it could blend down excess stocks of highly enriched uranium and plutonium to make them less bomb-worthy while devising ways to dispose of them more permanently.

Some $2.5 billion in Nunn-Lugar money has been expended on these tasks over the past seven years. That is little more than the price of a single B-2 bomber and not nearly enough to cope with the dan-ger. Far too much, nearly two-thirds of that sum, has gone to cover administrative costs and pay U.S. contractors. Russia has been grudg-ing about cooperating, in part because so little funding has trickled down to it and in larger part because American cooperation has been so crabbed.

Russia has a backlog of warheads to dismantle. One quick way to disable the warheads awaiting disassembly is "pit stuffing," which is already used to prevent unsafe warheads from detonating accidentally, according to Matthew Bunn, who served in the Office of Science and Technology Policy. Warheads have a "pit" at their core, a hollow sphere of highly enriched uranium or plutonium. Each pit has a tiny tube running through it, allowing tritium, used to boost the yield of the warhead, to be fed into the sphere. If steel wire is instead fed through the tube until the pit is "stuffed" with wire, the pit cannot be compressed to form a critical mass needed for a chain reaction. Inspectors could verify that warheads had been rendered useless without exposing warhead design information.[8]

Once the warheads are disassembled, the extracted HEU can be blended down and stored for eventual disposal. U.S. purchases of such HEU have stalled dangerously as a result of putting a quasi-private firm, the U.S. Enrichment Corporation, in charge. The U.S. government should take over the job and agree to pay Russia in advance to blend down all its excess HEU and buy any HEU it is willing to sell. It should do the same with Russia's plutonium, starting with the nuclear material at vulnerable research labs and on board decommissioned nuclear submarines.[9]

Disposing of plutonium extracted from warheads is more difficult because it cannot be denatured like HEU, rendering it useless for bomb making. A National Academy of Sciences study preferred two options: combine plutonium and uranium into MOX fuel for use in existing reactors; or else mix plutonium with radioactive waste and molten glass in a process called vitrification and fabricate the mixture into chemically inert logs to be placed in long-term storage.[10]

It also makes sense to help pay for Russia to downsize its nuclear arms complex and find civilian jobs and housing for those who work in it. That will require aid for economic development of the formerly closed nuclear cities around Russia.[11]

It would be prudent to negotiate elimination of Russian and American fissile material stocks in excess of what each country needs to maintain a stockpile of 1,000 warheads. To impede the production of new fissile material, all reactors, reprocessing facilities, and uranium enrichment plants would be safeguarded under the International Atomic Energy Agency or bilateral auspices. This could be done as part of, or in advance of, a fissile material cutoff now under negotiation in the UN Conference on Disarmament. To impede the production of new warheads, other than those being remanufactured for safety and reliability reasons, Steve Fetter has proposed strict monitoring of all warheads and pits entering and exiting all such production facilities.[12]

Such measures have been resisted by guardians of the nuclear arsenals on both sides, who see them as threats to their essential roles and missions and infringements on their autonomy. Some career officials regard the nuclear legacy of the cold war as a crown jewel, a keepsake to be treasured and retained at all costs. In 1995 the guardians of Russia's nuclear arsenal even exploited the reluctance to cooperate in Washington and growing national assertiveness in Moscow to block agreement to exchange sensitive nuclear data.

TACTICAL NUCLEAR DISARMAMENT

Tactical warheads are much more liable to theft and misuse than strategic warheads. Russia still has 3,000 to 4,000 tactical nuclear warheads in its arsenal. Few are mated with their delivery vehicles. As many as 6,000 more—the exact number is uncertain—are kept at fifty storage sites around Russia. Most have outlived their expected service life. None are likely to last another decade. The sooner they are taken out of service and disassembled, the safer the world will be. That will take time, however, because of the backlog of tactical warheads slated for dismantling. Meanwhile, they might be disabled by pit stuffing.

It would be useful to consolidate storage sites and arrange for mutual monitoring of them. An exchange of data on each side's tactical nuclear stockpile is imperative.[13] Russia's total remains in doubt because in response to President Bush's initiative they were withdrawn unilaterally. No common ceilings were ever negotiated. A baseline count of warheads would be a helpful precursor to such negotiations.

It also would make sense to begin negotiating a verification regime for tactical warheads, including short-notice inspections of deployment and storage sites.[14] Once warheads are declared, joint teams would authenticate and "tag" them with unique, tamper-proof seals. They would then be stored for disassembly at dismantling sites under perimeter monitoring by international inspectors. Prior notification would be required to remove any warheads from storage.

As inducement for reciprocal reductions by Russia, the United States could unilaterally withdraw the last 400 of its air-delivered tactical warheads from Europe. A National Academy of Sciences study in 1997 questioned their military utility.[15] The armed services are more than willing to get rid of them, along with all other tactical warheads. Their withdrawal could set the stage for talks to reduce such warheads or ban them altogether. Negotiated ceilings will be essential as strategic nuclear reductions proceed and the tactical arsenal gains prominence. A low ceiling of no more than 500 warheads might be negotiable as an interim step toward a ban.

Bureaucratic interests have been the main impediment to mutual monitoring of tactical arms. Resisting any perceived infringement on their own autonomy, guardians of the U.S. arsenal, especially civilians in the Pentagon, balk at putting the proposition to Russia. Similar interests in Russia may impede a positive response. As a result, reductions have been taken unilaterally without negotiating verifiable ceilings to bound the uncertainty about the size of the stockpiles. A debt-for-security swap might ease bureaucratic impediments. Forgiving part of Russia's debt in return for its cooperation on nuclear transparency might bring new stakeholders with different bureaucratic interests into the action. But the interests of Minatom and the displaced nuclear scientists and workers in Russia also will have to be addressed.

A NUCLEAR STAND-DOWN

A deteriorating nuclear infrastructure in Russia has left command and control of its deterrent in patchy shape. The survival of its retaliatory force would be precarious, which drives Russia to launch on warning in a crisis. As a result, its strategic nuclear forces remain poised on hair-trigger alert, capable of being launched within minutes of a warning of attack. So do American nuclear forces. That posture greatly increases the risk of accidental or unauthorized launch. The 1994 agreement between Presidents Clinton and Yeltsin not to aim nuclear missiles at each other did little to reduce the risk: targets for the land-based ballistic missile force can be reactivated in seconds and targets for the submarine-launched force in minutes without the knowledge of the other side. An ultranationalist regime in Russia would likely do just that.

To ease the danger of unintended nuclear strikes, Washington should unilaterally eliminate its launch-on-warning option from its nuclear war plans and invite Moscow to do likewise. This step would permit nuclear forces to be taken off high alert. It would return to the practice at the height of cold war, from 1945 until 1952, when all U.S. warheads were separated from their means of delivery and kept in the custody of civilians in the Atomic Energy Commission. The president would have to order them to be turned over to the armed services and loaded onto missiles and bombers for delivery.

In 1991 President Bush unilaterally took all strategic bombers off alert. Now the president should order a stand-down of all land-based missiles so that it would take weeks, even months—not minutes—to launch them. To ensure that the United States is not caught napping, two Trident missile-carrying submarines would remain at sea at all times. Instead of keeping them on station, with their missiles armed and ready for prompt reaction, however, they would remain out of range of Russia on low-level alert, lengthening the time it would take for the missiles on board to be readied for launch to at least eighteen hours. Again, Russia would be asked to reciprocate. Once the two sides took these unilateral steps in parallel, they would stand down their forces. Provisions in START could be readily extended to verify the stand-down.[16] In the event of fundamental changes in the world, the stand-down could be reversed only after timely notification to the other side.

As added inducement for Russia to reciprocate, the United States should end its dangerous practice of tailing Russian missile-carrying submarines. In a notorious incident, an American sub and a Russian sub collided in the Barents Sea. Yet the risk of accident at sea pales in comparison to the nuclear instability posed by the provocative game of undersea hide-and-seek. With most of its missile-carrying submarines penned up in the Sea of Okhotsk and just two on patrol at any time, Russia worries that the least vulnerable leg of its deterrent remains at the mercy of American antisubmarine warfare. Tailing Russian subs makes the United States less secure. Safety lies in reciprocity—in American acceptance of a submarine exclusion zone in the Sea of Okhotsk, reassuring Russia that its second-strike capability is not at risk. That might allow it to dispense with its launch-on-warning posture.

In the past, political impediments, both bureaucratic and domestic, would have ruled out such far-reaching changes. They no longer do. The main impediment is now sheer inertia, especially among civilian officials in the Pentagon.

FURTHER CUTS IN STRATEGIC ARMS

The sooner Russia's nuclear arsenal is reduced, the safer the world will be. Yet Russia cannot be expected to make deep cuts without reciprocal U.S. cuts. Such cuts have proved laborious to negotiate and even more laborious to ratify. There is no reason to hold up further reductions for another prolonged round of strategic arms talks.

Yet, instead of forging ahead, the Clinton administration at first held START III hostage to Duma ratification of START II, then agreed belatedly with Russia to seek a common ceiling of 2,000 to 2,500 warheads in START III once negotiations begin.[17] Yet the Russians want to go lower—to 1,000 warheads or fewer.[18] U.S. requirements under current nuclear policy guidelines can be met with an arsenal of 1,500 warheads. Reduction to that level was among the options proposed by the armed services in 1991. The United States can simply announce it is willing to implement cuts to that level and invite Russia to reciprocate. Verification rules currently in practice will suffice to monitor compliance.

Russia would be willing to reduce to much lower levels. Authoritative officials there have spoken in track II discussions of a ceiling of 500 warheads. Even that may exceed the level that Russia can afford to maintain in the next decade. Reductions to the 500 level would necessitate changes in nuclear strategy by both sides. No longer would they be capable of shooting first in a crisis in hopes of destroying large numbers of a rival's missiles before they can be launched. They would have to abandon as well their current strategy of threatening first use of nuclear arms to deter attack by nonnuclear means.

Reductions below the 500 level would require expanding the negotiations to include all other nuclear-armed countries. While that is possible, it will require much more amicable political relations among them. Although reduction to much below 500 warheads may not yet be feasible, it remains a worthy goal.

STEERING A COOPERATIVE COURSE

The United States can do little on its own to reduce the new nuclear dangers. Russia's cooperation is essential. That will require a midcourse correction in American policy toward Russia—a greater willingness to satisfy Russia's security needs and much more comprehensive political and economic engagement with the aim of promoting democracy and prosperity there. Such a course will encounter strong headwinds in Washington unless the American foreign policy establishment rethinks its approach to security.

Politically, the United States continues to take actions that undermine the supporters of cooperative security in Russia. One was to expand NATO to Poland, Hungary, and the Czech Republic, and eventually elsewhere in Eastern Europe. Another is to test and deploy ballistic missile defenses that will require revising the ABM Treaty or scrapping it if Russia does not agree to the revisions. Whether these actions serve American interests is open to serious doubt. It is one thing to ignore Russia's interests while acting in America's interests and quite another to jeopardize American security by acting unilaterally when cooperation would provide better protection.

Allying with Eastern European states is hardly warranted, even on realist grounds. Russia currently poses no danger to their security. As the war in Chechnya shows, it is barely strong enough to preserve its own territorial integrity, let alone to threaten its neighbors. With memories of Afghanistan still fresh, Russia's leaders and generals, not just its people, have little appetite for foreign adventure. Even if vengeful nationalists bent on aggression were to come to power in Moscow, they would first have to restore Russia's military might, leaving ample time for the United States to extend security guarantees to Eastern Europe.

"Expand or die" may have been a popular slogan for some NATO traditionalists, but it was inaction in Bosnia, not elsewhere in Eastern Europe, that was marginalizing the alliance in the early 1990s. The Partnership for Peace, promoting military-to-military contact and joint training for peacekeeping, was an adequate response to Eastern Europe's security needs.

The most plausible grounds for expanding NATO were a fear of renewed rivalry for influence in Eastern Europe between Germany and Russia and the hope that American involvement could head it off. Yet it did not follow that the competition would take military form. Indeed, by expanding NATO, the United States was itself militarizing the competition. Poles, Czechs, Hungarians, and other Eastern Europeans were not attracted to Germany but to Europe. The European Union or a new economic community was a more appropriate way to satisfy their political desire to join a Western club.

Leaving Russia out, however, will needlessly alienate Russia's westernizers and antagonize its ultranationalists, making cooperation to reduce the new nuclear dangers and to meet other pressing security concerns unsustainable.

NATO expansion was driven by American domestic politics, not American national interests. Pressure to expand came from those of Eastern European extraction, who understandably wanted the United States to embrace their native lands and whose partisan allegiance, once solidly Democratic, has been hotly contested in the past five presidential elections. The concentration of Polish-Americans and other East European ethnic groups in states with substantial electoral votes like Illinois, Michigan, New York, and Wisconsin was a major consideration in President Clinton's decision to endorse NATO expansion in October 1996, a month before the election.[19] Republicans eager to court the ethnic vote to secure their majority in Congress and Pentagon contractors desperate for new markets to offset the shrinking global demand for arms also backed expansion.

The foreign policy establishment was divided. On one side were realists like Henry Kissinger, who sought to head off renewed competition for influence in Eastern Europe and who saw no need to defer to a weak Russia, and Eastern European émigrés like UN ambassador Madeleine Albright and State Department adviser Charles Gati, whose sympathies lay with their homelands. On the other side were realists like George Kennan and Paul Nitze, who believed the best way to ease Eastern Europe's insecurity was to strengthen Westernoriented, democratic-minded forces in Russia. The Clinton administration was itself divided, with Secretary of Defense William Perry and the joint chiefs of staff opposed to NATO expansion and National Security Adviser Lake in favor. A September 1993 speech by Lake kicking off the campaign for "enlargement of the world's free community of market democracies"—the word "expansion" was rejected as too aggressive—rationalized NATO expansion in terms of liberal internationalism, not realism.[20] In the end the president was moved to put Eastern Europe first.

To assuage Russian amour propre, the Clinton administration crafted a Founding Act on Mutual Relations and Security between NATO and Russia. The act, signed on April 27, 1997, in Paris, has been a dead letter ever since. Having pledged to cooperate "to the broadest possible degree" on arms control, nonproliferation, theater missile defense, conflict prevention, and peacekeeping and to exchange information on military doctrines, budgets, and programs, the parties did little of the sort. The act established a NATO-Russian permanent joint council as a "mechanism for consultations, coordination, and to the maximum extent possible, where appropriate, for joint decisions and joint action with respect to security issues of common concern." It has become, in the words of former administration officials William Perry and Ashton Carter, "more of a diplomatic debating society than a catalyst for practical NATO-Russia cooperation."[21] The reason is that the United States refuses to take up serious issues in it.

One such issue is ballistic missile defense. The American impulse for unilateralism is no more evident than its premature pursuit of this technologically unproven protection against an over-the-horizon threat. Ballistic missile defense may excite the imaginations of go-it-alone Republicans and whet the appetites of Pentagon contractors, but it will only get in the way of dealing with more clear and present nuclear dangers in Russia. Such defenses can easily be overwhelmed. Deploying them gives China an incentive to add to its nuclear force and Russia a disincentive to reduce its own. It will also arouse animosity in both countries and bring disrepute on officials there who favor cooperation with United States.

Like NATO expansion, ballistic missile defense is largely being driven by partisan politics. Hypersensitive to accusations of weakness and eager to deny the Republicans a campaign issue, the Clinton administration adopted "hugging tactics." Like infantry units on a battlefield trying to avoid bombardment, it maneuvered to stay as close as it could to its G.O.P. opponents by accelerating the development of missile defenses.

Avoiding actions that cause a neuralgic reaction in Russia is necessary but not sufficient to create political conditions conducive to cooperative security. The United States also needs to be more proactive in helping Russia's democrats lay the institutional foundations of Russian democracy. Political reform should have a higher priority for the United States than economic restructuring in Russia. It has not.

The American approach to economic reform in Russia has been comparable to the one it adopted for many developing countries. Its advice often has been doctrinaire—prescribing bitter medicine it would not be willing to swallow itself. Hiding behind the IMF, which set the terms for economic aid, the United States confined itself largely to humanitarian and technical assistance on a bilateral basis. The paltry amount it provided was hardly commensurate with Russia's importance to American security.

The question is, Should Russia be treated like any another developing country, or do the nuclear dangers it poses require something more? An apt comparison might be the treatment of South Korea, where the United States did not let free market dogma stand in the way of meeting that country's needs. Despite understandable qualms about many of its ally's economic practices, it provided South Korea substantial assistance for years. During the Asian economic crisis of 1997, when South Korea got in trouble because of excessive foreign borrowing by its private sector and the unregulated profligacy of its banks, the United States put together a $57 billion rescue package to help inoculate it from further financial contagion. IMF aid was initially conditioned on tough terms that Washington had been seeking in bilateral trade talks with Seoul, but the United States relaxed the conditions when they proved so onerous that they threatened to embitter Korean-American relations.

Consonant with a cooperative security approach, the United States could advance American objectives by more comprehensive economic engagement with Russia. Targeted economic aid could be devoted to such purposes as reform of Russia's criminal code and judicial procedure, improvements in law enforcement to undercut protection rackets by organized crime, securities and bank regulation and proper accounting practices, fiscal reform to institute regular and fair tax collection, and development of a state-run social security system.

Cooperative security must extend beyond nuclear and military matters to address Russia's broader political and economic needs. Above all, it requires the United States to forgo taking temporary advantage of Russia and to seek mutual and reciprocal ways to solve common problems. That, in turn, will require overcoming the political impediments to cooperative security in the United States. The concluding chapter suggests ways to do that.

10

A MIDCOURSE CORRECTION
WITH RUSSIA

The combination of laissez-faire ideas, social Darwinism, and geopolitical realism that prevailed in the United States and the United Kingdom stood in the way of any hope for an open society in Russia. If the leaders of these countries had had a different view of the world, they could have established firm foundations for a global open society.

—George Soros, February 1997[1]

Even with the brutal war in Chechnya near a dead end, Russia still seethes with communal and social tensions. As the economy sputters, then plunges to new depths, and investors take flight, millions of impoverished Russians eke out a mean existence alongside a tiny class of nouveaux riches. In such circumstances, some observers fear a restoration of autocracy or the coming of neofascism and urge American preparedness for a new cold war. Others believe that Russia will muddle through and that, a generation from now, it will resemble the rest of Europe, perhaps poorer but no more aggressive and no less democratic.

Russia's future, in short, is unknowable. So, too, is the best course for the United States to take with respect to it. Like sailing a ship on a cloudy night with a malfunctioning Global Positioning System, one way to cope with uncertainty is to steer by dead reckoning. That requires a navigator to know where he wants to go and where he has been. If a ship does not have a destination, any course will take it there. The more accurately the navigator can chart where the ship has been, the better his fix on its present location and the less likely he is to stray very far off course.

The United States has never set a clear goal, however. The breakup of the Soviet Union has vied for priority with control of loose nukes, promotion of democracy, and reform of the economy. That has made it difficult to steer a steady course.

Today, the United States has two overriding objectives in Russia: to prevent proliferation in the immediate future and to foster a peaceful and prosperous democracy over the long haul. It is arguable how much the United States could have done in the past to foster democracy or prosperity in Russia, although it might have tried much harder. What is incontestable is that it could have done much more to reduce the new nuclear dangers.

That would have required the United States to plot a common course with Russia. Yet close tracking of U.S.-Russian relations during the period 1985–94 shows U.S. unwillingness to engage in sustained cooperation:

◆ The United States hailed the Soviet Union's withdrawal from Eastern Europe and Afghanistan while doing little to ease Gorbachev's way out.

◆ The United States encouraged German unification while insisting that a united Germany remain in NATO. It facilitated Gorbachev's acquiescence by promising not to expand NATO eastward, then reneged on its promise. That could play into the hands of ultra-nationalists in Russia who are bent on avenging its humiliation, much as the Nazis exploited the Peace of Paris to advance their cause in Germany after World War I.

◆ Taking advantage of Moscow's willingness to cooperate, Washington pushed it to the limit in every negotiation to reduce arms. Now it wants to renegotiate, even violate, the Anti-Ballistic Missile Treaty, the keystone of arms control that has remained in force since 1972. Revanchists in Russia could exploit the unequal arms treaties as a rallying cry in the future, much as rightists in Japan did in the 1930s when they rebelled against Shidehara diplomacy and renounced Washington and London Treaties' limits on Japan's navy.

◆ Washington was slow to cooperate in purchasing nuclear material from Russia and taking other prudent steps to control loose nukes there.

◆ The United States preached the benefits of democracy and free markets. While it was liberal with its advice, it was not as free with aid that Russia desperately needed to attain those aims. That has helped to poison the politics of reform in Russia for some time to come.

To the American foreign policy establishment, these judgments may sound harsh. Unfortunately, they are warranted.

Washington's fitful cooperation with Moscow had unintended consequences not only in Russia but also in faraway places. For instance, it may have hardened North Korea's determination to obtain firm quid pro quos before agreeing to give up nuclear arming and to retain some of its nuclear leverage in order to ensure that the United States lived up to its end of the bargain. "We watched how you dealt with the Russians," said a senior North Korean diplomat in 1993. "We will not let that happen to us."[2]

THE POLITICS OF COOPERATIVE SECURITY

What accounts for American failure to cooperate? First, most U.S. officials had common beliefs or assumptions—*shared images*—about Soviet behavior and international relations generally. These shared images were suffused with realism, blinding officials to the evidence that Gorbachev and Shevardnadze meant what they said about common security. Such preconceptions fueled American skepticism about the chances of cooperating with the Soviet Union to advance U.S. security interests, leading Washington to act unilaterally or else to push to the limit in negotiations instead of trying to meet Moscow partway. While the American foreign policy establishment did give the Bush and Clinton administrations leeway for deal making with Moscow, it was so imbued with realism that it never quite overcame its skepticism to lend all-out support to cooperative security.

A second explanation is *domestic politics*. The American public was mostly supportive of cooperation with Moscow.[3] Ethnic groups with roots in Eastern Europe were actively opposed, however. So were unilateralists on the right wing of the Republican Party. Unilateralism has been a particular passion of dispensationalists on the Christian right who take the United Nations, the Council on Foreign Relations, "global governance," and "the new world order" as signs of the imminent coming of an Antichrist who will impose dictatorship on the world.[4]

A third explanation is *bureaucratic politics*. Government agencies have organizational interests that impeded cooperation with Moscow or disinclined them to bear the costs.

Table 1 lists instances when Moscow offered to cooperate and Washington did or did not reciprocate, and why. Examining the impediments to cooperative security reveals the potential for overcoming some of them.

ORGANIZATIONAL INTERESTS

In bureaucratic politics within the executive branch, the main impediment remains the unwillingness of agencies to sacrifice a portion of their budgets to pay the price of cooperation. Other organizational interests antithetical to cooperative security have weakened since the cold war's end. That applies especially to agency resistance to dealing with the new nuclear dangers.

The State Department has an interest in good relations with other governments. That inclines it to favor cooperation with all but enemy governments, like the Soviet Union during the cold war. Advocating accommodation with the Soviets was no way to advance a career in the Foreign Service. Moreover, Moscow was hardly a pleasant place to be posted during the cold war. The experience left many Soviet specialists with an abiding antagonism toward their host government. With the coming of Gorbachev and the collapse of communism, that antagonism dissipated, and the State Department's interest in good relations with the host government of the day reasserted itself. Because the United States did not recognize the other Soviet republics, maintaining good relations meant, in practice, dealing with Moscow. Indeed, as the Soviet Union began to come apart, the Foreign Service suffered somewhat from a Moscow-centric view of the republics.

The State Department also has an interest in negotiating with other governments. That interest does not necessarily lead career officials to favor diplomatic give-and-take, especially when they expect that negotiations will prove contentious at home or fruitless and that the negotiators will take the blame. That was decidedly so with arms control talks with the Soviet Union during much of the cold war. Purges of arms controllers by the Nixon and Reagan administrations reinforced the inclination of professional diplomats to delegate that treacherous task to outsiders.[5]

TABLE 1. COOPERATIVE SECURITY: DID THE UNITED STATES PLAY AND WHY?

DATE	SOVIET UNION	UNITED STATES	EXPLANATION
10/11–12/86	Accepts zero option on INF at Reykjavik, agrees to abolish nuclear arms on condition of no SDI tests for ten years	Agrees to nuclear abolition but wants to test SDI after five years	Bureaucratic politics
1986–87	Seeks negotiated end to war in Afghanistan	Rejects	Realism
4/13–15/87	Asks for political accord, coalition government in Kabul	Insists Soviet Union withdraw first	Realism
12/8/87	INF Treaty signed at Washington Summit		Cooperative security
2/8/88	Sets deadline for withdrawal from Afghanistan	Insists Moscow end arming, reneging on its 1985 pledge to stop arms flow when Soviet troops leave; seeks fall of Najibullah	Realism, domestic politics
12/7/88	Unilateral cut of 500,000 troops	Bush dismisses as "small but a good start," pushes FOTL	Realism
	Agrees to deep cuts in strategic arms	Bush delays START	Realism
2/89	Seeks international conference on Afghan civil war	Tacit cooperation to let Afghans "stew in their own juices"	Realism
5/11, 5/30/89	Proposes asymmetric cuts in conventional forces to equal level	Reversing long-held stand on equal ceilings, seeks higher ceiling of 30,000 troops for U.S. in Europe	Realism
	Unilaterally removes 500 tactical warheads and proposes ban	Opposes short-range nuclear arms talks	Realism

(cont. on next page)

TABLE 1. COOPERATIVE SECURITY (CONT.)

DATE	SOVIET UNION	UNITED STATES	EXPLANATION
5/89–9/89	Urges Communists to enter coalition in Poland, loosens restrictions on German emigration	Status quo-plus policy sets new tests for cooperation	Realism
9/21/89	Will dismantle radar at Krasnoyarsk, sign START without limits on SDI; proposes side letter on SLCMs	Focuses on chemical arms ban instead of START; turns down limits on SLCMs	Realism
11/9/89	Berlin Wall falls	Low-key reaction in public but privately urges rapid German unification, united Germany in NATO	Realism
12/2–3/89	At Malta shows itself "malleable" on unification, asks for easing on trade	Agrees to MFN but conditionally and not now	Domestic politics
	Seeks expanded role for CSCE	Rejects	Realism
1/31/90	Unilateral cut in conventional forces, seeks deeper cuts	Seeks 225,000 ceiling on U.S. troops in Europe, 30,000 higher than for Soviet Union	Realism, domestic politics
2/4/90	Demands no NATO expansion to east if united Germany in NATO	Agrees, then reneges	Realism
2/7–9/90–3/19/90	Accepts side letter on SLCMs instead of START limits, ALCM counting rule	Wants ban on land-based MIRVs	Bureaucratic politics, domestic politics
5/31–6/3/90	Accepts united Germany in NATO	Nine assurances; asks Lithuania to suspend declaration of independence, negotiate with Moscow	Cooperative security

TABLE 1. COOPERATIVE SECURITY (CONT.)

DATE	SOVIET UNION	UNITED STATES	EXPLANATION
	Seeks MFN, aid	No change in nuclear strategy	Realism
		Agrees if emigration laws eased, embargo on Lithuania lifted, talks with Vilnius held	Domestic politics
7/9–10/90	Seeks aid	Aid only if Moscow reforms economy first and cuts aid to Cuba, defense spending	Realism, liberalism
8/2–4/90	Signs joint statement condemning Iraqi aggression	Invites Soviet military to join Gulf coalition	Cooperative security
9/9/90	Agrees to threaten "additional steps," demands cease-fire, wants Mideast peace conference if Iraq withdraws	Accepts Soviet collaboration in Middle East "to resolve all conflicts" there	Cooperative security
	Asks $4–5 billion in aid	Gets Saudi Arabia to extend $4 billion line of credit	Cooperative security
1/28/91	Agrees to insist on Iraqi withdrawal	Agrees to Mideast peace conference in joint statement	Cooperative security
2/15/91	Seeks negotiated settlement to head off ground war	Sets nonnegotiable demands	Realism
3/91, 6/11/91	Asks for $1.5 billion credit guarantee to buy grain	Approves	Domestic politics
5/31/91	Asks aid for reform, membership in G-7, World Bank, I.M.F.	Rejects grand bargain, invites Gorbachev to G-7	Realism, liberalism

(cont. on next page)

TABLE 1. COOPERATIVE SECURITY (CONT.)

DATE	SOVIET UNION	UNITED STATES	EXPLANATION
9/25/91	Unilateral arms cuts reciprocated	Global, unilateral withdrawal of certain nuclear arms, partial deactivation	Bureaucratic politics
1/92	Russia seeks cuts to 2,000 warheads	Wants 4,700 ceiling on warheads	Realism, bureaucratic politics
1/92	Ukraine balks at signing START, NPT, shipping out warheads	Withholds aid, threatens isolation	Realism
2/92–9/93	Russia revives grand bargain of aid for reform	Grants humanitarian aid but no grand bargain	Domestic politics
	Russia seeks aid for securing, dismantling of nuclear arms	Slow to provide aid	Domestic politics
5/6/92	Russia sells cryogenic rocket engines to India	Imposes economic sanctions	Domestic politics
2/23/93	Ukraine deactivates some SS-19 missiles	Promises aid, security partnership if Kiev begins dismantling	Cooperative security
4/3–4/94	Russia agrees not to transfer technology to India for making rocket engines	Relents on engine sales to India	Cooperative security
1/14/94	Ukraine to transfer warheads to Russia for proceeds of their HEU if Russia forgives oil, gas debts	Advances Russia $60 million for warhead dismantling	Cooperative security
	Russia agrees to sell U.S. 500 metric tons of HEU for $11.5 billion	Reneges	Domestic politics
10/9–12/94	Kazakhstan gives U.S. 600 kg of HEU	Gives humanitarian aid to Kazakhstan	Cooperative security

The State Department has an interest in preventing proliferation as well, but that interest was never close to its essence, the roles and missions deemed critical by career members of the Foreign Service. It mattered much less than maintaining good relations with other governments, as is all too evident in past U.S. dealings with Israel, Pakistan, India, and South Africa. Nonproliferation has low status among generalists in the Foreign Service, who were content to let technical experts in the civil service or the Arms Control and Disarmament Agency (A.C.D.A.) take on this chore. With the demise of A.C.D.A. and its absorption by State, this function may assume higher status, but it is still not seen as essential. To the extent that cooperation with Russia to prevent proliferation has come to be seen as a way of advancing the department's interests in good relations and negotiating, however, career officials favor it.

The Department of Energy has a conflict of interest in regard to the new nuclear dangers. Traditionally, it has had responsibility for designing and building nuclear warheads and for promoting nuclear power. Neither of these responsibilities inclined it to see the prevention of proliferation as a pressing concern. Quite to the contrary, some in the weapons labs have seen proliferation as a rationale for continued nuclear arming, even resumption of nuclear testing.

With the collapse of the Soviet Union, however, the demand for new warhead designs from the armed services has contracted, and a comprehensive ban on nuclear tests has led the labs to gravitate to new roles and missions. One area of congressional concern and budgetary growth is preventing proliferation, which can take advantage of the labs' expertise in warhead security and dismantling as well as intelligence assessment.

While the labs' interest in nonproliferation has grown, it is still far from their dominant role, or raison d'être. That remains "stockpile stewardship," the current euphemism for ensuring that the warheads still in the nuclear arsenal are safe and reliable and retaining the expertise to replace them when they decay.

Perhaps the most notable shift in interests in favor of coping with the new nuclear dangers has occurred in the army, navy, and air force. Acquiring the capabilities they need to carry out their responsibilities is the armed services' constant preoccupation in a world without the Red Army. As the defense budget has declined from its cold war peak, they cannot afford to waste money on nuclear capabilities they never expect to use.

That is no longer a problem for the army, which gave up the last of its nuclear arms in 1991. It is a major concern of the navy, which is internally riven among the carrier navy, the surface navy, and the undersea navy. Naval aviators were only too happy to remove all nuclear arms from surface ships in 1991 to free them for conventional missions. The sailors have always resented the submariners and initially resisted civilian pressure to purchase nuclear-armed Polaris submarines forty years ago. The navy now prefers to operate fewer missile-carrying submarines, especially if that lets it keep all ten of its expensive carrier battle groups instead.

The most dramatic redefinition of interest has taken place in the air force, whose organizational essence since its inception has been strategic bombing: striking targets in urban industrial areas instead of targets on the battlefield. In the belief that strategic bombing would degrade the enemy's ability and will to resist, it acquired substantial numbers of nuclear arms during the cold war. Since the collapse of the Soviet threat, however, it has seen the value in conventional bombing, which has become its essence. That shift was evident in the promotion of aviators from the Tactical Air Command to top posts in the air force, including the command of its intraservice rival, the Strategic Air Command. It also was evident in the mid-1980s in the change of S.A.C.'s motto from "Peace Is Our Profession," which implied nuclear deterrence, to "We Are Warriors," which strongly implied the use of conventional weapons. This revived interest, aided by improvements in guidance technology, has led the air force to tout its effectiveness at precision bombing of strategic targets without having to resort to nuclear arms.

To sustain their capabilities and budgets, the armed services need threats, not wars, and Russia is no longer much of a threat. Nuclear proliferation is one, but nuclear sites, as the air force learned to its dismay in Iraq, are not easy targets to locate or to strike, and no amount of threat inflation can turn the most likely proliferators—North Korea, Iran, and Iraq—into foes of any consequence. The American public has never supported war simply to prevent a state from developing nuclear arms, nor has the government ever seriously contemplated launching a war solely for that purpose.[6] Counterproliferation is not enough of a mission to justify the excessive forces that the Pentagon has retained since the demise of the Red Army.

Cooperation with Russia to reduce the new nuclear dangers would undergird American conventional superiority and make it easier for the armed services to justify acquisition of new conventional weapons without having to waste money on nuclear arms they do not need. The services prefer not to pay for such cooperation out of the defense budget, but resistance in recent years to reducing the number and role of nuclear arms in American strategy has come from civilians in the Pentagon, not the uniformed military.

DOMESTIC POLITICS

To judge from what they tell pollsters, most Americans support cooperation with Russia, especially to deal with the new nuclear dangers. The Republican leadership in Congress does not. Unilateralism, not cooperative security, has long been a staple of the right wing of the party, especially in its southern and western strongholds. So long as the Democrats shrink from openly challenging the Republican majority on this issue, partisan politics will remain a key impediment to cooperation.

Yet partisan politics does not operate in a vacuum. Russia lacks a well-organized constituency in the United States. That is not the case for Poland, Ukraine, and, to a lesser extent, other Eastern European countries. Divided between Russia-firsters and Eastern Europe-firsters, the foreign policy establishment also was slow to warm up to Moscow. Most Soviet experts in the establishment were initially skeptical of Gorbachev's intentions and hostile to cooperation. Many did come around to dealing with Moscow, but they tended to offer fewer proposals worth trying than reasons why none of them would work.

The foreign policy establishment, supposedly a bastion of liberal internationalism, has been surprisingly lukewarm about cooperative security. Most experts in the academic world, think tanks, and other nongovernmental organizations have been antagonistic to the idea if they thought about it at all.

Proliferation experts are a prime example. They tend to concentrate on denying states the means of bomb making. Yet denial is inadequate. It can buy time and provide early warning, but it cannot succeed forever. The interdiction of supply has to be supplemented by efforts to reduce demand. Unlike a strategy of pure denial, which threatens proliferators with economic and political isolation, convincing countries not to build the Bomb requires cooperating with them, however unsavory they may be. Countries that seek nuclear arms are insecure. They need reassurance to ease their insecurity. Trying to isolate them or force them to forgo nuclear arming could well backfire. Yet proliferation experts spend most of their time drawing attention to the circumvention of export controls, for instance, the flow of nuclear material and missile components to Iran. By calling attention to the problem instead of seeking a solution, they help mobilize support for coercive measures, ranging from economic sanctions and antimissile defenses to air strikes and other forms of counterproliferation. That puts them on the side of those who oppose cooperative efforts to reduce the demand for such arms, even though that is not necessarily their intention.

SHARED IMAGES OF REALISM

Why was the American foreign policy establishment so slow to recognize the shifts in Soviet policy under Gorbachev and Shevardnadze and even slower to favor cooperation with Moscow? The widely shared belief in realism among foreign policy practitioners in the government and outsiders who try to influence them is the main reason. So strong was its hold, especially among true believers, that they tried to reinterpret changes in Soviet policy as a sign of weakness, a temporary expediency designed to buy time for the Soviet Union to regain its strength. So resilient is the faith in realism even today that the dominant interpretations of recent history fail to acknowledge that the Soviet Union acted on the basis of common security and that the United States failed to reciprocate—with adverse consequences for American security. The widely held belief in realism remains the principal impediment to cooperative security with Russia.

Shared images of realism also pervade American news coverage of Russia and the rest of the world. That is understandable because American sources, especially U.S. officials and members of the foreign policy establishment, dominate American news.

News is not what happened. News is what somebody says has happened. That is especially so when the happenings are invisible to all but the participants, as most foreign policy events are. News gathering consists of organizational routines, or standard operating procedures, for selecting and excluding news sources. Among the most important of these procedures are legwork, interviewing sources in person or by telephone rather than poring over documents or analyzing statistics, and beats and bureaus, sites that reporters regularly cover, where news is produced and disseminated routinely through press releases, news conferences, or background briefings. Reinforcing these routines are journalists' conventions for selecting the stories that they consider newsworthy and the sources they consider authoritative.[7] Covering a beat means making occasional checks with a network of contacts or potential news sources—above all, authoritative sources, people in formal positions of authority in the institutions where reporters are routinely located.

American journalists regarded the president of the United States as a more authoritative source about the Soviet Union than the general secretary of the Communist Party of the Soviet Union. Undue reliance on authoritative American sources is only partly offset by another journalistic convention, balance or fairness, which obliges reporters to cite sources from various sides of a controversy.

As a result of the routines and conventions of journalism, much of the news about the Soviet Union did not originate in Moscow but in Washington, where American officials made policy pronouncements, leaked intelligence assessments, and floated trial balloons, and members of Congress, experts, and interest groups criticized and offered policy alternatives. News of the Soviet Union was reflected and refracted through the lenses of outsiders, mostly U.S. officials or American experts who had a vested interest in their characterizations. Insofar as reporters and editors are part of the American foreign policy establishment and rely on it as a source for news, it is not surprising that their facts and interpretation largely reflect establishment beliefs.

Perhaps the most important convention is that news consists of "stories." Once a story line becomes established, it is quite impervious to change, and one of the longest-running stories was the cold war. Journalists kept trying to fit the Soviet-American story into that cold war frame even as Gorbachev was shattering it.

It is a convention of journalism as well that stories about conflict are more newsworthy than stories about cooperation, and stories about war, even cold war, are the most newsworthy of all. That helps explain why, even though cooperation between foes may be more unexpected than conflict—and thus more newsworthy—news coverage concentrated on the continuing differences between Russia and the United States more than on their occasional resolution.

Tough talk makes headlines. Official sources in favor of coercion dominate the news. The more forceful their policy, the more attention they get. In this sense, the news is hostile to cooperation.

The news media act as the central nervous system of the body politic. If they do not perform this function well, they disorient the political system—blinding it to impending trouble overseas, muffling or distorting reactions from home and abroad, and misinforming audiences about government actions. To the extent that news coverage of the world is dominated by American news sources, news making creates a closed circle of Americans talking to themselves. In so doing, the news mutes and distorts information from abroad, in this case, efforts by the Soviet Union, and later Russia, to cooperate with the United States.

MAKING USE OF NGOS

One way to get around the political impediments to government-to-government cooperation is to make use of nongovernmental organizations (NGOs). In coping with the new nuclear dangers, NGOs have shown that they can go where governments fear to tread. They have been instrumental in nurturing the seeds of democracy in Russia. They also have mustered political support for a more cooperative course by the United States. To promote change in Russia it is essential to harness the NGO community.

With support from private foundations, American NGOs, along with their Russian and European counterparts, are protecting the rights of minorities and strengthening the rule of law in Russia. They are helping to educate and train thousands of Russians in law, accounting, journalism, and other professions.[8] They are providing financial and technical support to a host of human rights, legal, environmental, educational, and other indigenous organizations. They are operating online news networks and promoting business ventures.

In the field of security, a private initiative by financier George Soros funded research grants for scientists in Russia and the other former Soviet republics for two years to work on civilian projects to discourage them from selling their nuclear know-how abroad.

One of the most significant contributions by NGOs has been track II diplomacy by nonofficials, former officials, and officials acting in their unofficial capacity. Some track II talks served as extragovernmental channels of communication that had little direct effect on U.S. or Soviet policy but did inform a circle of experts in and out of government on nuclear and economic matters. Other track II efforts went beyond exchanging ideas and floated proposals for reforming the Soviet economy. A few even instituted ways to deal with the new nuclear dangers.

Pugwash was one of the early examples of track II. Founded by American, Soviet, and European nuclear scientists in 1957 and later enlarged to include social and political scientists from top Soviet institutes and American and European think tanks, Pugwash broke down communication barriers to play a pivotal role in the Limited Test Ban Treaty and to help prepare the ground for strategic arms talks.[9] Another key forum for track II was the Socialist International, where European socialists developed personal ties and exchanged ideas with Soviet "new thinkers." Other influential track II channels were the Committee on International Security and Arms Control of the National Academy of Sciences, the Soviet-American Disarmament Study group (known as the "Doty Group" for its founder, Professor Paul Doty of Harvard), the International Physicians for the Prevention of Nuclear War, the Dartmouth Group, and the United Nations Association.[10]

Once Gorbachev assumed power, such channels proliferated. Prominent former officials like Richard Nixon, Brent Scowcroft, Henry Kissinger, and Zbigniew Brzezinski and businessmen like Henry Kendall served as important informants and go-betweens for the Reagan and Bush administrations.[11] The information imparted in track II served as a corrective to intelligence assessments and diplomatic dispatches and was instrumental in persuading Secretary of State Shultz to reopen talks with Moscow.[12] Kissinger pressed President Bush to support rapid unification of Germany, and Nixon and Brzezinski urged him to aid the Soviet Union.[13]

Track II diplomacy by outside experts Graham Allison, Robert Blackwill, Jeffrey Sachs, and Grigory Yavlinsky and by officials acting in an unofficial capacity tried but failed to arrange a "grand bargain" of U.S. aid for Soviet and later Russian reform. Track II discussions initiated in 1987 by the Federation of Atomic Scientists with the Soviet Academy of Sciences devised ways of verifying warhead dismantlement and fissile material controls. In an effort to arrange cooperative verification, the Natural Resources Defense Council and the Federation of Atomic Scientists held track II discussions in Moscow in October 1991 and in Kiev in December 1991 with scientists from Los Alamos and Livermore national laboratories, representatives of the Soviet and Russian foreign ministries, the scientific directors of the two Soviet weapons labs, and senior officials from the Ministry of Atomic Power and Industry acting in their unofficial capacity.[14] In track II talks in October 1991 with Viktor Mikhailov, Soviet minister of atomic energy, M.I.T. physicist Thomas Neff tried to broker a deal for the United States to buy highly enriched uranium that Russia was extracting from its warheads. Track II talks sponsored by the W. Alton Jones Foundation in June 1992 inspired Clinton administration officials to reverse course and try cooperative security with both Ukraine and Russia on denuclearization and Foreign Minister Andrei Kozyrev to push for lower levels of alert on Russia's strategic forces.

Some track II contacts brought about change more directly. One of the most unusual was arranged by the National Resources Defense Council (N.R.D.C.) in 1986. The Threshold Test Ban Treaty signed in 1974, which limited underground nuclear weapons tests to an explosive force of 150 kilotons of TNT, and a related treaty signed two years later similarly limiting peaceful nuclear explosions remained unratified. The Reagan administration was refusing to submit them to the Senate. Opponents in the Pentagon, the weapons labs, and Congress, eager to test new nuclear warheads as well as directed-energy devices for use in ballistic missile defenses, claimed the limits were unverifiable and that Soviet tests had exceeded them. The first claim was disputed by reputable seismologists and the second by the intelligence community. In May 1986, after track II talks with Evgeny Velikov of the Soviet Academy of Sciences, Adrian DeWind, chairman of the N.R.D.C., who had helped negotiate the treaty, and staff physicist Thomas Cochran arranged for permission to install seismic monitoring devices at three points near the Soviet test site in Kazakhstan, 100 miles west of Semipalatinsk, an area previously off-limits to foreigners. They arranged for similar monitoring by Soviet scientists in Nevada.[15] By comparing the shock waves emitted by natural seismic activity to those from underground nuclear tests, the monitors could better calibrate the size of Soviet tests and help determine whether or not the unratified treaties could be verified without renegotiating them, opening the way to a Comprehensive Test Ban Treaty outlawing all underground nuclear tests. It was a triumph of track II diplomacy.

These are just some of the private initiatives in the period 1985–94 to stimulate cooperative security between the U.S. government and the Soviet Union and its successors or to undertake cooperative security in the face of government inaction.

Track II initiatives often kindle the resentment of government officials. It is not just that, as George Bernard Shaw once put it, "every profession is a conspiracy against the laity." Officials look upon outsiders as meddlesome sources of political pressure rather than as helpful informants and intermediaries, and in some cases, like former President Nixon on Soviet aid and the N.R.D.C. seismic monitoring, pressure was certainly the intent. Outsiders do desire to get their way, or at least demonstrate influence, and too often tend to hear what they want to hear from foreigners. Officials, who have access to a wide range of information sources on other countries, worry that outsiders may be exploited by foreign governments, which can disown an unofficial contact more readily than they can an official one. For these reasons, officials may be all too ready to discount or discredit nongovernmental sources of information, especially when they are discrepant with their own.

Still, there is much to be gained from track II diplomacy. Outsiders are freer to speak their minds to foreigners than are officials. They can sometimes probe more deeply than officials, who know that a probe may reveal as much as it gathers and who therefore are required to act under instruction, keeping them on a short leash. In cases where U.S. intelligence gathering is limited by lack of assets or blinkered by preconceptions, track II diplomacy can open a window onto a closed society.

NGOs cannot function without foundation support. Nurturing democracy and the rule of law in Russia will take at least a generation, and prosperity perhaps will require longer. Yet many program officers and boards of foundations have time horizons almost as short as those of political leaders, driven by the headlines in the *New York Times* and the latest polls. The "been there-done that" frame of mind in foundations is detrimental to sustained effort.

Because track II is usually risky and not always productive, most foundations are reluctant to invest "venture capital" in it. Track II diplomacy also has been adversely affected by dwindling foundation support for peace and security studies. Funding had grown as national security became a headline issue during the Reagan administration. Liberal internationalist foundations responded to the rise of well-financed and highly politicized right-wing foundations. The high point came in 1988, when 171 foundations awarded $123.8 million in grants in the field of peace, security, and international relations, broadly defined. Seventeen foundations accounted for 80 percent of the total. Just two, Ford and MacArthur, provided 30 percent, a sum matched by seven leading right-wing foundations. Ten years later, total funding had dropped to $100 million, of which just $40 million was devoted strictly to peace and security grants.[16] Foundations need to reexamine their patterns of giving not only to support track II efforts but also to fill a larger need: the lack of political support for cooperative security.

Changing Course

Ultimately, NGOs are no substitute for governments. For the United States to achieve its goals with respect to Russia, the government needs to chart a new course of cooperative security. For that to happen it is essential to overcome the political impediments to cooperative security. Above all, that means directly challenging the shared images of realism prevalent in the academic and expert community, the news media, and the rest of the foreign policy establishment.

The United States will not try cooperative security unless it learns from its mistakes. That places a special burden on Russia specialists, arms control experts, and international relations scholars in the academic community, where learning is supposed to take place.

Soviet studies in the United States were well funded during the cold war and enjoyed considerable prestige and some influence outside the academy. It was, however, an area of ideological disputation where dogma all too often displaced empiricism, with the consequence that Soviet specialists, with some notable exceptions, were not especially enlightening about the Gorbachev revolution or its dispiriting aftermath. Now, as new opportunities for studying Russia on the ground, not just in the library, have opened up, funding for research has been cut back. Foundations need to reconsider and grant support for empirical scholarly fieldwork in Russia and collaborative projects with Russians.

Arms controllers have treated proliferation as a technical and functional problem, not a political one. They tend to study the details of a country's nuclear infrastructure but not its internal politics, its foreign policy, or its motives for arming or helping others to do so. Instead of concentrating on coercive ways to stanch the supply of nuclear materials and missile components, they need to encourage cooperative ways of reducing the demand for nuclear arms. That will take a shift in the direction of foundation support.

The study of international relations in the United States is far too theoretical and far less empirical than it should be. Theorists are awarded professorships at the most prestigious universities, while careful empirical work is dismissed as mere journalism. The same is true to a lesser extent for comparative politics. Area studies have fallen into disfavor, and painstaking work on a single country no longer has the cachet of comparative theory. One consequence is that fewer of the best scholars are getting out of the ivory tower and into the field.

Those who are knowledgeable about the politics, culture, and interests of other countries also contribute less to public discourse in the United States than they might. As the academic job market has tightened, schools of thought have become more relentlessly imperialistic, and professional journals less catholic in their taste and more hidebound. Realists have dominated the discourse on security in the nonacademic journal with the largest circulation, *Foreign Affairs.*

A division of labor has developed between the public domain and the academy, with only a small number of scholars, many in think tanks rather than universities, involving themselves in the public debate as authors of op-eds and as sources for reporters. That is partly a function of the narrow reach of journalists' Rolodexes, but it also springs from scholarly disdain for public discourse and the self-promotion of think tanks and institutes that depend on foundation funding and are rewarded for the public attention they get. The foreign policy establishment takes experts seriously. It could benefit by hearing from a broader sample of them.

Foundations may want to reconsider whether publicity is an appropriate measure of whether projects warrant support. They also need to reexamine the pattern of grant making in peace and security. Foundations have increasingly responded to the latest fashion in security studies, broadening security to encompass environment, population growth and migration, economic redistribution, and other issues that affect it. Funding of these concerns has come at the expense of core security matters. To the extent that this work can be

dismissed as tangential or irrelevant by the realists in the foreign policy establishment, however, it may fail to challenge conventional
thinking. More consideration needs to be given to foundation support for cooperative as opposed to coercive ways of attaining traditional security goals.

News coverage will change only when establishment attitudes
do. Journalistic routines and conventions could generate stories on
the domestic political struggle between those who favor coercion
and those who advocate cooperation in dealing with other countries.
That would satisfy the journalists' appetite for conflict. It also would
satisfy their convention of balance.

The cold war was a highly conflictual era of international relations in which antagonism was intensified by ideological difference,
the security dilemma was heightened by the threat of nuclear war,
and American foreign policy was driven by realism. The dominance
of realism is an anachronism in the current era when antagonism is
muted and war among the great powers is highly improbable.
Cooperation can ease the security dilemma. Extensive political and
economic engagement can dissolve what is left of it. Absent cooperation, how long will a renascent Russia, whether ruled by moderate or vengeful nationalists, tolerate the military inferiority that
developed under Gorbachev? Cooperation is both possible and
essential in the rest of the world as well. Absent cooperation, how
will Japan, India, and the rest of Asia adjust to a rising China? Absent
cooperation, how will North and South Korea, or China and Taiwan,
move from confrontation to reconciliation? Absent cooperation,
how will the community of Europe grow without alienating the
United States?

Realists who continue to engage in pure power politics emphasize American military superiority and the need to maintain it. They
understate the costs of using force, not only in terms of the sacrifice
of life and treasure but also in the erosion of public support for foreign involvement. They resist further reduction in military spending. Yet the United States far outspends the rest of the world. Russia,
which ranks second, devotes less than one-third the sum that the
United States does to defense. China, which ranks third, spends less
than one-fourth. Seven of the top ten spenders are U.S. allies.[17] The
United States could afford substantial cuts in defense spending and
still retain its military advantage and its technological edge as insurance against a failure of cooperative security.

Realists also underestimate the opportunity cost of not engaging in cooperative security, where American advantages are even greater than they are in the military realm. Cooperative security is cheap compared to military superiority. No historic enmities stand in the way of American cooperation with other nations. The United States is home to people from many lands, a potential source of understanding about other countries. It has allies who are willing to follow its lead. It is rich enough to pay for more than its share of cooperation. It stands to benefit most from a low-threat environment because it can save more than any other country if it can safely reduce its defense burden.

Realists also misread recent history. In their quest for simplicity, they attach too much importance to the balance of power and the structure of the international system and downplay the inextricable relationship between domestic and foreign policy. In particular, they ignore the power of values and beliefs, which do not march across borders and cannot be deterred by a balance of power. In so doing, realists failed to predict or explain the end of the cold war.[18] Nor have they appreciated much of what has been happening in relations among the great powers since. Another way of thinking about the world is to start at home, to understand state behavior primarily in terms of bureaucratic and domestic politics, and to regard international politics as the projection of domestic forces on the larger arena. That understanding is essential to making cooperative security work.

American unwillingness to cooperate with strangers has been an important impediment to achieving American interests in the world. Time after time, the United States has tried threats to get its way when promises seemed more likely to succeed. Even when it has made promises, it has not always kept them. If the American impulse toward coercive unilateralism is not restrained, the United States will be the loser.

Businessmen grasp what has eluded most realists: that the way to get ahead in the world is to make deals and live up to them. Threats are not ruled out in business—ask any newsdealer—but driving a hard bargain is not the best way to build a lasting relationship, and predatory behavior that drives other firms to ruin is not always the most profitable business practice.

Cooperative security worked when the United States tried it with the Soviet Union and later Russia. It can work elsewhere as well. It can succeed where coercion would fail, and at lower cost. Coercive measures like economic embargoes are costly to the sanctioner as well as to the sanctioned. The burden often falls disproportionately on sectors of the American economy with the political power to undo sanctions. Military force is even more expensive. The foreign policy establishment believes that the United States should be willing to act unilaterally abroad. By a three-to-one majority, though, the American people reject unilateralism.[19] A majority of the foreign policy establishment believes that the United States has less clout in the world today than it did a decade ago and wants it to show more muscle abroad. Again, the American public does not share that view.[20] Most Americans are much more amenable to other forms of overseas engagement, even giving foreign aid, than to military intervention.[21] For policymakers to define America's role in the world in military terms—to emphasize coercion instead of conciliation—may feed the fires of isolationism.

Arms control is premised on an immanent threat of war among the great powers and the need for nuclear deterrence to ensure security. Arms control focuses on numerical reductions and qualitative restraints on the arms race, with the object of stabilizing the nuclear balance of power. Today, the need to prevent the spread of nuclear weapons requires moving beyond traditional arms control to create the political climate needed for a sharp reduction in the number of nuclear arms and a radical diminution in the role that they play in American strategy. Nuclear arms will need to become like gold in international economics: not serving as a store of value or the currency of last resort but being locked up in Fort Knox and ignored. Bringing this about will require countries to take the security interests of other states into account and to satisfy those interests, even at some sacrifice to their own. Although that may be difficult to accomplish, it is politically possible. Failure to do so will imperil America's well-being.

NOTES

CHAPTER 1

1. *This Week with David Brinkley*, ABC-TV, January 22, 1989.
2. George P. Shultz, *Turmoil and Triumph: My Years as Secretary of State* (New York: Charles Scribner's Sons, 1993), pp. 5–6.
3. Gorbachev first used the word "crisis" at a Central Committee plenum on January 1, 1987.
4. The concept was a prominent feature of the report of the Independent Commission on Disarmament and Security Issues, known as the Palme Commission after its chairman, Olof Palme, former prime minister of Sweden. It was first formulated in May 1981 by Egon Bahr, a West German Social Democrat who was a member of the commission: "Security can now only be achieved in common. No longer against each other but only with each other shall we be secure." The commission report, drafted by Johan Jorgen Holst, Emma Rothschild, and Barry Blechman, was prepared for the Second UN Special Session on Disarmament in May 1982. Among the commission members and a signer of the report was Georgy Arbatov.
5. Don Oberdorfer, *The Turn: From the Cold War to a New Era* (New York: Poseidon Press, 1991), p. 321. Gorbachev's remarks are from an Oberdorfer interview with National Security Adviser Colin Powell, who was present; Shultz's reflection is from an interview with Shultz, p. 471. Cf. Shultz, *Turmoil and Triumph*, p. 1106; Mikhail S. Gorbachev, *Memoirs* (New York: Doubleday, 1996), p. 496. After the December 1987 summit, Bush had accompanied Gorbachev to the airport. In the course of their conversation, he had "assured Gorbachev that there should be no doubt about his commitment to cooperation with the Soviet Union." Pavel Palazchenko, *My Years with Gorbachev and Shevardnadze: The Memoir of a Soviet Interpreter* (University Park, Pa.: Pennsylvania State University Press, 1997), pp. 79–80.
6. The term "shared images" is used in Morton H. Halperin, *Bureaucratic Politics and Foreign Policy* (Washington, D.C.: Brookings Institution, 1977), p. 11.
7. Kenneth Waltz, *Theory of International Politics* (Reading, Mass.: Addison-Wesley, 1979), p. 116.
8. Ibid., pp. 102–14. Cf. Edward Hallett Carr, *The Twenty Years' Crisis, 1919–1939* (New York: Harper and Row, 1964), chs. 8, 13.

9. Waltz, *Theory of International Politics*, p. 105.

10. Carr, *Twenty Years' Crisis*, pp. 177–78.

11. Realists try to discredit cooperative security by drawing parallels to the failure of collective security after World War I. For instance, see Barry R. Posen and Andrew L. Ross, "Competing Visions for U.S. Grand Strategy," *International Security* 21, no. 3 (Winter 1996/97): 23–32. Yet cooperative security has nothing to do with collective security, which regards peace as indivisible and requires nations, whether or not they are allied, to band together to deter and resist aggression, by means of economic embargo or war. The era of collective security was short-lived, lasting no more than a decade. The reasons for its failure were set out by Carr in 1939 in his classic work, *The Twenty Years' Crisis*. The League of Nations, he argued, rested on utopian assumptions, all of them tenets of classical liberalism. The principal assumption was that international politics was based on a harmony of interests, in particular, an overriding interest of all nations in peace. The harmony of interest ensured that peace was the normal condition of the world and war an aberration and that the rest of the world would willingly ally against any aggressor nation. A second assumption was that autarky would give way to interdependence because free trade made all nations more prosperous and that free trade gave all nations a stake in peace. An end to autarky also would guarantee the efficacy of economic sanctions against any nation that waged war. A third assumption was that people everywhere shared the same morality and put a high value on peace, prosperity, and the sanctity of contracts (treaties), ensuring the efficacy of international law. A final assumption was that, although leaders might favor war, the people believe in peace, and that democracy would make public opinion an effective force, precluding states from waging war.

12. For an early and elegant statement of cooperative security, see Richard H. Ullman, *Securing Europe* (Princeton, N.J.: Princeton University Press, 1991), especially chs. 3–4.

13. On the concept of a security community, see Karl Deutsch, *Political Community and the North Atlantic Area: International Organization in the Light of Historical Experience* (Princeton, N.J.: Princeton University Press, 1957).

CHAPTER 2

1. Vaclav Havel, "The Power of the Powerless," in *Living in Truth*, ed. Jan Vladislav (London: Faber and Faber, 1986), p. 56.

2. Colin L. Powell, *My American Journey* (New York: Random House, 1995), p. 392.

3. Leon V. Sigal, "Signs of a Soviet Shift: Conventional Forces in Europe," *Bulletin of the Atomic Scientists* 43, no. 10 (December 1987): 16–20.

4. Archie Brown, *The Gorbachev Factor* (New York: Oxford University Press, 1996), p. 124.

5. Ibid., p. 156. Cf. Mikhail S. Gorbachev, *Memoirs* (New York: Doubleday, 1996), pp. 278–79.

6. Coit Blacker, *Hostage to Revolution: Gorbachev and Soviet Security Policies, 1985–1991* (New York: Council on Foreign Relations, 1993), p. 168.

7. Gorbachev, *Memoirs*, pp. 24–27.

8. Stephen F. Cohen, "Gorbachev and the Soviet Reformation," in *Voices of Glasnost: Gorbachev's Reformers Speak*, ed. Stephen F. Cohen and Katrina vanden Heuvel (New York: W. W. Norton, 1989), pp. 15–16.

9. Brown, *Gorbachev Factor*, pp. 78–80, 123–27.

10. For an inside account of his election by a onetime ally, see Yegor Ligachev, *Inside Gorbachev's Kremlin*, trans. Catherine A. Fitzpatrick, Michele A. Berdy, and Dobrochna Dyrcz-Freeman (New York: Pantheon, 1993), pp. 72–79.

11. John W. Parker, *Kremlin in Transition*, vol. 2: *Gorbachev, 1985–1989* (London: Routledge, 1991), pp. 103–4. An expurgated version of the speech was published in the ministry's house organ, *Vestnik*, on August 5, 1987, more than a year after he gave it, perhaps because of his blunt criticism.

12. Don Oberdorfer, *The Turn: From the Cold War to a New Era* (New York: Poseidon Press, 1991), p. 164.

13. William E. Odom, *The Collapse of the Soviet Military* (New Haven: Yale University Press, 1998), pp. 107–10.

14. Parker, *Kremlin in Transition*, vol. 2, p. 181.

15. Anatoly Chernyaev's diary, *Shest' let s Gorbachevym: Po dnevnikovym zapisiam* (Moscow: Progress, 1993), p. 256.

16. Roald Z. Sagdeev, *The Making of a Soviet Scientist: My Adventures in Nuclear Fusion and Space from Stalin to Star Wars* (New York: John Wiley and Sons, 1994), p. 194.

17. Speech to the Federal Assembly of Yugoslavia, *Pravda*, March 17, 1988, pp. 1–2, reprinted in Foreign Broadcast Information Service, FBIS-SOV-88-052, March 17, 1988, p. 28.

18. Clifford G. Gaddy, *The Price of the Past: Russia's Struggles with the Legacy of a Militarized Economy* (Washington, D.C.: Brookings Institution, 1996), pp. 55–56.

19. Ibid., pp. 56–61.

20. Odom, *Collapse of the Soviet Military*, p. 91.

21. Quoted in Dusko Doder and Louise Branson, *Gorbachev: Heretic in the Kremlin* (New York: Viking, 1990), p. 207.

22. Pavel Palazchenko, *My Years with Gorbachev and Shevardnadze: The Memoir of a Soviet Interpreter* (University Park, Pa.: Pennsylvania State University Press, 1997), p. 94.

23. Matthew Evangelista, *Unarmed Forces: The Transnational Movement to End the Cold War* (Ithaca, N.Y.: Cornell University Press, 1999), pp. 156–61, 187–203,

312–16. Gorbachev himself acknowledged the influence of Felipe González, Willy Brandt, Egon Bahr, and other European socialists on his thinking. Thomas Risse-Kappen, "Ideas Do Not Float Freely: Transnational Coalitions, Domestic Structures, and the End of the Cold War," *International Organization* 48, no. 2 (Spring 1994): 201.

24. Brown, *Gorbachev Factor*, pp. 19–21, 48–49, 112–13, 341n93; Cohen and vanden Heuvel, *Voices of Glasnost*, pp. 115–16, 141–42, 160–61, 176–78, 310–11; David Deudney and G. John Ikenberry, "The International Sources of Soviet Change," *International Security* 16, no. 3 (Winter 1991/92): 100–18; Jeff Checkel, "Ideas, Institutions, and the Gorbachev Foreign Policy Revolution," *World Politics* 45, no. 2 (January 1993): 283–85; Risse-Kappen, "Ideas Do Not Float Freely," pp. 185–214; Robert G. Herman, "Identity, Norms and National Security: The Soviet Foreign Policy Revolution and the End of the Cold War," in *The Culture of National Security: Norms and Identity in World Politics*, ed. Peter Katzenstein (New York: Columbia University Press, 1996), pp. 291–98; Sarah E. Mendelsohn, *Changing Course: Ideas, Politics, and the Soviet Withdrawal from Afghanistan* (Princeton, N.J.: Princeton University Press, 1998), pp. 61, 71–91, 103–10; Evangelista, *Unarmed Forces*, pp. 307–12.

25. Some assumed that the zero option was put forth in order to be rejected and that its proponents would succeed in their aim, for instance, Leon V. Sigal, "Kennan's Cuts," *Foreign Policy*, no. 44 (Fall 1981): 70–81.

26. Oberdorfer, *Turn*, p. 158.

27. Parker, *Kremlin in Transition*, vol. 2, p. 60.

28. Mikhail S. Gorbachev, *Perestroika: New Thinking for Our Country and the World* (New York: Harper and Row, 1987), pp. 145–51.

29. Ibid., p. 11.

30. Oberdorfer, *Turn*, p. 161.

31. "Gorbachev CPSU Central Committee Report," *Pravda*, February 26, 1986, reprinted in Foreign Broadcast Information Service, FBIS-SOV-86-038, February 26, 1986, pp. 8–9.

32. Raymond L. Garthoff, *The Great Transition: American-Soviet Relations and the End of the Cold War* (Washington, D.C.: Brookings Institution, 1994), p. 256. For his own understanding of the doctrinal issues, see Gorbachev, *Perestroika*, pp. 133–34.

33. Eduard Shevardnadze, *The Future Belongs to Freedom* (New York: Free Press, 1991), p. 47.

34. Mikhail S. Gorbachev, speech to International Forum for a Nuclear-Free World, *Pravda*, February 14, 1987, excerpted in *Current Digest of the Soviet Press* 39, no. 7 (March 18, 1987): 11. In August 1987 Andrei Kokoshin, deputy director of IMEMO, and Major General Valentin Larionov of the General Staff Academy publicly surfaced the rationale for a change in doctrine by reexamining defensive operations in the 1943 battle of Kursk. Parker, *Kremlin in Transition*, vol. 2, p. 184.

35. Garthoff, *Great Transition*, p. 572.

36. Gorbachev, *Memoirs*, pp. 464–65; Garthoff, *Great Transition*, p. 571; Anatoly Chernyaev, "Gorbachev and the Reunification of Germany: Personal Recollections," in *Soviet Foreign Policy, 1917–1991*, ed. Gabriel Gorodetsky (London: Frank Cass, 1994), p. 158.

37. Brown, *Gorbachev Factor*, p. 242.

38. Garthoff, *Great Transition*, pp. 297, 573–74.

39. Ibid., pp. 574, 588; Gorbachev, *Memoirs*, p. 482.

40. "On the Strategic Line of the USSR with Respect to the UN and Related International Organizations," Central Committee Doc. no. 164/177, August 28, 1989, quoted in Garthoff, *Great Transition*, pp. 401–2.

41. Shevardnadze, *Future Belongs to Freedom*, p. 51.

42. Jack F. Matlock, Jr., *Autopsy on an Empire: The American Ambassador's Account of the Collapse of the Soviet Union* (New York: Random House, 1995), pp. 144–47. Cf. Garthoff, *Great Transition*, pp. 361–62.

43. Palazchenko, *My Years with Gorbachev and Shevardnadze*, p. 101.

44. Speech at the U.S.S.R. Ministry of Foreign Affairs Workers' *Activ* [an *activ* is like a union], July 4, 1997, published September 10, 1987, reprinted in Foreign Broadcast Information Service, FBIS-SOV-87-102, November 3, 1987, p. 89.

45. Carolyn McGiffert Ekedahl and Melvin A. Goodman, *The Wars of Eduard Shevardnadze* (University Park, Pa.: Pennsylvania State University Press, 1997), p. 70.

46. Cohen and vanden Heuvel, *Voices of Perestroika*, p. 327.

47. Garthoff, *Great Transition*, p. 587.

48. Brown, *Gorbachev Factor*, pp. 77–78.

49. Hans-Dietrich Genscher, *Rebuilding a House Divided: A Memoir by the Architect of Germany's Reunification* (New York: Broadway Books, 1998), p. 201.

50. In early 1985, one historian remembers raising the possibility before a group of foreign policy specialists in Washington that the cold war might end some day and suggesting the need to begin thinking about the sort of order that might follow, only to be met with awkward silence. John Lewis Gaddis, *The United States and the End of the Cold War: Implications, Reconsiderations, Provocations* (New York: Oxford University Press, 1992), p. vii.

51. "Will the Cold War Fade Away?" *Time*, July 27, 1987, p. 32.

52. George P. Shultz, *Turmoil and Triumph: My Years as Secretary of State* (New York: Charles Scribner's Sons, 1993), p. 1003.

53. Henry S. Rowen, "Living with a Sick Bear," *National Interest*, no. 2 (Winter 1985/86): 25. For an alternative realist assessment, that Soviet decline would stimulate the loosening of the Western alliance and the spread of nuclear arms, see Kurt M. Campbell, "Prospects and Consequences of Soviet Decline," in *Fateful Visions: Avoiding Nuclear Catastrophe*, ed. Joseph S. Nye, Jr., Graham T. Allison, and Albert Carnesale (Cambridge, Mass.: Ballinger, 1988), pp.

166–69. A cautiously optimistic appraisal came from an adviser to Canada's foreign minister, Franklyn Griffiths, "'New Thinking' in the Kremlin," *Bulletin of the Atomic Scientists* 43, no. 3 (April 1987): 720–24. In 1983 Royal Dutch/Shell, trying assess whether rising prices for energy would make it worthwhile to spend more on oil and natural gas exploration and development, decided not to do so based on a strikingly different scenario for the Soviet Union. Peter Schwartz, *The Art of the Long View: Planning for the Future in an Uncertain World* (New York: Doubleday, 1991), pp. 48–49, 56–59, 64–65.

54. Moshe Lewin, *The Gorbachev Phenomenon: A Historical Interpretation* (Berkeley, Calif.: University of California Press, 1989).

55. For instance, Jack Snyder, "The Gorbachev Revolution: A Waning of Soviet Expansionism?" *International Security* 12, no. 3 (Winter 1987–88): 93–131; Robert Legvold, "Soviet Learning in the 1980s," in *Learning in U.S. and Soviet Foreign Policy*, ed. George W. Breslauer and Philip E. Tetlock (Boulder, Colo.: Westview Press, 1991), especially pp. 694–720.

56. Matlock, *Autopsy on an Empire*, p. 91.

57. Ibid., p. 144. The recollection of the reaction to Gorbachev's UN speech of Robert Hutchings, a key N.S.C. staffer in the Bush years, also is instructive. "While we in the Bush administration paid considerable attention to the passage" on freedom of choice, "what we probably underestimated was the extent to which Gorbachev's rhetorical shift was meant, for internal Soviet consumption, to prepare the ideological ground for radical departures yet to come in Soviet foreign policy." In fact, Gorbachev had been preparing the ground at home since 1985, but Washington remained unimpressed. Robert L. Hutchings, *American Diplomacy and the End of the Cold War: An Insider's Account of U.S. Policy in Europe, 1989–1992* (Washington, D.C.: Woodrow Wilson Center Press, 1997), p. 9.

58. Shultz, *Turmoil and Triumph*, p. 864. See also p. 586. For a defense of C.I.A. estimates, which provides unintended support for the Shultz criticism, see Robert M. Gates, *From the Shadows: The Ultimate Insider's Story of Five Presidents and How They Won the Cold War* (New York: Simon and Schuster, 1996), pp. 289–91, 328–35, 337, 344–45, 375–78, 384–88, 409, 422–23, 441–43, 449, 562–66.

59. Powell, *My American Journey*, pp. 375–76. He not only made his own assessment but acted on it, anticipating the implications for the defense budget. A year later, in a speech entitled "The Future Just Ain't What It Used to Be," Powell warned the Army Association that "our bear is now wearing a Smokey hat and carries a shovel to put out fires. Our bear is now benign." Upon becoming chairman of the Joint Chiefs of Staff, he headed off deeper cuts in the defense budget by devising the so-called Base Force embodying a 25 percent cut and then convincing a reluctant secretary of defense and resistant service chiefs to endorse it. See also pp. 402, 436–40, 444, 448, 451–52, 454–56.

60. National Intelligence Estimate, NIE 11-23-88, "Gorbachev's Economic Programs: The Challenges Ahead," December 1988, p. iii.

61. National Intelligence Estimate, NIE 11-4-89, "Soviet Policy toward the West: The Gorbachev Challenge," April 1989, p. 18.

62. "Rising Political Instability under Gorbachev: Understanding the Problem and Prospects for Resolution," Office of Soviet Analysis, Central Intelligence Agency, April 1989, National Security Archive 00600, p. v.

63. Powell, *My American Journey*, p. 376.

64. Patrick E. Tyler, "New Pentagon 'Guidance' Cites Soviet Threat in Third World," *Washington Post*, February 13, 1990, p. A-1.

65. Hutchings, *American Diplomacy and the End of the Cold War*, p. 3.

66. James A. Baker III, *The Politics of Diplomacy: Revolution, War, and Peace, 1989–1992* (New York: G. P. Putnam's Sons, 1995), p. 41.

67. Ibid., p. 68.

68. Philip Zelikow and Condoleezza Rice, *Germany Unified and Europe Transformed: A Study in Statecraft* (Cambridge, Mass.: Belknap Press, 1995), p. 20.

69. Paul H. Nitze, "Gorbachev's Plan for a Communist Comeback," *Washington Post*, January 10, 1990, p. A-19.

70. Strobe Talbott, "Rethinking the Red Menace," *Time*, January 1, 1990, p. 69.

71. Raymond L. Garthoff, *Detente and Confrontation: American-Soviet Relations from Nixon to Reagan* (Washington, D.C.: Brookings Institution, 1985), pp. 1017–18.

72. Jack F. Matlock, Jr., "Gorbachev: Lingering Mysteries," *New York Review of Books*, December 19, 1996, p. 39.

73. Angus Roxburgh, *The Second Russian Revolution: The Struggle for Power in the Kremlin* (New York: Pharos Books, 1992), p. 49.

74. Snyder, "Gorbachev Revolution," p. 119.

75. "An Interview with Gorbachev," *Time*, September 9, 1985, p. 23.

76. Garthoff, *Great Transformation*, pp. 600–1.

77. As he said in Bucharest on May 27, 1987, "In developing perestroika, the C.P.S.U. naturally proceeds from the concrete conditions of the Soviet Union, from our understanding of the theory of socialism, taking into account the needs and will of the Soviet people. At the same time we study with intense interest the experience of friends, their trials in the realm of theory and practice of socialist construction, and we strive to utilize widely all that suits our conditions." Garthoff, *Great Transition*, pp. 574–75. Cf. interview with Aleksandr Tsipko in Oberdorfer, *Turn*, p. 356. Also in May, Shevardnadze went to Budapest to discuss Gorbachev's dissatisfaction with the pace of change there, and a month later Karoly Grosz ousted Janos Kadar as general secretary. Burlatsky's phrase is from his speech at the University of Pennsylvania on January 28, 1991. Rey Koslowski and Friedrich V. Krachtowil, "Understanding Change in International Politics: The Soviet Empire's Demise and the International System," in *International Relations*

Theory and the End of the Cold War, ed. Richard Ned Lebow and Thomas Risse-Kappen (New York: Columbia University Press, 1995), p. 152.

78. Serge Schmemann, "Rallying Cry of East Berliners: 'Gorbachev!'" *New York Times,* June 10, 1987, p. A-7.

79. George Bush and Brent Scowcroft, *A World Transformed* (New York: Alfred A. Knopf, 1998), p. 137. Cf. Oberdorfer, *Turn,* pp. 360–61; Hutchings, *American Diplomacy and the End of the Cold War,* p. 73. Communists retained the defense and interior portfolios.

80. Garthoff, *Great Transition,* p. 602n154.

81. Hutchings, *American Diplomacy and the End of the Cold War,* pp. 60–61, cites more ominous statements in "the official Soviet dailies" *Pravda* and *Izvestia* as evidence that "Soviet attitudes were still in evolution and far from uniform." Yet the dailies were mouthpieces of the opposition; Gorbachev was making policy.

82. Robert G. Kaiser, *Why Gorbachev Happened: His Triumphs and His Failure* (New York: Simon and Schuster, 1991), p. 306n; Oberdorfer, *Turn,* pp. 384–86.

83. Ekedahl and Goodman, *Wars of Eduard Shevardnadze,* pp. 245–47, 296n56, 315n36; Baker, *Politics of Diplomacy,* p. 147; Palazchenko, *My Years with Gorbachev and Shevardnadze,* pp. 124–25; Shevardnadze, *Future Belongs to Freedom,* pp. 192–93; Ligachev, *Inside Gorbachev's Kremlin,* pp. 190–95.

84. Matlock, *Autopsy on an Empire,* pp. 299–300, 323, 339–40, 343, 356, 424, 449–63, 607.

85. Ibid., pp. 300–5.

86. Oberdorfer, *Turn,* pp. 389–90.

87. Ronald D. Asmus, J. F. Brown, and Keith Crane, *Soviet Foreign Policy and the Revolutions of 1989 in Eastern Europe* (Santa Monica, Calif.: RAND, 1991), p. 85. On the challenges to East Germany's legitimacy by well-placed Soviet reformers, see Jeffrey Gedmin, *The Hidden Hand: Gorbachev and the Collapse of East Germany* (Washington, D.C.: A.E.I. Press, 1992), pp. 46–53.

88. Memorandum of conversation between Gorbachev and Krenz, cited in Zelikow and Rice, *Germany Unified and Europe Transformed,* p. 90.

CHAPTER 3

1. The reformers had personal memories of the war: Germans had occupied Gorbachev's village, and his father had served five years on the western front; Shevardnadze had lost his brother, and a grenade wound had left Yakovlev with a limp. Carolyn McGiffert Ekedahl and Melvin A. Goodman, *The Wars of Eduard Shevardnadze* (University Park, Pa.: Pennsylvania State University Press, 1997), p. 164.

2. Shevardnadze made that comparison in rebutting critics of new thinking in an article published in *Pravda* on June 26, 1990. Ibid., p. 162.

3. Anatoly Chernyaev and Aleksandr Bessmertnykh told Raymond Garthoff of these concerns: Raymond L. Garthoff, *The Great Transition: American-Soviet Relations and the End of the Cold War* (Washington, D.C.: Brookings Institution, 1994), p. 609n170. Shevardnadze raised this concern in a telephone call to West Germany's foreign minister, Hans-Dietrich Genscher, immediately after the dismantling of the Berlin Wall in November 1989, according to Robert Zoellick. Ekedahl and Goodman, *Wars of Eduard Shevardnadze*, p. 164. Reports of near confrontations and Stasi provocations prompted Washington to draw up contingency plans at this time. Robert L. Hutchings, *American Diplomacy and the End of the Cold War: An Insider's Account of U.S. Policy in Europe, 1989–1992* (Washington, D.C.: Woodrow Wilson Center Press, 1997), pp. 100–2.

4. Mikhail S. Gorbachev, *Perestroika: New Thinking for Our Country and the World* (New York: Harper and Row, 1987), p. 201.

5. Timothy Garton Ash, *In Europe's Name: Germany and the Divided Continent* (New York: Random House, 1993), p. 108. Cf. Mikhail S. Gorbachev, *Memoirs* (New York: Doubleday, 1996), pp. 517–18.

6. Archie Brown, *The Gorbachev Factor* (New York: Oxford University Press, 1997), pp. 244–45; Anatoly Chernyaev, "Gorbachev and the Reunification of Germany: Personal Recollections," in *Soviet Foreign Policy, 1917–1991*, ed. Gabriel Gorodetsky (London: Frank Cass, 1994), pp. 159–60; Hans-Dietrich Genscher, *Rebuilding a House Divided: A Memoir by the Architect of Germany's Reunification* (New York: Broadway Books, 1998), pp. 209, 273. Gorbachev repeats the formula in his book *Perestroika*, p. 200. On the eve of the von Weizsacker visit, Vyacheslav Dashichev, who chaired the foreign ministry's Academic Consultative Council, wrote a provocative twenty-six-page paper arguing that "the model of socialism, as established and developed in the G.D.R., has been unable to prove its advantages to the common people in the two German states" and that sentiment for unification was increasing "markedly." With unification on the table, he argued, "Moscow should take the initiative while it was still able, without waiting until the course of events forced it to act." The June council meeting was postponed and did not take place until November 27. An edited version of the paper was published on May 18, 1988, in *Literaturnaya Gazeta*. Ambassador Matlock sent copies to President Reagan and Secretary of State Shultz. Vyacheslav Dashichev, "On the Road to German Reunification: The View from Moscow," in Gorodetsky, *Soviet Foreign Policy*, pp. 171–73.

7. Eduard Shevardnadze, *The Future Belongs to Freedom* (New York: Free Press, 1991), p. 131. Starting in 1987, Erich Honecker was being told by Ambassador Gerd König in Moscow of Shevardnadze's view that overcoming Germany's division "would constitute a contribution to the construction of

a 'European home.'" Reinhold Andert and Wolfgang Herzberg, *Der Sturz: Erich Honecker im Kreuzverhor* (Berlin: Weimar, 1990), p. 21.

8. Ekedahl and Goodman, *Wars of Eduard Shevardnadze*, p. 152.

9. Among those who interpret German unification as a case of cooperation are Philip Zelikow and Condoleezza Rice, *Germany Unified and Europe Transformed: A Study in Statecraft* (Cambridge, Mass.: Belknap Press, 1995); Elizabeth Pond, *Beyond the Wall: Germany's Road to Unification* (Washington: Brookings Institution, 1993), chs. 12–15; Thomas Risse, "The Cold War's Endgame and German Unification," *International Security* 21, no. 4 (Spring 1997): 159–85.

10. "Gorbachev's Domestic Gambles and Instability in the U.S.S.R.," SOV-89-1077, Office of Soviet Analysis, Central Intelligence Agency, September 1989, National Security Archive 00602, p. 3.

11. Thomas Risse-Kappen, "Ideas Do Not Float Freely: Transnational Coalitions, Domestic Structures, and the End of the Cold War," *International Organization* 48, no. 2 (Spring 1994): 195, 197–98, 204–5.

12. Ash, *In Europe's Name*, p. 48.

13. Zelikow and Rice, *Germany Unified and Europe Transformed*, p. 26.

14. Ibid., p. 28.

15. Ibid., pp. 28, 380n66.

16. Ibid., p. 29.

17. Ekedahl and Goodman, *Wars of Eduard Shevardnadze*, p. 167.

18. Lou Cannon, "Reagan Is Concerned about Bush's Indecision," *Washington Post*, May 6, 1989, p. A-21.

19. "The Talk of the Town," *New Yorker*, May 29, 1989, pp. 27–28.

20. Zelikow and Rice, *Germany Unified and Europe Transformed*, pp. 26–27. Cf. Garthoff, *Great Transition*, p. 377.

21. National Security Directive 23, "United States Relations with the Soviet Union," September 22, 1989, excerpted in Hutchings, *American Diplomacy and the End of the Cold War*, p. 35.

22. Hutchings, *American Diplomacy and the End of the Cold War*, p. 11.

23. Bernard Weinraub, "Bush Urges East to Join in Ending Division of Europe," *New York Times*, June 1, 1989, p. A-1.

24. Hutchings, *American Diplomacy and the End of the Cold War*, p. 38.

25. Ibid., pp. 32–33. The theme was first sounded by Foreign Minister Genscher in a widely misinterpreted speech at Davos in 1987. See also p. 17.

26. Michael Beschloss and Strobe Talbott, *At the Highest Levels: The Inside Story of the End of the Cold War* (Boston: Little, Brown, 1993), pp. 59–60.

27. Ibid., p. 60.

28. Horst Teltschik, "Gorbachev's Reform Policy and the Outlook for East-West Relations," *Aussenpolitik* (Hamburg) 40, no. 3 (June 1989): 203, 214.

29. Jeffrey Gedmin, *The Hidden Hand: Gorbachev and the Collapse of East Germany* (Washington, D.C.: A.E.I. Press, 1992), pp. 44, 51–52.

30. Ash, *In Europe's Name*, p. 118. Gorbachev had no such recollection of the conversation, according to Zelikow and Rice, *Germany Unified and Europe Transformed*, p. 34.

31. Charles S. Maier, *Dissolution: The Crisis of Communism and the End of East Germany* (Princeton, N.J.: Princeton University Press, 1997), p. 222.

32. Ash, *In Europe's Name*, p. 115.

33. Genscher, *Rebuilding a House Divided*, p. 269.

34. Don Oberdorfer, *The Turn: From the Cold War to a New Era* (New York: Poseidon Press, 1991), p. 360.

35. Maier, *Dissolution*, pp. 59–60, 72; Genscher, *Rebuilding a House Divided*, p. 264.

36. Ekedahl and Goodman, *Wars of Eduard Shevardnadze*, p. 248; Jim Hoagland, "Hungary Had Soviet Approval: U.S. Reportedly Informed of Plans for East Germans," *Washington Post*, September 17, 1989, p. A-1; Genscher, *Rebuilding a House Divided*, p. 281.

37. Zelikow and Rice, *Germany Unified and Europe Transformed*, pp. 71–72.

38. Maier, *Dissolution*, pp. 139–41.

39. Zelikow and Rice, *Germany Unified and Europe Transformed*, p. 74.

40. Ibid., pp. 74, 80.

41. Ibid., p. 83.

42. Hannes Adomeit, "Gorbachev and German Unification: Revision of Thinking, Realignment of Power," *Problems of Communism* 39, no. 4 (July/August, 1990): 6; Gorbachev, *Memoirs*, pp. 523–25; Gunther Schabowski, *Das Politburo* (Hamburg: Rohwohlt Taschenbuch Verlag, 1990), p. 74; Gedmin, *Hidden Hand*, p. 99; Robert M. Gates, *From the Shadows: The Ultimate Insider's Story of Five Presidents and How They Won the Cold War* (New York: Simon and Schuster, 1996), p. 467; Genscher, *Rebuilding a House Divided*, p. 286. For a different account, see Zelikow and Rice, *Germany Unified and Europe Transformed*, p. 84.

43. Maier, *Dissolution*, pp. 142–45.

44. Zelikow and Rice, *Germany Unified and Europe Transformed*, p. 84. The Soviet ambassador received instructions not to interfere, according to Oberdorfer, *Turn*, p. 364. For an alternative view, see Pond, *Beyond the Wall*, p. 119.

45. Gedmin, *Hidden Hand*, p. 102.

46. Genscher, *Rebuilding a House Divided*, p. 298; Pond, *Beyond the Wall*, p. 116.

47. Pond, *Beyond the Wall*, pp. 121–24; Gedmin, *Hidden Hand*, pp. 104–5.

48. James A. Baker III, *The Politics of Diplomacy: Revolution, War, and Peace, 1989–1992* (New York: G. P. Putnam's Sons, 1995), p. 163.

49. Dashichev, "On the Road to German Reunification," p. 173.

50. Marc Fisher, "One Year Later, World Is Learning How Berlin Wall Opened," *Washington Post*, November 10, 1990, p. A-23.

51. Zelikow and Rice, *Germany Unified and Europe Transformed*, p. 99.

52. Ibid., pp. 99–100.

53. Oberdorfer, *Turn*, p. 364. Cf. Gedmin, *Hidden Hand*, pp. 114–15.

54. Gedmin, *Hidden Hand*, pp. 6–7, 85–86, 112–15.

55. Pond, *Beyond the Wall*, p. 158.

56. "Wir mussen Kurs halten," *Der Spiegel*, September 25, 1989, pp. 16–17. Cf. Pond, *Beyond the Wall*, p. 157. On British opposition to unification, see Margaret Thatcher, *The Downing Street Years* (New York: HarperCollins, 1993), pp. 792, 796–98.

57. R. W. Apple, Jr., "Possibility of a Reunited Germany Is No Cause for Alarm, Bush Says," *New York Times*, October 25, 1989, p. A-1.

58. Zelikow and Rice, *Germany Unified and Europe Transformed*, p. 95.

59. Chernyaev, "Gorbachev and the Reunification of Germany," p. 164. Cf. Gorbachev, *Memoirs*, p. 527.

60. Zelikow and Rice, *Germany Unified and Europe Transformed*, pp. 120–21.

61. Hutchings, *American Diplomacy and the End of the Cold War*, p. 99.

62. Ibid., p. 100.

63. Zelikow and Rice, *Germany Unified and Europe Transformed*, pp. 122–23.

64. Ibid., p. 98.

65. Hutchings, *American Diplomacy and the End of the Cold War*, p. 104.

66. "Thatcher Sees East European Progress as More Important than Germans' Unity," *Wall Street Journal*, January 26, 1990, p. A-12. Cf. Zelikow and Rice, *Germany Unified and Europe Transformed*, pp. 115–16. On her efforts to get Mitterrand to slow down unification, see Thatcher, *Downing Street Years*, pp. 796–98.

67. Chernyaev, "Gorbachev and the Reunification of Germany," p. 166.

68. Interview by Fedor Burlatsky, *Literaturnaya Gazeta*, April 10, 1991, reprinted in Foreign Broadcast Information Service, FBIS-SOV-91-071, April 12, 1991, p. 32.

69. On the origins of Malta, see George Bush and Brent Scowcroft, *A World Transformed* (New York: Alfred A. Knopf, 1998), pp. 129–30, 132–33; Baker, *Politics of Diplomacy*, p. 168.

70. Zelikow and Rice, *Germany Unified and Europe Transformed*, p. 127; Chernyaev, "Gorbachev and the Reunification of Germany," p. 165.

71. Beschloss and Talbott, *At the Highest Levels*, p. 157.

72. Baker, *Politics of Diplomacy*, pp. 170–71.

73. Zelikow and Rice, *Germany Unified and Europe Transformed*, pp. 128–29.

74. Oberdorfer, *Turn*, p. 385.

75. Zelikow and Rice, *Germany Unified and Europe Transformed*, p. 130. West Germany's foreign minister came to a similar conclusion after a testier meeting with Gorbachev in Moscow two days later. Genscher, *Rebuilding a House Divided*, p. 317.

76. Zelikow and Rice, *Germany Unified and Europe Transformed*, pp. 130–31.

77. Pavel Palazchenko, *My Years with Gorbachev and Shevardnadze: The Memoir of a Soviet Interpreter* (University Park, Pa.: Pennsylvania State University Press, 1997), p. 165; Dashichev, "On the Road to German Reunification," p. 176.

78. Palazchenko, *My Years with Gorbachev and Shevardnadze*, pp. 165–66.

79. Dashichev, "On the Road to German Reunification," p. 176.

80. Zelikow and Rice, *Germany Unified and Europe Transformed*, p. 148.

81. Paul B. Stares, *The New Germany and the New Europe* (Washington, D.C.: Brookings Institution, 1992).

82. Zelikow and Rice, *Germany Unified and Europe Transformed*, p. 155; Genscher, *Rebuilding a House Divided*, p. 299.

83. Bush and Scowcroft, *World Transformed*, p. 235.

84. Genscher, *Rebuilding a House Divided*, p. 335.

85. Zelikow and Rice, *Germany Unified and Europe Transformed*, p. 168. The differences persisted because the choice of forum did not eliminate the risk. See pp. 209–11. Cf. Bush and Scowcroft, *World Transformed*, p. 234; Hutchings, *American Diplomacy and the End of the Cold War*, pp. 107–8.

86. Ash, *In Europe's Name*, pp. 364–65.

87. Chernyaev, "Gorbachev and the Reunification of Germany," p. 166; Gorbachev, *Memoirs*, p. 528; Zelikow and Rice, *Germany Unified and Europe Transformed*, pp. 162–63.

88. Gorbachev, *Memoirs*, p. 528.

89. Zelikow and Rice, *Germany Unified and Europe Transformed*, p. 172.

90. Ibid.

91. Ibid., p. 166.

92. Ibid., p. 171.

93. Ibid., p. 173.

94. Hutchings, *American Diplomacy and the End of the Cold War*, p. 111.

95. Ibid., pp. 111–12.

96. Bush and Scowcroft, *World Transformed*, p. 237.

97. Beschloss and Talbott, *At the Highest Levels*, p. 182.

98. Oberdorfer, *Turn*, p. 395. Cf. Zelikow and Rice, *Germany Unified and Europe Transformed*, pp. 181–84; Baker, *Politics of Diplomacy*, p. 235; Gorbachev, *Memoirs*, pp. 529, 675; Garthoff, *Great Transition*, p. 414.

99. Zelikow and Rice, *Germany Unified and Europe Transformed*, pp. 186–87.

100. Bush and Scowcroft, *World Transformed*, p. 241.

101. Zelikow and Rice, *Germany Unified and Europe Transformed*, p. 184.

102. Ibid., p. 187.

103. Ibid., pp. 188–89. Kohl was prepared to go further. On February 19 Bonn endorsed demilitarization: "no formations or institutions of the Western Alliance should be moved forward to the present territory of the G.D.R." This included both "NATO-assigned and non-assigned military forces of the Bundeswehr." See also p. 204. Cf. Chernyaev, "Gorbachev and the Reunification of Germany," p. 167.

104. "Meeting of M. S. Gorbachev with H. Kohl," *Pravda*, February 11, 1990, cited in Garthoff, *Great Transition*, p. 414.

105. Zelikow and Rice, *Germany Unified and Europe Transformed*, pp. 190, 205.

106. Baker, *Politics of Diplomacy*, p. 234.

107. Zelikow and Rice, *Germany Unified and Europe Transformed*, p. 203.

108. Ibid., pp. 196–97.

109. Baker, *Politics of Diplomacy*, pp. 213–15; Bush and Scowcroft, *World Transformed*, p. 243. Cf. Genscher, *Rebuilding a House Divided*, pp. 345–46.

110. Genscher, *Rebuilding a House Divided*, pp. 347–48.

111. Pond, *Beyond the Wall*, p. 172.

112. Zelikow and Rice, *Germany Unified and Europe Transformed*, pp. 203–4; Pond, *Beyond the Wall*, p. 182.

113. Zelikow and Rice, *Germany Unified and Europe Transformed*, p. 211. Cf. Hutchings, *American Diplomacy and the End of the Cold War*, pp. 120–23.

114. Bush and Scowcroft, *World Transformed*, p. 248. Cf. Thatcher, *Downing Street Years*, pp. 798–99.

115. Bush and Scowcroft, *World Transformed*, p. 252. Cf. Baker, *Politics of Diplomacy*, p. 234.

116. Zelikow and Rice, *Germany Unified and Europe Transformed*, p. 215.

117. Hutchings, *American Diplomacy and the End of the Cold War*, p. 115.

118. Martin Weil, "Can the Blacks Do for Africa What the Jews Did for Israel?" *Foreign Policy*, no. 15 (Summer 1974): 118.

119. Bush and Scowcroft, *World Transformed*, pp. 252, 260–62. Cf. Zelikow and Rice, *Germany Unified and Europe Transformed*, pp. 216–22.

120. Baker, *Politics of Diplomacy*, p. 235.

121. Beschloss and Talbott, *At the Highest Levels*, p. 198.

122. Palazchenko, *My Years with Gorbachev and Shevardnadze*, pp. 95, 182, 194.

123. Anatoly Chernyaev, "The Phenomenon of Gorbachev in the Context of Leadership," *International Affairs* (Moscow) 39, no. 6 (June 1993): 48. Cf. Dashichev, "On the Road to German Reunification," p. 177.

124. Garthoff, *Great Transition*, pp. 612, 417n19.

125. Ibid., p. 417n19. Cf. Chernyaev, "Gorbachev and the Reunification of Germany," p. 167; Zelikow and Rice, *Germany Unified and Europe Transformed*, pp. 244–45.

126. *New York Times* editorials on November 25, December 13, and December 16, 1989; January 28, February 6, February 28, April 16, April 26, April 30, May 2, May 7, May 20, May 23, June 4, June 18, June 30, July 5, July 16, July 17, July 20, and July 28, 1990, addressed issues relating to German unification.

127. "In Germany: 4+2=5," *New York Times*, May 2, 1990, p. A-26.

128. McGeorge Bundy, "From Cold War to Trusting Peace," *Foreign Affairs* 69, no. 1 (Winter 1989–90): 205.

129. George F. Kennan, "This Is No Time to Talk of Reunification," *Washington Post*, November 12, 1989, p. D-1.

130. Zelikow and Rice, *Germany Unified and Europe Transformed*, p. 199.

131. Pond, *Beyond the Wall*, p. 189.

132. Ibid., p. 188.

133. Beschloss and Talbott, *At the Highest Levels*, pp. 140–41.

134. Zelikow and Rice, *Germany Unified and Europe Transformed*, p. 252.

135. Ibid., p. 254.

136. Baker, *Politics of Diplomacy*, pp. 246–47.

137. Zelikow and Rice, *Germany Unified and Europe Transformed*, pp. 248–49; Shevardnadze, *Future Belongs to Freedom*, p. 138. Cf. Genscher, *Rebuilding a House Divided*, pp. 372–75

138. Bush and Scowcroft, *World Transformed*, pp. 224–27.

139. Beschloss and Talbott, *At the Highest Levels*, p. 206. Cf. Jack F. Matlock, Jr., *Autopsy on an Empire: The American Ambassador's Account of the Collapse of the Soviet Union* (New York: Random House, 1995), pp. 323–30, 337–59, 379–80.

140. Zelikow and Rice, *Germany Unified and Europe Transformed*, pp. 258–60; Bush and Scowcroft, *World Transformed*, p. 270.

141. For the German view, see Genscher, *Rebuilding a House Divided*, pp. 218–19.

142. The details of the assurances are drawn from Zelikow and Rice, *Germany Unified and Europe Transformed*, pp. 262–65.

143. Baker, *Politics of Diplomacy*, p. 251n.

144. Bush and Scowcroft, *World Transformed*, p. 271.

145. Zelikow and Rice, *Germany Unified and Europe Transformed*, p. 266.

146. Ibid., p. 278. The authors suggest it was a last-minute conversion, but Gorbachev had repeatedly favored self-determination for Germany.

147. Zelikow and Rice, *Germany Unified and Europe Transformed*, pp. 283–85.

148. Pond, *Beyond the Wall*, p. 218; Zelikow and Rice, *Germany Unified and Europe Transformed*, p. 293.

149. Zelikow and Rice, *Germany Unified and Europe Transformed*, pp. 296–97.

150. Ibid., pp. 299–300. Cf. Palazchenko, *My Years with Gorbachev and Shevardnadze*, p. 198.

151. The following discussion is drawn from Zelikow and Rice, *Germany Unified and Europe Transformed*, pp. 303–14.

152. John Steinbruner and Leon V. Sigal, eds., *Alliance Security: NATO and the No-First-Use Question* (Washington, D.C.: Brookings Institution, 1983), chs. 1, 2, 4.

153. Zelikow and Rice, *Germany Unified and Europe Transformed*, pp. 316–17.

154. Ibid., pp. 318, 320.

155. Ibid., pp. 321–22; Thatcher, *Downing Street Years*, p. 811.

156. Zelikow and Rice, *Germany Unified and Europe Transformed*, pp. 324–25.

157. Ibid., p. 289. Cf. Genscher, *Rebuilding a House Divided*, pp. 434–35.

158. Zelikow and Rice, *Germany Unified and Europe Transformed*, pp. 325–26.

159. Ibid., p. 334.

160. Pravda, July 5, 1990, quoted in Angus Roxburgh, *The Second Russian Revolution: The Struggle for Power in the Kremlin* (New York: Pharos Books, 1992), p. 159.

161. Zelikow and Rice, *Germany Unified and Europe Transformed*, p. 331.

162. Ibid., p. 329.

163. Ibid., pp. 335–37.

164. Pond, *Beyond the Wall*, p. 222.

165. Genscher, *Rebuilding a House Divided*, p. 429.

166. Zelikow and Rice, *Germany Unified and Europe Transformed*, pp. 338–42.

167. Palazchenko, *My Years with Gorbachev and Shevardnadze*, p. 204.

168. Zelikow and Rice, *Germany Unified and Europe Transformed*, pp. 349–52.

169. Hutchings, *American Diplomacy and the End of the Cold War*, p. 138.

170. Zelikow and Rice, *Germany Unified and Europe Transformed*, pp. 356–62; Hutchings, *American Diplomacy and the End of the Cold War*, pp. 138–39; Genscher, *Rebuilding a House Divided*, pp. 447–53.

171. Thucydides, *The Peloponnesian War*, book V, ch. 7, "The Melian Debate."

172. Mikhail Gorbachev, "Will NATO's Enlargement Be Its Last?" *Washington Times*, March 11, 1999, p. 18.

173. Gedmin, *Hidden Hand*, p. 121.

174. Matlock, *Autopsy on an Empire*, p. 386.

CHAPTER 4

1. Recalling "ruminations" with President Bush while fishing off Walker's Point, Maine, August 23, 1990, in George Bush and Brent Scowcroft, *A World Transformed* (New York: Alfred A. Knopf, 1998), pp. 354–55.

2. George Shultz, "U.S.-Soviet Relations: Where Do We Want to Be and How Do We Get There?" memo to the president, cited in George P. Shultz, *Turmoil and Triumph: My Years as Secretary of State* (New York: Charles Scribner's Sons, 1993), p. 266.

3. Ronald Reagan, speech on "Soviet-American Relations," January 16, 1984, *Weekly Compilation of Presidential Documents* 20, no. 3 (January 23, 1984): 40–45. Recognizing that "most of these conflicts have their origins in local problems" and acknowledging the need "for both of us to defuse tensions and regional conflicts" was a far cry from Reagan's earlier, more confrontational condemnation of Soviet expansionism. Raymond L. Garthoff, *The Great Transition: American-Soviet Relations and the End of the Cold War* (Washington, D.C.: Brookings Institution, 1994), p. 144.

4. Jack F. Matlock, Jr., *Autopsy on an Empire: The American Ambassador's Account of the Collapse of the Soviet Union* (New York: Random House, 1995), p. 148. See also p. 84.

5. Robert M. Gates, *From the Shadows: The Ultimate Insider's Story of Five Presidents and How They Won the Cold War* (New York: Simon and Schuster, 1996), p. 346.

6. Eduard Shevardnadze, *The Future Belongs to Freedom* (New York: Free Press, 1991), p. 26. Gorbachev said much the same to President Reagan at their first summit meeting in Geneva and to Chancellor Kohl at Stavropol. Ronald Reagan, *An American Life* (New York: Simon and Schuster, 1990), p. 639; Hans-Dietrich Genscher, *Rebuilding a House Divided: A Memoir by the Architect of Germany's Reunification* (New York: Broadway Books, 1998), p. 427.

7. Robert H. Johnson, "'Rollback' Revisited—A Reagan Doctrine for Insurgent Wars?" *ODC Policy Focus*, no. 1, Overseas Development Council, Washington, D.C., January 1986, pp. 3, 5.

8. "U.S. Relations with the USSR," Robert C. McFarlane and Zofia Smardz, *Special Trust: Pride, Principle and Politics Inside the White House* (New York: Cadell and Davies, 1994), pp. 372, 375.

9. Garthoff, *Great Transition*, p. 712.

10. Gates, *From the Shadows*, pp. 143–49; Diego Cordóvez and Selig Harrison, *Out of Afghanistan: The Inside Story of the Soviet Withdrawal* (New York: Oxford University Press, 1995), pp. 38–39. Even before that, although President Carter ruled out direct aid for the mujahideen, National Security Adviser Zbigniew Brzezinski had authorized the C.I.A. to encourage Zia Ul-Haq's military dictatorship in Pakistan to support the insurgency and to work with Pakistan's Inter-Services Intelligence directorate to plan training and co-ordinate Chinese, Saudi, Egyptian, and Kuwaiti aid (see pp. 33–34). Direct arms aid began in 1980. David Binder, "U.S. Supplying Afghan Insurgents with Arms in a Covert Operation," *New York Times*, February 16, 1980, p. A-1.

11. On aid levels to the insurgents and to Pakistan, see Cordóvez and Harrison, *Out of Afghanistan* pp. 54, 56–58, 65–70, 206–7.

12. Sarah E. Mendelsohn, *Changing Course: Ideas, Politics, and the Soviet Withdrawal from Afghanistan* (Princeton, N.J.: Princeton University Press, 1998), pp. 81–82.

13. Mikhail Gorbachev, "Revolutionary Perestroika—An Ideology of Renewal," speech to the Soviet Central Committee plenum, February 18, 1988, quoted in Garthoff, *Great Transition*, pp. 725–26.

14. Cordóvez and Harrison, *Out of Afghanistan*, pp. 183–84, 189.

15. William E. Odom, *The Collapse of the Soviet Military* (New Haven: Yale University Press, 1998), p. 103. Cf. Garthoff, *Great Transition*, pp. 726–27; Steve Coll, "Anatomy of a Victory," *Washington Post*, July 19–20, 1992, p. A-1.

16. Cordóvez and Harrison, *Out of Afghanistan*, p. 188.

17. Reagan, *American Life*, pp. 618–19.

18. Letter from Mikhail Gorbachev, quoted in ibid., p. 648.

19. Odom, *Collapse of the Soviet Military*, pp. 103–4.

20. Cordóvez and Harrison, *Out of Afghanistan*, pp. 152–54, 202–5.

21. Garthoff, *Great Transition*, p. 727; Archie Brown, *The Gorbachev Factor* (New York: Oxford University Press, 1997), p. 234.

22. Brown, *Gorbachev Factor*, p. 234.

23. Shevardnadze, *Future Belongs to Freedom*, p. 47. On October 10 Shevardnadze had expressed willingness to make a time frame for Soviet withdrawal an integral part of the Afghan accords. Cordóvez and Harrison, *Out of Afghanistan*, pp. 225–26.

24. John W. Parker, *Kremlin in Transition*, vol. 2: *Gorbachev, 1985–1989* (London: Routledge, 1991), pp. 84–85.

25. Ronald Reagan, "Freedom, Regional Security, and Global Peace," message to Congress, March 14, 1986, *Weekly Compilation of Presidential Documents* 22, no. 11 (March 17, 1986): 357, 363.

26. Coll, "Anatomy of a Victory."

27. Shultz, *Turmoil and Triumph*, pp. 692, 1087; Gates, *From the Shadows*, pp. 349–51; Garthoff, *Great Transition*, pp. 272; Cordóvez and Harrison, *Out of Afghanistan*, pp. 194–98.

28. Parker, *Kremlin in Transition*, vol. 2, p. 263.

29. Shultz, *Turmoil and Triumph*, p. 895. Cf. Cordóvez and Harrison, *Out of Afghanistan*, pp. 198–201; Mendelsohn, *Changing Course*, pp. 97–100.

30. Cordóvez and Harrison, *Out of Afghanistan*, pp. 103–4, 155–58.

31. Garthoff, *Great Transition*, pp. 713–14, 723.

32. Ibid., p. 714. Resistance to a diplomatic solution dated back to the Carter administration, when National Security Adviser Brzezinski blocked an attempt by Secretary of State Cyrus Vance to arrange for the Soviet Union to withdraw. Cordóvez and Harrison, *Out of Afghanistan*, pp. 54–55.

33. Cordóvez and Harrison, *Out of Afghanistan*, pp. 183–84, 189.

34. Ibid., pp. 189–94, 214, 216, 220.

35. Ronald Reagan, "A Foundation for Enduring Peace," address to UN General Assembly, October 24, 1985. On American unwillingness to engage in talks, Cordóvez and Harrison, *Out of Afghanistan*, pp. 53, 85, 103–7, 180.

36. Shultz, *Turmoil and Triumph*, p. 870.

37. Politburo records cited in Mendelsohn, *Changing Course*, p. 112.

38. Parker, *Kremlin in Transition*, vol. 2, p. 264. Cf. Garthoff, *Great Transition*, p. 729; Gates, *From the Shadows*, pp. 429–30; Cordóvez and Harrison, *Out of Afghanistan*, pp. 207–9.

39. Parker, *Kremlin in Transition*, vol. 2, pp. 264–65.

40. Cordóvez and Harrison, *Out of Afghanistan*, pp. 248–51.

41. Shultz, *Turmoil and Triumph*, p. 895.

42. Special National Intelligence Estimate, SNIE 11/37-88, "U.S.S.R.: Withdrawal from Afghanistan," March 1988, p. 1.

43. Gates, *From the Shadows*, p. 431; Shultz, *Turmoil and Triumph*, p. 1088; George P. Shultz quoted in *Retrospective on the End of the Cold War*, ed.

Fred I. Greenstein and William C. Wohlforth, Monograph Series no. 6, Center of International Studies, Princeton University, 1994, p. 37. In March 1988 the C.I.A. predicted "an unstable coalition of traditionalist and fundamentalist groups" would succeed Najibullah. "It will be Islamic—possibly strongly fundamentalist, but not as extreme as Iran." Special National Intelligence Estimate, "U.S.S.R.: Withdrawal from Afghanistan," p. 1. On Pakistani reliance on the fundamentalists and doubts raised in Washington, see Cordóvez and Harrison, *Out of Afghanistan*, pp. 162–63.

44. Aleksandr Yakovlev interview on Central Television, reprinted in Foreign Broadcast Information Service, FBIS-SOV-91-251, December 31, 1991, p. 4.

45. Ibid., pp. 3–4.

46. Parker, *Kremlin in Transition*, vol. 2, p. 268.

47. Shultz, *Turmoil and Triumph*, p. 987.

48. Ronald Reagan, "United Nations Address before the 43rd Session of the General Assembly," September 21, 1987, *Weekly Compilation of Presidential Documents* 23, no. 38 (September 28, 1987): 1053–54.

49. Shultz, *Turmoil and Triumph*, p. 1003.

50. Gates, *From the Shadows*, p. 430.

51. Parker, *Kremlin in Transition*, vol. 2, p. 270.

52. "Statement of the General Secretary M. S. Gorbachev on Afghanistan," *Pravda*, February 8, 1988, reprinted in Foreign Broadcast Information Service, FBIS-SOV-88-025, February 8, 1988, pp. 34–35.

53. Don Oberdorfer, *The Turn: From the Cold War to a New Era* (New York: Poseidon Press, 1991), p. 276.

54. Ibid., p. 278. On Zia's shift, see Cordóvez and Harrison, *Out of Afghanistan*, pp. 258–59, 328.

55. Shultz, *Turmoil and Triumph*, p. 1087. Cf. Cordóvez and Harrison, *Out of Afghanistan*, pp. 260–65.

56. Pavel Palazchenko, *My Years with Gorbachev and Shevardnadze: The Memoir of a Soviet Interpreter* (University Park, Pa.: Pennsylvania State University Press, 1997), p. 89.

57. Shultz, *Turmoil and Triumph*, pp. 1089–90.

58. Ibid., p. 1090.

59. Ibid.

60. Palazchenko, *My Years with Gorbachev and Shevardnadze*, pp. 89–90; Shevardnadze, *Future Belongs to Freedom*, pp. 97–98.

61. Oberdorfer, *Turn*, p. 280. Cf. interview with George Shultz in Carolyn McGiffert Ekedahl and Melvin A. Goodman, *The Wars of Eduard Shevardnadze* (University Park, Pa.: Pennsylvania State University Press, 1997), p. 189.

62. Oberdorfer, *Turn*, p. 281.

63. Ekedahl and Goodman, *Wars of Eduard Shevardnadze*, p. 193.

64. James A. Baker III, *The Politics of Diplomacy: Revolution, War, and Peace, 1989–1992* (New York: G. P. Putnam's Sons, 1995), p. 74.

65. Palazchenko, *My Years with Gorbachev and Shevardnadze*, p. 117.

66. Mikhail S. Gorbachev, *Memoirs* (New York: Doubleday, 1996), pp. 541–42.

67. Baker, *Politics of Diplomacy*, p. 528.

68. Ekedahl and Goodman, *Wars of Eduard Shevardnadze*, p. 193.

69. Palazchenko, *My Years with Gorbachev and Shevardnadze*, p. 117.

70. Garthoff, *Great Transition*, p. 713.

71. Bush and Scowcroft, *World Transformed*, p. 135.

72. Shevardnadze, *Future Belongs to Freedom*, p. 100.

73. Baker, *Politics of Diplomacy*, p. 10.

74. Ibid., pp. 11–12.

75. Ibid., p. 10.

76. Ibid., p. 11.

77. Ibid., p. 14.

78. Palazchenko, *My Years with Gorbachev and Shevardnadze*, pp. 212, 214, 222–23. Cf. Baker, *Politics of Diplomacy*, p. 397.

79. Shevardnadze, *Future Belongs to Freedom*, pp. 100–1, 103. Cf. Palazchenko, *My Years with Gorbachev and Shevardnadze*, p. 209.

80. Baker, *Politics of Diplomacy*, p. 15. On the ensuing friction with Gorbachev, see Palazchenko, *My Years with Gorbachev and Shevardnadze*, pp. 214–15, 219.

81. Baker, *Politics of Diplomacy*, p. 15.

82. Michael R. Gordon and Bernard E. Trainor, *The Generals' War* (Boston: Little, Brown, 1995), pp. 47–48.

83. Baker, *Politics of Diplomacy*, p. 282.

84. Ibid.

85. Bush and Scowcroft, *World Transformed*, p. 338.

86. Baker, *Politics of Diplomacy*, p. 283.

87. Ibid., p. 286.

88. Bush and Scowcroft, *World Transformed*, p. 352.

89. Ibid., p. 362.

90. Gorbachev, *Memoirs*, pp. 552–53.

91. Bush and Scowcroft, *World Transformed*, p. 364.

92. Ibid., pp. 364–66.

93. Ibid., pp. 365–66. Cf. Gorbachev, *Memoirs*, p. 554.

94. Baker, *Politics of Diplomacy*, p. 292.

95. Bush and Scowcroft, *World Transformed*, p. 367.

96. Baker, *Politics of Diplomacy*, pp. 292–93.

97. Palazchenko, *My Years with Gorbachev and Shevardnadze*, pp. 213–14; Baker, *Politics of Diplomacy*, p. 293.

98. Baker, *Politics of Diplomacy*, pp. 294–95. Tarasenko warned Ross about the mounting criticism in Moscow over Iraq. See Palazchenko, *My Years with Gorbachev and Shevardnadze*, p. 215.

99. Bush and Scowcroft, *World Transformed*, p. 370.

100. Baker, *Politics of Diplomacy*, pp. 295–96.

101. Interview with an American participant, December 15, 1995.

102. Baker, *Politics of Diplomacy*, pp. 297–98.

103. Bush and Scowcroft, *World Transformed*, pp. 377–78. Cf. Baker, *Politics of Diplomacy*, pp. 398–400.

104. Bush and Scowcroft, *World Transformed*, pp. 394–95.

105. Baker, *Politics of Diplomacy*, p. 310.

106. Palazchenko, *My Years with Gorbachev and Shevardnadze*, p. 225.

107. Baker, *Politics of Diplomacy*, pp. 312–13.

108. Bush and Scowcroft, *World Transformed*, pp. 403–4.

109. Palazchenko, *My Years with Gorbachev and Shevardnadze*, pp. 226–28.

110. Bush and Scowcroft, *World Transformed*, pp. 408–9.

111. Palazchenko, *My Years with Gorbachev and Shevardnadze*, p. 231.

112. Ibid.

113. Baker, *Politics of Diplomacy*, p. 321.

114. Ibid., p. 384.

115. Bush and Scowcroft, *World Transformed*, p. 454.

116. Baker, *Politics of Diplomacy*, pp. 391–92.

117. Ibid., p. 392; Palazchenko, *My Years with Gorbachev and Shevardnadze*, pp. 256–57.

118. "US-USSR and the Persian Gulf," *Dispatch* (U.S. Department of State) 2, no. 5 (February 4, 1991): 71.

119. Baker, *Politics of Diplomacy*, p. 393.

120. Michael Beschloss and Strobe Talbott, *At the Highest Levels: The Inside Story of the End of the Cold War* (Boston: Little, Brown, 1993), p. 331.

121. Bush and Scowcroft, *World Transformed*, p. 461.

122. Gordon and Trainor, *Generals' War*, p. 415.

123. Ibid., p. 456.

124. Gorbachev has categorically rejected the "suspicions that Americans had" that Primakov was pursuing "his own line" of policy toward Iraq. David Hoffman, "A Soviet Bureaucrat in a Capitalist World," *Washington Post*, March 19, 1999, p. A-1.

125. Baker, *Politics of Diplomacy*, pp. 402–3.

126. Bush and Scowcroft, *World Transformed*, p. 470.

127. Ibid., pp. 470–72.

128. Ibid., p. 472.

129. Ibid., p. 473.

130. Ibid., p. 475.

131. Ibid., p. 476. Cf. Gorbachev, *Memoirs*, pp. 562–63, 565.

132. Bush and Scowcroft, *World Transformed*, p. 355.

Chapter 5

1. Colin L. Powell, *My American Journey* (New York: Random House, 1995), p. 375.

2. The most formidable realist of all, Hans Morgenthau, was consistently critical of the cold war as an ideological crusade and called for self-limitation in Hans J. Morgenthau, *Politics among Nations: The Struggle for Power and Peace*, 3d ed. (New York: Alfred A. Knopf, 1962), pp. 207–21, 349–59. Cf. Hans J. Morgenthau, "Old Superstitions, New Realities," *New Republic*, January 22, 1977, pp. 50–65.

3. David Alan Rosenberg, "The Origins of Overkill: Nuclear Weapons and American Strategy, 1945–1960," *International Security* 7, no. 4 (Spring 1983): 3–71.

4. Bruce G. Blair, *Global Zero Alert for Nuclear Forces* (Washington, D.C.: Brookings Institution, 1995).

5. William W. Kaufmann, "Nonnuclear Deterrence," in *Alliance Security: NATO and the No-First-Use Question*, ed. John Steinbruner and Leon V. Sigal (Washington, D.C.: Brookings Institution, 1983), pp. 43–90.

6. Michael MccGwire, *Perestroika and Soviet National Security* (Washington, D.C.: Brookings Institution, 1987), chs. 2, 7.

7. Steinbruner and Sigal, *Alliance Security*, chs. 2, 6.

8. Leon V. Sigal, "The Case for Eliminating Battlefield Nuclear Weapons," in *Battlefield Nuclear Weapons: Issues and Options*, ed. Stephen D. Biddle and Peter D. Feaver (Cambridge, Mass.: Harvard University Center for Science and International Affairs, 1989), pp. 33–53. This was understood at the highest levels in Moscow. In December 1975, as the United States was introducing new laser-guided bombs and missiles with pinpoint accuracy, K.G.B. chief Yuri Andropov reported to the Central Committee that these new weapons could be armed with low-yield nuclear warheads as well as conventional ones. That made it difficult for the Soviet Union to distinguish readiness for nuclear from conventional attack and would, said Andropov, "simplify the procedure of making a decision on military use of tactical nuclear weapons." Matthew Evangelista, *Unarmed Forces: The Transnational Movement to End the Cold War* (Ithaca, N.Y.: Cornell University Press, 1999), p. 293.

9. James G. Blight and David A. Welch, *On the Brink: Americans and Soviets Reexamine the Cuban Missile Crisis* (New York: Hill and Wang, 1989), pp. 29–33, 52, 61–63, 69–75, 84–88, 90–92, 100–1, 178, 186, 192–93, 198–200, 242, 273–74; McGeorge Bundy, *Danger and Survival: Choices about the Bomb in the First Fifty Years* (New York: Random House, 1988), pp. 417–21; and Aleksandr G. Savel'yev and Nikolay N. Detinov, *The Big Five: Arms Control Decision-Making in the Soviet Union* (Westport, Conn: Praeger, 1995), p. 3.

10. Interviews with senior Russian officials, June 25, 1990, and April 15, 1997.

11. Thomas C. Schelling and Morton H. Halperin, *Strategy and Arms Control* (New York: Twentieth Century Fund, 1961), p. 1.

12. This goes beyond "cooperative security" as first used in John D. Steinbruner, "The Prospect of Cooperative Security," *Brookings Review*, Winter 1988/89, pp. 53–62, where it is applied to a extensive set of U.S.-Soviet arms control arrangements. The concept is elaborated in Janne E. Nolan, ed., *Global Engagement: Cooperation and Security in the 21st Century* (Washington, D.C.: Brookings Institution, 1994), ch. 1, where it is extended somewhat beyond arms control.

13. Raymond L. Garthoff, "New Thinking in Soviet Military Doctrine," *Washington Quarterly*, Summer 1988, pp. 131–58. Cf. Michael MccGwire, *Military Objectives in Soviet Foreign Policy* (Washington, D.C.: Brookings Institution, 1987).

14. This draws on Nolan, *Global Engagement*, pp. 4–5. This chapter was drafted by Nolan based on contributions from Ashton B. Carter, William J. Perry, Wolfgang H. Reinicke, and John D. Steinbruner, among others.

15. Michael Mandelbaum, *The Dawn of Peace in Europe* (New York: Twentieth Century Fund Press, 1996), p. 105.

16. Among the earliest exceptions were Bruce G. Blair, *Strategic Command and Control: Redefining the Nuclear Threat* (Washington, D.C.: Brookings Institution, 1985); Daniel F. Ford, *The Button: The Pentagon's Strategic Command and Control System* (New York: Simon and Schuster, 1985); Ashton B. Carter, John D. Steinbruner, and Charles A. Zraket, eds., *Managing Nuclear Operations* (Washington, D.C.: Brookings Institution, 1987); Sigal, "Case for Eliminating Battlefield Nuclear Weapons," pp. 33–53.

17. Some of Reagan's repeated references to nuclear abolition in public and private and Shultz's efforts toward this goal are chronicled in Ronald Reagan, *An American Life* (New York: Simon and Schuster, 1990), pp. 257–58, 268, 549–50, 605–6; George P. Shultz, *Turmoil and Triumph: My Years as Secretary of State* (New York: Charles Scribner's Sons, 1993), pp. 189, 258, 358–60, 372, 376, 466–67, 484, 511–12, 519, 537, 576, 699–705, 754; Robert C. McFarlane and Zofia Smardz, *Special Trust: Pride, Principle and Politics inside the White House* (New York: Cadell and Davies, 1994), p. 296. Cf. Martin Anderson, *Revolution* (New York: Harcourt Brace Jovanovich, 1987), pp. 72–73; Edwin Meese III, *With Reagan: The Inside Story* (Washington, D.C.: Regnery Gateway, 1992), pp. 186–87.

18. Ronald Reagan, address to the Japanese Diet, November 10, 1983, in Shultz, *Turmoil and Triumph*, p. 189.

19. On public attitudes toward defenses, see Thomas W. Graham, "The Politics of Failure: Strategic Nuclear Arms Control, Public Opinion, Domestic Politics in the United States, 1945–1980," Ph.D. diss., M.I.T., 1989, ch. 6.

20. Shultz, *Turmoil and Triumph*, p. 258. Cf. Reagan, *American Life*, pp. 549–50.

21. The author himself was one of those arms controllers who assumed, incorrectly, that the zero option and other deep cuts proposals were foisted on the president by advisers who were determined to avoid arms limitations. He wrongly dismissed the president's public utterances about getting rid of nuclear arms as oratorical flourishes, not a serious commitment. Leon V. Sigal, "Kennan's Cuts," *Foreign Policy*, no. 44 (Fall 1981): 70–81; Leon V. Sigal, "Getting Over the Summit," *Bulletin of the Atomic Scientists* 43, no. 1 (January/February 1987): 12–13.

22. Shultz, *Turmoil and Triumph*, p. 490.

23. Strobe Talbott, *The Master of the Game: Paul Nitze and the Nuclear Peace* (New York: Alfred A. Knopf, 1988), pp. 217–18.

24. Strobe Talbott, *Deadly Gambits: The Reagan Administration and the Stalemate in Nuclear Arms Control* (New York: Alfred A. Knopf, 1984), p. 256.

25. McFarlane and Smardz, *Special Trust*, p. 226.

26. Talbott, *Master of the Game*, p. 204. The K.G.B. was aware of this possibility and sought to collect intelligence on it. Raymond L. Garthoff, *The Great Transition: American-Soviet Relations and the End of the Cold War* (Washington, D.C.: Brookings Institution, 1994), p. 515n22.

27. Shultz, *Turmoil and Triumph*, p. 575.

28. Ibid., p. 258.

29. Talbott, *Deadly Gambits*, p. 221.

30. Benjamin I. Page and Robert Y. Shapiro, *The Rational Public: Fifty Years of Trends in Policy Preferences* (Chicago: University of Chicago Press, 1992), pp. 264–74, 280–81.

31. Those who thought the United States should "get tough" with the Soviet Union dropped from 74 percent in 1980 to 40 percent in May 1982. In July 1982 68 percent said the Reagan administration was "going too far" in its nuclear buildup. In April 1983 the public preferred a nuclear freeze to a buildup by a margin of 64 to 25 percent. Robert Y. Shapiro and Benjamin I. Page, "Foreign Policy and the Rational Public," *Journal of Conflict Resolution* 32, no. 2 (June 1988): 243; Leslie H. Gelb, "Poll Finds Doubt over Response to Soviet Threat," *New York Times*, April 15, 1983, p. A-1.

32. Leon V. Sigal, "Warming to the Freeze," *Foreign Policy*, no. 48 (Fall 1982): 54. Cf. Reagan, *American Life*, pp. 295, 297.

33. Talbott, *Deadly Gambits*, p. 80.

34. Ibid., chs. 11–14.

35. Shultz, *Turmoil and Triumph*, p. 258.

36. Graham, "Politics of Failure," ch. 6.

37. Reagan, *American Life*, p. 570.

38. Ronald Reagan, for one, made that connection. Ibid., p. 584.

39. The Soviet delegation, in a presentation cleared with Moscow, had read a statement saying only that, with the start of deployments, the current round of talks was over and that it would not set a date for resumption of talks,

leaving the door open for such a resumption. But another statement, issued over Andropov's name that day, said the talks could resume only when the missiles were withdrawn, making it more difficult for the Soviets to climb down. Pavel Palazchenko, *My Years with Gorbachev and Shevardnadze: The Memoir of a Soviet Interpreter* (University Park, Pa.: Pennsylvania State University Press, 1997), p. 19.

40. National Intelligence Estimate, NIE 11-18-91, "The Implications of Recent Soviet Military-Political Activity," June 1991, in Robert M. Gates, *From the Shadows: The Ultimate Insider's Story of Five Presidents and How They Won the Cold War* (New York: Simon and Schuster, 1996), pp. 272–73.

41. President Reagan viewed the tape on October 10. Shortly thereafter, he was fully briefed on the Single Integrated Operational Plan, or SIOP, for the first time. A "most sobering experience," he noted in his diary. Reagan, *American Life*, p. 585.

42. Gates, *From the Shadows*, p. 258.

43. Geoffrey Howe, *Conflict of Loyalty* (London: Macmillan, 1994), p. 350. Cf. Christopher Andrew and Oleg Gordievsky, *KGB: The Inside Story of Its Foreign Operations from Lenin to Gorbachev* (London: Hodder and Stoughton, 1990), pp. 488–507.

44. Gates, *From the Shadows*, pp. 270–73. Cf., Oleg Gordievsky, *Next Stop Execution: The Autobiography of Oleg Gordievsky* (London: Macmillan, 1995), pp. 271–73.

45. Don Oberdorfer, *The Turn: From the Cold War to a New Era* (New York: Poseidon Press, 1991), p. 67. See also pp. 65–68. Cf. Garthoff, *Great Transition*, pp. 138–40. Shultz, who was not briefed by the C.I.A. on its findings, dismisses the tension as just talk. Shultz, *Turmoil and Triumph*, pp. 464.

46. Reagan, *American Life*, pp. 588–89. See also pp. 257–58, 268, 595, 602, and his expression of concern cited by Margaret Thatcher, *The Downing Street Years* (New York: HarperCollins, 1993), p. 324. Cf. Beth A. Fischer, *The Reagan Reversal: Foreign Policy and the End of the Cold War* (Columbia, Mo.: University of Missouri Press, 1997), pp. 120–37.

47. Reagan, *American Life*, pp. 13, 268–70, 567, 588–89, 592, 594, 603, 616, 636, 644.

48. David A. Stockman, *The Triumph of Politics: Why the Reagan Revolution Failed* (New York: Harper and Row, 1986), pp. 100–9, 269–99.

49. Roald Z. Sagdeev, *The Making of a Soviet Scientist: My Adventures in Nuclear Fusion and Space from Stalin to Star Wars* (New York: John Wiley and Sons, 1994), p. 273.

50. Savel'yev and Detinov, *Big Five*, pp. 172–73; Matthew Evangelista, "The Paradox of State Strength: Transnational Relations, Domestic Structures, and Security Policy in Russia and the Soviet Union," *International Organization* 49, no. 1 (Winter 1995): 16–17.

51. Reagan's March 1983 letter to Yuri Andropov invited the direct correspondence. "Historically, our predecessors have made better progress when

communicating has been private and candid. If you wish to engage in such communication, you will find me ready." McFarlane and Smardz, *Special Trust*, pp. 293–94, 297–98. He renewed the invitation in a letter to Konstantin Chernenko in July 1984. Reagan, *American Life*, pp. 594–95. On Shultz's role, see p. 606.

52. Shultz, *Turmoil and Triumph*, p. 466. Cf. p. 376 and Kenneth L. Adelman, *The Great Universal Embrace: Arms Summitry—A Skeptic's Account* (New York: Simon and Schuster, 1989), p. 65. Robert Gates, one of Shultz's well-placed opponents, confirms his pivotal role. Gates, *From the Shadows*, pp. 281–82, 292, 323.

53. Shultz, *Turmoil and Triumph*, pp. 466–67.

54. Reagan, *American Life*, pp. 591–92.

55. McFarlane and Smardz, *Special Trust*, p. 296.

56. Shultz, *Turmoil and Triumph*, p. 507.

57. Thatcher, *Downing Street Years*, pp. 247, 462, 466–68, 473.

58. Ibid., p. 468. The president remained unconvinced. Afterward, he pulled McFarlane aside and and told him, "Bud, you know, she's really missing the point on SDI. And she's doing a lot of damage with all this sniping about it." McFarlane and Smardz, *Special Trust*, p. 306.

59. McFarlane and Smardz, *Special Trust*, pp. 303–4.

60. Fred I. Greenstein and William C. Wohlforth, eds., *Retrospective on the End of the Cold War*, Monograph Series no. 6, Center of International Studies, Princeton University, 1994, pp. 15–16.

61. Talbott, *Master of the Game*, pp. 213–14. On the fight over instructions, see Jay Winik, *On the Brink: The Dramatic, Behind-the-Scenes Saga of the Reagan Era and the Men and Women Who Won the Cold War* (New York: Simon and Schuster, 1996), pp. 320–21.

62. Shultz, *Turmoil and Triumph*, p. 519. Cf. McFarlane and Smardz, *Special Trust*, pp. 304–5.

63. Talbott, *Master of the Game*, p. 265.

64. Max M. Kampelman, *Entering New Worlds: The Memoirs of a Private Man in Public Life* (New York: HarperCollins, 1991), p. 311.

65. William E. Odom, *The Collapse of the Soviet Military* (New Haven: Yale University Press, 1998), pp. 99–100. The C.I.A. characterized Shevardnadze as someone with "flamboyant style, courageous, decisive, intelligent, and with an imaginative approach to problem solving," in short, as "anything but a faceless implementer of policy." Gates, *From the Shadows*, p. 341.

66. Savel'yev and Detinov, *Big Five*, p. 29. See also p. 20.

67. Ibid., pp. 16–18, 21, 28–29.

68. Ibid., pp. 35–39.

69. Ibid., pp. 60, 111, 113, 115–17.

70. Ibid., p. 120. Cf. Mikhail S. Gorbachev, *Memoirs* (New York: Doubleday, 1996), pp. 404–5.

71. Talbott, *Master of the Game*, p. 274; McFarlane and Smardz, *Special Trust*, p. 314; Gorbachev letter to Reagan, September 12, 1985, quoted in Reagan, *American Life*, p. 626.

72. Oberdorfer, *Turn*, p. 136. On the origins of the INF initiative, see Savel'yev and Detinov, *Big Five*, p. 127.

73. Gorbachev, *Memoirs*, p. 407. See also p. 411.

74. Greenstein and Wohlforth, *Retrospective on the End of the Cold War*, p. 13.

75. Shultz, *Turmoil and Triumph*, p. 603. Cf. McFarlane and Smardz, *Special Trust*, pp. 317–18.

76. Oberdorfer, *Turn*, p. 157.

77. "Text of the Joint U.S.-Soviet Statement," *New York Times*, November 22, 1985, p. A-15. In his response of October 31, 1985, Reagan had picked up on the suggestion in Gorbachev's letter of September 12 to underscore the inadmissibility of nuclear war. Reagan, *American Life*, pp. 624, 629.

78. McFarlane and Smardz, *Special Trust*, pp. 319–20. Cf. Shultz, *Turmoil and Triumph*, p. 700; Palazchenko, *My Years with Gorbachev and Shevardnadze*, p. 43. Reagan repeated the formulation in a February 1986 letter to Gorbachev. Oberdorfer, *Turn*, p. 169.

79. Talbott, *Master of the Game*, pp. 263–64.

80. Savel'yev and Detinov, *Big Five*, p. 92.

81. Ibid., pp. 92–93. On Gorbachev's motives, see Anatoly Chernyaev, quoted in Greenstein and Wohlforth, *Retrospective on the End of the Cold War*, p. 41.

82. Shultz, *Turmoil and Triumph*, p. 700. Cf. George P. Shultz, quoted in Greenstein and Wohlforth, *Retrospective on the End of the Cold War*, p. 42.

83. Shultz, *Turmoil and Triumph*, pp. 716, 718.

84. McFarlane and Smardz, *Special Trust*, p. 223.

85. Shultz, *Turmoil and Triumph*, p. 717. For an account of the decision-making by one proponent of abandoning SALT II, see Adelman, *Great Universal Embrace*, pp. 268–77, 282–85.

86. As Gorbachev would suggest in an August interview in *Time*, he intended to prohibit field testing, which comported with the understanding that Gerard Smith, the American negotiator, had conveyed to the Senate in 1972, at the time the ABM Treaty was ratified. Talbott, *Master of the Game*, pp. 277–78.

87. Shultz, *Turmoil and Triumph*, pp. 718, 720. The idea originated with Under Secretary of Defense Fred Iklé and was backed by Richard Perle, who had been looking for a "boffo" counterproposal to Gorbachev's headline-grabbing proposal of January and thought it "would expose the theoretical basis for Soviet objections to SDI, thus putting them on the defensive." Admiral John Poindexter, the president's national security adviser, married the idea to the State Department's proposal to abide by the ABM Treaty. Oberdorfer, *Turn*, pp. 170–74; Talbott, *Master of the Game*, p. 307; Winik, *On the Brink*, p. 413; Adelman, *Great Universal Embrace*, pp. 27–29.

88. Adelman, *Great Universal Embrace*, pp. 28, 30.

89. Shultz, *Turmoil and Triumph*, p. 723. Unilateralist supporters of SDI tried to keep Reagan from sharing it. Adelman, *Great Universal Embrace*, pp. 314–15, 317–21.

90. Gorbachev, *Memoirs*, p. 414.

91. Talbott, *Master of the Game*, p. 315. The idea had come from Chernyaev, according to Archie Brown, *The Gorbachev Factor* (New York: Oxford University Press, 1996), p. 231.

92. Gates, *From the Shadows*, pp. 404–5.

93. Savel'yev and Detinov, *Big Five*, pp. 152–53.

94. Shultz, *Turmoil and Triumph*, p. 758.

95. Garthoff, *Great Transition*, p. 286.

96. "Directive to the Foreign Ministers of the USSR and the USA Concerning the Drafting of Agreements on Nuclear Disarmament," in Oberdorfer, *Turn*, pp. 445–46. The proposal was prepared by Sergei Akhromeyev, chief of the Soviet general staff, along with Yuli Vorontsov of the Foreign Ministry and Georgi Kornienko of the International Department of the Central Committee. Brown, *Gorbachev Factor*, p. 232. Chernyaev raised objections. Cf. his diary reference in Odom, *Collapse of the Soviet Military*, p. 131.

97. Shultz, *Turmoil and Triumph*, p. 760. Cf. Adelman, *Great Universal Embrace*, p. 55.

98. Garthoff, *Great Transition*, p. 288.

99. Shultz, *Turmoil and Triumph*, p. 761.

100. The C.I.A. had told Shultz not to expect a significant Soviet military role at Reykjavik, according to Carolyn McGiffert Ekedahl and Melvin A. Goodman, *The Wars of Eduard Shevardnadze* (University Park, Pa.: Pennsylvania State University Press, 1997), p. 112.

101. The Americans believed Soviet chief of staff Akhromeyev was the key to winning over the Soviet delegation, but Akhromeyev says he contemplated resigning when Gorbachev decided to accept the U.S. proposal. Garthoff, *Great Transition*, p. 287n102.

102. Oberdorfer, *Turn*, p. 95. Cf. Adelman, *Great Universal Embrace*, pp. 60–61.

103. Savel'yev and Detinov, *Big Five*, pp. 130–31; Gorbachev, *Memoirs*, pp. 439–40.

104. Oberdorfer, *Turn*, p. 196.

105. Shultz, *Turmoil and Triumph*, p. 768.

106. Ibid. Cf. Oberdorfer, *Turn*, p. 197.

107. Bernard Gwertzman, "Shultz Details Reagan's Arms Bid at Iceland to Clarify U.S. Position," *New York Times*, October 18, 1986, p. 5.

108. Shultz, *Turmoil and Triumph*, p. 769.

109. Oberdorfer, *Turn*, p. 201.

110. Adelman, *Great Universal Embrace*, p. 20.

111. Ibid., pp. 71–72.

112. Gwertzman, "Shultz Details Reagan's Arms Bid at Iceland," p. 5.

113. Oberdorfer, *Turn*, p. 202. Cf. Shultz, *Turmoil and Triumph*, p. 772.

114. Oberdorfer, *Turn*, p. 203.

115. Savel'yev and Detinov, *Big Five*, pp. 129–30.

116. Garthoff, *Great Transition*, p. 298n124.

117. Shultz, *Turmoil and Triumph*, pp. 772–73.

118. Ibid., pp. 772, 774.

119. Adelman, *Great Universal Embrace*, pp. 80–81.

120. "Draft Interim Report," Special Committee on Nuclear Strategy and Arms Control, North Atlantic Assembly, Brussels, May 1987, p. 8.

121. Karen DeYoung, "British Confident They've Curbed U.S. Excesses," *Washington Post*, November 19, 1986, p. A-1. Cf. Thatcher, *Downing Street Years*, pp. 472–73.

122. Shultz, *Turmoil and Triumph*, p. 777.

123. James Schlesinger, "Nuclear Deterrence, the Ultimate Reality," *Washington Post*, October 21, 1986, p. A-17, a position he amplified in "Reykjavik and Revelations: A Turn of the Tide?" *Foreign Affairs* 65, no. 3 (America and the World 1986/87): 426–46.

124. Shultz, *Turmoil and Triumph*, p. 777.

125. Garthoff, *Great Transition*, p. 292; Palazchenko, *My Years with Gorbachev and Shevardnadze*, p. 68.

126. John W. Parker, *Kremlin in Transition*, vol. 2: *Gorbachev, 1985–1989* (London: Routledge, 1991), p. 144.

127. Shultz, *Turmoil and Triumph*, p. 776; Adelman, *Great Universal Embrace*, pp. 85–86.

128. Michael R. Gordon, "U.S. Ideas on Arms Offered in Iceland Are Being Refined," *New York Times*, November 2, 1986, p. 1; Garthoff, *Great Transition*, p. 292; Palazchenko, *My Years with Gorbachev and Shevardnadze*, p. 60; Adelman, *Great Universal Embrace*, pp. 54–55.

129. Shultz, *Turmoil and Triumph*, p. 871; Kampelman, *Entering New Worlds*, p. 340.

130. Garthoff, *Great Transition*, p. 309. Weinberger also tried to get Reagan to back away from the agreement on 100 INF missiles a side and to insist on zero, but the president, at Shultz's urging, refused. "On May 15," wrote Shultz, "in what I could interpret only as an act of defiance and sabotage of a president weakened by the Iran-Contra affair, Cap engineered a statement in the communiqué of a meeting of NATO defense ministers calling for the elimination of *all* long-range INF missiles." Shultz, *Turmoil and Triumph*, p. 899.

131. Raymond L. Garthoff, *Policy versus the Law: The Reinterpretation of the ABM Treaty* (Washington, D.C.: Brookings Institution, 1987), pp. 2–3, 12–13.

132. Oberdorfer, *Turn*, pp. 216–17.

133. Talbott, *Master of the Game*, p. 360; Evangelista, "Paradox of State Strength," pp. 19–20. Cf. Garthoff, *Great Transition*, p. 515n22; Palazchenko, *My Years with Gorbachev and Shevardnadze*, pp. 55, 69; Evangelista, *Unarmed Forces*, pp. 328–29, 333. In 1993 Palazchenko disclosed that some at working levels of the Foreign Ministry urged that "we should deemphasize SDI in our positions." Greenstein and Wohlforth, *Retrospective on the End of the Cold War*, p. 15.

134. Celestine Bohlen, "Soviets Separate SDI from Missile Accord," *Washington Post*, March 1, 1987, p. A-1.

135. Kampelman, *Entering New Worlds*, pp. 319–20. Emphasis added.

136. John Deutch, Brent Scowcroft, and R. James Woolsey, "The Danger of the Zero Option," *Washington Post*, March 31, 1987, p. A-21.

137. Henry Kissinger, "Forget the 'Zero Option,'" *Washington Post*, April 5, 1987, p. C-2.

138. Savel'yev and Detinov, *Big Five*, pp. 51–52.

139. Shultz, *Turmoil and Triumph*, p. 884.

140. Ibid., pp. 890–91; Hans-Dietrich Genscher, *Rebuilding a House Divided: A Memoir by the Architect of Germany's Reunification* (New York: Broadway Books, 1998), p. 221. On the origins of the proposal, see Savel'yev and Detinov, *Big Five*, pp. 131–32.

141. Thatcher, *Downing Street Years*, pp. 771–72.

142. Savel'yev and Detinov, *Big Five*, pp. 133–34. Cf. Palazchenko, *My Years with Gorbachev and Shevardnadze*, p. 67.

143. Reagan, *American Life*, p. 686. On May 28 Horst Teltschik told Robert Linhard that the Pershing I-As must be removed "at the end of the process." On June 1, Kohl, after a delay to placate opposition from some Christian Democrats, notified Washington of his acceptance of zero shorter-range missiles. This was formalized at a meeting of NATO foreign ministers on June 12, which also insisted on a "firebreak" against yet a third zero, eliminating all battlefield nuclear arms. Shultz, *Turmoil and Triumph*, pp. 905, 984n; Genscher, *Rebuilding a House Divided*, pp. 226–28.

144. Thatcher, *Downing Street Years*, p. 770.

145. Garthoff, *Great Transition*, p. 324; Shultz, *Turmoil and Triumph*, p. 997.

146. Shultz, *Turmoil and Triumph*, p. 999. Cf. Palazchenko, *My Years with Gorbachev and Shevardnadze*, p. 73.

147. Shultz, *Turmoil and Triumph*, p. 1086.

148. Thatcher, *Downing Street Years*, p. 775.

149. George F. Will, "How Reagan Changed America," *Newsweek*, January 9, 1989, p. 16.

150. Shultz, *Turmoil and Triumph*, p. 1086. That judgment needs one qualification: it applies to the objectives of Reagan, not as originally laid out but as eventually clarified by Shultz.

151. Jack F. Matlock, Jr., *Autopsy on an Empire: The American Ambassador's Account of the Collapse of the Soviet Union* (New York: Random House, 1995), p. 98.

CHAPTER 6

1. George Bush and Brent Scowcroft, *A World Transformed* (New York: Alfred A. Knopf, 1998), p. 28.

2. Michael Beschloss and Strobe Talbott, *At the Highest Levels: The Inside Story of the End of the Cold War* (Boston: Little, Brown, 1993), p. 205. Bush made the remark to a group of contractors visiting the White House on April 24, 1990, in the context of discussing the crisis in Lithuania and the possibility a reactionary coup in Moscow.

3. "Rising Political Instability under Gorbachev: Understanding the Problem and Prospects for Resolution," Office of Soviet Analysis, Central Intelligence Agency, April 1989, pp. iii, 15, quoted in Robert M. Gates, *From the Shadows: The Ultimate Insider's Story of Five Presidents and How They Won the Cold War* (New York: Simon and Schuster, 1996), p. 511.

4. Gates, *From the Shadows*, p. 526. Cf. Raymond L. Garthoff, *The Great Transition: American-Soviet Relations and the End of the Cold War* (Washington, D.C.: Brookings Institution, 1994), p. 388n30. On the president's recollection, see Bush and Scowcroft, *World Transformed*, p. 154.

5. For Bush's own views, see Don Oberdorfer, *The Turn: From the Cold War to a New Era* (New York: Poseidon Press, 1991), p. 329.

6. Philip Zelikow and Condoleezza Rice, *Germany Unified and Europe Transformed: A Study in Statecraft* (Cambridge, Mass.: Belknap Press, 1995), p. 20; Robert L. Hutchings, *American Diplomacy and the End of the Cold War: An Insider's Account of U.S. Policy in Europe, 1989–1992* (Washington, D.C.: Woodrow Wilson Center Press, 1997), pp. 27–28, 31–32.

7. Carolyn McGiffert Ekedahl and Melvin A. Goodman, *The Wars of Eduard Shevardnadze* (University Park, Pa.: Pennsylvania State University Press, 1997), p. 101.

8. Ibid., p. 95.

9. Bush and Scowcroft, *World Transformed*, p. 12.

10. James A. Baker III, *The Politics of Diplomacy: Revolution, War, and Peace, 1989–1992* (New York: G. P. Putnam's Sons, 1995), p. 69.

11. Beschloss and Talbott, *At the Highest Levels*, p. 24.

12. William Safire, "Baker's First Blunder," *New York Times*, January 5, 1989, p. A-23.

13. Beschloss and Talbott, *At the Highest Levels*, p. 24.

14. Ibid., p. 17.

15. Garthoff, *Great Transition*, pp. 339–40.

16. Beschloss and Talbott, *At the Highest Levels*, p. 25.

17. Bernard Weinraub, "Cheney Remarks on Soviet Future Ruffle the White House's Feathers," *New York Times*, May 2, 1989, p. A-1.

18. Baker, *Politics of Diplomacy*, p. 70.

19. Jack F. Matlock, Jr., *Autopsy on an Empire: The American Ambassador's Account of the Collapse of the Soviet Union* (New York: Random House, 1995),

pp. 186–88. One point in Matlock's cable did register with Scowcroft, "that we might have leverage over Moscow because of its need for Western economic resources and know-how." It became the basis of a memorandum drafted by the N.S.C. staff laying out a four-part strategy for dealing with the Soviet Union. After shoring up its position at home and in NATO, the administration would focus its attention on Eastern Europe and Soviet actions in the third world. Bush and Scowcroft, *World Transformed*, pp. 40–41.

20. Beschloss and Talbott, *At the Highest Levels*, p. 34.

21. Ibid., p. 31.

22. Eduard Shevardnadze, *The Future Belongs to Freedom* (New York: Free Press, 1991), p. 122.

23. Garthoff, *Great Transition*, pp. 529–30. That April a revised version of the *Soviet Military Encyclopedia* contained a key conclusion under the entry for Military Strategy: "The most important task for Soviet military strategy in contemporary conditions is working out the problems of preventing war." John W. Parker, *Kremlin in Transition*, vol. 2: *Gorbachev, 1985–1989* (London: Routledge, 1991), p. 171.

24. Garthoff, *Great Transition*, pp. 354, 359.

25. Leon V. Sigal, "Signs of a Soviet Shift: Conventional Forces in Europe," *Bulletin of the Atomic Scientists* 43, no. 10 (December 1987): 16–20.

26. Garthoff, *Great Transition*, pp. 359–60. On General Akhromeyev's recollection of the military's role, see Matthew Evangelista, *Unarmed Forces: The Transnational Movement to End the Cold War* (Ithaca, N.Y.: Cornell University Press, 1999), pp. 301–2, 313.

27. Evangelista, *Unarmed Forces*, pp. 311–15.

28. Parker, *Kremlin in Transition*, vol. 2, pp. 286–87, 292n37.

29. Ibid., pp. 278–79. Defense Minister Dmitri Yazov added further details in an interview in *Izvestia*, reprinted in Foreign Broadcast Information Service, FBIS-SOV-89-038, February 28, 1989, pp. 1–4.

30. National Intelligence Estimate, NIC M 89-10005, "Soviet Theater Forces in 1991: The Impact of Unilateral Withdrawals on Structure and Capabilities," November 1989, p. 2. The cuts would give NATO seven days' additional warning time, according to Sam Nunn, "Responding to Gorbachev," *Washington Post*, December 18, 1988, p. C-7.

31. Bush and Scowcroft, *World Transformed*, p. 6. An intelligence estimate that October had a different characterization: the withdrawal "will result in a significant reduction in the combat capability of Soviet forces in Eastern Europe." National Intelligence Estimate, NIC M 89-10003, "Status of Soviet Unilateral Withdrawals," October 1989, p. iii.

32. Hans-Dietrich Genscher, *Rebuilding a House Divided: A Memoir by the Architect of Germany's Reunification* (New York: Broadway Books, 1998), p. 255. Cf. Pavel Palazchenko, *My Years with Gorbachev and Shevardnadze: The Memoir of a Soviet Interpreter* (University Park, Pa.: Pennsylvania State University Press,

1997), pp. 67, 132; Aleksandr G. Savel'yev and Nikolay N. Detinov, *The Big Five: Arms Control Decision-Making in the Soviet Union* (Westport, Conn: Praeger, 1995), pp. 133–34.

33. Beschloss and Talbott, *At the Highest Levels*, p. 36.

34. John Newhouse, "The Diplomatic Round: Eternal Severities," *New Yorker*, October 23, 1989, p. 108.

35. Margaret Thatcher, *The Downing Street Years* (New York: HarperCollins, 1993), pp. 784–86.

36. Bush and Scowcroft, *World Transformed*, p. 65; Genscher, *Rebuilding a House Divided*, p. 240. Genscher already had spoken out in the Bundestag for postponing new deployments. Cf. p. 233.

37. Baker, *Politics of Diplomacy*, p. 87.

38. Newhouse, "Diplomatic Round," p. 106

39. Ibid., pp. 106–7; Genscher, *Rebuilding a House Divided*, pp. 244–45.

40. Genscher, *Rebuilding a House Divided*, pp. 245–46.

41. Thomas L. Friedman, "U.S. Anger Rising Against Germans over NATO Stand," *New York Times*, April 30, 1989, p. 1.

42. Bush and Scowcroft, *World Transformed*, p. 68.

43. Ibid., p. 69.

44. Ibid., p. 70.

45. Thatcher, *Downing Street Years*, p. 786.

46. Newhouse, "Diplomatic Round," pp. 107–8.

47. Leon V. Sigal, "The Case for Eliminating Battlefield Nuclear Weapons," in *Battlefield Nuclear Weapons: Issues and Options*, ed. Stephen D. Biddle and Peter D. Feaver (Cambridge, Mass.: Harvard University Center for Science and International Affairs, 1989), pp. 33–53.

48. Michael R. Gordon, "Reagan Arms Adviser Says Bush Is Wrong on Short-Range Missiles," *New York Times*, May 3, 1989, p. A-1. Nitze elaborated his views in an op-ed, Paul Nitze, "What Bush Should Do to Solve the NATO Flap," *Washington Post*, May 14, 1989, p. C-1.

49. Michael R. Gordon, "U.S. Ex-Officials Urge Talks on NATO Missiles," *New York Times*, May 2, 1989, p. A-10.

50. George C. Wilson, "NATO 'Shooting Itself in the Foot,' Nunn Says," *Washington Post*, May 4, 1989, p. A-30; Michael R. Gordon, "Bush Is Criticized on Capitol Hill over NATO Dispute," *New York Times*, May 4, 1989, p. A-1.

51. Baker, *Politics of Diplomacy*, pp. 90, 93.

52. Bush and Scowcroft, *World Transformed*, p. 38. Cf. p. 65.

53. Baker, *Politics of Diplomacy*, p. 91.

54. France, which had troops in West Germany but refused to participate in MBFR, now relented, but it still opposed bloc-to-bloc talks, preferring to participate in CFE on its own. As in MBFR, NATO wanted CFE to cover only ground forces, while the Warsaw Pact sought to extend the talks to air and naval forces in the region and chemical and nuclear arms. The Soviet

Union wanted to exempt some parts of the Transcaucasus military district, and NATO in turn sought to exempt parts of Turkey.

55. Mikhail S. Gorbachev, *Memoirs* (New York: Doubleday, 1996), pp. 455–56.

56. Beschloss and Talbott, *At the Highest Levels*, p. 39. Aspin's criticism also was felt in the White House. Cf. Bush and Scowcroft, *World Transformed*, p. 59.

57. Newhouse, "Diplomatic Round," p. 108.

58. Beschloss and Talbott, *At the Highest Levels*, pp. 37–38; Bush and Scowcroft, *World Transformed*, p. 43.

59. Hutchings, *American Diplomacy and the End of the Cold War*, p. 3.

60. Bush and Scowcroft, *World Transformed*, p. 44.

61. Ibid., p. 43.

62. Ibid., p. 44. Cf. Gates, *From the Shadows*, p. 462.

63. Beschloss and Talbott, *At the Highest Levels*, pp. 55, 59–60.

64. Baker, *Politics of Diplomacy*, p. 74.

65. Ibid., pp. 80–81. Gorbachev, *Memoirs*, p. 501, has a somewhat different wording, "Let the fruit ripen and fall into our lap."

66. Thomas L. Friedman, "Gorbachev Hands a Surprised Baker an Arms Proposal," *New York Times*, May 12, 1989, p. A-1.

67. Baker, *Politics of Diplomacy*, p. 82.

68. Ibid., p. 83.

69. Gates, *From the Shadows*, p. 462.

70. Baker, *Politics of Diplomacy*, p. 93.

71. Take Me to Your Leader," *New York Times*, May 21, 1989, sec. IV, p. 26.

72. Beschloss and Talbott, *At the Highest Levels*, p. 74.

73. Ibid., p. 76.

74. Bush and Scowcroft, *World Transformed*, p. 73.

75. Beschloss and Talbott, *At the Highest Levels*, p. 77; Baker, *Politics of Diplomacy*, pp. 93–94.

76. Bush and Scowcroft, *World Transformed*, p. 74.

77. Beschloss and Talbott, *At the Highest Levels*, p. 77.

78. Bush and Scowcroft, *World Transformed*, p. 74.

79. Hutchings, *American Diplomacy and the End of the Cold War*, p. 54.

80. Thatcher, *Downing Street Years*, p. 788.

81. Baker, *Politics of Diplomacy*, pp. 94–96. The administration agreed to negotiate on three conditions: talks on short-range missiles would not begin until a CFE accord had been concluded, reductions agreed to would not be carried out until conventional force cuts were under way, and elimination of short-range nuclear missiles was ruled out. Michael R. Gordon, "New U.S. Arms Line Would Slow NATO Cuts," *New York Times*, May 21, 1989, p. 11.

82. Bush and Scowcroft, *World Transformed*, pp. 72, 81–82. Cf. Genscher, *Rebuilding a House Divided*, pp. 257–58.

83. Beschloss and Talbott, *At the Highest Levels*, p. 80; Oberdorfer, *Turn*, p. 371.

84. "Points of Mutual Advantage: *Perestroika* and American Foreign Policy," October 16, 1989, *Department of State Bulletin* 89, no. 2153 (December 1989): 10. Emphasis added.

85. "Prerequisites and Principles for Arms Control," October 23, 1989, *Department of State Bulletin* 89, no. 2153 (December 1989): 15.

86. Baker, *Politics of Diplomacy*, p. 156. See also pp. 157–58. Cf. Gates, *From the Shadows*, pp. 480–81.

87. Baker, *Politics of Diplomacy*, p. 156.

88. Beschloss and Talbott, *At the Highest Levels*, p. 123. Cf. Baker, *Politics of Diplomacy*, pp. 156–57; Gates, *From the Shadows*, pp. 473–74.

89. Colin L. Powell, *My American Journey* (New York: Random House, 1995), pp. 436–37. Cf. pp. 444–45, 451–52, 454–55.

90. Bush and Scowcroft, *World Transformed*, p. 208.

91. Gates, *From the Shadows*, p. 487; Bush and Scowcroft, *World Transformed*, p. 209.

92. Bush and Scowcroft, *World Transformed*, pp. 209–10.

93. Ibid., p. 210.

94. Zelikow and Rice, *Germany Unified and Europe Transformed*, p. 170.

95. Bush and Scowcroft, *World Transformed*, pp. 211–14.

96. Hutchings, *American Diplomacy and the End of the Cold War*, p. 128.

97. Bush and Scowcroft, *World Transformed*, p. 214.

98. Bob Woodward, "The Conversion of Gen. Powell," *Washington Post*, December 21, 1989, p. A-1.

99. The treaty would not be revised to take the new political realities into account until 1999. Jeffrey D. McCausland, "Endgame: CFE Adaptation and the OSCE Summit," *Arms Control Today* 29, no. 7 (September–October 1999): 15–19.

100. Baker, *Politics of Diplomacy*, p. 212.

101. Hutchings, *American Diplomacy and the End of the Cold War*, p. 133.

102. James Macintosh, "Confidence-Building Measures in Europe: 1975 to the Present," in *Encyclopedia of Arms Control*, ed. Richard Dean Burns, vol. 2 (New York: Charles Scribner and Sons, 1993), pp. 929–45. Cf. Jonathan Dean, *Watershed in Europe: Dismantling the East-West Military Confrontation* (Lexington, Mass.: D. C. Heath, 1987).

103. Beschloss and Talbott, *At the Highest Levels*, p. 363.

104. On the original number of sites, see Ekedahl and Goodman, *Wars of Eduard Shevardnadze*, p. 125. Most of the underreporting seems to have been the result of removing all treaty-limited equipment from divisions with small amounts of it, allowing the Soviets to exclude the division from monitoring. The effect was to reduce the Soviet Union's quota of annual inspections. P. Terrence Hopmann, "From MBFR to CFE: Negotiating Conventional Arms Control in Europe," in Burns, *Encyclopedia of Arms Control*, vol. 2, p. 983.

105. Ekedahl and Goodman, *Wars of Eduard Shevardnadze,* p. 243.

106. Beschloss and Talbott, *At the Highest Levels,* p. 290.

107. Ibid., pp. 292.

108. Ekedahl and Goodman, *Wars of Eduard Shevardnadze,* p. 244. Cf. Shevardnadze, *Future Belongs to Freedom,* p. 214.

109. Shevardnadze, *Future Belongs to Freedom,* p. xiv. See also p. 212.

110. Beschloss and Talbott, *At the Highest Levels,* p. 294.

111. Shevardnadze, *Future Belongs to Freedom,* p. xix.

112. Beschloss and Talbott, *At the Highest Levels,* p. 293.

113. Shevardnadze may also have resigned before Gorbachev, trying to appease the hard-liners, replaced him. Archie Brown, *The Gorbachev Factor* (New York: Oxford University Press, 1996), p. 279.

114. The rise of realism among Soviet foreign ministry officials is documented in Steven Kull, *Burying Lenin: The Revolution in Soviet Ideology and Foreign Policy* (Boulder, Colo.: Westview Press, 1992), pp. 67–80.

115. Ekedahl and Goodman, *Wars of Eduard Shevardnadze,* p. 106. Cf. Palazchenko, *My Years with Gorbachev and Shevardnadze,* pp. 30, 248.

116. Anatoly Dobrynin, *In Confidence: Moscow's Ambassador to America's Six Cold War Presidents* (New York: Times Books, 1995), p. 628.

117. Beschloss and Talbott, *At the Highest Levels,* p. 115.

118. Palazchenko, *My Years with Gorbachev and Shevardnadze,* pp. 126–27. Gorbachev sometimes expressed similar doubts about the Bush administration's intentions. Cf. p. 131.

119. Ekedahl and Goodman, *Wars of Eduard Shevardnadze,* p. 121.

120. Garthoff, *Great Transition,* pp. 384–85. See also pp. 518–19. Palazchenko, *My Years with Gorbachev and Shevardnadze,* p. 130, identifies the other members of the "group of five" as K.G.B. chief Vladimir Kryuchkov, Defense Minister Dmitri Yazov, Oleg Baklanov, the Central Committee secretary responsible for the defense industry, and Yuri Maslyukov, the deputy prime minister responsible for the defense industry.

121. Beschloss and Talbott, *At the Highest Levels,* p. 118.

122. Baker, *Politics of Diplomacy,* p. 151.

123. Garthoff, *Great Transition,* p. 539. The U.S. number, 880, was the arithmetic mean between the Soviet proposal of 760 and the arbitrary round number of 1,000.

124. Garthoff, *Great Transition,* p. 385.

125. Ekedahl and Goodman, *Wars of Eduard Shevardnadze,* p. 121. Korniyenko later made his criticism public in a diatribe published in *Sovetskaya Rossiya* in mid-February 1991. Palazchenko, *My Years with Gorbachev and Shevardnadze,* p. 272.

126. "U.S.-Soviet Relations: A Discussion of Perestroika and Economic Reform," *Department of State Bulletin* 89, no. 2153 (December 1989): 26.

127. "Prerequisites and Principles for Arms Control," *Department of State Bulletin* 89, no. 2153 (December 1989): 15.

128. Beschloss and Talbott, *At the Highest Levels*, pp. 144, 155. For the president's own view, see Bush and Scowcroft, *World Transformed*, p. 150.
129. Beschloss and Talbott, *At the Highest Levels*, p. 145.
130. Ibid., p. 146.
131. Ibid., p. 147.
132. Ibid., pp. 155, 162.
133. Bush and Scowcroft, *World Transformed*, p. 208.
134. Ibid., p. 499.
135. Ibid., p. 500.
136. Beschloss and Talbott, *At the Highest Levels*, pp. 188–89.
137. Bush and Scowcroft, *World Transformed*, p. 501.
138. Savel'yev and Detinov, *Big Five*, pp. 156–58.
139. Baker, *Politics of Diplomacy*, pp. 236–37.
140. Garthoff, *Great Transition*, p. 423.
141. Beschloss and Talbott, *At the Highest Levels*, pp. 212–13; Oberdorfer, *Turn*, pp. 407–10; Baker, *Politics of Diplomacy*, p. 252n.
142. Beschloss and Talbott, *At the Highest Levels*, p. 363.
143. Palazchenko, *My Years with Gorbachev and Shevardnadze*, p. 257.
144. Ibid., pp. 249–50.
145. Beschloss and Talbott, *At the Highest Levels*, p. 365.
146. Ibid., p. 367. See also pp. 366–70. Palazchenko recalled how the irony of having Moiseyev cast as "an arms control knight in shining armor" prompted laughter in the foreign ministry, in Fred I. Greenstein and William C. Wohlforth, eds., *Retrospective on the End of the Cold War*, Monograph Series no. 6, Center of International Studies, Princeton University, 1994, p. 23.
147. Beschloss and Talbott, *At the Highest Levels*, p. 373.
148. Ibid., p. 402.
149. Ibid., pp. 404–5.
150. Ibid., p. 406. Cf. Palazchenko, *My Years with Gorbachev and Shevardnadze*, pp. 291–92; Bush and Scowcroft, *World Transformed*, p. 508.
151. National Intelligence Estimate, NIE 11-18-90, "The Deepening Crisis in the U.S.S.R.: Prospects for the Next Year," November 1990, pp. 7, 16. Emphasis added.
152. Hans A. Bethe, Kurt Gottfried, and Robert S. McNamara, "The Nuclear Threat: A Proposal," *New York Review of Books*, June 27, 1991, pp. 48–50.
153. "Don't Stop with START," *New York Times*, July 19, 1991, p. A-26.

CHAPTER 7

1. As documented in Anatoly Chernyaev's notes of the lunch, in Jack F. Matlock, Jr., *Autopsy on an Empire: The American Ambassador's Account of the Collapse of the Soviet Union* (New York: Random House, 1995), p. 553.

2. Aleksandr Yakovlev, "Ethics and Reformation," speech at the Vatican, January 14, 1992, reprinted in Yakovlev, *The Fate of Marxism in Russia*, trans. Catherine A. Fitzpatrick (New Haven: Yale University Press, 1993), p. 228.

3. Anders Åslund, *How Russia Became a Market Economy* (Washington, D.C.: Brookings Institution, 1995), p. 34. Many others went into business for themselves while seldom showing up to work at their erratically paid jobs in the bureaucracy.

4. Anders Åslund, *Gorbachev's Struggle for Economic Reform*, rev. ed. (Ithaca, N.Y.: Cornell University Press, 1991), p. 147.

5. For a graphic description by a conservative who broke with Gorbachev, see Yegor Ligachev, *Inside Gorbachev's Kremlin*, trans. Catherine A. Fitzpatrick, Michele A. Berdy, and Dobrochna Dyrcz-Freeman (New York: Pantheon, 1993), pp. 109–15.

6. Interview with Jonathan Steele, *The Guardian*, London, December 12, 1992.

7. Allan R. Meyerson, "The Soviet Economic Morass," *New York Times*, September 16, 1990, sec. III, p. 5.

8. Åslund, *How Russia Became a Market Economy*, pp. 47–48.

9. Åslund, *Gorbachev's Struggle for Economic Reform*, p. 197.

10. Mikhail S. Gorbachev, "The Socialist Idea and Revolutionary Perestroika," *Pravda*, November 26, 1989, pp. 1–3, quoted in Matlock, *Autopsy on an Empire*, pp. 289–90.

11. Archie Brown, *The Gorbachev Factor* (New York: Oxford University Press, 1996), p. 102. Cf. Anatoly Chernyaev, quoted in *Retrospective on the End of the Cold War*, ed. Fred I. Greenstein and William C. Wohlforth, Monograph Series no. 6, Center of International Studies, Princeton University, 1994, p. 28.

12. Matlock, *Autopsy on an Empire*, p. 122.

13. Max M. Kampelman, *Entering New Worlds: The Memoirs of a Private Man in Public Life* (New York: HarperCollins, 1991), pp. 5–6.

14. George Bush and Brent Scowcroft, *A World Transformed* (New York: Alfred A. Knopf, 1998), p. 48.

15. Robert L. Hutchings, *American Diplomacy and the End of the Cold War: An Insider's Account of U.S. Policy in Europe, 1989–1992* (Washington, D.C.: Woodrow Wilson Center Press, 1997), p. 211.

16. Bush and Scowcroft, *World Transformed*, p. 49.

17. Ibid., pp. 49, 51–52.

18. Hutchings, *American Diplomacy and the End of the Cold War*, p. 211.

19. Bush and Scowcroft, *World Transformed*, p. 51; "Remarks to the Citizens of Hamtramck, Michigan," April 17, 1989, *Weekly Compilation of Presidential Documents* 25, no. 16 (April 24, 1989): 563.

20. Bush and Scowcroft, *World Transformed*, pp. 113–14.

21. Ibid., p. 139.

22. Ibid.

23. Hutchings, *American Diplomacy and the End of the Cold War*, pp. 69, 211.

24. Matlock, *Autopsy on an Empire*, pp. 180–81.

25. Åslund, *Gorbachev's Struggle for Economic Reform*, p. 204.

26. Brown, *Gorbachev Factor*, p. 149.

27. Åslund, *Gorbachev's Struggle for Economic Reform*, p. 67. On the politics of economic decision making in 1985–90, pp. 62–67.

28. On his political style, Anatoly Chernyaev, "The Phenomenon of Gorbachev in the Context of Leadership," *International Affairs* 39, no. 6 (June 1993): 48.

29. Matlock, *Autopsy on an Empire*, p. 190.

30. "Rising Political Instability Under Gorbachev: Understanding the Problem and Prospects for Resolution," Office of Soviet Analysis, Central Intelligence Agency, April 1989, National Security Archive 00600, pp. iii, iv.

31. "Gorbachev's Domestic Gambles and Instability in the U.S.S.R.," SOV-89-1077, Office of Soviet Analysis, Central Intelligence Agency, September 1989, National Security Archive 00602, pp. v, 3. Cf. Michael Beschloss and Strobe Talbott, *At the Highest Levels: The Inside Story of the End of the Cold War* (Boston: Little, Brown, 1993), pp. 141–43.

32. Matlock, *Autopsy on an Empire*, p. 187.

33. James A. Baker III, *The Politics of Diplomacy: Revolution, War, and Peace, 1989–1992* (New York: G. P. Putnam's Sons, 1995), pp. 73, 75.

34. Don Oberdorfer, *The Turn: From the Cold War to a New Era* (New York: Poseidon Press, 1991), p. 343.

35. Ibid., p. 370. When Baker saw Shevardnadze in July in Paris, that was all he had to offer.

36. Bush and Scowcroft, *World Transformed*, p. 129.

37. Pavel Palazchenko, *My Years with Gorbachev and Shevardnadze: The Memoir of a Soviet Interpreter* (University Park, Pa.: Pennsylvania State University Press, 1997), p. 284.

38. Matlock, *Autopsy on a Empire*, p. 196.

39. Bush and Scowcroft, *World Transformed*, p. 144.

40. Palazchenko, *My Years with Gorbachev and Shevardnadze*, p. 148.

41. Beschloss and Talbott, *At the Highest Levels*, p. 143.

42. Ibid., pp. 140–41.

43. Carolyn McGiffert Ekedahl and Melvin A. Goodman, *The Wars of Eduard Shevardnadze* (University Park, Pa.: Pennsylvania State University Press, 1997), p. 122.

44. Bush and Scowcroft, *World Transformed*, pp. 162–63.

45. Beschloss and Talbott, *At the Highest Levels*, pp. 154–56, 164.

46. Ibid., pp. 159, 159n, 167.

47. Matlock, *Autopsy on an Empire*, p. 272.

48. Bush and Scowcroft, *World Transformed*, p. 227.

49. Ibid., p. 284.

50. Ibid., pp. 284–85. Cf. Mikhail S. Gorbachev, *Memoirs* (New York: Doubleday, 1996), p. 540.

51. Raymond L. Garthoff, *The Great Transition: American-Soviet Relations and the End of the Cold War* (Washington, D.C.: Brookings Institution, 1994), p. 415.

52. Baker, *Politics of Diplomacy*, p. 249.

53. Beschloss and Talbott, *At the Highest Levels*, p. 210.

54. Philip Zelikow and Condoleezza Rice, *Germany Unified and Europe Transformed: A Study in Statecraft* (Cambridge, Mass.: Belknap Press, 1995), p. 259.

55. Bush and Scowcroft, *World Transformed*, p. 287.

56. Beschloss and Talbott, *At the Highest Levels*, pp. 236–37.

57. Baker, *Politics of Diplomacy*, pp. 294–95.

58. Interview with Grigory Yavlinsky, Moscow, November 14, 1991.

59. Brown, *Gorbachev Factor*, p. 151. Cf. Åslund, *Gorbachev's Struggle for Economic Reform*, pp. 204–5.

60. For Gorbachev's view of the linkage, see Gorbachev, *Memoirs*, pp. 378–82.

61. Robert M. Gates, *From the Shadows: The Ultimate Insider's Story of Five Presidents and How They Won the Cold War* (New York: Simon and Schuster, 1996), p. 496.

62. Åslund, *Gorbachev's Struggle for Economic Reform*, pp. 207–8.

63. Ibid., pp. 214–15.

64. Ibid., pp. 212–13.

65. *Moscow News*, no. 43 (1990); interview with Oleg Bogomolov, Moscow, November 12, 1991.

66. Palazchenko, *My Years with Gorbachev and Shevardnadze*, p. 217.

67. Matlock, *Autopsy on an Empire*, p. 415. Matlock had tried to postpone the mission. See also pp. 413–14.

68. Bush and Scowcroft, *World Transformed*, p. 500.

69. "The Soviet Cauldron," SOV-M-91-20177, Office of Soviet Analysis, Central Intelligence Agency, April 25, 1991, National Security Archive 00603, pp. 1–3.

70. Matlock, *Autopsy on an Empire*, p. 502.

71. Clifford G. Gaddy and Barry W. Ickes, "Russia's Virtual Economy," *Foreign Affairs* 77, no. 5 (September/October 1998): 56.

72. Matlock, *Autopsy on an Empire*, p. 509.

73. Gates, *From the Shadows*, p. 504; Palazchenko, *My Years with Gorbachev and Shevardnadze*, pp. 274–78, has an account of the Gorbachev-Nixon encounter.

74. Matlock, *Autopsy on an Empire*, pp. 510–11. Cf. Bush and Scowcroft, *World Transformed*, p. 503; Beschloss and Talbott, *At the Highest Levels*, p. 377.

75. Beschloss and Talbott, *At the Highest Levels*, p. 378.

76. Ibid.

77. Matlock, *Autopsy on an Empire*, pp. 525–26.

78. Beschloss and Talbott, *At the Highest Levels*, p. 376.

79. Matlock, *Autopsy on an Empire*, p. 530. Cf. Beschloss and Talbott, *At the Highest Levels*, pp. 380–81.

80. Matlock, *Autopsy on an Empire*, p. 439.

81. Ibid., pp. 534–36.

82. Joint Working Group on Western Cooperation in the Soviet Transition to Democracy and the Market Economy, *Window of Opportunity: The Grand Bargain for Democracy in the Soviet Union* (New York: Pantheon, 1991), and a shorter version, Graham Allison and Robert Blackwill, "America's Stake in the Soviet Future," *Foreign Affairs* 70, no. 3 (Summer 1991): 77–97.

83. Beschloss and Talbott, *At the Highest Levels*, p. 385.

84. Matlock, *Autopsy on an Empire*, pp. 537–38.

85. Ibid., p. 539.

86. Baker, *Politics of Diplomacy*, p. 478.

87. Matlock, *Autopsy on an Empire*, pp. 547–48.

88. Beschloss and Talbott, *At the Highest Levels*, p. 389.

89. Baker, *Politics of Diplomacy*, p. 478.

90. Gates, *From the Shadows*, p. 502.

91. Bush and Scowcroft, *World Transformed*, p. 507.

92. Beschloss and Talbott, *At the Highest Levels*, p. 390.

93. Baker, *Politics of Diplomacy*, p. 478.

94. Bush and Scowcroft, *World Transformed*, p. 503.

95. Matlock, *Autopsy on an Empire*, pp. 551–52.

96. Bush and Scowcroft, *World Transformed*, p. 506.

97. Ibid., pp. 507.

98. Gorbachev, *Memoirs*, p. 612.

99. As documented in Anatoly Chernyaev's notes of the lunch, in Matlock, *Autopsy on an Empire*, p. 553.

100. Beschloss and Talbott, *At the Highest Levels*, pp. 393–95.

101. Bush and Scowcroft, *World Transformed*, p. 522.

102. Baker, *Politics of Diplomacy*, pp. 535–36.

103. Åslund, *How Russia Became a Market Economy*, pp. 216–17.

104. Baker, *Politics of Diplomacy*, pp. 654–55.

105. Ibid., pp. 656–57.

106. Hutchings, *American Diplomacy and the End of the Cold War*, p. 334.

107. Åslund, *How Russia Became a Market Economy*, pp. 217–18.

108. Ibid., p. 217.

109. Hutchings, *American Diplomacy and the End of the Cold War*, p. 334.

CHAPTER 8

1. Memorandum to the president, September 11, 1945, quoted in Henry L. Stimson and McGeorge Bundy, *On Active Service in Peace and War* (New York: Harper, 1948), p. 644.

2. George Bush and Brent Scowcroft, *A World Transformed* (New York: Alfred A. Knopf, 1998), pp. 520–21.

3. David Albright, Frans Berkhout, and William Walker, *World Inventory of Plutonium and Highly Enriched Uranium, 1992* (New York: Oxford University Press, 1993), pp. 36, 40.

4. Brian G. Chow and Kenneth A. Solomon, *Limiting the Spread of Weapons-Usable Fissile Materials* (Santa Monica, Calif.: RAND, 1993), pp. 12–13.

5. James A. Baker III, *The Politics of Diplomacy: Revolution, War, and Peace, 1989–1992* (New York: G. P. Putnam's Sons, 1995), p. 139.

6. Jack F. Matlock, Jr., *Autopsy on an Empire: The American Ambassador's Account of the Collapse of the Soviet Union* (New York: Random House, 1995), pp. 540–45; Bush and Scowcroft, *World Transformed*, pp. 504–6.

7. "The Soviet Cauldron," SOVM91-20177, Office of Soviet Analysis, Central Intelligence Agency, April 25, 1991, National Security Archive 00603, pp. 1, 4, 5. Cf. Michael Beschloss and Strobe Talbott, *At the Highest Levels: The Inside Story of the End of the Cold War* (Boston: Little, Brown, 1993), p. 360; Robert M. Gates, *From the Shadows: The Ultimate Insider's Story of Five Presidents and How They Won the Cold War* (New York: Simon and Schuster, 1996), p. 520.

8. Special National Intelligence Estimate, "Gorbachev's Future," May 23, 1991, National Security Archive 00604, pp. 1, 2. Cf. Gates, *From the Shadows*, p. 520.

9. Baker, *Politics of Diplomacy*, p. 143.

10. Ibid., p. 475.

11. Bush and Scowcroft, *World Transformed*, p. 525.

12. William J. Broad, "Nuclear Designers from East and West Plan Bomb Disposal," *New York Times*, December 17, 1991, p. C-1. Cf. Seymour M. Hersh, "The Wild East," *Atlantic Monthly*, June 1994, pp. 68–69. That December, the two NGOs cosponsored a conference in Moscow on ways to cope with loosening nuclear control in the Soviet Union. Among the topics discussed were disabling nuclear weapons, tagging all warheads to ensure accurate accounting and make them easier to locate, secure storage, and warhead dismantling.

13. Thomas L. Neff, "A Grand Uranium Bargain," *New York Times*, October 24, 1991, p. A-25.

14. James Collins, quoted in Celestine Bohlen, "American Vows Millions to ex-Soviet Science," *New York Times*, December 10, 1992, p. A-17.

15. George Soros, "Who Lost Russia?" *New York Review of Books*, April 13, 2000, p. 12.

16. Leon V. Sigal, "Buy Down the Red Army," *New York Times*, December 9, 1991, p. A-16.

17. Christopher Paine and Thomas B. Cochran, "Kiev Conference: Verified Warhead Controls," *Arms Control Today* 22, no. 1 (January/February 1992): 16.

18. "Now Reduce the 'Renegade' Risk," *New York Times*, August 1, 1991, p. A-20. The increasing sense of urgency can be seen by comparing *Times* editorials on June 18, August 15, and September 13, 1989; January 16, February 14, April 12, May 15, and May 26, 1990; May 11 and July 19, 1991.

19. Gates, *From the Shadows*, p. 528.

20. Kurt M. Campbell et al., *Soviet Nuclear Fission: Control of the Nuclear Arsenal in a Disintegrating Soviet Union* (Cambridge, Mass.: M.I.T. Press, 1991).

21. Ashton B. Carter and William J. Perry, *Preventive Defense: A New Security Strategy for America* (Washington, D.C.: Brookings Institution Press, 1999), pp. 71–72.

22. Colin L. Powell, *My American Journey* (New York: Random House, 1995), p. 540.

23. Philip Zelikow and Condoleezza Rice, *Germany Unified and Europe Transformed: A Study in Statecraft* (Cambridge, Mass.: Belknap Press, 1995), p. 238. It held out the possibility of deploying the tactical air-to-surface missile (TASM).

24. Michael R. Gordon, "Bush Plans to Cut Short-Range Arms in Germany," *New York Times*, April 19, 1990, p. A-12.

25. Margaret Thatcher, *The Downing Street Years* (New York: HarperCollins, 1993), pp. 788, 810.

26. Don Oberdorfer, *The Turn: From the Cold War to a New Era* (New York: Poseidon Press, 1991), p. 408.

27. Interview with a Ukrainian officer, Kiev, November 18, 1991.

28. Zelikow and Rice, *Germany Unified and Europe Transformed*, pp. 304–5, 312–13. Cf. R. Jeffrey Smith, "U.S. to Seek to Eliminate Most A-Arms in Europe," *Washington Post*, May 3, 1990, p. A-1.

29. Zelikow and Rice, *Germany Unified and Europe Transformed*, p. 263.

30. Thatcher, *Downing Street Years*, p. 811.

31. Jim Hoagland, "Bush's NATO Success Advances U.S. Goals," *Washington Post*, July 7, 1990, p. A-18.

32. Catherine Kelleher, "Short-Range Nuclear Weapons: What Future in Europe?" *Arms Control Today* 21, no. 1 (January/February 1991): 18.

33. Interviews with senior Bush administration officials, Washington, D.C., February 27, 1996, and June 28, 1996.

34. Baker, *Politics of Diplomacy*, p. 526.

35. Bruce G. Blair, *Global Zero Alert for Nuclear Forces* (Washington, D.C.: Brookings Institution, 1995), pp. 20–21.

36. Powell's skepticism about nuclear arms is abundantly apparent in his memoir; Powell, *My American Journey*, pp. 45, 47, 112–13, 323–24, 452, 485–86.

37. Interview with a senior Bush administration official, Washington, D.C., June 28, 1996.

38. Gates, *From the Shadows*, p. 530. Cf. Bush and Scowcroft, *World Transformed*, pp. 541–43; Andrew Rosenthal, "Arms Plan Germinated in Back-Porch Sessions," *New York Times*, September 29, 1991, sec. I, p. 14.

39. Bush and Scowcroft, *World Transformed*, p. 542.

40. Powell, *My American Journey*, p. 541.

41. Bush and Scowcroft, *World Transformed*, p. 542.

42. Interview with senior Bush administration official, June 28, 1996. Cf. Bush and Scowcroft, *World Transformed*, p. 545.

43. On November 5, 1991, Bush signed NSD-64 on nuclear deployments for fiscal years 1991–92, authorizing the return of all land-based and sea-based tactical nuclear warheads to the United States. U.S. Commander-in-Chief, Pacific, Command History, 1991, I, pp. 90–93, excerpted in Peter Hayes and Steven Noerper, "The Future of the U.S.-R.O.K. Alliance," in *Peace and Security in Northeast Asia: The Nuclear Issue and the Korean Peninsula*, ed. Young Whan Kihl and Peter Hayes (Armonk, N.Y.: M. E. Sharpe, 1996), pp. 259–61. On July 2, 1992, in a statement issued by the White House, Bush declared that "all ground-launched tactical nuclear weapons have been returned to U.S. territory, as have all naval tactical nuclear weapons." "U.S. Completes Pullback of Nuclear Weapons," *Washington Post*, July 3, 1992, p. A-6.

44. Serge Schmemann, "Soviets Hail U.S. Arms Plan and Signal Their Own Cuts; Britain and France Join In," *New York Times*, September 29, 1991, p. 1.

45. Pavel Palazchenko, *My Years with Gorbachev and Shevardnadze: The Memoir of a Soviet Interpreter* (University Park, Pa.: Pennsylvania State University Press, 1997), pp. 328–29.

46. "Gorbachev Remarks on Arms Cuts," *New York Times*, October 5, 1991, p. 12.

47. Hersh, "Wild East," p. 68.

48. Baker, *Politics of Diplomacy*, p. 527.

49. Bush and Scowcroft, *World Transformed*, p. 555.

50. James A. Baker III, "America and the Collapse of the Soviet Empire: What Has to Be Done," speech at Princeton University, December 12, 1991, prepared text from the Office of the Assistant Secretary/Spokesman, U.S. Department of State.

51. Baker, *Politics of Diplomacy*, pp. 571–72. This was a change, according to the director of central intelligence, Robert Gates, who testified before the Senate Governmental Affairs Committee on January 15, 1992, that in the past there were "three nuclear briefcases. They were held by the president, the defense minister, and the chief of the general staff. Today, there appear to be only two."

52. Ibid., p. 574.

53. Palazchenko, *My Years with Gorbachev and Shevardnadze*, pp. 360–61.

54. Baker, *Politics of Diplomacy*, p. 575.

55. Ibid., p. 576.

56. Ibid., pp. 580–81.

57. Ibid., pp. 582–83.

58. Interviews with the deputy leader of the parliament, Ivan Plyuschch, and Defense Minister Konstantin Morozov, Kiev, November 22, 1991; Rukh legislators Serhij Kolyschnyk, Kiev, November 18, 1991, and Serhij Holovaty, Kiev, November 19, 1991; Rukh leaders Wladimir Muljava, Kiev, November 18, 1991, and Les Taniuk, Kiev, November 22, 1991; Republican Party leader Mykhailo Horyn, Kiev, November 22, 1991.

59. Baker, *Politics of Diplomacy*, p. 585.

60. Matlock, *Autopsy on an Empire*, pp. 3–4. Cf. Bush and Scowcroft, *World Transformed*, p. 559.

61. Baker, *Politics of Diplomacy*, p. 659. Bush also announced several unilateral steps, including a halt in production of all Midgetman missiles and reassignment of a sizable portion of the bomber fleet to purely conventional roles.

62. Ibid.

63. Ibid., p. 660.

64. Mitchell Reiss, *Bridled Ambition: Why Countries Constrain Their Nuclear Capabilities* (Washington, D.C.: Woodrow Wilson Center Press, 1995), pp. 92, 154n6.

65. Matlock, *Autopsy on an Empire*, pp. 565–71; Beschloss and Talbott, *At the Highest Levels*, p. 409n.

66. Bush and Scowcroft, *World Transformed*, p. 543.

67. Reiss, *Bridled Ambition*, pp. 93–94.

68. Sherman W. Garnett, "Ukraine's Decision to Join the NPT," *Arms Control Today* 25, no. 1 (January/February 1995): 8.

69. Nuclear Backsliding in Ukraine," *New York Times*, May 4, 1992, p. A-16.

70. Reiss, *Bridled Ambition*, p. 97.

71. Ibid., pp. 95–96.

72. Ibid., pp. 96–97.

73. Baker, *Politics of Diplomacy*, p. 664.

74. Ibid., p. 669.

75. Ibid.

76. Ibid., p. 670.

77. Ibid.

78. Ashton B. Carter, "Memorandum on Meetings in Moscow on International Security, June 24–25, 1992: High Points," author's copy, July 1, 1992.

79. George Perkovich, "Trip Report: Moscow Nuclear Arms Reduction Workshop," author's copy, July 2, 1992.

80. Natalia A. Feduschak, "U.S. Stance on Ukraine Pushes It Closer to Declaring Itself a Nuclear Nation," *Wall Street Journal*, May 3, 1993, p. A-10.

81. Reiss, *Bridled Ambition*, pp. 101–2.

82. Paul Quinn Judge, "Yeltsin Weighed Nuclear Strike on Ukraine, Soviet Report Says," *Boston Globe*, October 25, 1991; Cf. Steve Coll and R. Jeffrey Smith, "Is Ukraine Reaching for Control over Nuclear Arms?" *Washington Post*, June 3, 1993, p. A-1.

83. Matlock, *Autopsy on an Empire*, p. 700.

84. Daniel Williams, "Russia Asserts Role in Ex-Soviet Republics," *Washington Post*, September 29, 1993, p. A-1.

85. Kathleen Mihalisko, "Defense, the CIS, and Ukrainian Public Opinion," Radio Free Europe/Radio Liberty *Research Report*, September 4, 1992; Bohdan Nahaylo, "The Shaping of Ukrainian Attitudes toward Nuclear Arms," Radio Free Europe/Radio Liberty *Research Report*, February 19, 1993.

86. John J. Mearsheimer, "The Case for a Ukrainian Nuclear Deterrent," *Foreign Affairs*, 72, no. 3 (Summer 1993): 50–51.

87. Reiss, *Bridled Ambition*, p. 105.

88. Ibid., p. 156n14.

89. Steven Erlanger, "Ukraine and Arms Accords: Kiev Reluctant to Say 'I Do,'" *New York Times*, March 31, 1993, p. A-1.

90. Statement by President Clinton, "Advancing U.S. Relations with Russia and Other New Independent States," April 23, 1993; testimony of Strobe Talbott and Under Secretary of Defense Walt Slocombe before the Subcommittee on European Affairs, U.S. Congress, Senate, Committee on Foreign Relations, June 24, 1993.

91. Chrystia Freeland, "U.S. Shifts Policy on Ukraine," *Washington Post*, May 11, 1993, p. A-12.

92. Michael R. Gordon, "Russians Fault U.S. on Shifting Ukraine's Arms," *New York Times*, June 7, 1993, p. A-1.

93. News conference on June 18, *Holos Ukrayiny*, reprinted in Foreign Broadcast Information Service, FBIS-SOV-93-121, June 25, 1993, p. 41.

94. R. Jeffrey Smith, "Ukraine Begins to Dismantle Nuclear Missiles Aimed at U.S.," *Washington Post*, July 28, 1993, p. A-13.

95. In Ukraine's interpretation, the START Treaty required only partial elimination of the strategic arms on its territory. The Lisbon Protocol, as spelled out in a letter from President Kravchuk, required it to be nuclear-free. Massandra foundered on whether the treaty or the Kravchuk letter was governing. James E. Goodby, *Europe Undivided: The New Logic of Peace in U.S.-Russian Relations* (Washington, D.C.: U.S. Institute of Peace, 1998), p. 82.

96. Reiss, *Bridled Ambition*, p. 109. Cf. Fred Hiatt, "Russia, Ukraine Differ on Deal," *Washington Post*, September 5, 1993, p. A-42; and Pavel Shinkarenko, "The Truth about Nuclear Weapons," *Rossiykiye Vesti*, September 22, 1993,

reprinted in Foreign Broadcast Information Service, FBIS-SOV-93-104, September 24, 1993, pp. 7–8.

97. Reiss, *Bridled Ambition*, pp. 109–10.

98. Ibid., p. 108.

99. Robert Seely, "Ukrainian Retreats on A-Pledge," *Washington Post*, October 20, 1993, p. A-31.

100. Telephone interview with a senior Clinton administration official, November 2, 1993. Cf. Reiss, *Bridled Ambition*, pp. 111–12.

101. Dunbar Lockwood, "Russia Revises Nuclear Policy, Ends Soviet 'No-First-Use' Pledge," *Arms Control Today* 23, no. 10 (December 1993): 19.

102. Russia Warns Ukraine of Decay of Warheads," *New York Times*, November 6, 1993, p. 5.

103. "Resolution of the Verkhovna Rada of Ukraine," *Survival* 36, no. 1 (Spring 1994): 168–70.

104. Ann Devroy, "Clinton Presses Ukraine on Disarming," *Washington Post*, November 30, 1993, p. A-4.

105. Michael R. Gordon, "Kiev Acts Quickly on Pledge to Disarm Nuclear Weapons," *New York Times*, December 21, 1993, p. A-14.

106. Reiss, *Bridled Ambition*, p. 115.

107. Ibid., pp. 116–17. Cf. the trilateral statement and annex in *Arms Control Today* 24, no. 1 (January/February 1994): 21–22.

108. Goodby, *Europe Undivided*, pp. 88–89.

109. Dunbar Lockwood, "Ukrainian Rada Clears Way for START I, NPT Accession," *Arms Control Today* 24, no. 2 (March 1994): 32. The text of the resolution is on p. 41.

110. Text of the Memorandum on Security Assurances in Connection with Ukraine's Accession to the NPT, December 5, 1994, *Arms Control Today* 25, no. 1 (January/February 1995): 21.

111. For a summary of the various actions, see Graham T. Allison et al., *Avoiding Nuclear Anarchy: Containing the Threat of Loose Russian Nuclear Weapons and Fissile Material* (Cambridge, Mass.: M.I.T. Press, 1996), ch. 3.

112. Thomas Neff, "Privatizing U.S. National Security: The U.S.-Russian HEU Deal At Risk," *Arms Control Today* 28, no. 6 (August/September 1998): 8.

113. Richard A. Falkenrath, "The HEU Deal," in Allison et al., *Avoiding Nuclear Anarchy*, p. 231.

114. Joseph Stiglitz, a member of the Council of Economic Advisers, was among those who argued against the arrangement on these grounds; Jonathan Chait, "Shoeless Joe Stiglitz," *American Prospect* July–August 1999, p. 54.

115. Falkenrath, "HEU Deal," pp. 237, 240–41, 243n.

116. John C. Baker, "Nonproliferation Incentives for Russia and Ukraine," *Adelphi Papers* no. 309, International Institute for Strategic Studies, London, 1997.

117. Falkenrath, "HEU Deal," p. 249.

118. Ibid., pp. 245, 251–52. Cf. I. M. Destler, *American Trade Politics: System under Stress* (Washington, D.C.: Institute for International Economics, 1986), pp. 111–25.

119. Falkenrath, "HEU Deal," pp. 253–55.

120. Ibid., p. 260.

121. Ibid., p. 264.

122. Michael R. Gordon, "U.S., in a Secret Deal, Removes Bomb Fuel in Ex-Soviet Republic," *New York Times*, November 23, 1994, p. A-1. Cf. White House fact sheet and briefing by Secretary of Defense William Perry and Secretary of Energy Hazel O'Leary, November 23, 1994.

123. "U.S. Security Assistance to the Former Soviet Union," *Arms Control Today* 25, no. 3 (April 1995): 24.

124. Steven Kull, I. M. Destler, and Clay Ramsay, *The Foreign Policy Gap: How Policymakers Misread the Public* (College Park, Md.: University of Maryland, Center for International and Security Studies, 1997), chs. 2, 5.

125. Allison et al., *Avoiding Nuclear Anarchy*, pp. 80–82.

126. Testimony of Under Secretary of Energy Charles B. Curtis before the Committee on Armed Services, U.S. Congress, Senate, April 19, 1994.

127. The idea had come from Thomas Cochran of the National Resources Defense Council, experts at Los Alamos, and Frank von Hippel of the White House Office of Science and Technology Policy. Frank von Hippel, "Working in the White House on Nuclear Nonproliferation and Arms Control: A Personal Report," *Journal of the Federation of American Scientists* 48, no. 2 (March/April 1995).

128. Telephone interview with a National Academy of Sciences official, February 15, 1995.

129. Allison et al., *Avoiding Nuclear Anarchy*, pp. 82–86.

130. Glenn E. Schweitzer, *Moscow DMZ: The Story of the International Effort to Convert Russian Weapons Science to Peaceful Purposes* (Armonk, N.Y.: M. E. Sharpe, 1996), pp. 100, 103.

131. Ibid., p. 69.

132. Ibid., pp. 19, 44.

133. Ibid., pp. 20, 32.

134. Ibid., pp. 57–58.

135. Alexander A. Pikayev et al., "Russia, the U.S. and the Missile Technology Control Regime," *Adelphi Papers* no. 317, International Institute for Strategic Studies, London, 1998, p. 8.

136. Ibid., pp. 46–47, 53–55.

137. By early in the next century, according to C.I.A. director James Woolsey, in *Hearing: Global Threat Assessment*, testimony before the Select Committee on Intelligence, U.S. Congress, Senate, January 10, 1995. Estimates in previous years were eight to ten years. In seven to fifteen years, according to

Defense Secretary William Perry, in Clyde Haberman, "U.S. and Israel See Iranians 'Many Years' from A-Bomb," *New York Times*, January 10, 1995, p. A-3. Perry was contradicting Israeli and American officials who contended it would take Iran just five years; these were quoted in Chris Hedges, "Iran May Be Able to Build an Atomic Bomb in 5 Years, U.S. and Israeli Officials Fear," *New York Times*, January 5, 1995, p. A-10.

138. "The Nunn-Lugar Cooperative Threat Reduction Program: Donor and Recipient Country Perspectives," conference at the Center for Non-proliferation Studies, Monterey Institute of International Studies, Monterey, Calif., August 20–22, 1995.

139. Jane Wales, text of remarks to the Carnegie Endowment Conference on Nuclear Nonproliferation in 1995: "Renewal, Transition, or Decline?" Carnegie Endowment for International Peace, Washington, D.C., January 31, 1994.

140. James Goldgeier, "NATO Expansion: The Anatomy of a Decision," *Washington Quarterly*, Winter 1998, p. 87; James M. Goldgeier, *Not Whether but When: The U.S. Decision to Enlarge NATO* (Washington, D.C.: Brookings Institution Press, 1999), p. 38.

141. Goldgeier, *Not Whether But When*, pp. 21, 167.

142. Douglas Brinkley, "Democratic Enlargement: The Clinton Doctrine," *Foreign Policy*, no. 106 (Spring 1997): 108.

143. Goldgeier, "NATO Expansion," pp. 93–94; Goldgeier, *Not Whether But When*, pp. 52, 54, 57–58.

144. Goldgeier, *Not Whether But When*, pp. 32–37, 77–84.

145. Carter and Perry, *Preventive Defense*, pp. 30–32.

CHAPTER 9

1. Kissinger was complaining about Clinton's carefully caveated commitment to no "permanent stationing of substantial combat forces" on the territory of new NATO members "in the current and foreseeable security environment." William Drozdiak, "Poland Urges NATO Not to Appease Russia: The Smell of Yalta Is Always with Us," *Washington Post*, March 17, 1997, p. A-13.

2. These points are developed in Leon V. Sigal, *Disarming Strangers: Nuclear Diplomacy with North Korea* (Princeton, N.J.: Princeton University Press, 1998), ch. 1.

3. Frans Berkhout et al., "A Cutoff in the Production of Fissile Material," *International Security* 19, no. 3 (Winter 1994/95): 174.

4. "Plutonium: The First 50 Years" U.S. Department of Energy, February 1996.

5. Testimony of Lawrence Gershwin before the Subcommittee on Defense, U.S. Congress, House, Committee on Appropriations, May 6, 1992.

6. Testimony of General Eugene Habinger, commander of STRATCOM, before the Committee on Armed Services, U.S. Congress, Senate, March 13, 1997.

7. Conversations with Steve Fetter, University of Maryland. Cf. Steve Fetter, "A Comprehensive Transparency Regime for Warheads and Fissile Materials," *Arms Control Today* 29, no. 1 (January/February 1999): 3–7.

8. Matthew Bunn, "'Pit-Stuffing': How to Disable Thousands of Warheads and Easily Verify Their Dismantlement," *Federation of Atomic Scientists Public Interest Report* 51, no. 2 (March/April 1998): 3–5.

9. Matthew Bunn and Kenneth Luongo, "Urgently Needed Next Steps for Fissile Material and Warhead Controls," author's copy, December 1, 1998.

10. Committee on International Security and Arms Control, National Academy of Sciences, *Management and Disposition of Excess Weapons Plutonium* (Washington, D.C.: National Academy Press, 1994), ch. 6 and executive summary, pp. 12–17. Cf. Frank von Hippel et al., "Eliminating Nuclear Warheads," *Scientific American*, August 1993, pp. 47–49.

11. Matthew Bunn et al.,"Retooling Russia's Nuclear Cities," *Bulletin of the Atomic Scientists* 55, no. 5 (September/October 1999): 44–50.

12. Fetter, "Comprehensive Transparency Regime for Warheads," p. 7.

13. Matthew Bunn, "Act Now, Mr. President," *Bulletin of the Atomic Scientists* 54, no. 2 (March/April 1998): 4.

14. Spurgeon M. Keeny, Jr., and Wolfgang Panovsky, "Controlling Nuclear Warheads and Materials: Steps toward a Comprehensive Regime," *Arms Control Today* 22, no. 1 (January/February 1992): 5–6.

15. Committee on International Security and Arms Control, National Academy of Sciences, *The Future of U.S. Nuclear Weapons Policy* (Washington, D.C.: National Academy Press, 1997).

16. Bruce Blair, "Russia's Nuclear Collapse: The Case for a Mutual Standdown," paper prepared for Pugwash meeting no. 241, London, November 6–8, 1998.

17. White House press release, "Joint Statement on Parameters of Future Reductions in Nuclear Forces," March 21, 1997.

18. Interview with a senior Russian official, April 15, 1997.

19. James M. Goldgeier, *Not Whether but When: The U.S. Decision to Enlarge NATO* (Washington, D.C.: Brookings Institution Press, 1999), pp. 53–54, 61–62, 77–83, 106.

20. James Goldgeier, "NATO Expansion: The Anatomy of a Decision," *Washington Quarterly*, Winter 1998, p. 87.

21. Ashton B. Carter and William J. Perry, *Preventive Defense: A New Security Strategy for America* (Washington, D.C.: Brookings Institution Press, 1999), p. 60.

CHAPTER 10

1. George Soros, "The Capitalist Threat," *Atlantic Monthly*, February 1997, p. 53.

2. Interview with a senior North Korean diplomat, March 9, 1993.

3. "Overall," concluded the Chicago Council on Foreign Relations based on its 1990 survey, "favorability toward the Soviet Union has risen dramatically, with majorities of the public endorsing peaceful, cooperative policies." Only 28 percent favored trade restrictions, down 19 percent from 1982; 40 percent favored providing economic aid to help the Soviet Union modernize its economy (by comparison, 45 percent wanted to reduce aid to Israel); and 82 percent favored negotiating arms control agreements. In a view that would have been unthinkable at the beginning of the decade, a substantial majority (69 percent) favored "working with Soviet military units to increase stability in the Middle East." John E. Rielly, ed., *American Public Opinion and U.S. Foreign Policy, 1991* (Chicago: Chicago Council on Foreign Relations, 1991), pp. 20, 29, 37.

4. William Martin, "The Christian Right and American Foreign Policy," *Foreign Policy*, no. 114 (Spring 1999): 78–79.

5. For the Nixon purge, see William Bundy, *A Tangled Web: The Making of Foreign Policy in the Nixon Presidency* (New York: Hill and Wang, 1998), pp. 346–47, 405–6.

6. Benjamin I. Page and Robert Y. Shapiro, *The Rational Public: Fifty Years of Trends in Policy Preferences* (Chicago: University of Chicago Press, 1992), p. 222.

7. This way of thinking about news making is elaborated in Leon V. Sigal, *Reporters and Officials: The Organization and Politics of Newsmaking* (Lexington, Mass.: Lexington Books, 1973).

8. In the school year 1997–98, 6,424 students from Russia were enrolled in American colleges and universities. By contrast, the three countries with the highest number of students were Japan with 47,073, China with 46,958, and South Korea with 42,890. Data from the Institute of International Education, in Paul Desruisseaux, "2-Year Colleges at Crest of Wave in U.S. Enrollments by Foreign Students," *Chronicle of Higher Education*, December 11, 1998, p. A-67.

9. Matthew Evangelista, *Unarmed Forces: The Transnational Movement to End the Cold War* (Ithaca, N.Y.: Cornell University Press, 1999), ch. 3.

10. Gloria Duffy, "Track-Two Diplomacy and the Revolution in the Soviet Union," *Nuclear Times* 10, nos. 2–3 (Autumn/Winter 1992): 48–51. On the Soviet-American Disarmament Study group and the Committee on International Security and Arms Control, see Evangelista, *Unarmed Forces*, pp. 36–39, 134–38, 144–47, 200–211, 228. On the International Physicians for the Prevention of Nuclear War, see pp. 147–55, 271–73, 355–57, 375–76, 383.

11. Michael Beschloss and Strobe Talbott, *At the Highest Levels: The Inside Story of the End of the Cold War* (Boston: Little, Brown, 1993), pp. 6–7, 13–17, 138; Raymond L. Garthoff, *The Great Transition: American-Soviet Relations and the End of the Cold War* (Washington, D.C.: Brookings Institution, 1994), pp. 605–6; Don Oberdorfer, *The Turn: From the Cold War to a New Era* (New York: Poseidon Press, 1991), pp. 82, 239.

12. Conversation with a senior State Department official in the Reagan administration, Washington, D.C., December 9, 1998.

13. Beschloss and Talbott, *At the Highest Levels*, p. 138. The Germans had their own Track II channels with both the Soviet Union and East Germany. Timothy Garton Ash, *In Europe's Name: Germany and the Divided Continent* (New York: Random House, 1993), p. 132.

14. Christopher Paine and Thomas B. Cochran, "Kiev Conference: Verified Warhead Controls," *Arms Control Today* 22, no. 1 (January/February 1992): 15.

15. William J. Broad, "Westerners Reach Soviet to Check Atom Site," *New York Times*, July 6, 1986, sec. I, p. 1. Cf. Evangelista, *Unarmed Forces*, pp. 279–88.

16. Anne Allen, ed., *Search for Security: The ACCESS Guide to Foundations in Peace, Security, and International Relations* (Washington, D.C.: ACCESS, 1989). The 1998 estimate was compiled by a foundation program officer.

17. U.S. Arms Control and Disarmament Agency, *World Military Expenditures and Arms Transfers, 1996* (Washington, D.C.: U.S. Government Printing Office, 1997), p. 36.

18. An early statement is Isabelle Grunberg and Thomas Risse-Kappen, "A Time of Reckoning? Theories of International Relations and the End of the Cold War," in *The End of the Cold War: Evaluating Theories of International Relations*, ed. Pierre Allan and Kjell Goldmann (Dordrecht: Martinus Nijhoff, 1992), pp. 104–46.

19. John E. Rielly, *American Public Opinion and U.S. Foreign Policy, 1999* (Chicago: Chicago Council on Foreign Relations, 1999), pp. 24–25. This is no passing fad, to judge from the Council's past surveys and trend data on support for the United Nations in Page and Shapiro, *Rational Public*, pp. 215–19.

20. A 1993 poll found 54 percent of the establishment believed the United States had lost influence; 30 percent of the public did. Seventy-five percent of the establishment wanted the United States to play the most active role in the world, compared to 37 percent of the public. Andrew Kohut, "Societal Change in the United States and Its Transatlantic Consequences from an Empirical Perspective," in Max Kaase and Andrew Kohut, eds., *Estranged Friends? The Transatlantic Consequences of Societal Change* (New York: Council on Foreign Relations Press, 1996), pp. 81, 88. Again, this is not a momentary mood but a long-standing tendency. For trend data on public attitudes toward cooperation with the Soviet Union and China, see Page and Shapiro,

Rational Public, pp. 223, 246–50, 262, 268, 273, 280. The view is especially prevalent among congressional staff members, to judge from a survey, *America's Place in the World, II*, undertaken by the Pew Research Center for the People and the Press, Washington, D.C., September 4–11, 1997, questions 15–16.

21. For instance, while 79 percent of the foreign policy establishment favored use of U.S. troops if North Korea invaded South Korea, just 30 percent of the general public did. The figures were 69 and 38 percent if Arab forces invaded Israel, 58 and 28 percent if Russia invaded Poland, 51 and 27 percent if China invaded Taiwan. Public support for economic aid stands at 47 percent, a level that has held for twenty-five years. A majority favors cutbacks in military aid. Rielly, *American Public Opinion and U.S. Foreign Policy, 1999*, pp. 21, 24, 26. Cf. Kohut, "Societal Change in the United States," p. 78; Stephen Kull, "What the Public Knows that Washington Doesn't," *Foreign Policy*, no. 101 (Winter 1995–96): 102-15. Again, this stance is not a passing fancy. For trend data on American attitudes toward foreign aid, military spending, and military involvement, see Page and Shapiro, *Rational Public*, pp. 224–25, 240, 252, 262–67, 270–72, 274–79.

INDEX

Note: Page numbers followed by letters *n* and *t* refer to notes and tables, respectively.

ABOUT THE AUTHOR

Leon V. Sigal is director of the Northeast Asia Cooperative Security Project at the Social Science Research Council and an adjunct professor at the School of International and Public Affairs at Columbia University. A former member of the New York Times editorial board, he is the author of a number of books, most recently, *Disarming Strangers: Nuclear Diplomacy with North Korea* (Princeton University Press, 1998) and *Fighting to the Finish: The Politics of War Termination in the United States and Japan, 1945* (Cornell University Press, 1988).